"*ProLife Answers to ProChoice Arguments* offers up-to-date answers to the tough questions. It pulls back the thin veil of 'right and choices' with the truth about how abortions are marketed to the nation and to women in crisis pregnancies. Every reader should give it to his or her acquaintances so they can understand the truth about abortion. **This book is must reading for every citizen in our nation—prolife or prochoice.**"—CAROL EVERETT, former abortion clinic owner and author of *Blood Money: Getting Rich Off a Woman's Right to Choose*

"This book should end the debate over abortion in this country once and for all. It probably won't, but it should. Its logic is unassailable; its research is impeccable; and its scope is monumental. Simply, precisely, and objectively, Randy Alcorn answers every argument that could possibly be raised by abortion advocates. **If you have room for only one prolife book in your library, make sure it is this one.**"—GEORGE GRANT, executive director, Legacy Communications; author of *Grand Illusions: The Legacy of Planned Parenthood*

"**I've never come across a book that has spoken to my heart like this one.** I couldn't put it down. I read it in one day, but I'll be going over it again and again. It is an accurate, powerful, compassionate, and biblical book. With passion and truth, Randy Alcorn courageously reveals the reality behind the exploitation and agony of abortion."—KATHY WALKER, international president, Women Exploited by Abortion, Inc.

"**Randy Alcorn's book is in a class by itself.** It is exhaustively researched, thoroughly documented, and logically organized for easy access. It demolishes abortion distortions with the most compelling prolife arguments yet developed. We must all learn to speak out on this issue. This book is the place to begin. If you're serious about stopping the killing of children, buy this book!"—GREGG CUNNINGHAM, former Pennsylvania legislator and U.S. Justice Department congressional liaison official; director, the Center for Bio-Ethical Reform

"Randy Alcorn has written a definitive book on America's greatest of all tragedies—legalized abortion. A 'must read' for all Americans, *ProLife Answers to ProChoice Arguments* is excellently researched and documented. This book should be the desktop reference book for every pastor, politician, and layman who needs the best researched answer for any question pertaining to the prolife issue. There's nothing better out there."—GAYLE AT̶̶̶̶̶̶̶̶̶̶̶̶
Right to Life

"Randy Alcorn has used scientific facts and common sense logic in addressing all of the prochoice arguments. He has carefully put to rest the idea that unborn children are disqualified from the constitutional protection enjoyed by already born people. **The author brilliantly exposes the truth that abortion involves not merely another 'choice,' but a living, human child.**"—JEANNIE HILL, R.N., director, Sidewalk Counselors for Life

"We highly recommend this book for health professionals and others confronted by the dilemmas surrounding abortion. Packed with data and reference, it is topically organized for quick use. We find the contents very helpful for those earnestly trying to answer critical questions, including **'When does life begin?' We sincerely recommend this book to anyone desiring accurate information about the most significant ethical question of this age.**"—RANDALL L. MARTIN, M.D. and CYNTHIA L. MARTIN, R.N.

"**Clear, crisp, and incisive, _ProLife Answers to ProChoice Arguments_ is the master handbook, the ultimate reference** that Life Advocates, teachers, and media directors have long desired. It is ideal for teachers, students, pastors, policy makers, undecided observers, and readers everywhere. With his consummate wallop of prochoice mythology, Randy Alcorn has filled a notable void in the abortion debate."—ROYCE DUNN, president, Please Let Me Live; national director, Life Chain

"**This book thoroughly documents the strength of the prolife position.** As a guide to debating the issue, it sets forth the prolife answers to prochoice arguments in a compelling and convincing manner. It will find fertile soil in the hearts of many who are presently undecided."—THOMAS A. GLESSNER, president, National Institute of Family and Life Advocates

Randy Alcorn

Pro*Life*
Answers to
Pro*Choice*
Arguments

MULTNOMAH
BOOKS

PROLIFE ANSWERS TO PROCHOICE ARGUMENTS

© 1992, 1994, 2000 by Eternal Perspective Ministries
International Standard Book Number: 978-1-57673-751-4

Cover design by Uttley/DouPonce DesignWorks
Cover image by Tony Stone Images

Scripture quotations are from: *The Holy Bible*, New International Version
© 1973, 1984 by International Bible Society,
used by permission of Zondervan Publishing House.
New American Standard Bible (NASB)
© 1960, 1977, 1995 by the Lockman Foundation.

Published in the United States by Multnomah, an imprint of the Crown
Publishing Group, a division of Penguin Random House LLC, New York.

MULTNOMAH® and the mountain colophon are trademarks
of Penguin Random House LLC.

Printed in the United States of America

To my parents,
Arthur Loren Alcorn and Lucille Vivian Alcorn,
who, by the hand of God, gave me the gift of life,
and never made me feel they regretted it.

ACKNOWLEDGMENTS

Some highly qualified people gave their valuable time to examine this manuscript and make insightful corrections and comments. Their expertise helped to ensure accuracy as well as clarity and logical consistency. My heartfelt thanks to David J. Sargent, M.D.; Jeannie Hill, R.N.; Kathy Rodriguez, Ph.D.; Randall L. Martin, M.D.; Cynthia L. Martin, R.N.; Rainy Takalo, R.N.; Gary Lovejoy, Ph.D.; Carol Everett, former abortion clinic owner; Jennifer Eastberg, Licensed Clinical Social Worker and former abortion clinic counselor; Kathy Walker of Women Exploited by Abortion. All these gave valuable input to the original work.

I am indebted to Dr. Francis Beckwith, Dr. Walt Larimore, Mark Crutcher, Steven Ertelt, Gregg Cunningham, Judie Brown and a host of others for their writings and the hundreds of resources I've drawn on for the new edition.

Ron and Kathy Norquist, my friends and coworkers, helped substantially in compiling information for both the original and revised books. Kathy spent long hours assisting in revisions. Bonnie Hiestand and Janet Albers did lots of typing, editing, and assisting in updating research. Ruth King proofread the galleys. Paul deParrie helped on the original and Cathy Ramey on the revision. Both were great sources of information. Special thanks to Rod and Diane Meyer for permission to include their story in Appendix G.

My friend Rod Morris faithfully edited both books. Nanci, Karina, and Angela Alcorn remain my best friends and most valued consultants. I am deeply grateful for the privilege of their companionship, support, and commitment to our Lord. To Him belongs all credit and praise for any value this book may have.

CONTENTS

Part One: Arguments Concerning Life, Humanity, and Personhood

2. "The fetus is just a part of the pregnant woman's body, like her tonsils or appendix. You can't seriously believe a frozen embryo is an actual person."　56

2a. A body part is defined by the common genetic code it shares with the rest of its body; the unborn's genetic code differs from his mother's.

2b. The child may die and the mother live, or the mother may die and the child live, proving they are two separate individuals.

2c. The unborn child takes an active role in his own development, controlling the course of the pregnancy and the time of birth.

2d. Being inside something is not the same as being part of something.

2e. Human beings should not be discriminated against because of their place of residence.

2f. There is substantial scientific reason to believe that frozen embryos are persons and should be granted the same rights as older, larger, and less vulnerable persons.

3. "The unborn is an embryo or a fetus—just a simple blob of tissue, a product of conception—not a baby. Abortion is terminating a pregnancy, not killing a child."　63

3a. Like *toddler* and *adolescent*, the terms *embryo* and *fetus* do not refer to nonhumans, but to humans at particular stages of development.

3b. Semantics affect perceptions, but they do not change realities; a baby is a baby no matter what we call her.

3c. From the moment of conception, the unborn is not simple, but very complex.

3d. Prior to the earliest abortions, the unborn already has every body part she will ever have.

3e. Every abortion stops a beating heart and terminates measurable brain waves.

3f. Even in the earliest surgical abortions, the unborn child is clearly human in appearance.

3g. Even before the unborn is obviously human in appearance, she is what she is—a human being.

3h. No matter how much better it sounds, "terminating a pregnancy" is still terminating a life.

4. "The fetus may be alive, but so are eggs and sperm. The fetus is a potential human being, not an actual one; it's like a blueprint, not a house; an acorn, not an oak tree."   71

4a.   The ovum and sperm are each a product of another's body; unlike the conceptus, neither is an independent entity.

4b.   The physical remains after an abortion indicate the end not of a potential life, but of an actual life.

4c.   Something nonhuman does not become human by getting older and bigger; whatever is human must be human from the beginning.

4d.   Comparing preborns and adults to acorns and oaks is dehumanizing and misleading.

4e.   Even if the analogy were valid, scientifically speaking an acorn is simply a little oak tree, just as an embryo is a little person.

5. "The unborn isn't a person, with meaningful life. It's only inches in size and can't even think; it's less advanced than an animal, and anyway, who says people have a greater right to live than animals?"   74

5a.   Personhood is properly defined by membership in the human species, not by stage of development within that species.

5b.   Personhood is not a matter of size, skill, or degree of intelligence.

5c.   The unborn's status should be determined on an objective basis, not on subjective or self-serving definitions of personhood.

5d.   It is a scientific fact that there are thought processes at work in unborn babies.

5e.   If the unborn's value can be compared to that of an animal, there is no reason not to also compare the value of born people to animals.

5f.   Even if someone believes that people are no better than animals, why would they abhor the killing of young animals, while advocating the killing of young children?

5g.   It is dangerous when people in power are free to determine whether other, less powerful lives are meaningful.

5h.   Arguments against the personhood of the unborn are shrouded in rationalization and denial.

6. "A fetus isn't a person until implantation...or until quickening or viability or when it first breathes." 83

6a. Implantation is a gauge of personhood only if location, nutrition, and interfacing with others make us human.

6b. Quickening is a gauge of personhood only if someone's reality or value depends upon being noticed by another.

6c. Viability is an arbitrary concept. Why not associate personhood with heartbeat, brain waves, or something else?

6d. The point of viability changes because it depends on technology, not the unborn herself. Eventually babies may be viable from the point of conception.

6e. In a broad sense, many born people are not viable because they are incapable of surviving without depending on others.

6f. A child's "breathing," her intake of oxygen, begins long before birth.

6g. Someone's helplessness or dependency should motivate us to protect her, not to destroy her.

7. "Obviously life begins at birth. That's why we celebrate birthdays, not conception days, and why we don't have funerals following miscarriages." 89

7a. Our recognition of birthdays is cultural, not scientific.

7b. Some people *do* have funerals after a miscarriage.

7c. Funerals are an expression of our subjective attachment to those who have died, not a measurement of their true worth.

7d. There is nothing about birth that makes a baby essentially different than he was before birth.

8. "No one can really know that human life begins before birth." 91

8a. Children know that human life begins before birth.

8b. Pregnant women know that human life begins before birth.

8c. Doctors know that human life begins before birth.

8d. Abortionists know that human life begins before birth.

8e. Prochoice feminists know that human life begins before birth.

8f. Society knows that human life begins before birth.

8g. The media know that human life begins before birth.

8h. Prochoice advocates know that human life begins before birth.

8i. If we can't know that human life begins before birth, how can we know whether it begins at birth or later?

Part Two: Arguments Concerning Rights and Fairness

9. "Even if the unborn are human beings, they have fewer rights than the woman. No one should be expected to donate her body as a life-support system for someone else."   103

9a. Once we grant that the unborn are human beings, it should settle the question of their right to live.

9b. The right to live doesn't increase with age and size; otherwise toddlers and adolescents have less right to live than adults.

9c. The comparison between a baby's rights and a mother's rights is unequal. What is at stake in abortion is the mother's lifestyle, as opposed to the baby's life.

9d. It is reasonable for society to expect an adult to live temporarily with an inconvenience if the only alternative is killing a child.

10. "Every person has the right to choose. It would be unfair to restrict a woman's choice by prohibiting abortion."   110

10a. Any civilized society restricts the individual's freedom to choose whenever that choice would harm an innocent person.

10b. "Freedom to choose" is too vague for meaningful discussion; we must always ask, "Freedom to choose *what?*"

10c. People who are prochoice about abortion are often not prochoice about other issues with less at stake.

10d. The one-time choice of abortion robs someone else of a lifetime of choices and prevents him from ever exercising his rights.

10e. Everyone is prochoice when it comes to the choices prior to pregnancy and after birth.

10f. Nearly all violations of human rights have been defended on the grounds of the right to choose.

11. "Every woman should have control over her own body. Reproductive freedom is a basic right."   113

11a. Abortion assures that 650,000 females each year do *not* have control over their bodies.

11b. Not all things done with a person's body are right, nor should they all be legally protected.

11c. Prolifers consistently affirm true reproductive rights.

11d. Even prochoicers must acknowledge that the "right to control one's body" argument has no validity if the unborn is a human being.

11e. Too often "the right to control my life" becomes the right to hurt and oppress others for my own advantage.

11f. Control over the body can be exercised to prevent pregnancy in the first place.

11g. It is demeaning to a woman's body and self-esteem to regard pregnancy as an unnatural, negative, and "out of control" condition.

12. "Abortion is a decision between a woman and her doctor. It's no one else's business. Everyone has a constitutional right to privacy."   116

12a. The Constitution does not contain a right to privacy.

12b. Privacy is never an absolute right, but is always governed by other rights.

12c. The encouragement or assistance of a doctor does not change the nature, consequences, or morality of abortion.

12d. The father of the child is also responsible for the child and should have a part in this decision.

12e. The father will often face serious grief and guilt as a result of abortion. Since his life will be significantly affected, shouldn't he have something to say about it?

13. "It's unfair for an unmarried woman to have to face the embarrassment of pregnancy or the pain of giving up a child for adoption."   120

13a. Pregnancy is not a sin. Society should not condemn and pressure an unmarried mother into abortion, but should help and support her.

13b. The poor choice of premarital sex is never compensated for by the far worse choice of killing an innocent human being.

13c. One person's unfair or embarrassing circumstances do not justify violating the rights of another person.

13d. Adoption is a fine alternative that avoids the burden of child raising, while saving a life and making a family happy; it is tragic that adoption is so infrequently chosen as an alternative to abortion.

13e. The reason that adoption may be painful is the same reason that abortion is wrong—a human life is involved.

14. "Abortion rights are fundamental for the advancement of women. They are essential to having equal rights with men."   124

14a. Early feminists were prolife, not prochoice.

14b. Some active feminists still vigorously oppose abortion.

14c. Women's rights are not inherently linked to the right to abortion.

14d. The basic premises of the abortion-rights movement are demeaning to women.

14e. Many of the assumptions that connect women's welfare with abortion, the pill, and free sex have proven faulty.

14f. Some of the abortion-rights strategies assume female incompetence and subject women to ignorance and exploitation.

14g. Abortion has become the most effective means of sexism ever devised, ridding the world of multitudes of unwanted females.

15. "The circumstances of many women leave them no choice but to have an abortion."   129

15a. Saying they have no choice is not being prochoice, but proabortion.

15b. Those who are truly prochoice must present a woman with a number of possible choices instead of just selling the choice of abortion.

15c. "Abortion or misery" is a false portrayal of the options; it keeps women from pursuing—and society from providing—positive alternatives.

16. "I'm personally against abortion, but I'm still prochoice. It's a legal alternative and we don't have the right to keep it from anyone. Everyone's free to believe what they want, but we shouldn't try to impose it on others."   132

16a. To be prochoice about abortion is to be proabortion.

16b. The only good reason for being personally against abortion is a reason that demands we be against other people choosing to have abortions.

16c. What is legal is not always right.

16d. How can we tell people that they are perfectly free to believe abortion is the killing of children but that they are not free to act as if what they believe is really true?

Part Three: Arguments Concerning Social Issues

17. "'Every child a wanted child.' It's unfair to children to bring them into a world where they're not wanted." 139

17a. Every child is wanted by someone; there is no such thing as an unwanted child.

17b. There is a difference between an unwanted pregnancy and an unwanted child.

17c. "Unwanted" describes not a condition of the child, but an attitude of adults.

17d. The problem of unwantedness is a good argument for wanting children, but a poor argument for eliminating them.

17e. What is most unfair to unwanted children is to kill them.

18. "Having more unwanted children results in more child abuse." 142

18a. Most abused children were wanted by their parents.

18b. Child abuse has not decreased since abortion was legalized, but has dramatically increased.

18c. If children are viewed as expendable before birth, they will be viewed as expendable after birth.

18d. It is illogical to argue that a child is protected from abuse through abortion since abortion *is* child abuse.

19. "Restricting abortion would be unfair to the poor and minorities, who need it most." 146

19a. It is not unfair for some people to have less opportunity than others to kill the innocent.

19b. The rich and white, not the poor and minorities, are most committed to unrestricted abortion.

19c. Prochoice advocates want the poor and minorities to have abortions, but oppose requirements that abortion risks and alternatives be explained to them.

19d. Planned Parenthood's abortion advocacy was rooted in the eugenics movement and its bias against the mentally and physically handicapped and minorities.

20. "Abortion helps solve the problem of overpopulation and raises the quality of life."   150

20a. The current birthrate in America is less than what is needed to maintain our population level.

20b. The dramatic decline in our birthrate will have a disturbing economic effect on America.

20c. Overpopulation is frequently blamed for problems with other causes.

20d. If there is a population problem that threatens our standard of living, the solution is not to kill off part of the population.

20e. Sterilization and abortion as cures to overpopulation could eventually lead to mandatory sterilization and abortion.

20f. The "quality of life" concept is breeding a sense of human expendability that has far-reaching social implications.

21. "Even if abortion were made illegal, there would still be many abortions."   157

21a. That harmful acts against the innocent will take place regardless of the law is a poor argument for having no law.

21b. The law can guide and educate people to choose better alternatives.

21c. Laws concerning abortion have significantly influenced whether women choose to have abortions.

22. "The antiabortion beliefs of the minority shouldn't be imposed on the majority."   159

22a. Major polls clearly indicate that the majority, not the minority, believes that there should be greater restrictions on abortion.

22b. Many people's apparent agreement with abortion law stems from their ignorance of what the law really is.

22c. Beliefs that abortion should be restricted are embraced by a majority in each major political party.

22d. In 1973 the Supreme Court imposed a minority morality on the nation, ignoring the votes of citizens and the decisions of state legislatures.

23. "The antiabortion position is a religious belief that threatens the vital separation of church and state." *165*

23a. Many nonreligious people believe that abortion kills children and that it is wrong.

23b. Morality must not be rejected just because it is supported by religion.

23c. America was founded on a moral base dependent upon principles of the Bible and the Christian religion.

23d. Laws related to church and state were intended to assure freedom *for* religion, not freedom *from* religion.

23e. Religion's waning influence on our society directly accounts for the moral deterioration threatening our future.

Part Four: Arguments Concerning Health and Safety

---

24. "If abortion is made illegal, tens of thousands of women will again die from back-alley and clothes-hanger abortions." *173*

24a. For decades prior to its legalization, 90 percent of abortions were done by physicians in their offices, not in back alleys.

24b. It is not true that tens of thousands of women were dying from illegal abortions before abortion was legalized.

24c. The history of abortion in Poland invalidates claims that making abortion illegal would bring harm to women.

24d. Women still die from *legal* abortions in America.

24e. If abortion became illegal, abortions would be done with medical equipment, not clothes hangers.

24f. We must not legalize procedures that kill the innocent just to make the killing process less hazardous.

24g. The central horror of illegal abortion remains the central horror of legal abortion.

25. "Abortion is a safe medical procedure—safer than full-term pregnancy and childbirth." *178*

25a. Abortion is not safer than full-term pregnancy and childbirth.

25b. Though the chances of a woman's safe abortion are now greater, the number of suffering women is also greater because of the huge increase in abortions.

25c. Even if abortion were safer for the mother than childbirth, it would still remain fatal for the innocent child.

25d. Abortion can produce many serious medical problems.

25e. Abortion significantly raises the rate of breast cancer.

25f. The statistics on abortion complications and risks are often understated due to the inadequate means of gathering data.

25g. The true risks of abortion are rarely explained to women by those who perform abortions.

26. "Abortion is an easy and painless procedure." 184

26a. The various abortion procedures are often both difficult and painful for women.

26b. Abortion is often difficult and painful for fathers, grandparents, and siblings of the aborted child.

26c. Abortion is often difficult and painful for clinic workers.

26d. Abortion is difficult and painful for the unborn child.

26e. Even if abortion were made easy or painless for everyone, it wouldn't change the bottom-line problem that abortion kills children.

27. "Abortion relieves women of stress and responsibility, and thereby enhances their psychological well-being." 192

27a. Research demonstrates abortion's adverse psychological effects on women.

27b. The many postabortion therapy and support groups testify to the reality of abortion's potentially harmful psychological effects.

27c. The suicide rate is significantly higher among women who have had abortions than among those who haven't.

27d. Postabortion syndrome is a diagnosable psychological affliction.

27e. Many professional studies document the reality of abortion's adverse psychological consequences on a large number of women.

27f. Abortion can produce both short- and longer-term psychological damage, especially a sense of personal guilt.

27g. Most women have not been warned about and are completely unprepared for the psychological consequences of abortion.

28. "Abortion providers are respected medical professionals working in the woman's best interests."   201

28a. Abortion clinics do not have to maintain the high standards of health, safety, and professionalism required of hospitals.

28b. Many clinics are in the abortion industry because of the vast amounts of money involved.

28c. Clinic workers commonly prey on fear, pain, and confusion to manipulate women into getting abortions.

28d. Clinic workers regularly mislead or deceive women about the nature and development of their babies.

28e. Abortionists engage in acts so offensive to the public that most media outlets refuse to describe them even in the abortionist's own words.

28f. Abortionists, feminists, a past president of the United States, many congressmen, and the Supreme Court have defended partial-birth abortion, one of the most chilling medical atrocities in human history.

28g. Abortion clinics often exploit the feminist connection, making it appear that their motive is to stand up for women.

28h. Doctors doing abortions violate the fundamental oaths of the medical profession.

Part Five: Arguments Concerning the Hard Cases

---

29. "What about a woman whose life is threatened by pregnancy or childbirth?"   221

29a. It is an extremely rare case when abortion is required to save the mother's life.

29b. When two lives are threatened and only one can be saved, doctors must always save that life.

29c. Abortion for the mother's life and abortion for the mother's health are usually not the same issue.

29d. Abortion to save the mother's life was legal before convenience abortion was legalized and would continue to be if abortion were made illegal again.

30. "What about a woman whose unborn baby is diagnosed as deformed or handicapped?"   223

30a. The doctor's diagnosis is sometimes wrong.

30b. The child's deformity is often minor.

30c. Medical tests for deformity may cause as many problems as they detect.

30d. Handicapped children are often happy, always precious, and usually delighted to be alive.

30e. Handicapped children are not social liabilities, and bright and "normal" people are not always social assets.

30f. Using dehumanizing language may change our thinking, but not the child's nature or value.

30g. Our society is hypocritical in its attitude toward handicapped children.

30h. The adverse psychological effects of abortion are significantly more traumatic for those who abort because of deformity.

30i. The arguments for killing a handicapped unborn child are valid only if they also apply to killing born people who are handicapped.

30j. Abortions due to probable handicaps rob the world of unique human beings who would significantly contribute to society.

30k. Abortions due to imperfections have no logical stopping place; they will lead to designer babies, commercial products to be bred and marketed, leaving other people to be regarded as inferior and disposable.

31. "What about a woman who is pregnant due to rape or incest?"   231

31a. Pregnancy due to rape is extremely rare, and with proper treatment can be prevented.

31b. Rape is never the fault of the child; the guilty party, not an innocent party, should be punished.

31c. The violence of abortion parallels the violence of rape.

31d. Abortion does not bring healing to a rape victim.

31e. A child is a child regardless of the circumstances of his conception.

31f. What about already-born people who are "products of rape"?

31g. All that is true of children conceived in rape is true of those conceived in incest.

1. No adverse circumstance for one human being changes the nature and worth of another human being.
2. Laws must not be built on exceptional cases.

Part Six: Arguments Against the Character of Prolifers

32. "Antiabortionists are so cruel that they insist on showing hideous pictures of dead babies."   239

32a. What is hideous is not the pictures themselves, but the reality they depict.

32b. Pictures challenge our denial of the horrors of abortion. If something is too horrible to look at, perhaps it is too horrible to condone.

32c. Nothing could be more relevant to the discussion of something than that which shows what it really is.

32d. It is the prochoice position, not the prolife position, that is cruel.

33. "Prolifers don't care about women, and they don't care about babies once they're born. They have no right to speak against abortion unless they are willing to care for these children."   245

33a. Prolifers are actively involved in caring for women in crisis pregnancies and difficult child-raising situations.

33b. Prolifers are actively involved in caring for unwanted children and the other "disposable people" in society.

33c. It is abortion providers who do not provide support for women choosing anything other than abortion.

34. "The antiabortionists are a bunch of men telling women what to do."   250

34a. There is no substantial difference between men and women's views of abortion.

34b. Some polls suggest that more women than men oppose abortion.

34c. The great majority of prolife workers are women.

34d. If men are disqualified from the abortion issue, they should be disqualified on both sides.

34e. Men are entitled to take a position on abortion.

34f. There are many more women in prolife organizations than there are in proabortion organizations.

34g. Of women who have had abortions, far more are prolife activists than prochoice activists.

35. "Antiabortionists talk about the sanctity of human life, yet they favor capital punishment." 253

35a. Not all prolifers favor capital punishment.

35b. Capital punishment is rooted in a respect for innocent human life.

35c. There is a vast difference between punishing a convicted murderer and killing an innocent child.

36. "Antiabortion fanatics break the law, are violent, and bomb abortion clinics." 255

36a. Media coverage of prolife civil disobedience often bears little resemblance to what actually happens.

36b. Prolife civil disobedience should not be condemned without understanding the reasons behind it.

36c. Peaceful civil disobedience is consistent with the belief that the unborn are human beings.

36d. Prolife protests have been remarkably nonviolent, and even when there has been violence, it has often been committed by clinic employees and escorts.

36e. Abortion clinic bombing and violence are rare, and are neither done nor endorsed by prolife organizations.

37. "The antiabortionists distort the facts and resort to emotionalism to deceive the public." 261

37a. The facts themselves make abortion an emotional issue.

37b. It is not the prolife position, but the prochoice position that relies on emotionalism more than truth and logic.

37c. The prolife position is based on documented facts and empirical evidence, which many prochoice advocates ignore or distort.

37d. The prochoice movement consistently caricatures and misrepresents prolifers and their agenda.

37e. The prochoice movement, from its beginnings, has lied to and exploited women, including the "Roe" of *Roe* v. *Wade* and the "Doe" of *Doe* v. *Bolton*.

38. "Antiabortion groups hide behind a profamily facade, while groups such as Planned Parenthood are truly profamily because they assist in family planning." 266

38a. The prochoice movement's imposition of "family planning" on teenagers has substantially contributed to the actual cause of teen pregnancy.

38b. Through its opposition to parental notification and consent, Planned Parenthood consistently undermines the value and authority of the family.

38c. Planned Parenthood makes huge financial profits from persuading people to get abortions.

38d. Planned Parenthood has been directly involved in the scandals of trafficking baby body parts.

38e. As demonstrated in the case of Becky Bell, the prochoice movement is willing to distort and exploit family tragedies to promote its agenda.

38f. Planned Parenthood, the prochoice movement, and the media ignore family tragedies that do not support the prochoice agenda.

Summary Argument

---

39. "The last three decades of abortion rights have helped make our society a better place to live." 275

39a. Abortion has left terrible holes in our society.

39b. Abortion has made us a nation of schizophrenics concerning our children.

39c. Abortion is a modern holocaust which is breeding unparalleled violence and to which we are accomplices.

39d. Abortion is taking us in a direction from which we might never return.

39e. Abortion has ushered in the brave new world of human pesticides.

39f. Abortion has led us into complete moral subjectivism in which we are prone to justify as ethical whatever it is we want to do.

Final Appeals

Appendices

INTRODUCTION TO THE REVISED EDITION

When I wrote the first edition of this book in the early 1990s, I wanted to supply people with a carefully researched, highly useable resource. I had no idea the impact it would have. The book sold over 75,000 copies, a huge number for a book on this subject. Most importantly, it has been repeatedly used by thousands of people in their attempts to speak up for those who cannot speak for themselves.

Many prolife groups use the book to train their volunteers and their speakers. College ethics classes use it as a textbook. I have received letters from hundreds of high school and college students who've used the book to help them prepare speeches or write term papers and editorials for their school newspapers. I've spoken to three thousand public high school students at a single convention, distributing free copies of the book, which they eagerly snatched up.[1] Pastors have asked to use it in their sermons; people write and ask if they can use it to construct letters to newspapers, family members, and representatives. (The answer is always yes.)

One church took out full-page ads in its city's daily newspaper, each ad presenting the answers to various prochoice arguments. Internet groups have posted portions of the book, and discussion groups have systematically gone over its logic. Individuals have bought hundreds of copies and donated them to public libraries across the country. *ProLife Answers to ProChoice Arguments* has been translated into several languages and won a national book award in Italy.[2]

Some readers have completely changed their mind about abortion. While working on this revision I received an e-mail from a young woman saying, "After reading your prolife book, I went through a belief change. I used to be strongly prochoice. Now, I'm strongly prolife." (She then asked for a recommendation of a local prolife group where she could volunteer.)

A large number of nominally prolife readers have picked up the book to discover that they have never understood the issues, arguments, and strength of the prolife case. They had been intimidated by the prochoice assumptions in the media, on campuses, and in workplaces. Many have written to say that, for the first time, they've been equipped to defend the prolife position. They say they are now speaking up for those who cannot speak for themselves.

For the last four years, I've been acutely aware of the need for a new edition of this resource. While the overall structure of the book remains the same, updates and revisions have been made on virtually every page. Dated materials have been removed and treatment of current issues added. About three hundred of the nearly eight hundred endnotes are brand new, from more current sources, many of those in the 2000s.

Because of all the speaking opportunities, radio interviews, panel discussions, and personal conversations that came as a result of the first edition, I felt much more prepared to write this revision. Having received a steady stream of input from people about what is most helpful in the book, I know what people are looking for and what they can use. This book is a tool, a resource not only to be read and contemplated, but to be *used*. As I complete the exhausting process involved in this extensive revision, I honestly believe it is a more helpful resource than ever, perhaps the most thorough and useable prolife resource available. In any case, I hope readers will make frequent use of it.

How Has the Book Changed?

Statistics have been updated and new charts have been added. The resource materials in Appendix K have all been double-checked and corrected, with many new additions, including Internet web sites. The four appendices from the original book are now accompanied by seven new ones, and the old ones have been revised. Some people may find the appendices to be the most useable resources in this book. (See additional resources at www.epm.org.)

New subjects have been added, including partial-birth abortion, fetal tissue research, and frozen embryos. I've included significant material on the Hippocratic Oath. I've included the remarkable court testimony of abortionist Leroy Carhart. I've added the accounts of Norma McCorvey (Jane Roe of *Roe* v. *Wade*) and Sandra Cano (Mary Doe of *Doe* v. *Bolton*), who in 1995 both came forward to tell their stories of having been deceived and used by their attorneys and abortion advocates (see answer 37e). I've quoted from the unforgettable speech the late Mother Teresa made in 1994 at the annual Prayer Breakfast in Washington, D.C. Standing tiny and hunched over before some of the most powerful political figures in America, including the president and many members of Congress who pride themselves on their prochoice viewpoint, she rebuked them for their callousness to the unborn and called upon them to change their hearts and actions and reach out their arms to embrace our tiniest children (see answer 20f). It was a breath of fresh air, one of the finest messages of hope in the recent history of a nation's capital that has been under a shroud of darkness on both sides of the political aisle.[3]

In stark contrast to Mother Teresa's words, a year later Jocelyn Elders, then Surgeon General of the United States, said, "America needs to get over its love affair with the fetus." The two women held up to the country two different visions of our moral obligation to our weak and small citizens.

Several significant books and articles have been written since the first edition of this book, among them philosophy professor Francis J. Beckwith's *Politically Correct Death*[4] and Mark Crutcher's *Lime 5*[5], a startling exposé of abortion clinics in America. What may be the most significant essay on abortion ever written is feminist Naomi Wolf's 1995 article in the *New Republic,* acknowledging that pro-choice advocates such as herself must finally admit truths about the unborn they have long denied.[6] I quote from each of these writings in this book.

How Has the Nation Changed in Regard to Life Issues?

Every day news clippings remind us of our moral decline in the respect for human life:

> Doorsteps and trash bins are more suitable for daily newspapers than what many Houston residents found in those places last year—abandoned babies. Residents found thirteen discarded babies over a period of ten months in the nation's fourth largest city. Three of the thirteen were found dead. The sheer number of abandonments left citizens and city officials stunned.[7]

In November 1996 a teenage girl delivered a child in a Delaware motel, then she and her boyfriend allegedly put the living baby in a plastic bag and dropped it in a dumpster.[8]

In June 1997 a New Jersey teenager gave birth in a bathroom stall at her high school prom. She dropped the baby in the trash, then returned to the dance floor and asked the band to play her favorite song, "The Unforgiven."[9]

In June 2000 a seventeen-year-old mother who was attending night school hurled her baby into the Passaic River after she couldn't find a baby sitter.[10]

In the wake of the school shootings and a generation of violent and self-absorbed children, many Americans have become less flippant about the moral reference points offered by the Christian faith and are taking them more seriously than ever. Some are realizing that we are facing the terrible consequences of a generation that has grown up under abortion on demand.

The power of the strong to determine the fate of the weak has been inbred through laws and policies and classroom discussions on abortion. What would have been repellant to previous generations simply seems normal to them—and it is we who have made it seem normal. In August 2000 a Florida mother made headlines by pulling a gun on her sixteen-year-old and forcing her to an abortion clinic.

But there is good news. Among both the young and the old, a backlash is taking place. People are sensing that something is desperately wrong when the strong dehumanize and kill the weak, inventing sanctimonious slogans to justify it. Included in this backlash is a reexamination of the possibility that prolife advocates, many of them Christians, may have been correct to defend the rights of unborn children and to warn that if we fail to do so, our society will lose its soul.

In 1994 my home state of Oregon became the first jurisdiction on the planet to officially legalize physician assisted suicide.[11] In 1997 it reaffirmed the decision by another popular vote. The warnings of Francis Schaeffer in the 1970s—that abortion was part of a slippery slope that would surely lead to the legalization of killing adults—were fulfilled right before our eyes. For the moment, this killing remains voluntary. But we have already seen cases where family members are coercing elderly parents to agree to be killed by their doctors.

A recent Oregon case involved an eighty-five-year-old woman with growing dementia. She was originally denied eligibility for assisted suicide by the psychiatrist who evaluated her, due to her cognitive impairments and the fact that her family appeared to be pressuring her. A second opinion was sought, and although this psychologist admitted that the patient's "choices may be influenced by her family's wishes and her daughter, Erika, may be somewhat coercive" she nevertheless approved the suicide.[12] The final call came down to a single hospital administrator. He approved the lethal overdose for this elderly woman.[13]

Some states have passed special laws against partial-birth abortion and fetal tissue research. State laws requiring twenty-four-hour waiting periods, informed consent, and parental consent for abortion have made limited strides in reducing the numbers of children killed. Beginning in May 1998 the Genocide Awareness Project (GAP) brought to twenty-three college campuses a startling depiction of abortion that visually connected it with the holocaust, the killing fields, and the racial atrocities in American history (see answer 32b). The revival of moral discourse has encouraged the Center for Bio-Ethical Reform to bring GAP off the college campus and into mainstream America. A new project is in the formative stage, "The Reproductive Choice Campaign," which involves semitrucks displaying large graphic abortion billboards and traveling on densely populated freeways in an effort to reach larger numbers of people and "make it impossible to ignore and impossible to trivialize the horror of abortion."[14]

Feminists for Life has provided pregnancy resource kits to college health clinics, advisors, and counselors across the country and is leading a discussion on developing practical resources for pregnant and parenting students on college campuses—including housing, child care, and maternity coverage in health care. Planned Parenthood's *Insider* calls Feminists for Life's College Outreach Program the "newest and most challenging concept" in student organizing and predicts that it "could have a profound impact" on colleges "as well as on Planned Parenthood's education and advocacy efforts."[15]

In the midst of an ethic dominated by Darwinian thought, one of the most significant recent developments is the intelligent design movement within the field of biochemistry. Scientists who include Michael Behe are arguing that Darwinian evolution simply cannot begin to account for the extreme complexity of the machinery within cells, which is now visible at the subatomic level.[16] A number of mainstream scientists have now gone on record as rejecting the randomness of evolution in favor of intelligent design.[17]

This movement away from Darwinian evolution may serve at the very least to challenge people to rethink their fatalistic and nihilistic assumptions about human behavior. The unspoken but underlying premise of abortion is survival of the fittest. That dogma is being challenged as people reconsider whether there is in fact an intelligent Designer behind our intelligent design. By acknowledging a Creator some are beginning to return to the concept of a moral Judge who will hold us accountable for our actions toward the youngest and weakest of our kind.

In the first edition of this book I quoted several times from Peter Singer, who was then still a fringe figure in bioethics. I cite him a number of times in the revised edition, now that he has become bioethics professor at Princeton University, a platform he is using to give credibility to beliefs that the unborn and many infants and handicapped people don't deserve to live and should be eliminated. (The scariest thing about Singer is not that he is so far "out there," but that he is one of the few people willing to honestly take the abortion mentality to its logical conclusions.)

There are some positive developments related to the status of the unborn. A 2000 Gallup poll indicated that 19 percent of Americans believe that abortion should be "illegal in all circumstances."[18] That is the highest percentage in the previous fifteen years. While the same Gallup poll indicated that Americans are evenly split on the issue, it said that "two-thirds of those who hold the prolife view say they feel very strongly about it compared to just over half of prochoice adherents."[19]

States are routinely allowing prosecutions for acts that result in the death of the unborn. Kentucky's House of Representatives Judiciary Committee approved a 2000 bill giving legal status to unborn children. It will allow parents to sue for the wrongful deaths of babies in the womb. Under the bill, the unborn would be recognized as a "person" from the moment of conception, "without regard to age, health, or condition of dependency."[20] The proposal would allow parents to file lawsuits claiming that wrongful acts by others led to their unborn babies' deaths. Significantly, abortionists would be specifically exempted from liability! But surely some people will begin to see the moral schizophrenia reflected in this exemption.

On a national level, a bill called the Unborn Victims of Violence Act would dictate that if an unborn child is injured or killed during an act of violence, the attacker could be charged for both harm to the mother and to the unborn child. This means that an assailant who kills a pregnant woman and her unborn child would be guilty of two murders, not one. The House passed this bill by a 254–172 margin and as this book goes to press, it is scheduled to appear before the Senate.[21] In July 2000 the House also unanimously passed a bill prohibiting states from executing a pregnant woman.

Every day about eight thousand American young people are infected with a sexually transmitted disease.[22] Despite this fact, there is some very good news. A third of all school districts now require abstinence-only sex education programs, and more than 80 percent require that their programs emphasize abstinence. Only 14 percent still require comprehensive safer-sex programs.

"Abstinence has exploded over the last ten years," says Peter Brandt, who serves as acting director of the National Coalition for Abstinence Education. The new emphasis comes alongside a drop in teen pregnancy and sexual activity rates, which have fallen for the first time in two decades. The Centers for Disease Control report a 9 percent decrease in teen pregnancy and 28 percent decrease in teen abortions during the 1990s. According to the CDC, the percentage of teens abstaining from sex rose from 46 to 52 percent from 1995 to 1997.[23]

Adults tend to underestimate young people's ability to stand up for what's right and to hold to high standards. We tend to lower the bar, but many of them want to raise it. The extreme popularity of Joshua Harris's *I Kissed Dating Goodbye* (over 800,000 copies sold) testifies to this fact.

Fetal Tissue Research

In 2000 paralyzed actor Christopher Reeve asked a Senate subcommittee hearing, "Is it more ethical for a woman to donate unused embryos that will never become human beings, or to let them be tossed away as so much garbage when they could help save thousands of lives?"[24]

Reeve's question supplies a noble-sounding reason for aborting babies, one which will likely persuade many women wrestling with their consciences that abortion, after all, will really help save other lives. It appears to take the moral high ground by making it sound as if one side in the debate wanted embryos to "be tossed away as so much garbage," while his side wants to save thousands of lives.

The logic was reminiscent of those who justified the Nazi doctors' experimentation on prisoners by saying that people were being killed anyway, so why not help others by benefiting from the research and remains?

Stem cells are versatile master cells from which a variety of tissues and organs develop. They are considered prime prospects for effective biomedical research. They are available from a variety of benign human sources, including consenting adults, umbilical cord blood, and placentas.

But government scientists in the National Institute of Health are determined to use stem cells from embryonic human babies who lose their lives in the harvesting. As I write, debate is raging, and the NIH is forging new policy on use of the unborn in stem cell research.[25] The NIH promises that federally funded human embryonic stem cell research will be "conducted in an ethical and legal manner." It also claims that it "understands and respects the ethical, legal, and social issues" associated with it.[26] The question is whether it is possible to deliberately destroy a human embryo—meaning a small young human being—in an ethical manner.

Frozen People

In February 2000, Dr. Bernard Nathanson testified before Congress on reproductive technologies. He said:

> There is a very large market in frozen embryos. There are about 50,000 embryos in various cryobanks across the country. What are we to do? Freezing can only preserve an embryo five or six years. Some entrepreneurs have the answer: Sell them. One enterprising reporter showed that if you go to Columbia University, you can tell them what kind of baby

you want, matching your physique, your ethnic background and your educational background, and they will pick out a frozen embryo that perfectly matches what you want and sell it to you and implant the embryo in the womb of your wife or girlfriend for all of $2,750....

There is technology such as posthumous sperm removal. If a man dies and the widow wants to become pregnant, within a reasonable period of time, the urologist puts a needle into the testes, pulls out some sperm and fertilizes her egg. So the dead man is a new father, reversing all normal familial relationships and procedures.[27]

Gonads are being sold for $550 each, and research has been done to extract ova from aborted girls and use them for in vitro fertilization.[28] How would you like to explain to a child that his biological mother was an aborted baby?

The much-heralded two hundred fifty million dollar Human Genome Project has sequenced over 90 percent of the human genetic code.[29] In March 2000, the British government announced that it will begin conducting routine genetic testing on pregnant women. Health authorities have been instructed to offer a range of genetic tests to pregnant women who could be carrying a disorder. They have also been advised that proabortion counseling should be given as a matter of course if the unborn child is found to be abnormal.[30] Bioethics professor C. Ben Mitchell says that prenatal genetic screening "targets fetuses for destruction, since we don't have cures or treatments for most genetic anomalies."[31]

Genetic manipulation and the abortion mentality are combining to pave the way to designer babies, commercial products to be bred and marketed, leaving other people—both unborn and born—to be regarded as inferior and disposable.

In 2000 an Ohio couple filed suit against their two doctors because the doctors allegedly did not warn them of their daughter's spina bifida, for which they would have aborted her:

"They are saying the child should be dead," attorney Michael Lyon stated. "What would have avoided the damages to this child? Death, termination. I can't imagine the child standing here ten years from now saying, 'I want to be dead.'" Ann Ruley Combs, lawyer for the other doctor, Leela Dwivedi, warned that if the family wins its suit, "we're creating an expectation that every child has a right to be born perfect."[32]

Baby Sarah and Baby Samuel

In 1999 an unborn child named Sarah Marie Switzer, twenty-four weeks after conception, was operated on for spina bifida. A photograph published in *Life* magazine captured the world's attention. That photograph appears on the back cover of this book. It won *Life*'s award for picture of the year in science and technology. Sarah was put back inside her mother and was born two months later, nine weeks premature.

In 1999 another unborn child, Samuel Armas, was operated on for spina bifida at twenty-one weeks. When he saw a picture similar to the one on the back cover, family advocate James Dobson called it "the photograph of the decade." Chuck Colson described it this way:

As the surgeon was closing the womb, the miracle happened. Baby Samuel pushed his hand out of the womb and grabbed the surgeon's finger. Photographer Michael Clancy caught this astonishing act on film. And in that instant, Clancy went from being prochoice to being prolife. As he put it, "I was totally in shock for two hours after the surgery.... I know abortion is wrong now—it's absolutely wrong."[33]

Samuel Armas was sewn back into his mother's womb, then born nearly four months later in December 1999. Unfortunately, many people have not looked at these pictures. Nor have they considered the implications of what it means for physicians to be treating a patient, giving him anesthetics to dull the pain, performing a lifesaving or life-enhancing surgery on him, watching him grasp the surgeon's finger, then turning around and saying it is perfectly acceptable to kill that same patient during the remaining four months until he is born.

The good news is that some people are finally starting to see the self-evident moral inconsistency of this position. The bad news is, other people remain blind. A stunning example of this (as I point out under answer 8d, "Abortionists know that human life begins before birth") is that the surgeon whose finger both Baby Samuel and Baby Sarah were grasping in the pictures performs abortions on spina bifida children of the same age!

It is not just abortionists who prefer not to deal with this evidence. Journalist Matt Drudge, author of the "Drudge Report," attempted to use Baby Samuel's photo on his Fox News Network television show, but was forbidden to do so by network management. They feared he might use the photo as "a jumping-off point to talk about partial-birth abortion."[34] Due to the network's censorship of the photograph, Drudge resigned.

20/20's Exposé on the Illegal Sale of Fetal Body Parts

One story provides an example of the good news/bad news aspects of the current discussions concerning abortion. The television news program *20/20* conducted a three-month investigation on the fetal body parts industry, and revealed their findings on the March 8, 2000 telecast. They reported that a black market industry has grown up around tissue and organs from aborted unborn children, donated "to help medical research," then marketed for hundreds or thousands of dollars.

Correspondent Chris Wallace interviewed a Missouri medical technician, Dean Alberty, who said that two tissue-retrieval companies he worked for encouraged him to take fetal tissue obtained from women who had not consented to donate their unborn children to medical research.

20/20 found that some companies are charging very high fees and showed price lists charging $325 for a spinal cord, $550 for a reproductive organ, and $999 for a brain.

How are these prices determined? One *20/20* producer went undercover as a potential investor to meet Dr. Miles Jones, a Missouri pathologist whose company, Opening Lines, obtains fetal tissue from clinics and ships it to research labs. "It's market force," Dr. Jones told the producer, explaining how he sets his prices. "It's what you can sell it for." He says that he hopes to run his own abortion facility in Mexico so he can get a greater supply of fetal tissue by offering cheaper abortions: "If you control the flow, it's probably the equivalent of the invention of the assembly line."

"That's trading in body parts. There's no doubt about it," said Arthur Caplan, director of the University of Pennsylvania's Center for Bioethics.[35]

While ABC's program was an eye-opener for many, it failed to air Alberty's eyewitness accounts of babies who were dissected and their organs harvested while still functioning. In these cases, according to the eyewitness, abortions were not performed—instead, babies were born alive in order to procure undamaged fetal specimens. ABC shed no light on the connection between partial-birth abortion and fetal tissue marketing, though evidence points to a direct connection between the late term abortion method that delivers a whole and unfragmented child for the intended procurement of limbs and organs....[36]

ABC also ignored other significant allegations brought to its attention by Life Dynamics, and chose not to identify Planned Parenthood's direct involvement in the scandal.[37]

Ironically, the report expressed no concern whatsoever that children were being brutally murdered and dismembered, only the concern that some people are improperly making money off donated body parts. This is equivalent to being upset not that Holocaust victims were dying to provide lampshades made of human skin, but only that entrepreneurs were making too much money from the sale of the lamps. As Life Dynamics put it, *"20/20's focus on the money trail is like pointing out that smoke from the ovens at Auschwitz violated Germany's Clean Air Act."*[38]

On the one hand, we must be grateful the abortion industry is finally being exposed. On the other hand, those exposing it are focusing on secondary issues which pale in comparison to the primary issue of what's being done to children.

Where Are We Going?

In his monumental work *How Now Shall We Live?* Chuck Colson points to indicators that the secularization of America is grinding to a halt. He suggests that despite many of our alarming social problems, "some of the most destructive pathologies are beginning to decline." These include the decline in birthrate among unmarried teens, the decline in surgical abortions, and the reductions in the number of people on welfare. Colson asks,

Why are cultural trends shifting? Because modernity has played out its destructive logical consequences. All the ideologies, all the utopian promises that have marked this century have proven utterly bankrupt. Americans have achieved what modernism presented as life's greatest shining purpose: individual autonomy, the right to do what one chooses. Yet this has not produced the promised freedom; instead, it has led to the loss of community and civility, to kids shooting kids in schoolyards, to citizens huddling in gated communities for protection.

We have discovered that we cannot live with the chaos that inevitably results from choice divorced from morality.

As a result, Americans are groping for something that will restore the shattered bonds of family and community, something that will make sense of life.[39]

My hope and prayer is that this book, in its new and improved form, will be a tool in the hands of both church and culture. May it, by God's grace, help us restore the respect for human life that resides near the core of any good nation.

WHY THIS BOOK IS NECESSARY

"Do we really need another book on abortion? What could be said that hasn't been said already?"

Given the number of books on abortion, why have I written yet another one, and why should you bother to read it?

This book is necessary because the stakes are so high in the abortion debate.

Abortion is the most frequently performed surgery on adults in America.[40] One out of four babies conceived in the United States is surgically aborted (with an unknown but growing number of chemical abortions).[41] Since about 49 percent of all pregnancies are unplanned,[42] this means about half of unplanned pregnancies are terminated by abortion. Abortions outnumber live births in fourteen major metropolitan areas.[43] There are about 1.37 million reported abortions in this country every year (down from 1.61 in 1990).[44] There have been nearly 40 million U.S. surgical abortions since abortion was legalized in 1973.

The abortion rate is the number of induced abortions per 1000 women aged 15 through 44 years. For 1996, the rate was 20.[45] That means 2 percent of all women of reproductive age in the United States had an induced abortion in 1996.

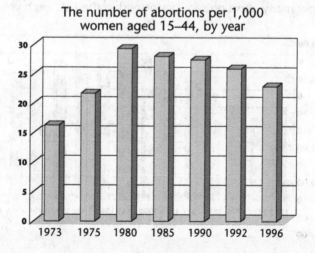

The number of abortions per 1,000 women aged 15–44, by year

The 1996 abortion ratio (the number of induced abortions per 1000 live births) was 314.[46] More than 30 million U.S. women have had induced abortions since nationwide legalization of abortion in 1973.[47]

The World Health Organization (WHO) estimates that each day between 100,000 and 150,000 induced abortions occur, or about 36 to 53 million worldwide each year.

If the prochoice position is correct, the freedom to choose abortion is an expression of equal rights, fairness, and justice. Abortion is a necessity, making society a better place for all. If we ever went back to a society in which abortion was not freely available, it would be a gigantic step backward in the history of human rights.

If the prolife position is correct, the 3,753 abortions occurring every day represent 3,753 human casualties. And though none of these deaths is reported on the evening news (though the same unborn child killed by a bullet would be), each aborted child is just as real and just as valuable as older children. If these unborn are really babies, then America has one of the highest infant mortality rates in the world.

If abortion does *not* kill children, the prolife mentality is at best a nuisance and at worst a serious threat to women's rights and personal liberty. If abortion *does* kill children, the prochoice mentality is responsible for the deaths of 1.3 million innocent people each year, more than the combined total of Americans who have died in all wars in our history. This is not a case where "it doesn't make a difference who's right and who's wrong." No matter who is right or wrong, the stakes are enormously high.

How many abortions are performed in the U.S. each year?

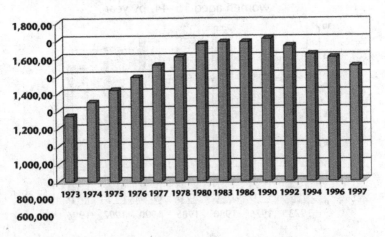

This book is necessary because there is so much tension and uncertainty about abortion.

In their extensive surveys of Americans, James Patterson and Peter Kim discovered that among issues people feel strongly about, abortion was number one—even above such hot issues as anti-Semitism, alcohol abuse, homelessness, the death penalty, pornography, and flag burning. A full 75 percent felt strongly about abortion one way or another.[48]

That many Americans feel strongly about abortion does not mean they have solid reasons for their feelings. A *Newsweek* poll asked, "Do you ever wonder whether your own position on abortion is the right one or not?" Significantly, 38 percent said yes and 7 percent didn't know, which indicates uncertainty as well.[49] Isn't it remarkable that an issue that is so important and that people feel so strongly about, is nonetheless so uncertain in the minds of so many? This book is written in part for that large number of uncertain people, in the hope that their uncertainty reflects openness to another point of view and to facts and logic that they may never have heard before.

This book is necessary because no single issue divides Americans as sharply as the issue of abortion.

In 1999 the Gallup News Service released a summary of current beliefs on the subject of abortion, with slightly different results than some of the information cited above:

> Three decades of extensive polling on the abortion issue have shown that Americans hold a complex set of opinions about the morality and legality of terminating a woman's pregnancy. However, when asked in a new Gallup poll to sum up their abortion views according to the labels favored by activists on each side, the public is almost evenly split on the issue, with 48% currently calling themselves "prochoice" and 42% identifying themselves as "pro-life." More than half of Americans in each group say they feel very strongly about their position, but just 19% insist they will support only candidates for major offices who share their abortion views.
>
> While adherence to the abortion labels tilts slightly in the prochoice direction, a follow-up question in the latest Gallup poll finds

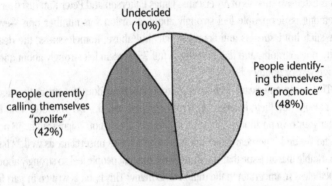

1999 Gallup poll summing up people's views on the issue of abortion

Undecided (10%)

People identifying themselves as "prochoice" (48%)

People currently calling themselves "prolife" (42%)

greater intensity of feeling on the part of prolife respondents. Two-thirds of those who hold the prolife view say they feel very strongly about it compared to just over half of prochoice adherents. The net result of these patterns is a nearly even division of Americans who feel very strongly on both sides of the issue, with a slight tilt in the prolife direction: 29% say they are very strongly prolife, while nearly as many, 26%, say they are very strongly prochoice. Taken together, 55% of Americans hold a very strong view on abortion. The rest indicate they feel less strongly about their positions on abortion, or have no opinion at all.[50]

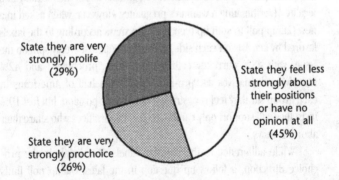

The intensity of feeling on the part of the respondents

State they are very strongly prolife (29%)

State they feel less strongly about their positions or have no opinion at all (45%)

State they are very strongly prochoice (26%)

Many of us have seen what happens when those who have strong opinions one way or the other try to discuss this issue. Sometimes the discussions are rational and productive. Sometimes they become quickly heated and accusatory. Many family gatherings have fallen into stone-cold silence when this issue has come up. It divides people not only on the streets and in workplaces, but in homes and churches. So, while abortion is hard to talk about, it is important to provide accurate information and a context in which that information can be discussed.

This book is necessary because the educational system does not present both sides of the abortion issue.

A representative of the National Abortion Rights Action League spoke in a high school social science class on the merits of abortion. Afterward, a student in the class asked the teacher if she could invite me to present a different view. When I arrived, the instructor, himself firmly prochoice, informed me that he had polled the students the day before and they had voted twenty-three to one for the prochoice position. Of course, they had made up their minds based on the information they'd been given. Unfortunately, that information was entirely one sided. It was certainly not complete, and much of it was not even accurate.

I presented the scientific, logical, and commonsense case for the humanity, value, and rights of unborn children. I showed the students intrauterine pictures demonstrating the development of the unborn at even the earliest stage that abortions occur. Some of the students were visibly shocked. Though these were objective and accessible scientific facts, no one had ever told them such things before. All they had ever heard were slogans and clichés about rights and privacy and choice, never tangible facts on which to build an accurate position.

After the presentation, the teacher said to me, "If we were to vote again, it would be different. Minds were changed today." Then he added something amazing: "You know, until now I had never heard the prolife position."

We must not miss this colossal irony. We live in what is supposed to be the most open-minded society in human history. We pride ourselves on giving our children an education that is broad, objective, and fact oriented. Yet here we have an intelligent, well-read social science teacher with a master's degree and decades of experience in the classroom, *who had never once heard a presentation of the prolife position*. Having never heard an alternative, how could he believe anything other than what he did? The poll of his students showed that just as he had accepted the prochoice position uncritically from others, they had done the same from him.

I, too, have never heard an accurate representation of the prolife position from any of the sources this teacher has relied upon for information, including public education and the media. Like most Americans, he has never studied the scientific evidence. He has never researched the nature and development of the unborn. He has not watched the movies of the unborn child in his mother's uterus. He has not looked thoughtfully at the pictures of aborted babies. He has not talked at length with women scarred by abortion.

The beliefs most people have about abortion do not come from research. They come indirectly, from hearing oft-repeated slogans and seeing movies such as the Oscar-winning *The Cider House Rules*:

> *The Cider House Rules* was billed as a tender coming-of-age saga about a young man who grew up in an orphanage. This institution was run by a kindly abortionist—back before abortion was even legal—a doctor who helped others by either caring for unwanted children in his orphanage or aborting them. "This man was to me the most compassionate creature I've ever played," said Michael Caine, who won best supporting actor for his role. When novelist John Irving, who wrote the script based on his book, won the Oscar for best adapted screenplay, his acceptance speech included a grandiose thank you to Planned Parenthood and the National Abortion Rights Action League—names that inspired roaring applause from the crowd.[51]

This is the nature of effective propaganda. Concepts that thinking citizens would find repugnant (such as cutting a little child to pieces) are wrapped in tender and compassionate packages. *The Cider House Rules* audiences walked away feeling warm about the work of an abortionist. This would never have occurred, of course, if the movie had shown what actually happens to a child in an abortion. The only way to make people feel good about abortion is to ignore or disguise what it actually is. Because the media and educational systems do this, most people never come to terms with the true nature of abortion.

But some will object, "I've heard what the antiabortionists think." In fact, the majority have heard at best a caricature of the prolife position—what prochoice advocates *say* is the prolife position.

This violates a fundamental rule of objective research. It's like listening to the Republican candidate for president explain the Democratic candidate's views, then thinking you've given the Democrat a fair hearing. It's like having a Ford dealer tell you about the difference between Ford and Toyota trucks, then saying you know all about Toyota trucks. *You will never get an accurate view of any position until you hear it directly from a person who actually holds that position.*

I have listened at length to prochoice advocates. I have heard and understood their position. Have you ever listened at length to a prolife advocate and really heard his or her position? Heard it to the point of understanding, even if you disagree? If not, this book is your opportunity.

This book is necessary because the media are biased against the prolife position.

For years the prochoice position has had a hot line to our brains. By reading newspapers and magazines and watching television, we have all earned the equivalent of a doctorate in prochoice thinking.

On some issues it's possible to get a balanced view. Given the variety of positions reflected in different media sources, we can compare and sift through the information from both sides. But in the case of abortion, the two sides are not represented to most Americans. A person who reads the newspaper, subscribes to one of the newsweeklies, listens to the radio, and watches national and local news programs may appear to be well informed. But when it comes to the abortion issue, in most cases he receives input from only one side.

Interviews with 240 journalists and editors in the media elite indicate that a full 90 percent of them approve of abortion for almost any reason, a much higher percentage than in the general public.[52] Numbers of these are prochoice activists, and one of their means of activism is the news service for which they work. Because they approve of abortion rights—often with a passion—they want viewers and readers to approve, too. Consequently they tell us things that make us approve and don't tell us things that would make us disapprove. Bias is a fact of life. I have it, and so do you. But most Americans don't get their information from you or me. Most get it from the popular media. Because of the extreme dominance of the prochoice position, the media is out of balance, and most Americans have not even begun to hear a fair representation of both sides in the abortion debate.

For example, the *Los Angeles Times* has required its writers to use the terms *prochoice* and *antiabortion*.[53] This lets one group start with the crucial semantic edge of sounding positive and the other with the deadly disadvantage of sounding negative. The *Times* gives editors, reporters, and readers no choice but prochoice.

Consider the comparative coverage of two demonstrations, one prochoice and one prolife, both in Washington, D.C., almost exactly one year apart. According to the park police, a prochoice rally had about 125,000 people. Nevertheless, the figure consistently used by the media was 300,000. The prolife rally a year later was attended by an estimated 300,000 people. It was at least twice as large as the prochoice event. Yet a major news network reported the crowd at 60,000 until it was embarrassed into raising the figure.

The day after the prochoice rally, the *Washington Post* gave it front page coverage. Every conceivable angle of the rally was featured in no less than a dozen separate stories, including the lead story that went more than fifteen columns. The *Post* had also printed a map and schedule for the march in its Sunday edition, which was the equivalent of tens of thousands of dollars in free advertising and recruiting.[54] Likewise, *USA Today* had run a front-page, full-color picture the Friday before.

A year later, the day after the much larger prolife rally, the *Washington Post* devoted to that event a grand total of one story and one photograph on page B3. *Time*, which gave a five-page cover story to the smaller rally, devoted no coverage whatsoever to the prolife rally.

The bias has been so blatant that people have begun to complain. To their credit, some in the media are listening. Lisa Myers of NBC said, "Some of the stories I have read or seen have almost seemed like cheerleading for the prochoice side."[55] Ethan Bronner of the *Boston Globe* said, "I think that when abortion opponents complain about a bias in newsrooms against their cause, they're absolutely right."[56] Richard Harwood of the *Washington Post* said that his paper's coverage of a prolife event was "shabby" and admitted, "This affair has left a blot on the paper's professional reputation."[57] David Shaw of the *Los Angeles Times* gave many illustrations of media bias on abortion, including this: "Abortion opponents are often described as 'militant' or 'strident.' Such characterizations are seldom used to describe abortion-rights advocates, many of whom can be militant or strident—or both."[58]

What happens when a reporter goes against the grain of the prochoice bias? Susan Okie of the *Washington Post* wrote a story that wasn't even about abortion—it concerned new procedures for saving premature babies. She was warned by colleagues that this kind of story was not good for the abortion rights movement. That the story was true and accurate was beside the point. When corrected, she said she felt like she was "being herded back into line."[59]

Susan Okie's experience is by no means unique. *Newsweek* warns us that the "thought police" are now everywhere, teaching us to be "politically correct."[60] PC has been called the "New McCarthyism" because it labels and punishes people who use terminology or take positions out of line with the progressive liberal establishment of education (which is normally mirrored by the media). *Newsweek* included a photograph of forty buttons with politically correct slogans; nine were abortion related, and every one was a prochoice slogan. As anyone in higher education and the media will tell you, it is PC to be prochoice and it isn't PC to be prolife.

It is not just the fault of the media and education establishments that they have been dominated by one perspective on abortion. Prolifers have, for the most part, failed to speak up with clarity and reason. They have let the other side frame the debate rather than taking care to frame it themselves. My hope is that this book will help another side—one based on facts and established ethical standards—to at last be heard.

This book is necessary because it is a comprehensive, documented, and accurate presentation of the prolife position.

Is this book biased? Of course it is. The question is not bias, the question is which bias is most solidly based on the facts. Which bias is the most reasonable and defensible?

I have tried to be fair. I have tried not to quote people out of context, and I have sought to accurately represent the prochoice position. I know many prochoice people whom I love and respect. I do not believe they are plotting to destroy society. I think they honestly believe that abortion is a necessary option that is ultimately best for women and for society.

Are the interactions between prochoicers and prolifers destined to be dialogues of the deaf? Or is there a common ground upon which they can meet? I believe there is at least a threefold common ground.

First, there is the common ground of empirical data—of scientific and psychological evidence that we need not and should not deny. Second, we share the ability (though it's hard to hold to in the face of our prejudices) to be logical and rational in applying this truth. Third, though it is not as large or solid as it was even two decades ago, most people still share a common ground of morality and some sense of justice, fairness, and compassion.

Francis Beckwith, formerly philosophy professor at the University of Nevada, Las Vegas, has long experience in this debate. He maintains that there is considerable common ground shared by prochoicers and prolifers:

First, both sides of the abortion debate believe that all human persons possess certain inalienable rights regardless of whether their governments protect these rights. That is why both sides appeal to what each believes is a fundamental right. The prolife advocate appeals to "life." The abortion-rights advocate appeals to "liberty"....

It is apparent then that the main dispute in the abortion debate does not involve differing values, but disagreement about both the application of these values and the truth of certain facts. The abortion-rights advocate does not deny that human beings have a fundamental right to life. He just believes that this right to life is not extended to the unborn since they are not fully human and/or their existence demands that another [the pregnant woman] is asked to make significant nonobligatory sacrifices. The prolife advocate does not deny that human persons have the liberty to make choices that they believe are in their best interests. He believes that this liberty does not entail the right to choose abortion since such a choice conflicts with the life, liberty, and interests of another human person [the unborn entity].

In summary, since there is a common ground between two moral positions that are often depicted as absolutely polarized, we can coherently reason and argue about this issue. And since there is a common ground of values, the question as to which position is correct rests on which one is best established by the facts and is consistent with our common values.[61]

Some readers will also share a confidence in the Bible as the Word of God and see it as the basis upon which morality must be built. Yet I have found that even among those who do not accept the Bible's authority, there is often enough common ground to discuss the abortion issue and to arrive at similar conclusions because of a mutual respect for the social justice and compassion reflected in the Scriptures, embodied in Jesus Christ, and traditionally respected throughout our nation's history. (Several of the appendices appeal to the teachings of Scriptures.)

I do not ask anyone to accept the prolife position without thinking. On the contrary, I ask that readers look at the evidence and weigh it on its own merit. I ask that stereotypes of the prolife position be set aside. I further ask the reader to be intellectually honest and resist the temptation to be politically correct by holding to the prochoice position even if it turns out that the evidence contradicts it.

I also ask that you not buy into ad hominem arguments. Many false accusations have been brought against prolifers (some of which are dealt with under arguments 32–38). However, I have certainly known some prolife jerks, just as I've known some very decent prochoice people. If you think some prolife people are out to lunch, you are no doubt correct. That has nothing to do, however, with whether or not the prolife position is accurate. Truth and winsomeness are not the same thing, and issues should be decided on the basis of truth, not personalities.

Do I encourage people to study the prochoice as well as the prolife position? Of course! Go to the prochoice sources and decide for yourself whether I'm stating their arguments accurately. I'm completely anticensorship on the abortion issue. Let's put all the cards on the table. Let's not hold back any of the evidence. Let's bring out the statistics, study the intrauterine pictures, show pictures of aborted unborns, hear from women who have had abortions, both prochoicers and prolifers. Let's listen to geneticists and biologists, as well as abortionists who are prochoice and former abortionists who are now prolife. Let each side present its case, and may the best case win. Truth is always served by a full disclosure of the facts. Error has good reason to fear such disclosure.

This book is necessary because it is an organized, logical, and easily referenced resource offering answers to every major prochoice argument.

This book presents prolife answers to the most frequently used prochoice arguments. Most readers will recognize these arguments, but many readers will never have heard answers to them.

This book is written in a clear, concise, and easily referenced format. I have designed it to be user-friendly, with the busy reader in mind. I use an outline style, with highlighted features that allow the reader to scan major points and subpoints. It is meant to be used and reused as a ready reference. The detailed table of contents allows you to locate any argument and response quickly. It is designed to help you find a quick answer to what the teacher, television personality, or secretary at work said earlier today.

If you are prochoice, I ask you to read this book with the open mind our society claims to value so highly. If the prolife side proves to be as senseless and irrational as you have been led to believe, fine. You can give it the firsthand rejection it deserves. But if the prolife position proves to be sensible and accurate, then you must rethink your position even if doing so is not politically correct or popular in your circles of influence. Fair enough?

If you are one of those "on the fence," I ask you to make this book part of a quest for truth. You can hear the prochoice position anywhere—just turn on a TV or read the paper. But this book may be your first opportunity to examine the prolife position. Please examine it carefully.

If you are prolife, I ask you to think through the foundations for the position you hold so that you will be able to hold to it more firmly in the face of continuous attack. It is not enough to say, "I know I'm right, though I'm not sure why." We must know how to defend our position intelligently and to educate others about the truth. If you already know what you believe, look in these pages for documentation as well as fresh and readily understandable ways to communicate that belief to others.

If the prolife position is wrong, we should abandon it immediately. If it is right, then innocent human lives depend on our ability and willingness at every opportunity to persuade others of the truth about the value, dignity, and rights of unborn children. I hope this book will serve you well in the task of education and communication as you speak up for those who cannot speak for themselves.

Part One

❦

Arguments Concerning

Life, Humanity,
& Personhood

1.

"It is uncertain when human life begins; that's a religious question that cannot be answered by science."

A 2000 Harris poll of 15,000 people revealed that among those who describe themselves as prolife, 88 percent say that life begins at conception, while among those who describe themselves as prochoice, only 23 percent believe life begins at conception.[62]

An article printed and distributed by the National Abortion Rights Action League (NARAL) describes as "antichoice" the position that "human life begins at conception." It says the prochoice position is, "Personhood at conception is a religious belief, not a provable biological fact."[63]

1a. If there is uncertainty about when human life begins, the benefit of the doubt should go to preserving life.

Suppose there is uncertainty about when human life begins. If a hunter is uncertain whether a movement in the brush is caused by a person, does his uncertainty lead him to fire or not to fire? If you're driving at night and you think the dark figure ahead on the road may be a child, but it may just be the shadow of a tree, do you drive into it, or do you put on the brakes? If we find someone who may be dead or alive, but we're not sure, what is the best policy? To assume he is alive and try to save him, or to assume he is dead and walk away?

Shouldn't we give the benefit of the doubt to life? Otherwise we are saying, "This may or may not be a child, therefore it's all right to destroy it."

1b. Medical textbooks and scientific reference works consistently agree that human life begins at conception.

Many people have been told that there is no medical or scientific consensus as to when human life begins. This is simply untrue. Among those scientists who have no vested interests in the abortion issue, there is an overwhelming consensus that human life begins at conception. (Conception is the moment when the egg is fertilized by the sperm, bringing into existence the zygote, which is a genetically distinct individual.)

51

Dr. Bradley M. Patten's textbook, *Human Embryology,* states, "It is the penetration of the ovum by a spermatozoan and the resultant mingling of the nuclear material each brings to the union that constitutes the culmination of the process of fertilization and *marks the initiation of the life of a new individual.*"[64] (Unless otherwise noted, quoted words in italics have been italicized by me, rather than the original author.)

Dr. Keith L. Moore's text on embryology, referring to the single-cell zygote, says, "The cell results from fertilization of an oocyte by a sperm and is *the beginning of a human being.*"[65] He also states, "Each of us started life as a cell called a zygote."[66]

Doctors J. P. Greenhill and E. A. Friedman, in their work on biology and obstetrics, state, "The zygote thus formed represents *the beginning of a new life.*"[67]

Dr. Louis Fridhandler, in the medical textbook *Biology of Gestation,* refers to fertilization as "that wondrous moment that marks the beginning of life for a new unique individual."[68]

Doctors E. L. Potter and J. M. Craig write in *Pathology of the Fetus and the Infant,* "Every time a sperm cell and ovum unite a new being is created which is alive and will continue to live unless its death is brought about by some specific condition."[69]

Popular scientific reference works reflect this same understanding of when human life begins. *Time* and Rand McNally's *Atlas of the Body* states, "In fusing together, the male and female gametes produce a fertilized single cell, the zygote, which is *the start of a new individual.*"[70] In an article on pregnancy, the *Encyclopedia Britannica* says, "*A new individual is created* when the elements of a potent sperm merge with those of a fertile ovum, or egg."[71]

These sources confidently affirm, with no hint of uncertainty, that life begins at conception. They state not a theory or hypothesis and certainly not a religious belief—every one is a secular source. Their conclusion is squarely based on the scientific and medical facts.

1c. Some of the world's most prominent scientists and physicians testified to a U.S. Senate committee that human life begins at conception.

A United States Senate judiciary subcommittee invited experts to testify on the question of when life begins. All of the quotes from the following experts come directly from the official government record of their testimony.[72]

- Dr. Alfred M. Bongioanni, professor of pediatrics and obstetrics at the University of Pennsylvania, stated:

  I have learned from my earliest medical education that human life begins at the time of conception.... I submit that *human life is present throughout this entire sequence from conception to adulthood* and that any interruption at any point throughout this time constitutes a termination of human life....

  I am no more prepared to say that these early stages [of development in the womb] represent an incomplete human being than I would be to say that the child prior to the dramatic effects of puberty...is not a human being. *This is human life at every stage.*

- Dr. Jerome LeJeune, professor of genetics at the University of Descartes in Paris, was the discoverer of the chromosome pattern of Down syndrome. Dr. LeJeune testified to the judiciary subcommittee, *"after fertilization has taken place a new human being has come into being."* He stated that this "is no longer a matter of taste or opinion," and "not a metaphysical contention; it is plain experimental evidence." He added, *"Each individual has a very neat beginning, at conception."*

- Professor Hymie Gordon, Mayo Clinic: "By all the criteria of modern molecular biology, life is present from the moment of conception."

- Professor Micheline Matthews-Roth, Harvard University Medical School: "It is incorrect to say that biological data cannot be decisive.... *It is scientifically correct to say that an individual human life begins at conception....* Our laws, one function of which is to help preserve the lives of our people, should be based on accurate scientific data."

- Dr. Watson A. Bowes, University of Colorado Medical School: "The beginning of a single human life is from a biological point of view a simple and straightforward matter—*the beginning is conception.* This straightforward biological fact should not be distorted to serve sociological, political, or economic goals."

A prominent physician points out that at these Senate hearings, "Pro-abortionists, though invited to do so, failed to produce even a single expert witness who would specifically testify that life begins at any point other than conception or implantation. Only one witness said no one can tell when life begins."[73]

1d. Many other prominent scientists and physicians have likewise affirmed with certainty that human life begins at conception.

- Ashley Montague, a geneticist and professor at Harvard and Rutgers, is unsympathetic to the prolife cause. Nevertheless, he affirms unequivocally, "The basic fact is simple: *life begins not at birth, but conception.*"[74]

- Dr. Bernard Nathanson, internationally known obstetrician and gynecologist, was a cofounder of what is now the National Abortion Rights Action League (NARAL). He owned and operated what was at the time the largest abortion clinic in the western hemisphere. He was directly involved in over sixty thousand abortions.

  Dr. Nathanson's study of developments in the science of fetology and his use of ultrasound to observe the unborn child in the womb led him to the conclusion that he had made a horrible mistake. Resigning from his lucrative position, Nathanson wrote in the *New England Journal of Medicine* that he was deeply troubled by his "increasing certainty that I had in fact presided over 60,000 deaths."[75]

  In his film, *The Silent Scream*, Nathanson later stated, "Modern technologies have convinced us that *beyond question the unborn child is simply another human being*, another member of the human community, indistinguishable in every way from any of us." Dr. Nathanson wrote *Aborting America* to inform the public of the realities behind the abortion rights movement of which he had been a primary leader.[76] At the time Dr. Nathanson was an atheist. His conclusions were not even remotely religious, but squarely based on the biological facts.

- Dr. Landrum Shettles was for twenty-seven years attending obstetrician-gynecologist at Columbia-Presbyterian Medical Center in New York. Shettles was a pioneer in sperm biology, fertility, and sterility. He is internationally famous for being the discoverer of male- and female-producing sperm. His intrauterine photographs of preborn children appear in over fifty medical textbooks. Dr. Shettles states:

> I oppose abortion. I do so, first, because I accept what is biologically manifest—*that human life commences at the time of conception*—and, second, because I believe it is wrong to take innocent human life under any circumstances. My position is scientific, pragmatic, and humanitarian.[77]

- The First International Symposium on Abortion came to the following conclusion:

> The changes occurring between implantation, a six-week embryo, a six-month fetus, a one-week-old child, or a mature adult are merely stages of development and maturation. The majority of our group could find no point in time between the union of sperm and egg, or at least the blastocyst stage, and the birth of the infant at which point we could say that this was not a human life.[78]

- The Official Senate report on Senate Bill 158, the "Human Life Bill," summarized the issue this way:

> Physicians, biologists, and other scientists agree that *conception marks the beginning of the life of a human being*—a being that is alive and is a member of the human species. There is overwhelming agreement on this point in countless medical, biological, and scientific writings.[79]

1e. The possibility of human cloning does nothing to discredit the fact that all humans conceived in the conventional manner began their lives at conception.

Since the original version of this book, the issue of human cloning has led to a new discussion. Throughout human history, a person's life in this world has always been a continuum which begins at conception and continues until death. But if human cloning is successful, it would bypass conception. A person created by cloning would enter the life continuum not at conception, but at another point.

This would do nothing, however, to change the person's human status.

Obviously, if you are not conceived, then your life cannot begin at conception. But once you have a human being (Homo sapiens) existing on this life continuum, you have a person of equal value to all other persons. How a person arrives on the continuum is not pertinent to his or her value as a person. If you found a one-year-old under a tree, you would not have to know any of her history to determine her value as a human being. If you wished to put her to a scientific test, all you would need to do to be certain you had a person would be to check her DNA to see if she is a Homo sapiens and her vital signs to see if she is alive.[80]

The possibility of clones does not alter in any way the reality that any person conceived in the conventional manner will have begun her life at the point of her conception. All human beings who *are* conceived begin precisely at that point.

Whether we *can* clone and whether we *should* are two very different matters. I believe this rightly resides within the prerogatives of God alone. But even if human cloning is ethically wrong, if it *can* be done by people, history demonstrates that it surely *will* be done. If it is, there would be no justification for considering the cloned person less valuable than the conceived person.

The ramifications of cloning are far-reaching and could have a profound effect on society. A *Time* article stated:

> Having sex is too much fun for us to stop, but religious convictions aside, it will be more for recreation than for procreation. Many human beings, especially those who are rich, vain and ambitious, will be using test tubes—not just to get around infertility and the lack of suitable partners, but to clone themselves and tinker with their genes.[81]

2. "The fetus is just a part of the pregnant woman's body, like her tonsils or appendix. You can't seriously believe a frozen embryo is an actual person."

Philosopher Mortimer Adler claimed that the unborn is "a part of the mother's body, in the same sense that an individual's arm or leg is a part of a living organism. An individual's decision to have an arm or leg amputated falls within the sphere of privacy—the freedom to do as one pleases in all matters that do not injure others or the public welfare."[82]

2a. A body part is defined by the common genetic code it shares with the rest of its body; the unborn's genetic code differs from his mother's.

Every cell of the mother's tonsils, appendix, heart, and lungs shares the same genetic code. The unborn child also has a genetic code, distinctly different from his mother's. Every cell of his body is uniquely his, each different than every cell of his mother's body. Often his blood type is also different, and half the time even his gender is different.

Half of the child's forty-six chromosomes come from his biological father, half from his mother. Except in the rare cases of identical twins, the combination of those chromosomes is unique, distinct even from that of a brother or sister coming from the same parents.

Just as no two people have identical fingerprints, no two people have identical genetic fingerprints. If one body is inside another, but each has its own unique genetic code, then there is not one person, but two separate people. John Jefferson Davis states:

> It is a well-established fact that a genetically distinct human being is brought into existence at conception. Once fertilization takes place, the zygote is its own entity, genetically distinct from both mother and father. The newly conceived individual possesses all the necessary information for a self-directed development and will proceed to grow in the usual human fashion, given time and nourishment. It is simply untrue that the unborn child is merely "part of the mother's body." In addition to being genetically distinct from the time of conception, the unborn possesses separate circulatory, nervous, and endocrine systems.[83]

A Chinese zygote implanted in a Swedish woman will always be Chinese, not Swedish, because his identity is based on his genetic code, not that of the body in which he resides. If the woman's body is the only one involved in a pregnancy, then she must have two noses, four legs, two sets of fingerprints, two brains, two circulatory systems, and two skeletal systems. Half the time she must also have testicles and a penis. In those 50 percent of pregnancies when the child is male, clearly his sexual organs are not part of his mother's body, but his own. It is a clear scientific fact that the mother is one distinctive and self-contained person, and the child is another.

2b. The child may die and the mother live, or the mother may die and the child live, proving they are two separate individuals.

The child-guest is a temporary resident of the mother-host. He will leave on his own as long as he is not prematurely evicted. There are many cases where a mother has been fatally injured, after which a doctor has delivered her child safely. The mother's body dies, the baby lives. Unmistakably, the baby was not merely a part of his mother's body, or he would have died with her. Children have been born several months after their mother has been declared "brain dead."[84] Obviously they must be two distinct individuals prior to the child's birth.

2c. The unborn child takes an active role in his own development, controlling the course of the pregnancy and the time of birth.

New Zealand professor A. W. Liley is known as the "father of fetology." Among his many pioneer achievements was the first intrauterine blood transfusion. Dr. Liley has stated:

> Physiologically, we must accept that the conceptus is, in a very large measure, in charge of the pregnancy.... Biologically, at no stage can we subscribe to the view that the fetus is a mere appendage of the mother.... It is the embryo who stops his mother's periods and makes her womb habitable by developing a placenta and a protective capsule of fluid for himself. He regulates his own amniotic fluid volume and although women speak of their waters breaking or their membranes rupturing, these structures belong to the fetus. And finally, it is the fetus, not the mother, who decides when labor should be initiated.[85]

Dr. Peter Nathanielsz of Cornell University concurs. He says that the unborn's brain sends a message to his own pituitary gland which in turn stimulates the adrenal cortex to secrete a hormone which stimulates the mother's uterus to contract.[86] A woman goes into labor not because her body is ready to surrender the unborn child, but because the unborn child is ready to leave her body.

2d. Being inside something is not the same as being part of something.

One's body does not belong to another's body merely because of proximity. A car is not part of a garage because it is parked there. A loaf of bread is not part of the oven in which it is baked. Louise Brown, the first test-tube baby, was conceived when sperm and egg joined in a petri dish. She was no more a part of her mother's body when placed there than she had been part of the petri dish where her life began. A child is not part of the body in which she is carried. As a person inside a house is not part of the house, so a person inside another's body is not part of that person's body.

This truth was overwhelmingly affirmed in July 2000 by the U.S. House of Representatives when they unanimously passed a bill making it illegal to execute a pregnant woman. The logical reason for this decision is that a preborn child is an individual person, distinct from his mother and with his own separate right to life. That hundreds of proabortion representatives could all agree to this bill demonstrates a profound failure to be morally consistent.

2e. Human beings should not be discriminated against because of their place of residence.

A person is a person whether she lives in a mansion or an apartment or on the street. She is a person whether she's trapped in a cave, lying dependently in a care center, or residing within her mother. We all believe a premature baby lying in a hospital incubator deserves to live. Would the exact same baby deserve to live any less simply because she was still in her mother?

Consider this true-to-life scenario. Two women become pregnant on the same day. Six months later Woman A has a premature baby, small but healthy. Woman B is still pregnant. One week later both women decide they don't want their babies anymore. Why should Woman B be allowed to kill her baby and Woman A not be allowed to kill hers?[87] Since there is no difference in the nature or development of the two babies, why would Woman B's action be exercising a legitimate right to choose, while Woman A's action would be a heinous crime subjecting her to prosecution for first-degree murder? It is irrational to recognize the one child as a baby and pretend the other one isn't.

I know a former prochoice nurse who was converted to a prolife position after seeing premature babies being frantically saved by a medical team in one room, while down the hall, babies the same age were being aborted.

2f. There is substantial scientific reason to believe that frozen embryos are persons and should be granted the same rights as older, larger, and less vulnerable persons.

In 1983 bioethical discussions were forever changed when Mario and Elsa Rios died in an airplane crash. They left behind two frozen embryos, in an in vitro fertilization clinic in Melbourne, Australia. Medical and legal journals suddenly had major issues to discuss, which had not begun to be resolved by the year 2000.[88] Currently there are more than 320 law review articles on the legal controversies surrounding frozen human embryos.[89]

Did the frozen embryos have property rights? If they were successfully implanted in a woman willing to bear them, would they stand to inherit the wealthy Rios estate? What were the ethical obligations of family and society? What should be done with the frozen embryos? Should they be discarded? Donated to another couple? Left frozen indefinitely?[90] Though it's very expensive and its success rate is low, many infertile couples are turning to in vitro fertilization (IVF) and artificial insemination. Fertility drugs given to women in IVF programs often produce more embryos than can safely be implanted at one time. It is standard practice to freeze the unused embryos through cryopreservation, in case they are needed later, when they can be thawed and implanted. Because of factors that include divorce, death, and changes of intention, the status of these embryos becomes uncertain.

More than ten million U.S. couples are infertile. In the last ten years the infertility industry has grown from about thirty to over three hundred clinics, with earnings exceeding one billion dollars—and the growth continues. In 1999 more than seventy-five thousand infants were born after IVF. This was more than twice as many as were available through traditional adoption.[91] At the same time, a 1999 *Washington Post* article reports that hundreds of thousands of human embryos are now frozen, suspended in liquid nitrogen tanks (with an estimated nineteen thousand more frozen embryos to be added each year).[92]

This should be of immense concern to all who believe human life begins at conception:

> Not all embryos survive the freeze-thaw process. A 50% survival rate is considered reasonable. After the thaw, embryos retaining 50% or more of the cells they had before freezing are cultured and placed back in the uterus via a tube inserted in the cervix. The number returned varies with the desires of the patient under the guidelines of age categories; under 35 years old, up to four embryos, 35 years and older, up to six embryos. National statistics for women 39 or less is 27% per embryo transfer, for women over 39, 14% per embryo transfer. Delivery rates will be lower due to miscarriage.[93]

Three to six embryos may be implanted in the hopes that one may live, but the majority die. In the best-case scenario, six embryos die, another six survive freezing, and at least two to five of these six die in the attempt to implant one. Often all of them die.

When, even under optimal conditions, physicians attempt to implant an embryo conceived in vitro, the success rate is startlingly low. According to Dr. Leon Speroff's widely regarded text in endocrinology and fertility, the success rate in any given cycle is 13.5 percent. Since typically three to six embryos may be used to attempt implantation, the actual survival rate is just over 3 percent. This means that twenty-nine out of thirty embryos die in order to implant a single child.[94]

Some people are quick to justify this on the basis that there is also a high rate of miscarriage in the natural reproductive process. But the difference is profound. What God does is up to Him, but we are not God. We do not have His prerogatives over human life and death. Spontaneous miscarriages are not our responsibility. What *is* our responsibility is child deaths caused by the overproduction of embryos in the hopes of a single implantation.

World-renowned geneticist Dr. Jerome LeJeune persuasively argued before the trial court in *Davis* v. *Davis* (a custody dispute involving seven human embryos) that the human embryo is in fact a human being, a real person.[95] After listening to various testimonies, the court's opinion was this: "Cryogenically preserved embryos are human beings.... Human embryos are not property. Human life begins at conception. Mr. and Mrs. Davis have produced human beings, in vitro, to be known as their child or children."[96]

To the argument "You can't seriously believe a frozen embryo is a human being," the proper response is, "Both scientifically and theologically, we can't seriously believe a frozen embryo is anything *other* than a human being."

In 1996 in Great Britain thirty-three hundred frozen embryos were thawed out, destroyed with saline solution, and incinerated as biological waste.[97] A study at two fertility clinics in Manchester, published in the *Lancet* medical journal, showed that 904 of 1344 frozen embryos had been thawed because couples had not requested another five-year extension or donated them to other couples or for research. "We are extremely concerned at the high rate of embryo destruction highlighted in this study," said Dr. Brian Lieberman of St. Mary's Hospital in Manchester. "This is the first time anyone in the world has reported the decisions made by a group of people with embryos in storage for five or more years."[98]

Can Christians, or any citizens with a respect for life, participate in good conscience in the supervised overproduction of human embryos that ultimately leads to such destruction? One prolife physician who is a fertility specialist and works with frozen embryos wrestled with this issue for years. Finally, he came to the conclusion that human life does not begin at conception, but at implantation. This was a convenient change in belief that allowed him to continue in his profession. Unfortunately, the notion that life begins at implantation has no biological basis (see answer 6a).

Dr. James Dobson, in his book *Solid Answers,* says this concerning in vitro fertilization:

> I believe most conservative Christians would agree this practice is morally indefensible from a biblical perspective. On the other hand, I feel that in vitro fertilization is less problematic when the donors are husband and wife—IF all the fertilized eggs are inserted into the uterus [i.e., no ova are wasted or disposed of after fertilization and no selection process by doctors or parents occurs]. As the woman's body then accepts one [or more] eggs and rejects the others, the process is left in God's hands and seems to violate no moral principles.[99]

3.

"The unborn is an embryo or a fetus—just a simple blob of tissue, a product of conception—not a baby. Abortion is terminating a pregnancy, not killing a child."

3a. Like *toddler* and *adolescent*, *the terms* embryo *and* fetus *do not refer to nonhumans, but to humans at particular stages of development.*

The word *embryo* is used of any living creature at an early stage of development. *Fetus* is a Latin word variously translated "offspring," "young one," or "little child."

It is scientifically inaccurate to say an embryo or a fetus is not a human being simply because he is at an earlier stage of development than a born infant. This is like saying that a toddler is not a human being—or is less of a human being—because he is not yet an adolescent. Or that an adolescent is not a human being because he is not yet an adult.

Stage of development has nothing to do with human worth. One of my daughters is two years older than the other. Does this mean she is two years better? Is a two-year-old child more precious now than he was a year ago? Is a child more worthy to live after birth than before birth?

3b. *Semantics affect perceptions, but they do not change realities; a baby is a baby no matter what we call her.*

"A rose by any other name would smell as sweet." A baby by any other name is still a baby. Though *fetus* was once a good word that spoke of a young human being, it is now used with a subhuman connotation. Referring to the fetus allows us not to use the B-word *(baby)*. The prochoice movement labors to avoid the B-word for it reminds us of the reality that abortion kills a child. This reality must be denied at all costs, because anyone who is understood to be arguing for the right to kill babies is fighting an uphill battle.

Product of conception (POC) goes a step further in depersonalizing the unborn child. In reality, the infant, the ten-year-old, and the adult are *all* "products of conception," no more nor less than the fetus. As the product of a horse's conception is always a horse, the product of human conception is always a human.

Still, the use of impersonal terminology allows us to overlook this reality.

Fertilized egg is a term frequently used of the newly conceived person. This term is dehumanizing and misleading. Neither egg nor sperm is in any sense a human being, but merely the product of a human being. However, at the point of fertilization someone brand new comes into existence, a unique human being. As the sperm no longer exists, neither does the egg per se. It is replaced by a new creation with unique DNA, rapidly growing and dividing on its own. This new human being is no more a mere "fertilized egg" than it is a "modified sperm." He or she is a newly created person with the equivalent of hundreds of volumes of distinct genetic programming.

Historically, the terms *conception* and *fertilization* have been virtually synonymous, both referring to the very beginning of human life. A contraceptive, just as it sounds, was something that prevented fertilization (*contra*dicted con*ception*). Unfortunately, in the last few decades alternative meanings of *conception* and *contraception* have emerged, a semantic shift which has greatly confused the issue. In *Physician* magazine, Dr. Eugene Diamond explains:

> Prior to 1976, a "contraceptive" was understood to be an agent that prevented the union of sperm and ovum. In 1976 the American College of Obstetricians and Gynecologists [ACOG], realizing that this definition didn't help its political agenda, arbitrarily changed the definition.
>
> A contraceptive now meant anything that prevented implantation of the blastocyst, which occurs six or seven days after fertilization. Conception, as defined by *Dorland's Illustrated Medical Dictionary* [27th edition], became "the onset of pregnancy marked by implantation of the blastocyst."
>
> The hidden agenda in ACOG's redefinition of "contraceptive" was to blur the distinction between agents preventing fertilization and those preventing implantation of the week-old embryo. Specifically, abortifacients such as IUDs, combination pills, minipills, progestin-only pills, injectables such as Provera and, more recently, implantables such as Norplant, all are contraceptives by this definition.[100]

This redefinition of "contraceptive" has gradually crept into the medical literature. Because of the change, many medical professionals refer to agents that sometimes prevent implantation as contraceptives, even though whenever they prevent implantation, they are in fact functioning as abortifacients. But because of some convenient semantic changes, this reality is hidden from the consumer. (See appendices D and E on chemical abortifacients and the birth control pill.)

Sometimes semantic shifts are made to depersonalize our smallest children; other times they are made to mask reality and confuse people. The National Institute of Health found that the public was reacting against the term "human embryonic stem cell research," referring to the destroying of human embryos by performing experiments on them. NIH actually chose to use a new term, "human pluripotent stem cell research," to describe the same thing. The new term masks the reality that human embryos are involved.[101]

Sometimes the characterization of the unborn is overtly hostile. I heard one prochoice advocate refer to unwanted pregnancy as a "venereal disease" and abortion as the "cure." Abortion-rights advocates have referred to unborn babies as debris,[102] garbage, and refuse[103] to justify abortion. Holocaust scholar Raul Hilberg argues that the key to the widespread destruction of the Jewish people was the use of degrading terminology such as "useless eaters" and "garbage," which blinded society to the fact that real people were being killed.[104]

3c. From the moment of conception, the unborn is not simple but very complex.

The newly fertilized egg contains a staggering amount of genetic information, sufficient to control the individual's growth and development for an entire lifetime. A single thread of DNA from a human cell contains information equivalent to a library of one thousand volumes, or six hundred thousand printed pages with five hundred words on a page. The genetic information stored in the new individual at conception is the equivalent of fifty times the amount of information contained in the *Encyclopedia Britannica*.[105]

3d. Prior to the earliest abortions, the unborn already has every body part she will ever have.

At eighteen days after conception the heart is forming, and the eyes start to develop. By twenty-one days the heart is not only beating, but pumping blood throughout the body. By twenty-eight days the unborn has budding arms and legs. By thirty days she has multiplied in size ten thousand times. She has a brain and blood flows through her veins.

By thirty-five days, mouth, ears, and nose are taking shape. At forty days the preborn child's brain waves can be recorded. The child's heartbeat, which began three weeks earlier, can already be detected by an ultrasonic stethoscope. By forty-two days the skeleton is formed, and the brain is controlling the movement of muscles and organs. The unborn reflexively responds to stimulus and may already be capable of feeling pain (see answer 26d). This is *before* the earliest abortions take place.

Famous intrauterine photographer Lennart Nilsson is best known for his photo essays in *Life* magazine and his bestselling book *A Child Is Born*. In his "Drama of Life Before Birth," he says this of the unborn at forty-five days after conception (this is just six-and-a-half weeks, when many women don't yet know they are pregnant): "Though the embryo now weighs only 1/30 of an ounce, it has all the internal organs of the adult in various stages of development. It already has a little mouth with lips, an early tongue and buds for 20 milk teeth. Its sex and reproductive organs have begun to sprout."[106] (See "tear drop" photograph of a miscarried child at this stage, on page 457.)

By eight weeks hands and feet are almost perfectly formed, and fingerprints are developing. Already, "Mother's movements stimulate the fetus's balance and motion detectors."[107] (See photograph of living child at eight weeks, on page 457.) By nine weeks a child will bend fingers around an object placed in the palm. Fingernails are forming, and the child is sucking his thumb. The nine-week baby has "already perfected a somersault, backflip and scissor kick."[108]

By ten weeks the child squints, swallows, and frowns. (See black and white photographs #1 and #2 at the center of this book.) By eleven weeks he urinates, makes a wide variety of facial expressions, and even smiles. By twelve weeks the child is kicking, turning his feet, curling and fanning his toes, making a fist, moving thumbs, bending wrists, and opening his mouth.[109]

All this happens in the first trimester, the first three months of life. In the remaining six months in the womb *nothing new develops or begins functioning*. The child only grows and matures.

3e. Every abortion stops a beating heart and terminates measurable brain waves.

Using figures dependent on abortion clinic records, about half of all abortions occur at eight weeks or less, 88 percent happen within twelve weeks, and 9 percent from thirteen to twenty weeks. The remainder (nearly fourteen thousand per year) are reported at beyond twenty-one weeks.[110]

However, abortion clinic workers say that clinics underreport later abortions. *Newsweek* states, "Statistics on abortion are notoriously suspect."[111] I have interviewed abortion clinic workers who say that no abortions occur before six weeks, and most do not occur until the baby's eighth week of development. Even when pregnancies are detected earlier, operators want to make sure the unborn is large enough to do a proper inventory of his severed body parts. (A hand or leg inadvertently left in the mother will cause a dangerous infection.)

What this means is that every description of an unborn child prior to fifty-six days gestation is true of the majority of aborted unborns. Every description prior to twenty-two days—including the beating heart—is true of every single aborted child. An actual audio tape of the clear, strong heartbeat of an infant at less than seven weeks was made by obstetrician-gynecologist Dr. Louis Hicks of Lexington, Kentucky.[112] It is sobering to listen to the beating heart of an unborn child who is at one of the *earliest* ages in which abortions are performed.

When women have abortions (in weeks)

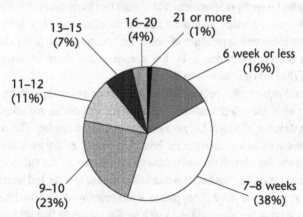

- 13–15 (7%)
- 16–20 (4%)
- 21 or more (1%)
- 6 week or less (16%)
- 11–12 (11%)
- 9–10 (23%)
- 7–8 weeks (38%)

Eighty-eight percent of abortions occur in the first 12 weeks of pregnancy.

What do we call it when a person no longer has a heartbeat or brain waves? Death. What should we call it when there *is* a heartbeat and there *are* brain waves? Life. *It is an indisputable scientific fact that each and every legal surgical abortion in America today stops a beating heart and stops already measurable brain waves.*

3f. Even in the earliest surgical abortions, the unborn child is clearly human in appearance.

The biggest disadvantage to the preborn child is that there is no window to the womb. His fate is in the hands of those who cannot see him. There are technologies, however, that have allowed us for almost thirty years to see into the womb. Both still and moving pictures show the startlingly clear humanity of the preborn. Watching obviously human unborn children through ultrasound convinced abortionist Bernard Nathanson that for years he had, unwittingly, been killing human beings.[113] A liberal Ivy League professor and his wife changed their minds on this issue when a sonogram of their amniocentesis showed their unborn child grabbing hold of the needle.

One of the photos on page 457 is of an unborn child at eight weeks of development. Notice the clearly discernible eyes, ears, mouth, nose, and hands. The tear-drop shaped picture below it is of an unruptured ectopic pregnancy six weeks after the mother's last menstrual period, taken after surgery by a medical photographer at the University of Minnesota. Notice again the clearly discernible features, especially eyes and hands. Remember that few abortions take place before this stage. This is the true appearance of one of the youngest of the 3,753 children killed in America every day. Sadly, few women getting abortions know this. Abortion clinics do not show them such pictures.

When I showed a picture of an eight-week developed unborn, a prochoice advocate—an intelligent college graduate—looked at me with disdain and asked, "Do you really think you're going to fool anyone with this trick photography?" This woman, whom I'm convinced was sincere in her belief, had been taught that the unborn was a blob of tissue, but when she looked at the actual picture, she saw that this was clearly a little human being. She was forced to conclude either that what she had been taught was wrong, or that this was a phony picture. It was easier to conclude the latter. Yet, as I pointed out to her, she could go to such secular sources as Harvard University Medical School textbooks, or *Life* magazine,[114] or Nilsson's *A Child Is Born*[115] and find exactly the same thing. I wonder if she ever investigated the scientific data.

Unfortunately, the problem is not just ignorance, but misinformation. An abortion clinic spokesperson told the *Winnipeg Sun* that the unborn is "a froglike thing...without a heartbeat, brain, eyes or internal organs."[116] A Kansas state representative, getting her information from a paid lobbyist of the abortion industry, stated that the unborn child at seven *months* "looks a lot like chopped liver."[117] (See photograph #3 at the center of this book, which shows the unborn at four months.)

I often hear people who believe and pass on such utterly false information.

A prochoice video aired on a cable television network showed a little pool of blood with no visible tissue, much less body parts, and said, "This is the contents of an emptied uterus after an eight-week abortion. It is clearly not a baby, despite what antiabortionists say in their propaganda."[118] Since the scientific facts of human development are indisputable, there are only two possible explanations: The video did not show the full remains of the abortion, or the child was so torn apart in the abortion that his body parts were no longer discernible. In either case, it is an attempt at deception, as one look at the photograph of the eight-week baby on the back cover of this book clearly shows.

Despite the widespread ignorance and misinformation on the subject, whenever we discuss abortion in this country, we are always discussing the death of a preborn with clearly discernible human features. In no way is it, nor does it even appear to be, "a blob of tissue."

3g. Even before the unborn is obviously human in appearance, she is what she is—a human being.

The cells of the new individual divide and multiply rapidly, resulting in phenomenal growth. There is growth precisely because there is a new and distinct life. Long before a woman knows she's pregnant, there is within her a living, growing human being. Between five and nine days the new person burrows into the wall of the womb for safety. Already his or her sex can be determined by scientific instruments. By fourteen days a hormone produced by the new child suppresses the mother's menstrual period. It will be two more weeks before his clearly human features are discernible and three more before they are obvious. Still, he is what he is, regardless of his appearance. As any of us know who have been around people terribly injured in accidents and fires, one need not look human to be human. At conception the unborn does not appear human to us who are used to judging humanity purely by appearance. Nevertheless, in the objective scientific sense he is every bit as human as any older child or adult.

Though I have emphasized the clearly human features of the unborn after six weeks of development, this does not mean babies are any less human before they look human. No matter how he or she looks, no matter which organs have developed and which haven't, *a child is a child, and abortion terminates that child's life*. The earliest means to cause abortion, including Mifepristone (RU-486) and all abortion pills, are—and will always be—still too late to avoid taking a life.

Even if someone takes the scientifically untenable position that the unborn is not a human being until it looks human and its heart and brain are functioning, he is still acknowledging the humanity of the twenty-eight million unborn killed by abortion in America in the last two decades.

3h. No matter how much better it sounds, "terminating a pregnancy" is still terminating a life.

Two years before abortion was legalized in America, a prochoice advocate instructed nurses in a prominent journal: "Through public conditioning, use of language, concepts and laws, the idea of abortion can be separated from the idea of killing."[119] The same year a symposium on abortion in Los Angeles offered this training: "If you say, 'Suck out the baby,' you may easily generate or increase trauma; say instead, 'Empty the uterus,' or 'We will scrape the lining of the uterus,' but never 'We will scrape away the baby.'"[120] Hitler's command to take the Jews to their death in the camps was couched in the phrase "empty the ghettos."

Language is not just the expression of minds, but the molder of minds. The ways words are used can tremendously influence someone's receptivity to an idea—even an idea that communicated in straightforward terms would be abhorrent.

Using words that focus on what happens to the pregnancy and the uterus takes attention away from the crux of the abortion issue—the individual residing in the uterus. But no matter how many words we use and how we use them, "terminating a pregnancy" is terminating a human life. The one may sound better than the other, but the realities are one and the same.

We must cut through the semantic fog and always find our way back to the bottom-line realities. As one prolife feminist says, "Prolifers don't object to terminating pregnancies. Pregnancies are only supposed to last a short while. We favor terminating them at around nine months. The objection is to killing children."[121]

4.

> "The fetus may be alive, but so are eggs and sperm. The fetus is a potential human being, not an actual one; it's like a blueprint, not a house; an acorn, not an oak tree."

4a. The ovum and sperm are each a product of another's body; unlike the conceptus, neither is an independent entity.

On a televised panel Faye Wattleton, former president of Planned Parenthood, countered the argument that an unborn baby is a living being by saying to a pro-life congressman, "Your sperm are alive too."[122] Similarly, in a widely read article in *Parade* magazine, the late Carl Sagan attacked the position that abortion kills children by asking, "So is masturbation mass murder?" and, "Why isn't it murder to destroy a sperm or an egg?"[123] The answer, as every scientist should know, is that there is a vast and fundamental difference between sperm and unfertilized eggs on the one hand, and fertilized eggs, or zygotes, on the other.

Neither egg nor sperm is complete. Like cells of one's hair or heart, neither egg nor sperm has the capacity to become other than what it is. Both are dead ends, destined to remain what they are until they die within a matter of days.

In contrast, when egg and sperm are joined, a new, dynamic, and genetically distinct human life begins. *This life is neither sperm nor egg nor a simple combination of both. It is independent, with a life of its own, on a rapid pace of self-directed development.* From the first instant of fertilization, that first single cell contains the entire genetic blueprint in all its complexity. This accounts for every detail of human development, including the child's sex, hair and eye color, height, and skin tone.[124] Take that single cell of the just conceived zygote, put it next to a chimpanzee cell or a gorilla cell, and "a geneticist could easily identify the human. Its humanity is already that strikingly apparent."[125]

4b. The physical remains after an abortion indicate the end not of a potential life, but of an actual life.

A film called "The Gift of Choice," produced by the Religious Coalition for Abortion Rights, claims that the unborn is "a probability of a future person," as opposed to the actuality of a present person. But what is left after an abortion are small but perfectly formed body parts—arms and legs, hands and feet, torso and head.

Photograph #4, at the center of this book, shows a hand taken from the discarded remains of an abortion, held in the hand of an adult. Look at it, then decide for yourself if this was a potential or actual human life.

In his how-to manual *Abortion Practice*, Colorado abortionist Dr. Warren Hern states, "A long curved Mayo scissors may be necessary to decapitate and dismember the fetus."[126] One must have a head in order to be decapitated and body parts in order to be dismembered. Lumps of flesh and blobs of tissue are neither decapitated nor dismembered.

Potential life cannot be ended because it hasn't begun. Human body parts are the product of actual human lives that have ended.

4c. Something nonhuman does not become human by getting older and bigger; whatever is human must be human from the beginning.

Dr. Thomas Hilgers states, "No individual living body can 'become' a person unless it already is a person. No living being can become anything other than what it already essentially is."[127]

Dr. Paul Ramsay says this:

> Thus it might be said that in all essential respects the individual is whoever he is going to become from the moment of impregnation. He already is this while not knowing this or anything else. Thereafter, his subsequent development cannot be described as becoming something he is not now. It can only be described as a process of achieving, a process of becoming the one he already is. Genetics teaches us that we were from the beginning what we essentially still are in every cell and in every generally human attribute and in every individual attribute.[128]

4d. Comparing preborns and adults to acorns and oaks is dehumanizing and misleading.

When an acorn is stepped on, the forest experiences no moral dilemma. When a "toddler" sapling or a "teenage" oak dies, the "mother tree" does not weep, nor do the sapling's siblings. We naturally value oak trees more than acorns.

Unfortunately, the comparison encourages us to make the quantum leap of concluding that we should value bigger and older people more than smaller and younger ones (specifically, the unborn). But what are our reasons for valuing the oak tree over the acorn? They are not moral or humanitarian, but simply pragmatic. The oak tree serves us well, either aesthetically or for the lumber or fire wood it can provide. Acorns are plentiful and expendable. But *why* are they expendable? For the same reason the oak tree is also ultimately expendable—it isn't a person; it's only a thing.

A baby, however, isn't a thing; it's a person. The unborn are not more expendable because they haven't developed into infants, nor infants more expendable because they haven't developed into toddlers, nor teenagers more expendable because they haven't developed into adults.

4e. Even if the analogy were valid, scientifically speaking an acorn is simply a little oak tree, just as an embryo is a little person.

Despite the dehumanizing elements of the acorn-oak analogy, those who understand what an acorn is will realize that, ironically, the analogy serves the opposite purpose it is intended for!

Blueprints are not houses, nor do they become houses no matter how long we care to wait, because by nature they are something else. But while the blueprint in no sense becomes the house, the acorn *does* become the oak tree. It can do so only because in the most basic sense it *is* the oak tree!

While no house was ever a blueprint, every oak tree was once an acorn. So it is with the person. Each person doesn't simply come from a zygote, embryo, or fetus. Each person *was* a zygote, an embryo, a fetus. As every oak tree was an acorn, every person was once a conceptus.

All the oak tree is or ever will be was in the acorn. If the acorn were destroyed, there would be no oak tree. Likewise, all that the adult is or ever will be was in the embryo. If the embryo were destroyed, there would be no baby, no teenager, and no adult. When the baby dies, the teenager dies. When the embryo dies, the baby dies. Abortion doesn't kill potential people. It kills actual people. And the loss of a person is a far greater loss than even an entire forest.

5.

"The unborn isn't a person, with meaningful life. It's only inches in size and can't even think; it's less advanced than an animal, and anyway, who says people have a greater right to live than animals?"

5a. Personhood is properly defined by membership in the human species, not by stage of development within that species.

> A living being's designation to a species is determined not by the stage of development, but by the sum total of its biological characteristics— actual and potential—which are genetically determined.... If we say that [the fetus] is not human, e.g. a member of Homo sapiens, we must say it is a member of another species. *But this cannot be.*[129]

Dictionaries define *person* as a "human being," "human individual," or "member of the human race." What makes a dog a dog is that he came from dogs. His father was a dog and his mother was a dog, and therefore he is a dog. What makes a human a human is that he came from humans. His father was a human person and his mother was a human person, so he can be nothing other than a human person.[130]

We must not be confused by statements such as Carl Sagan's:

> Despite many claims to the contrary life does not begin at conception: It is an unbroken chain that stretches back nearly to the origin of the Earth, 4.6 billion years ago. Nor does *human* life begin at conception: It is an unbroken chain dating back to the origin of species, tens or hundreds of thousands of years ago.[131]

Sagan missed the point entirely. When it comes to this issue, no one is talking about when the earth began or when the first humans began, but when each individual human being's life begins. None of us existed 150 years ago, but we do exist now. So somewhere between 150 years ago and now, your life began. How long your heritage goes back is irrelevant. The point is, your actual life started at a moment in time. Carl Sagan notwithstanding, the beginning of each human life is not a process, but an event. That event is conception.

5b. Personhood is not a matter of size, skill, or degree of intelligence.

Prochoice advocates often point out that a child aborted in the first trimester may be less than an inch or two in size, or less than an ounce or two in weight. But what measure of personhood is size? Is a professional basketball player more of a person than someone half his size? If a two-hundred-pound man loses fifty pounds, does he lose one fourth of his personhood? Scales and rulers are no measurement of human nature or worth. Intuitively, we all understand the truth put so simply by Dr. Seuss in *Horton Hears a Who*: "Because, after all, a person is a person, no matter how small."[132]

Joseph Fletcher, then professor at the University of Virginia, argued that an "individual" is not a "person" unless he has an IQ of at least 40, is self-aware, has self-control, with a sense of time (past, present, and future) and an ability to relate to others.[133]

One problem with these criteria is that they do not apply to an entire class of people, namely the comatose. Does anyone seriously believe that people lose their humanity when they go into a coma and regain it when they come out? If so, wouldn't the same be true when we sleep? Must one be awake, and therefore aware of self and time, to be a person? If one were asleep for five years rather than five hours, would this change the issue of his personhood?

British anthropologist Ashley Montague says that no one becomes human until he is molded by social and cultural influences. By this he means that more intelligent and educated people (such as himself) are more human than the inferior elements of society (such as some of the rest of us).[134]

If personhood is determined by one's current capacities, then someone who is unconscious or sick could be killed because he is not demonstrating superior intellect and skills. "But give the man time and he'll be able to function as a person." Give the baby time and so will she.

Age, size, IQ, or stage of development are simply differences in degree, not in kind. Our kind is humanity. We are people—human beings. We possess certain skills to differing degrees at different stages of development. When we reach maturation, there are many different degrees of skills and levels of IQ. But none of these make some people better or more human than others. None make some qualified to live and others unqualified.

There is no objective evidence to indicate that someone can be a member of the human race, but because he lacks certain qualities, he thereby fails to be a person.

5c. The unborn's status should be determined on an objective basis, not on subjective or self-serving definitions of personhood.

The Fourteenth Amendment says that the state shall not deprive any person of life without due process of law. When that was written, the word *human* was a synonym for *person* and could just as easily have been used. The Supreme Court admitted in *Roe* v. *Wade*: "If the suggestion of personhood [of the unborn] is established, the appellant's [proabortion] case, of course, collapses, for the fetus's right to life is then guaranteed specifically by the [fourteenth] amendment."[135]

To solve this problem, the court chose to abandon the historic meaning of personhood. In the years that have followed, a long series of subjective and artificial distinctions have been made by prochoice advocates to differentiate between humans and persons. Part of the reason for this is that the scientific fact that life begins at conception paints the prochoice movement into a corner. The old and still popular argument that "this isn't human life" is privately known to be erroneous by thinking prochoice people (see answers 8d–8h). They realize it's only a matter of time before the public learns the truth. The newer strategy is to say "Okay, this is human life, but it isn't really a person."

We must not reduce issues of life and death and basic human rights to a semantic game in which we are free to redefine our terms. Changing the meaning of words doesn't change reality. The concept of personhood is now virtually worthless as an ethical guide in the matter of abortion. The only objective questions we can ask are:

1. "Is it human; that is, did it come from human beings?"
2. "Is it a genetically unique individual?"
3. "Is it alive and growing?"

If the answers are yes, then "it" is a "he" or "she," a living person, possessing rights and deserving of protection.

5d. It is a scientific fact that there are thought processes at work in unborn babies.

The Associated Press reported a study showing "babies start learning about their language-to-be before they are born." University of North Carolina psychology professor Dr. Anthony DeCasper was quoted as saying, "Fetuses heard, perceived, listened and learned something about the acoustic structure of American English."[136]

Newsweek states, "Life in the womb represents the next frontier for studies of human development, and the early explorations of the frontier—through ultra-sound, fiber-optic cameras, miniature microphones—have yielded startling discoveries."[137] The same article says, "With no hype at all, *the fetus can rightly be called a marvel of cognition, consciousness and sentience.*" It also says that scientists have already detected sentience (self-awareness) in the second trimester.[138] Indeed, the extraordinary capacities and responses of preborn children have been well documented by scientific studies for years.[139]

By early in the second trimester the baby moves his hands to shield his eyes to bright light coming in through his mother's body. "The fetus also responds to sounds in frequencies so high or low that they cannot be heard by the human adult ear."[140] He hears loud music and may even cover his ears at loud noises from the outside world. At seventeen weeks, when abortions are still commonly performed, the child experiences rapid eye movement (REM) sleep, indicating that he is not only sleeping, but dreaming.[141] Can we say that someone capable of dreaming is incapable of thinking?

There is no doubt whatsoever that later abortions kill a sentient, thinking human being. By the end of the second and the start of the third trimester (at twenty-four weeks) the "brain's neural circuits are as advanced as a newborn's."[142] It seems unthinkable that anyone aware of the facts could favor the current legality of abortions in the second and third trimesters. That such abortions are adamantly defended by prochoice advocates should cause us to ask whether their position is based on facts at all, or merely on personal preference or wishful thinking.

But are earlier abortions any better than later ones? Since there is a functioning brain with measurable brain waves at forty days of development, who are we to say that these tiny brains can't do what brains do—think? Yet the vast majority of abortions legal in America occur after forty days. And even in the case of early chemical abortions which take the life before there's the capacity for thought, does this destroy the life in a way that is any less real or significant? Does it change the fact that a child who would have had a name and a family and a life will now have none of these?

5e. If the unborn's value can be compared to that of an animal, there is no reason not to also compare the value of born people to animals.

In 1975 Australian scientist and bioethicist Peter Singer wrote a book with a title that was to become the banner of a new movement: *Animal Liberation*. Singer said, "It can no longer be maintained by anyone but a religious fanatic that man is the special darling of the universe, or that animals were created to provide us with food, or that we have divine authority over them, and divine permission to kill them."[143]

Singer, now a professor at Princeton University, denounces what he calls "speciesism"—valuing humans above animals. He defines speciesism as "a prejudice or attitude of bias in favor of the interests of members of one's own species and against those of members of other species."[144] In his textbook, *Practical Ethics,* Singer says that speciesism is just as bad as sexism or racism. "It is speciesist to judge that the life of a normal adult member of our species is more valuable than the life of a normal adult mouse."[145]

Singer stretches the conventional definition of *person* beyond recognition by saying that not only can humans be nonpersons, but nonhumans can be persons:

> We should reject the doctrine that places the lives of members of our species above the lives of members of other species. Some members of other species are persons; some members of our own species are not. No objective assessment can give greater value to the lives of members of our species....[146]

Singer has also said:

> If we compare a severely defective human infant with a nonhuman animal, a dog or a pig, for example, we will often find the nonhuman to have superior capacities, both actual and potential, for rationality, self-consciousness, communication and anything else that can plausibly be considered morally significant.[147]

Once such logic is adopted, there is no stopping place. One nuclear physicist says, "It should be recognized that not all men are human.... It would seem to be more inhumane to kill an adult chimpanzee than a newborn baby, since the chimpanzee has greater mental awareness.[148] Of course, if our concern is for mental awareness, we could kill the chimpanzee or the baby or a teenager painlessly in his sleep, when he is not mentally aware. The real question is whether there is some reason to regard human life as inherently more valuable than nonhuman life. Our society has always acted on that premise. It is deeply rooted in the Judeo-Christian heritage of Western civilization. Abortion is both a cause and effect of this new "sliding scale" view of human worth.

The problem is not whether animals should be treated humanely. Of course they should. The problem is whether *humans* should be treated humanely. Here our double standard becomes obvious. In many places goldfish are no longer given as prizes at fairs because they were being flushed down toilets, and that was considered cruel. Abigail Van Buren of "Dear Abby" has said that people should not be allowed to put to death their pets for any reason. Yet she has repeatedly affirmed that she is prochoice about aborting babies.

When a Greenpeace activist came to a friend's house and asked for a donation to save the whales and seals, she responded, "I think your cause is worthy, but I give to one I think is even more worthy—saving the lives of baby humans." The activist scowled and walked away. His attitude is increasingly common in our society—Save the whales; kill the children.

5f. Even if someone believes that people are no better than animals, why would they abhor the killing of young animals, while advocating the killing of young children?

It is a serious crime, and strictly enforced, to break an eagle egg. Apparently, because there are plenty of unborn (parallel to unhatched) human babies, it is not a serious crime to kill them. Everyone knows that to break an eagle egg before it hatches is to kill an eagle. What is it to perform an abortion on a person?

The notion that human beings are different in degree but not in kind from animals is no longer a fringe notion. Many school children are now familiar with Singer's awkward term *speciesist*. Educated people—and generally speaking, only educated people—are seriously arguing that people have no more value than animals or that animals have just as much value as people. As the founder and director of People for the Ethical Treatment of Animals (PETA) puts it, "When it comes to feelings, a rat is a pig is a dog is a boy."[149]

Of course, many of these people, even those who are vegetarians, live inconsistently with their beliefs. (They usually swat mosquitoes rather than lovingly feed and nurture them.) But the most remarkable thing is that not only these people, but the public at large, looks the other way when human babies are killed at all stages of development. This includes the use of painful and horrific procedures that would cause a massive social outcry if done on dogs, cats, horses, whales, dolphins, or even rodents. While it seems too little to ask that preborn human babies be shown the same respect as preborn animal babies, if this were actually done, it would save the lives of countless children in America each year.

5g. It is dangerous when people in power are free to determine whether other, less powerful lives are meaningful.

Peter Singer says,

> When the death of a disabled infant will lead to the birth of another infant with better prospects of a happy life, the total amount of happiness will be greater if the disabled infant is killed. The loss of happy life for the first infant is outweighed by the gain of a happier life for the second. Therefore, if killing the hemophiliac infant has no adverse effect on others, it would, according to the total view, be right to kill him.[150]

Statements such as this explain why Singer was protested when he first came to teach at Princeton's Center for Human Values. The main protestors were Not Dead Yet, a disabilities rights group. They took offense at Singer's books, which say it should be legal to deliberately kill disabled infants, as well as children and adults with severe cognitive disabilities, which might include people with Down syndrome, mental retardation, or even A.D.D.

His ethics textbook also says, "The life of a fetus is of no greater value than the life of a nonhuman animal at a similar level of rationality, self-consciousness, awareness, capacity to feel, etc." He also says, "Since no fetus is a person, no fetus has the same claim to life as a person."[151] (Parents paying for their children to attend Singer's classes at Princeton might also want to consider that he believes there's justification for the elderly to be exterminated as well.)

George Will has this to say about the Princeton professor:

Peter Singer comes to campus to teach that truly ethical behavior will not flourish until humanity abandons the fallacy, as he sees it, of "the sanctity of life."

He comes trailing clouds of controversy because he argues, without recourse to euphemism or other semantic sleights-of-hand, the moral justification of some homicides, including infanticide and euthanasia. He rejects "the particular moral order" which supposes that human beings are extraordinarily precious because God made them so. He also rejects secular philosophies that depict human beings as possessing a unique and exalted dignity that sharply distinguishes them from, and justifies their "tyranny" over, other species of animals.

He appalls the right-to-life movement but actually he is the abortion-rights movement's worst nightmare. The logic of moral reasoning often is that he who says A must say B. Singer and other prochoice people say A. But he then says: A entails B, and B includes infanticide.[152]

Unfortunately, Singer isn't the only one who holds to his "only the smart and healthy and big deserve to live" worldview. A Portland, Oregon abortionist, Jim Newhall, said, "Not everybody is meant to be born. I believe, for a baby, life begins when his mother wants him."[153] To have heard fifty years ago that a human life begins and ends according to the desires of other human beings would have been unfathomable to thinking people. But apparently the reporter didn't even think to ask the abortionist a follow-up question.

Even organizations that do much good, such as the March of Dimes, have been heavily influenced by the eugenics movement. Dr. Marie Peeters-Ney, director for medical research of the Michael Fund points out, "The birth of a child with a chromosomal anomaly is now widely considered as a medical error and in certain countries lawsuits are filed against doctors because they failed to diagnose the 'condition' in utero. In an insidious manner, mentalities are changing and people now regard persons with a handicap as someone who should not be there."[154]

In the 1973 *Roe v. Wade* decision the Supreme Court questioned whether the unborn had "meaningful" lives. But meaningful to whom, and when? Is the fact that your life was not taken from you as an unborn meaningful to you now? If a mother wants her baby, his life is highly meaningful, which is why she mourns if there is a miscarriage. If the mother doesn't want her baby, then his life is not meaningful to her.

But does the worth of a human being depend upon whether others think his life is meaningful? Does the unborn transform from person to nonperson with each of his mother's changes of mind? And doesn't every human being regard the life he had in the womb as meaningful, since had it been terminated he would not now be alive?

Black people, women, Indians, Jews, and many others have been declared nonpersons or persons whose lives are not meaningful. But for whose benefit? That of the people in power, who have declared for their own economic, political, or personal advantage who is meaningful and who isn't. Whites decided that blacks were less human. Males decided that women had fewer rights. Now big people have decided that little people don't have rights.

Personhood is not something to be bestowed on living human beings, large or small, by an intellectual elite with vested interests in ridding society of undesirables. Personhood has an inherent value—a value that comes from being a member of the human race. For those who believe the Bible, this is linked to being created in the image of God. But even those who do not can hold to the position—though it is increasingly difficult to do so—that human life is valuable even when it is young or small or "less useful" to others.

This question is much broader than the issue of abortion. Exactly the same logic is being used with already born children. Dr. Charles Hartshorne of the University of Texas at Austin says, "Of course, an infant is not fully human.... I have little sympathy with the idea that infanticide is just another form of murder. Persons who are already functionally persons in the full sense have more important rights even than infants."[155]

Once it is acceptable to kill unborn children, no one who is weak or vulnerable can be safe. Is a handicapped person fully human? Is his life meaningful? How about the elderly? If those who cannot think do not deserve to live, what about those who think the wrong way?

Do we really want to live in this brave new world fostered by the skewed logic of the abortion rights movement?

5h. Arguments against the personhood of the unborn are shrouded in rationalization and denial.

Our ability to rationalize is demonstrated in the lengths we will go to to redefine what it means to be a person. First, we commit ourselves to do something we think is in our best interests. We start with our conclusion, the place we want to end up. Then we look for ways to get there while still keeping our sense of personal morality intact, so we don't have to be plagued by guilt. This is called rationalizing.

Simultaneously we reject information that would prohibit us from doing what we've already decided we want to do or that would make us feel guilty about what we've already done. When looking at abortion, the last thing we want to consider is information that would lead us to believe that we participated in the killing of a child. No one wants to face such a thing.

Distancing ourselves from information that contradicts our beliefs and actions is called denial. Rationalization and denial are methods we use to cope with unwanted, stressful information. This is why arguments for the prochoice position are saturated in rationalization and denial. At the end of the day, it is alarmingly easy for us to ignore evidence to the contrary, as well as the prompt-ings of our consciences, and simply believe whatever we want to believe.

6. "A fetus isn't a person until implantation...or until quickening or viability or when it first breathes."

6a. Implantation is a gauge of personhood only if location, nutrition, and interfacing with others make us human.

It is increasingly common for people to affirm that human life begins not at con-ception, but at implantation. This is especially true of physicians who wish to think of themselves as prolife while performing procedures or prescribing chemicals that can result in the destruction of those already conceived but not yet implanted.

To suggest that a newly conceived human being is not a living person just because she has not yet settled into her mother's endometrium is illogical. The endometrium is simply the source of "housing" and nourishment that will allow the already conceived child to continue living. Would we say the homeless and the hungry are not really people since they aren't living in a house or being fed? Just as we would do all we can to be sure adults who are homeless and hungry are not deprived of shelter and food, we should do all we can to be sure children are not deprived of the shelter and food provided by their mother's endometrium.

Some people argue that life begins at implantation, because the unborn is "lacking the essential element that produces life: an interface with the human community and communication of the fact that it is there."[156] But what does interfacing and communication have to do with whether or not someone is alive? If others are not aware of my existence (for instance, if I were stranded on a desert island or trapped in a cave), would that mean I would cease to exist?

Another argument comes from *twinning*, the division of a conceptus, and *recombination*, the reuniting of two concepti. These can occur up to fourteen days after conception, before or after implantation. Therefore some believe individual human life does not begin until that time. Robert Wennberg addresses this argument:

> Imagine that we lived in a world in which a certain small percentage of teenagers replicated themselves by some mysterious natural means, splitting in two upon reaching their sixteenth birthday. We would not in the least be inclined to conclude that no human being could therefore be considered a person prior to becoming sixteen years of age; nor would we conclude that life could be taken with greater impunity prior to replication than afterward. The real oddity—to press the parallel— would be two teenagers becoming one. However, in all of this we still would not judge the individual's claim to life to be undermined in any way. We might puzzle over questions of personal identity…but we would not allow these strange replications and fusions to influence our thinking about an individual's right to life. Nor therefore does it seem that such considerations are relevant in determining the point at which an individual might assume a right to life in utero.[157]

In the case of identical twins, the genetic code that each possesses is indistinguishable. If this meant that either were somehow less human because of that exceptional condition, it would also mean that they must be less human after birth. (And triplets less human still.)

6b. Quickening is a gauge of personhood only if someone's reality or value depends upon being noticed by another.

Quickening is an old term for when the mother first becomes aware of the movements of the child within her. Because the uterus is not highly sensitive to touch, quickening often happens in the second trimester, long after the child has started moving. Some women feel their children very early, others don't feel their presence until months later.

Surely we cannot believe that one child becomes human when his mother senses him at twelve weeks development, and another doesn't become human until his mother senses him at twenty. One person's ability or inability to recognize the presence of another has nothing whatsoever to do with the second person's reality. *Human life begins at conception, not at perception.*

6c. Viability is an arbitrary concept. Why not associate personhood with heartbeat, brain waves, or something else?

In *Roe v. Wade*, the Supreme Court defined viability as the point when the unborn is "potentially able to live outside the mother's womb, albeit with artificial aid."[158] The critical issue in when this point is reached is the development of the child's lungs.

But why make worthiness to live dependent upon the development of the child's lungs? Why not say he becomes human in the fourth week because that's when his heart beats? Or the sixth week because that's when he has brain waves? (Both are also arbitrary, yet both would eliminate all abortions currently performed.) Someone could argue that personhood begins when the unborn first sucks his thumb or responds to light and noise. Or why not say that personhood begins when the child takes his first step or is potty trained?

There is only one objective point of origin for any human being—only one point at which there was not a human being a moment ago, and there is now. That point is conception.

6d. The point of viability constantly changes because it depends on technology, not the unborn herself. Eventually babies may be viable from the point of conception.

Like all points other than conception, viability is arbitrary, but it is even more arbitrary than most. The point at which heart and brain develop—though unscientific as measurements of personhood—at least remain fairly constant. Yet in the last three decades, viability has been reduced from thirty weeks to less than twenty weeks of development. A child has actually been born at nineteen weeks and survived.

Viability depends not only on the child but on the ability of our technology to save his life. What will happen when we are able to save lives at fifteen weeks or less? Will those children suddenly become human and worthy to live? Can we honestly believe that children at twenty-one weeks were not human twenty years ago, but are human now simply because of improved technology? Or can we believe that the unborn at eighteen weeks, who is just barely nonviable, is not a human being, but ten years from now he will be because hospitals will have better equipment?

Does the baby's nature and worth also depend on which hospital—or country—he is in since some hospitals are equipped to save a nineteen-week-old child and others could save a child no earlier than twenty-eight weeks? Technologies change; babies do not. Surely we cannot believe that the sophistication of life-support systems determines the reality or worth of human life!

Dr. Landrum Shettles, a pioneer in fertility and sperm biology and contributor to fifty medical textbooks, made this assessment of the Supreme Court's arguments based on viability:

> An abortion law truly based on "viability" would require constant redefinition. What was not considered protectable human life last year might be this year. If we were to take the Court at its word, we would find ourselves with a law that makes last year's "abortions" this year's homicides in some cases. I have maintained human embryos in "laboratory wombs" for several days.... It appears inevitable that the day will come when the unborn will *always* be potentially viable outside the womb.[159]

Test-tube babies have already survived for days outside the womb before implantation. Shouldn't proponents of the viability theory then maintain that they were human from the point of conception since they were viable all along? As Dr. Shettles suggests, viability is ultimately an argument for the humanity of all preborn children since eventually science may find a way for an entire "pregnancy" to take place outside of a mother.

Despite all this, the Supreme Court cited viability as the point where the state has a compelling interest in the welfare of the unborn. (Ironically, the wording of the decision allowed abortion after viability anyway.) However, in the 1989 *Webster* v. *Reproductive Health Services* decision, the Supreme Court began to dismantle the illogical conclusions of *Roe* v. *Wade* when it said, "We do not see why the State's interest in protecting potential human life should come into existence only at the point of viability."

The tiniest baby to survive in Oregon weighed just ten ounces at birth. Born on March 5, 2000, she was able to be held in her mother's palm. Following her birth by Caesarian section, Sophia didn't have cranial bleeding, which often causes blindness, mental retardation, and other problems in premature infants. She was breathing by herself, and at five weeks, at one and a half pounds, she had more than doubled her weight.[160] Front page follow-up reports joyfully tracked the growth of little Sophia, showing her going home with her parents ninety-one days after birth.[161] By then she was four pounds.

Remarkably, the updates on little Sophia appeared in the *Oregonian,* a newspaper that has frequently printed editorials defending abortion. Every day that Sophia's life was being celebrated, many Oregon infants bigger than ten ounces, and some bigger than four pounds, were being cut to pieces in Portland abortion clinics. In all the media coverage, no one voiced the incongruity of why one child's life should be cherished and celebrated, while other children's lives, children of exactly the same kind and stage of development, were violently extinguished.

6e. In a broad sense, many born people are not viable because they are incapable of surviving without depending on others.

If viability is viewed in its broadest sense as the capacity to live without depending on other human beings, many people in our society are not viable. The premature baby still has to depend on someone for human care, even if it's a team of doctors and nurses who hover over him day and night.

What do the sick, the handicapped, Alzheimer's victims, infants, two-year-olds, many elderly, and the unborn all have in common? First, they are people. Second, they are not viable; they are dependent upon other people to live.

Many accident victims can't survive on their own without medical help. Is the person whose lungs are punctured now a nonperson? I am an insulin-dependent diabetic. I can't survive on my own. Without insulin I will die. Does that mean I'm not a person? The ability to survive without someone's help is a poor criterion by which to evaluate his humanity.

An infant won't survive two days without adult care. A two-year-old can't survive on his own either. Though these children can be very inconvenient and interfere with the desires and lifestyles of adults, most of us do not believe their parents have the right to kill them. I say "most of us" not facetiously, but in the interests of accuracy. Psychiatrist and anthropologist Virginia Abernethy of Vanderbilt

University's School of Medicine said in *Newsweek:* "I don't think abortion is ever wrong. As long as an individual is completely dependent upon the mother, it's not a person." The article goes on to explain:

> In this view, which is shared by other prochoice theorists, an individual becomes a person only when he or she becomes a responsible moral agent—around three or four, in Abernethy's judgment. Until then, she thinks, infants—like fetuses—are nonpersons; defective children, such as those with Down syndrome, may never become persons.[162]

Those who doubt the logical and inevitable consequences of the prochoice position should consider carefully these words. Even *Newsweek*, which has never been known as a mouthpiece for the prolife movement, cannot help but point out what a short jump there is from abortion to infanticide.

6f. A child's "breathing," her intake of oxygen, begins long before birth.

Some prochoice religious groups argue that as Adam's life began when God breathed into him, so each human life begins when the baby is born and takes his first breath. This demonstrates a misunderstanding of the nature of the unborn's respiration:

> While breathing in the usual sense does not begin until birth, the process of *respiration* in the more technical biological sense of the transfer of oxygen from the environment of the living organism occurs from the time of conception.... [I]t is the *mode* but not the *fact* of this oxygen transfer which changes at birth.[163]

The creation of Adam was historically unique, never again to be duplicated, and has no parallel to the birth of a child. As Harold O. J. Brown put it,

> If God took inanimate matter and made a man from it, as Genesis 2:7 seems to be saying, then obviously what he created was not a human being until it was given life. But the fetus is not "inanimate matter." It is already alive. And it is already human.... [T]o apply Genesis 2:7 to human beings who were carried for nine months in a mother's womb before birth is clearly ridiculous. This argument is seldom used by people who take Scripture seriously.[164]

6g. Someone's helplessness or dependency should motivate us to protect her, not to destroy her.

The issue of viability is that if someone is dependent upon an adult to survive, somehow she does not deserve to live. Yet this is contrary to our sense of what is right:

> Normally when we see someone mistreated, our sense of outrage, our urge to protect, is inversely related to the person's ability to protect himself: The more *dependent* he or she is, the more protective we become. With "viability" as our guide, we act completely contrary to our normal sense of moral responsibility. Rather than appealing to our best instincts, "viability" brings out the very worst in us.[165]

Some years ago the attention of our entire nation turned to Baby Jessica, the little girl trapped at the bottom of a deep well. The amount of human resources poured into saving her was vast, but no one doubted whether she was worth it. What touched our hearts more than anything was her helplessness and vulnerability.

When we are thinking accurately, we realize that a helpless person deserves help precisely because she is helpless. It is a sad commentary on society when a child's helplessness and dependence on another is used as an argument against her right to live.

---

7. "Obviously life begins at birth. That's why we celebrate birthdays, not conception days, and why we don't have funerals following miscarriages."

7a. Our recognition of birthdays is cultural, not scientific.

The Chinese calculate a person's age from the estimated time of his conception. Other societies celebrate birthdays to mark the day the already living child entered our world. On the day of birth we can first see, touch, and hold him. He has not come into being at this point, he has simply joined us on the outside. A birthday is not the beginning of a life, but the beginning of a face-to-face relationship. Our inability to see and hear an unborn child no more indicates he is not a person than our inability to hear someone in another part of the house indicates he is not a person.

7b. Some people do have funerals after a miscarriage.

A nonreligious couple came to me after their baby died before birth. The mother told me that she and her preborn daughter had become very close during her pregnancy. She said calmly, "No matter what anyone else says, I have lost a baby. We named her Mary Beth, and she will always be our daughter." There was no birth or death certificate, but this couple knew without a doubt that their preborn child was a human being. They asked to have a funeral. It was unforgettable. There wasn't a dry eye anywhere—everyone of us knew a child had died.

7c. Funerals are an expression of our subjective attachment to those who have died, not a measurement of their true worth.

Funerals are for the living, not the dead. The baby that dies in a miscarriage is a real baby, but we haven't gotten to know her yet. Therefore the sense of loss, though real, is often less than if she had been born and we had bonded with her. The difference, however, is not in her, but in *us*. Whether born or preborn, the less we know a person, the less we grieve her death. That's why we would be devastated if a close friend died today, but aren't devastated at the thousands of equally valuable people who did die today. Surely the fact that we do not grieve does not in any way lessen their personhood or worth.

7d. There is nothing about birth that makes a baby essentially different than he was before birth.

In 1983 a physician was accused of murder because he killed a baby who survived his attempt to abort him. Envision this scenario as it actually happened. Before the attempted abortion, the baby was normal and healthy. Five minutes later, he had been disfigured, poisoned, and burned with salt, all of which was perfectly legal. But since this child had been moved a few feet from where he was before (inside his mother), he was now considered a person.

The same physician, who went on to become a director of Planned Parenthood Federation of America, had full legal right to poison and kill the child moments earlier, but was now considered a murderer because he bungled his assigned task of killing inside the womb and finished the same job on the outside. He was prosecuted not for killing a child, but for doing such a poor job killing a child. Does anyone really believe that one of these attempted killings was right and the other was wrong?

I spent the night in a city where the news was dominated by the frightful story of a murdered infant estimated at three pounds. Only the top half of the child's body had been found. Doctors examining the baby said that he could have been born prematurely or aborted, but it was impossible to tell. The reason this was so newsworthy was that if it could be determined the child had been born, it would have been a murder of the worst kind.

But children of this size are killed by abortion every day, and it is a ho-hum affair to the media. Those who oppose the abortions that kill these children are regarded as antichoice and antirights. Yet anyone who would defend the bloody slaying of the child in the news—a child essentially no different than all aborted children of the same age—would be regarded as a monster. *What's the difference?*

If our concern is for the innocent child, why should anyone be relieved to find out the child was aborted rather than murdered? Either way, he was killed—and killed brutally! There would be no less pain, no less horror, and death would be no less real if this baby had been killed inside his mother by the doctor's knife or outside her by the knife of a psychopath.

There is simply no magic that somehow changes the nature and value of a child just because he has moved from inside his mother to outside.

8. "No one can really know that human life begins before birth."

8a. Children know that human life begins before birth.

I heard a radio news report of some children who found a dumpster full of aborted fetuses. When they ran to their parents in shock and fear, they said they had found "dead babies." They stated the obvious. For one not to believe the obvious, one has to be taught not to believe it. These children were too young to know not to believe what they saw.

Feminist Jean Garton tells the moving story of her three-year-old, who wandered into her room late at night and inadvertently saw a photo of a ten-week abortion. His mother describes his reaction:

> His small voice was filled with great sadness as he asked, "Who broke the baby?"
>
> How could this small, innocent child see what so many adults cannot see? How could he know instinctively that this which many people carelessly dismiss as tissue or a blob was one in being with him, was like him? In the words of his question he gave humanity to what adults call "fetal matter"; in the tone of his question he mourned what we exalt as a sign of liberation and freedom. With a wisdom which often escapes the learned, he asked in the presence of the evidence before his eyes, "Who broke the baby?"[166]

8b. Pregnant women know that human life begins before birth.

When have you ever heard a pregnant woman say, "The blob of tissue kicked me" or "That product of conception kicked me" or even "My fetus kicked me"? It's always, "My *baby* kicked me." Many pregnant women have worn T-shirts with big arrows pointing to their unborn child. Always they say, "Baby." Have you ever seen one that says "Blob," "POC," or "Fetus"?

My wife and I were outside an abortion clinic one dark, overcast day. Three women in a row came out of the clinic wearing sunglasses. We could see that all three had been crying. My wife said, "You don't grieve like that when you've just had a lump of tissue removed. You grieve like that when you've lost your baby."

8c. Doctors know that human life begins before birth.

Talk to any good doctor and he will say that when he is treating a pregnant woman, he has two patients, not just one. He shows great care and concern not only for the mother, but for the smaller less visible patient, checking his movement, his position, his heartbeat.

After a lifesaving surgery on an unborn child, the surgeon stated that such surgeries "make it clear that the fetus is a patient."[167] The Associated Press accompanied the story with a diagram from the *New England Journal of Medicine*, which clearly showed that the unborn was a baby.

"Surgery Before Birth," a remarkable cover story from *Discover* magazine, describes surgery on an unborn child:

A precise dose of anesthetic had put both the mother and the 24-week-old fetus safely and limply to sleep. And now, lifting the little arm gently to rotate the one-pound body into position, pediatric surgeon Michael Harrison poised his scalpel just under the rib cage. This astonishing intrusion on an unborn life took place on June 15, 1989; it was necessary because this tiny patient's diaphragm had failed to close as it should have.[168]

Note the reference to the unborn as a patient. If the unborn is not a person, who is the patient being operated on? If the surgery is unsuccessful and the unborn's heart stops beating, does the patient die? The patient is referred to as "an unborn life." His arm, rib cage, and diaphragm are referred to by name. An anesthetic was used to put him to sleep. Elsewhere in the article, the author refers to his gender, and occasionally comes right out and calls him a baby. The article ends by saying, "While fetal therapists wrestle with protocols...their efforts to save tiny lives continue." Yet that same tiny life, not to be born for another four months, can be legally killed by abortion up to the moment of birth.

A decade later, in 1999, an unborn child named Sarah Marie Switzer, twenty-four weeks after conception, was operated on for spina bifida while still in her mother's womb. The award-winning photograph on the back cover of this book, showing Sarah's extended arm before she was sewn back into her mother, was published in *Life* magazine.

Sarah was the patient; she was given anesthetics to dull the pain; and doctors acted to preserve and enhance her life. But had her parents decided later that they didn't want her, they could have legally had her killed any time in the following months (without anesthetics), right up until her moment of birth. Look again at this picture. Can anyone honestly believe this is not a human being? Or that it is morally acceptable to kill such a child? Yet children just like Sarah, invisible to us only because the womb has no window, are killed every day in the name of "choice."

A prochoice editorial in *California Medicine* recognized that the position that human life does not begin at conception is politically and socially expedient for the prochoice movement, but that "everyone" knows it is simply untrue:

Since the old ethic has not been fully displaced it has been necessary to separate the idea of abortion from the idea of killing, which continues to be socially abhorrent. The result has been a curious avoidance of the scientific fact, which everyone really knows, that human life begins at conception and is continuous whether intra- or extra-uterine until death.[169]

8d. Abortionists know that human life begins before birth.

Dr. Warren Hern, director of Boulder Abortion Clinic in Colorado, is the author of the abortion how-to manual, *Abortion Practice*. In it he says an abortionist may, in some second-trimester procedures, have to wait to make certain "fetal death has occurred" before continuing with the rest of the abortion process.[170]

Dr. Joseph Bruner is the name of the surgeon who lifted the arm of twenty-four-week-old baby Sarah Marie Switzer in the fetal surgery pictured on the back cover. He has performed eighty in utero spina bifida operations. Of all people, he could not be unaware of the humanity of that child grasping his finger. In fact, the April 2000 issue of the *Atlanta Journal Constitution* states, "to ease the strain Dr. Bruner often talks to the unborn children while he works—to soothe them and keep them quiet, and to let them know what is going on. Sometimes he conveys a message from the parents, 'We love you. We are trying our best to help.'"[171]

Yet the fact is, Dr. Bruner aborts children with spina bifida. He is paid to either save or kill children with the same condition, at the same age of development, according to the desires of the parent. He says this is "an increasingly difficult position to be in." He adds, "Because we are performing surgery to improve the lifestyle of fetuses who have spina bifida, it is difficult to justify an operation that could also take that life away. As we walk through this mine field, society is going to have to take a good, hard look at itself, because it is untenable to hold both views."[172]

8e. Prochoice feminists know that human life begins before birth.

In 1995 prominent feminist Naomi Wolf wrote a remarkable article for the *New Republic*. In it, she said to her fellow prochoice advocates:

By refusing to look at abortion within a moral framework, we lose the millions of Americans who want to support abortion as a legal right but still need to condemn it as a moral iniquity. Their ethical allegiances are then addressed by the prolife movement, which is willing to speak about good and evil.

But we are also in danger of losing something more important than votes; we stand in jeopardy of losing what can only be called our souls. Clinging to a rhetoric about abortion in which there is no life and no death, we entangle our beliefs in a series of self-delusions, fibs and evasions. And we risk becoming precisely what our critics charge us with being: callous, selfish and casually destructive men and women who share a cheapened view of human life....

The prolife warning about the potential of widespread abortion to degrade reverence for life does have a nugget of truth: a free-market rhetoric about abortion can, indeed, contribute to the eerie situation we are now facing, wherein the culture seems increasingly to see babies not as creatures to whom parents devote their lives but as accoutrements to enhance parental quality of life. Day by day, babies seem to have less value in themselves, in a matrix of the sacred, than they do as products with a value dictated by a market economy.

Stories surface regularly about "worthless" babies left naked on gratings or casually dropped out of windows, while "valuable," genetically correct babies are created at vast expense and with intricate medical assistance for infertile couples. If we fail to treat abortion with grief and reverence, we risk forgetting that, when it comes to the children we choose to bear, we are here to serve them—whomever they are; they are not here to serve us.[173]

8f. Society knows that human life begins before birth.

Public service advertisements urge women not to smoke, drink alcohol, or take drugs while pregnant because they could harm their unborn babies. Every establishment in the state of Oregon that serves alcohol is required to post this sign:

Pregnancy & Alcohol DO NOT MIX

Drinking alcoholic beverages, including wine, coolers and beer during pregnancy can cause birth defects

If this sign is accurate, shouldn't we also conclude "Abortion and Pregnancy Do Not Mix"? Shouldn't we also be saying, "Don't get an abortion; you've got a baby inside that will be killed."

If alcohol harms babies, what does abortion do to them? When it serves its purposes, society freely acknowledges that what's inside the mother is a child and nothing but a child. No intelligent person disputes that. In all the times I've gone to restaurants here in Oregon, I've never heard anyone point to that sign and say, "That's false. There aren't real babies inside pregnant women!"

A front-page headline of the *Oregonian* read, "Judge Sends Mother to Jail to Protect Unborn Child."[174] The same has happened in Washington, D.C., and many places in the country. Judges are taking radical steps to protect the lives of the unborn, even to the point of incarcerating women who take drugs or otherwise endanger their babies before birth.

South Carolina has used its child-endangerment law as the basis for arresting and prosecuting women who use illegal drugs while pregnant. Attorney General Charlie Condon said in 2000:

> South Carolina's policy of protecting unborn children from their mother's cocaine abuse will continue even at public hospitals. Search warrants can be used as well as consents to search.... There is no constitutional right for a pregnant mother to use drugs. The unborn child has a constitutional right to protection from its mother's drug abuse.[175]

The South Carolina law makes it a crime to "refuse or neglect to provide the proper care and attention" so that a child "is endangered or is likely to be endangered." The state's Supreme Court has ruled that a viable unborn child—one able to live outside the mother's womb—is a child under the law and has upheld the law's use against pregnant women. (In reality, the unborn child is just as much a human being prior to viability; see answer 6c.)

At the Medical University of South Carolina, a public hospital in Charleston, if a pregnant woman's urine test indicates cocaine use, she may be turned over to the authorities and arrested for distributing the drug to a minor. Similarly, in Illinois a pregnant woman who takes an illegal drug can be prosecuted for "delivering a controlled substance to a minor." This is an explicit recognition that the unborn is a person with rights of her own.

However, that same woman who is prosecuted and jailed in South Carolina or Illinois for endangering her child is perfectly free to abort that same child in those states and every other state. In America today, *it is illegal to harm your preborn child, but it is perfectly legal to kill him.*

If this sounds incredible, consider a proabortion *Newsweek* article that warns against do-it-yourself attempts at abortion. It says caution should be used with taking drugs to induce abortion because of the danger of "depriving the fetus of oxygen and causing fetal brain damage instead of abortion." The writer states, "Sadly, many home remedies could damage a fetus instead of kill it."[176] A damaged unborn child is a tragedy; a dead unborn child is a remedy. Does *Newsweek* understand what it is saying?

Several states have laws requiring that aborted babies be disposed of in a "humane" fashion. One does not dispose of tonsils or gall stones in a humane fashion. Similarly, the state of Minnesota has a law that requires hospitals and abortion clinics to bury or cremate aborted babies. Who but human beings are required to be buried or cremated?

A prolife speaker was detained by police for carrying with him the preserved body of an aborted baby. He was told it was illegal to transport human remains across state lines without special permission. When he realized that this meant the state would have to argue in court that the bodies of aborted babies are in fact human remains, he welcomed prosecution! The state dropped the charges. Though they knew these were human remains, how could a state that defends and funds abortions publicly admit—much less attempt to prove—that abortion kills human beings?

In 1988 a man stabbed a woman in the abdomen, thereby killing the "fetus" within her. Though the woman lived, the man was convicted of taking a human life, and his conviction was upheld in a higher court. Yet it was entirely legal for the woman to hire an abortionist to kill the same child. Why is an action that results in the death of the same preborn person considered murder on the one hand and a perfectly acceptable action on the other? This is society's schizophrenia about abortion—though it approves of it, there is an underlying knowledge that it kills children.

8g. The media know that human life begins before birth.

The evening news showed films of riots in another country. The reporter said that a number of innocent men and women had been shot down. Then with a look of horror he added, "Among those shot down was a pregnant woman."

Why was this any more tragic than shooting down the other women? Would anyone have reported, "They shot down a woman with a blob of tissue inside"? Of course not. The reason for the horror is because the bullet that killed the pregnant woman thereby killed a child. Ironically, the same newscaster is probably not at all horrified that nearly four thousand babies are deliberately cut to pieces in his country each day. Like 90 percent of his colleagues in the media, he is probably decidedly prochoice.[177] Yet, his reaction to the killing betrayed a gut-level realization that no amount of propaganda to the contrary could take from him: Inside every pregnant woman is an innocent child.

A *Time* magazine article arguing against drug use and for better prenatal care says, "Courts will never be able to ensure real protection to an unborn child. That will have to come from mothers who take responsibility for the lives they carry within them."[178] If the subject were abortion rather than drug use, would mothers be exhorted by *Time* to "take responsibility for the lives they carry within them"?

Both Chrysler and Volvo have run ads in major newsmagazines promoting their new cars equipped with air bags. The full-page Volvo ad showed a large ultrasound image of a preborn child, with the single message at the bottom: "Is Something Inside Telling You to Buy a Volvo?"[179] The Chrysler ad, two full pages, pictured a pregnant woman who had survived a serious automobile accident several months earlier. It said:

> Susan Reed was on her way to work when a drunk driver crashed into Susan's 1990 Dodge Spirit. Both cars were totally destroyed. But Mrs. Reed was wearing her lap/shoulder belt, and the Dodge Spirit was equipped with a driver's air bag. It worked. It saved her life. And it saved another life. Her baby's.[180]

Above another picture of the mother, this time with her newborn in arms, the large caption reads, "One Chrysler Air Bag, Two Lives Saved."

If a prolife organization had run these ads, they would have been dismissed as propaganda. Yet nothing a prolife ad could have said would have expressed more precisely the central message of the prolife movement. The ads simply stated what every thinking person knows: *Inside every pregnant woman is an inno-cent human being whose life is worthy of protection.*

8h. Prochoice advocates know that human life begins before birth.

A woman who was on television defending her abortions said, "I always carried my babies low." Despite her stated position, in that unguarded moment she showed her realization that her abortions had killed her babies.

A prochoice political candidate openly defended abortion. Yet in a television interview about his family he proudly said, "I'm a grandfather," even though his first grandchild was not due to be born for several months.

We visited a prochoice rally where one of the largest signs said, "My Body, My Baby, My Business." Think of what this message means. After birth the baby would still be hers. Would society then say it was her business what she did to him? If she has the right to kill her baby before birth, why not kill the same baby after birth? This demonstrator hadn't yet learned the cardinal rule of the prochoice movement: "Don't call them babies. Always pretend they aren't really children. Once you admit they are, your argument could be seen for what it is—an argument for baby killing."

An editorial in the *New Republic* concedes the humanity of the unborn and admits there is no essential difference between born and unborn. It then draws a conclusion refreshingly candid but chilling in its implications:

> There clearly is no logical or moral distinction between a fetus and a young baby; free availability of abortion cannot be reasonably distin-guished from euthanasia. Nevertheless we are for it. It is too facile to say that human life always is sacred; obviously it is not.[181]

Psychologist and prochoice advocate Magda Denes wrote, "I do think abor-tion is murder—of a very special and necessary sort. And no physician ever involved with the procedure ever kids himself about that."[182]

For many people, prochoice thinking is not primarily the result of ignorance, but of denial or ignorance-by-choice. What we all know to be true we refuse to admit or act upon as truth because of the difficulty it may create for us. By heap-ing up argument upon argument—as illogical and inconsistent as they may be—we try to bury the truth so deep that it will not resurface. And when it does, we quickly push it back down, hoping that our wishing it to go away will make it go away. But no matter how we ignore or deny it, the truth will still be the truth: Human life begins long before birth, and abortion kills children.

8i. If we can't know that human life begins before birth, how can we know whether it begins at birth or later?

Peter Singer and others have suggested that children should not be declared alive until some time after their birth so that parents can decide whether or not they have sufficient quality of life and whether they want them.[183] That way, if they decide to dispose of them, they would not have to face legal consequences.

This illustrates one of the problems with the claim that we can't know for sure that life begins before birth. Since there is no inherent difference in a child just before and just after birth, why not say he becomes alive or becomes a person, a day, month, year or ten years after birth? And why not say he ceases to be a person on his eightieth birthday? (The thought that someone might make such a claim may soon prove to be less ludicrous than it appears.) Francis Beckwith points out this fundamental problem of the agnostic "we don't know when it begins" approach to human life:

> It is a two-edged sword. If no one knows when full humanness is attained, then we cannot prevent a Satan-worshipping neighbor, who believes that full humanness begins at the age of two, from sacrificing his one-and-a-half-year-old son to the unholy one. After all, who knows when life begins? And who are we to push our "religious" views on others in a pluralistic society?[184]

Part Two

∞

Arguments Concerning

Rights
& Fairness

9. "Even if the unborn are human beings, they have fewer rights than the woman. No one should be expected to donate her body as a life-support system for someone else."

9a. Once we grant that the unborn are human beings, it should settle the question of their right to live.

One prochoice advocate, in the face of the overwhelming evidence, admitted to me that the unborn are human beings. He then added, "But that's irrelevant to the issue of a woman's right to have an abortion."

But how can one's humanity be irrelevant to the question of whether someone has the right to kill him? Wasn't the black person's humanity relevant to the issue of slavery, or the Jew's humanity relevant to the ethics of the Holocaust? Not only is the unborn's humanity relevant, *it is the single most relevant issue in the whole abortion debate*.

In the *Roe* v. *Wade* decision, Justice Harry Blackmun stated, "We need not resolve the difficult question of when life begins."[185] In fact, this question is not difficult at all, as the many scientists quoted under argument 1 attest. But no matter what answer we come to, isn't the question of whether living children are being killed by abortion *precisely* the question we must resolve?

Writing in the *New York Times*, prochoice Barbara Ehrenreich says, "A woman may think of her fetus as a person or as just cells depending on whether the pregnancy is wanted or not. This does not reflect moral confusion, but choice in action."[186]

In this Alice-in-Wonderland approach, one's choice is not made in light of scientific and moral realities. One's choice is itself the only important reality, overshadowing all matters of fact. But if society operated this way, every killing of a person would be justifiable. The real issue would not be the worth of the person killed, but the free choice of the one doing the killing. If a man doesn't want his wife, he can think of her as a nonperson. If he chooses to kill her, it would not be "moral confusion," but "choice in action."

Ms. Ehrenreich goes on to say, "Moreover, a woman may think of the fetus as a person and still find it necessary and morally responsible to have an abortion."[187]

We must not miss the implications of this viewpoint. It says that one may acknowledge the personhood of a fellow human being, yet feel that for one's personal benefit it is legitimate—even "morally responsible"—to kill that other person. Though this is a logical conclusion of abortion-rights thinking, if carried out in our society it would ultimately mean the end of all human rights and social justice.

Naomi Wolf admits that her fellow feminists have lied to themselves in depersonalizing and dehumanizing the unborn:

This has led to a bizarre bifurcation in the way we who are prochoice tend to think about wanted as opposed to unwanted fetuses: the unwanted ones are still seen in schematic black-and-white drawings while the wanted ones have metamorphosed into vivid and moving color. Even while Elders spoke of our need to "get over" our love affair with the unwelcome fetus, an entire growth industry—Mozart for your belly; framed sonogram photos; home fetal-heartbeat stethoscopes—is devoted to sparking fetal love affairs in other circumstances, and aimed especially at the hearts of over-scheduled yuppies. If we avidly cultivate love for the ones we bring to term, and "get over" our love for the ones we don't, do we not risk developing a hydroponic view of babies—and turn them into a product we can cull for our convenience?

Any happy couple with a wanted pregnancy and a copy of *What to Expect When You're Expecting* can see the cute, detailed drawings of the fetus whom the book's owner presumably is not going to abort, and can read the excited descriptions of what that fetus can do and feel, month by month. Anyone who has had a sonogram during pregnancy knows perfectly well that the 4-month-old fetus responds to outside stimulus—"Let's get him to look this way," the technician will say, poking gently at the belly of a delighted mother-to-be. The *Well Baby Book*, the kind of whole-grain holistic guide to pregnancy and childbirth that would find its audience among the very demographic that is most solidly prochoice reminds us that: "Increasing knowledge is increasing the awe and respect we have for the unborn baby and is causing us to regard the unborn baby as a real person long before birth...."

So, what will it be: Wanted fetuses are charming, complex REM-dreaming little beings whose profile on the sonogram looks just like

Daddy, but unwanted ones are mere "uterine material"? How can we charge that it is vile and repulsive for prolifers to brandish vile and repulsive images if the images are real? To insist that the truth is in poor taste is the very height of hypocrisy.[188]

"The height of hypocrisy" is one feminist's appraisal of this double standard. Yet, amazingly, in this same essay Wolf still defends abortion, saying it should be done with grief and mourning for the loss of the child. In some ways, her bottom-line message is even more frightening. She is telling people, "Stop lying to yourselves about the unborn...these are real babies, just as real and just as precious when we don't want them as when we do. Keep that tragic fact in mind as you go ahead and kill them."

9b. The right to live doesn't increase with age and size; otherwise toddlers and adolescents have less right to live than adults.

Francis Beckwith summarizes the gradualist viewpoint:

> They argue, however, that although the unborn entity is *human*, insofar as belonging to the species *homo sapiens*, it is not a *person* and hence not *fully* human.... Other philosophers take a gradualist position and argue that the unborn gradually gains more rights as it develops. Hence, a zygote has fewer rights than a six-month-old fetus, but this fetus has fewer rights than an adult woman.[189]

In a book called *Christian Ethics* one author justifies some abortions based on his belief that "human worth and human rights grow with the physiological development."[190] If this is true, then human worth and rights continue to grow after birth, since we know physiological development continues after birth. Physical development continues year after year and takes on dramatic changes during adolescence. If human worth and rights grow with physiological development, then adults have a greater right to live than adolescents, who have a greater right to live than infants. It is morally preferable to kill an infant than a toddler, a toddler than a teenager, and a teenager than an adult. Once we buy into the gradualist argument, there is absolutely no logical reason to stop at birth.

In their argument for letting handicapped infants die, two scientists and ethicists say this:

Prolife groups are right about one thing: the location of the baby inside or outside the womb cannot make such a crucial difference.... The solution, however, is not to accept the prolife view that the fetus is a human being with the same moral status as yours or mine. The solution is the very opposite: to abandon the idea that all human life is of equal worth.[191]

Can we accept a logic that ties human worth and rights to physiological development? Why are we so outraged when we read of child abductions and murders? Why do they seem even worse to us than when the same thing is done to an adult? Isn't it because children are small, vulnerable, and innocent? The idea of an older, stronger person using them, considering them expendable, is horrid and despicable. The right to live—the right not to be cut to pieces—is a basic right of every person. Surely it is no less a right for a child, whether born or unborn, than an adult.

The moral fabric of our society is woven around a premise stated in the Declaration of Independence: "We hold these truths to be self-evident, that all men are created equal, that they are endowed by their Creator with certain unalienable rights, that among these are life, liberty and the pursuit of happiness." Our fore-fathers did not say, "After a certain level of physiological development human beings gradually become equal, but until they do it's okay to take from them life, liberty, and the opportunity to pursue happiness." The concept that all are created equal stands in stark contrast to the notion that human rights evolve with age, size, or social status.

"We hold these truths to be self-evident" was an assertion that there are certain truths so basic, so foundational that we *must* hold to them if the social fabric of this country is to endure. There is a logical order here. The cornerstone is that all are created equal, then that there are certain rights given by God that we are not free to ignore. Then, that the first and most basic right is the right to life. The exercise of our right to liberty and our right to the pursuit of happiness naturally come after the foundational premise of the right to life. Our pursuit of happiness must not compromise any other person's right to live. The "right to life" is not some modern antiabortion slogan. It is the most fundamental assertion of the most significant founding document of our nation.

The three most consequential moral issues in American history have each hinged on an understanding of what it means that "all men are created equal." The first question: Does "all men" mean only the white race, or does it include blacks?

The second question: Does "all men" mean males, or does it mean all mankind, male and female? Laws were changed as our nation came to a correct answer to these questions. But the third question has every bit as much moral significance as the first two: Does "all men" mean only the bigger and older, or does it include the smaller and younger? Does it include our preborn children, our littlest boys and girls?

9c. The comparison between a baby's rights and a mother's rights is unequal. What is at stake in abortion is the mother's lifestyle, as opposed to the baby's life.

Of course a child does not have more rights than her mother. Any two people are equal, and any two people have equal rights. Hence, a mother has every bit as much right to live as any child. But in nearly all abortions, the woman's right to live is not an issue, because her life is not in danger (see argument 29).

The mother has not only the right to live, but also the right to the lifestyle of her choice—as long as that choice does not rob other people of even more fundamental rights, the most basic of which is the right to live. The right to a certain lifestyle is never absolute and unconditional. It is always governed by its effects on others.

Planned Parenthood states, "The desire to complete school or to continue working are common reasons women give for choosing to abort an unplanned pregnancy."[192] Completing school and working are desirable things in many cases, and pregnancy can make them difficult. But a woman normally can continue school and work during pregnancy. If she gives up a child for adoption, she need not give up school or work. If she chooses to raise the child herself, there are childcare options available if she must work outside the home.

I am not suggesting this is ideal, nor do I say it callously. I have worked with single mothers and know their difficulties. I am simply pointing out there are alternatives, any one of which is preferable to an innocent child's death. Regardless of the challenges, *one person's right to a preferred lifestyle is not greater than another person's right to a life*.

9d. It is reasonable for society to expect an adult to live temporarily with an inconvenience if the only alternative is killing a child.

Abortion-rights advocate Judith Jarvis Thomson invented an analogy that has been widely quoted in prochoice literature and debates. She compares pregnancy to a situation in which someone wakes up strapped to a famous but unconscious violinist. Imagine, Thomson says, that some group called the Society of Music Lovers has "kidnapped" you because you have a certain blood type. Now you are being forced to stay "plugged in" to the violinist's body for nine months until he is viable, or able to live on his own.

Thomson then asks what if it were not just nine months, but nine years or considerably longer? (Apparently this is a comparison to having to raise a child once he is born.) Thomson assumes that readers would find such a situation "outrageous" and would not consider it their obligation to be subjected to nine months—at least—of bondage and misery for the sake of the violinist, who is little more than a human parasite.[193]

This analogy is worth a closer examination, both because of its popularity and because it is typical of the way the abortion issue is framed by prochoice advocates. Here are six fallacies of this argument that cut to the heart of the abortion debate:

1. *Over 99 percent of all pregnancies are the result of sexual relations in which both partners have willingly participated*. One is rarely coerced into pregnancy. (See argument 31, "What about a woman who is pregnant due to rape or incest?") Though prolifers may be in Thomson's mind, neither they nor anyone else is parallel to the Society of Music Lovers. No one is going around forcing people to get pregnant. The outrage the reader feels at the idea of being kidnapped and coerced is an effective emotional device, but it is a distortion of reality.

2. *Pregnancy is a much different experience than the analogy depicts*. Pregnancy is portrayed as a condition in which one is unable to leave the room, to socialize, to have a job, or even to get out of bed. Carrying a child is depicted as a horrid, degrading, and debilitating situation. Both medical science and the personal experience of millions of women argue against this bleak and twisted picture. Carrying a child is a natural condition in which there is some inconvenience. But few women are bedridden during their pregnancies. Most are socially active, capable of working, traveling, and exercising almost to the day the child is delivered.

3. *Even when pregnancy is unwanted or difficult, it is a temporary condition*. Since the great majority of abortions take place from seven weeks to six months of development, the actual difference between the woman who aborts her child and the woman who doesn't is not nine months but three to seven months.

The analogy to nine years or even a lifetime of being chained to someone is obviously invalid since after birth a woman is free to give up her child to one of the hundreds of thousands of families waiting to adopt infants in this country. While pregnancy is a temporary condition, abortion produces a permanent condition—the death of a child.

4. *In this scenario, mother and child are pitted against each other as enemies.* The mother is at best merely a life-support system and at worst the victim of a crime. The child is a leech, a parasite unfairly taking advantage of the mother. Love, compassion, and care are nowhere present. The bonding between mother and child is totally ignored. The picture of a woman waking up in a bed, strapped to a strange unconscious man is bizarre and degrading to women, whose pregnancy and motherhood are natural.

5. *The child's presence during pregnancy is rarely more inconvenient than his presence after birth.* The burden of a born child is usually greater on a woman than the burden of an unborn. Yet if a parent of a two-year-old decides that she is tired of being a parent and that no one has the right to expect her to be one any longer, society nonetheless recognizes that she has certain responsibilities toward that child. She can surrender him for foster care or adoption, but she cannot abuse, neglect, or kill the child. If the solution to the stresses of pregnancy is killing the preborn child, is killing not also the solution to the stresses of parenting the preschooler?

6. *Even when there is no felt obligation, there is sometimes real obligation.* If a woman is being raped or murdered, what do we think of those who make no effort to rescue the woman? Don't we recognize that there is moral responsibility toward saving a life, even if it involves an inconvenience or risk we did not ask for or want?

For the woman carrying a child, isn't it a significant consideration that her own mother made the same sacrifice for her? Can we forget that every one of us was once that "leech," that "parasite," that "violinist" dependent on our mothers in order to live? Aren't you glad your mother looked at pregnancy—and looked at you—differently than portrayed by this prochoice analogy?

This argument for abortion is based in utilitarianism, the idea that whatever brings a person momentary happiness or relief is the right course of action. This is a shaky foundation for any society that hopes to be moral and just in its treatment of the weak and needy.

10. "Every person has the right to choose. It would be unfair to restrict a woman's choice by prohibiting abortion."

10a. Any civilized society restricts the individual's freedom to choose whenever that choice would harm an innocent person.

When I present the prolife position on school campuses, I often begin by saying, "I've been introduced as being prolife, but I want to make clear that I'm really prochoice. I believe that a person has the right to do whatever she wants with her own body. It's none of our business what choice she makes, and we have no right to impose our morals on others. Whether I like someone's choices or not is irrelevant. She should have the freedom to make her own choices."

I'm normally greeted by surprised looks and audible affirmation, including smiles, nods, and even applause. I have used the sacred buzzwords of the prochoice movement—rights, freedom, and choice. I have sounded tolerant, openminded, and fair. Then I say this:

"Yes, I'm prochoice. That's why I believe every man has the right to rape a woman if that is his choice. After all, it's his body, and neither you nor I have the right to tell him what to do with it. He's free to choose, and it's none of our business what choice he makes. We have no right to impose our morals on him. Whether I like the choice or not, he should have the freedom to make his own choices."

After I let the shock settle in a bit, I explain that I am not really prochoice when it comes to rape. I ask them to point out the fallacy of the "it's his body and he can choose what he wants" argument. They realize that in emphasizing the man's right to choose, I have completely ignored the rights of the innocent woman. My hope is that they also realize it is not always a virtue to be prochoice.

All laws impose a moral viewpoint and restrict the individual's behavior. This is true of laws against drunk driving and child abuse. Laws against false advertising restrict a businessman's right to free speech. Laws against discrimination infringe on the freedom of choice of those who would treat minorities unfairly. When others' rights are at stake—and particularly when their very lives are at stake—any decent society must restrict the individual's freedom of choice. Is an innocent person being damaged by a woman's choice to have an abortion? If not, no problem. If so, it is a major problem that society cannot afford to ignore. Any law that prohibits the fatal victimization of another person is by nature a just law.

10b. "Freedom to choose" is too vague for meaningful discussion; we must always ask, "Freedom to choose what?"

It is absurd to defend a specific choice merely on the basis that it is a choice. Yet if you read the literature and listen to the talk shows, you know that this is constantly done by prochoice activists. "The right to choose" is a magic slogan that seems to make all choices equally legitimate.

All of us are in favor of free choice when it comes to where people live, what kind of car they drive, and a thousand matters of personal preference that harm no one else. We are also prochoice in matters of religion, politics, and lifestyle, even when people choose beliefs and behavior we don't agree with. But most of us are decidedly not prochoice when it comes to murder, rape, kidnapping, armed robbery, and child abuse. When we oppose the right to choose rape or child abuse, we aren't opposing a right; we're opposing a wrong. And we're not narrow-minded and bigoted for doing so. We're just decent people concerned for the rights of the innocent. To be prochoice about someone's right to kill is to be antichoice about someone else's right to live.

Whenever we hear the term *prochoice,* we must ask the all-important question, "What choice are we talking about?" Given the facts about abortion, the question really becomes, "Do you think people should have the right to choose to kill innocent children if that's what they want to do?"

10c. People who are prochoice about abortion are often not prochoice about other issues with less at stake.

After I spoke at a public high school on the prolife position, the prochoice instructor took me to the faculty lounge for lunch. He pointed to a table where four teachers were smoking and said, "Fortunately, this is the last week smoking will be allowed in here. We've finally gotten the district to make the teachers lounge nonsmoking." Good-naturedly I said, "I see you're not really prochoice." With a surprised look, he explained, "But cigarette smoke hurts other people." I said, "So does abortion."

Many people who are prochoice about abortion support laws requiring people to wear seat belts. They are antichoice about seat belts because seat belts

111

save lives. When lives are at stake, "freedom to choose" can and is legitimately restricted by society. Both smokers and nonsmokers have rights over their bodies. But we recognize that the smoker's right to smoke ends at the moment it violates the nonsmoker's right to be healthy. Nonsmokers should not be subject to unhealthy fumes without their consent. Children should not be subject to dismemberment and death without their consent.

10d. The one-time choice of abortion robs someone else of a lifetime of choices and prevents him from ever exercising his rights.

How to deal with a pregnancy is one among thousands of choices a woman will make in her lifetime. But if that choice is abortion, her child will never have the opportunity to make any choices of his own. A woman will have opportunity to exercise many legal rights. But if one of those is abortion, her child will never be able to exercise a single right. The unborn have been a glaring exception in the efforts of the modern human rights movement:

> Although sensitive to the political needs of nearly every interest group, this movement tolerates *natalism:* the denial of the fundamental human right to life to a segment of human beings simply because they are not post-uterine. Just as skin color [racism], ethnic origin [ethnocentrism], gender [sexism], national power [imperialism], and birth date [ageism] are irrelevant to one's possession of fundamental human rights, so is one's degree of development and location inside or outside the womb [natalism].[194]

10e. Everyone is prochoice when it comes to the choices prior to pregnancy and after birth.

Men and women are free to choose to abstain from sex or to use birth control or to do neither. But when a woman is pregnant, the choice she has made has produced a new human being. As one woman points out, "After a woman is pregnant, she cannot choose whether or not she wishes to become a mother. She already is, and since the child is already present in her womb, all that is left to her to decide is whether she will deliver her baby dead or alive."[195] Once the baby is born, the woman is again free to choose: She can keep the child or give him up for adoption. The choice prolifers oppose is the choice that takes an innocent life.

10f. Nearly all violations of human rights have been defended on the grounds of the right to choose.

The slaveowners in this country a century and a half ago were prochoice. They said, "You don't have to own slaves if you don't want to, but don't tell us we can't choose to. It's our right." Those who wanted slaveholding to be illegal were accused of being antichoice and antifreedom, and of imposing their morality on others.

The civil rights movement, like the abolitionist movement one hundred years earlier, vehemently opposed the exercise of personal rights that much of society defended. It was solidly antichoice when it came to racial discrimination. Whites historically had a free choice to own slaves and later to have segregated lunch counters if they so chose. After all, America was a free country. But the civil rights movement fought to take away that free choice from them. Likewise, the women's movement fought to take away an employer's free choice to discriminate against women.

Nearly every movement of oppression and exploitation—from slavery, to prostitution, to pornography, to drug dealing, to abortion—has labeled itself prochoice. Likewise, opposing movements offering compassion and deliverance have been labeled antichoice by the exploiters. At least with prostitution, pornography, and drugs, the victim usually has some choice. In the case of abortion, the victim has no choice. He is society's most glaring exception to all the high-sounding rhetoric about the right to choose and the right to live one's life without interference from others.

The prochoice position always overlooks the victim's right to choose. The women don't choose rape. The blacks didn't choose slavery. The Jews didn't choose the ovens. And the babies don't choose abortion.

---

11. "Every woman should have control over her own body. Reproductive freedom is a basic right."

11a. Abortion assures that 650,000 females each year do not have control over their bodies.

Since about half of aborted babies are females, approximately 650,000 unborn females per year have their lives taken by surgical abortion in America. About twenty million females have died from abortion since it was legalized. A female who continues to be pregnant can still exercise basic control, though not absolute control, over her body and life. A female killed by abortion no longer has a body or a life and will never have the privilege of controlling one.

11b. Not all things done with a person's body are right, nor should they all be legally protected.

A man is not permitted to expose himself in public. Many places have laws against public urination. Prostitution is usually illegal. So is taking certain drugs. Most of us agree with these laws, yet they all restrict our freedom to do certain things with our bodies. My hand is part of my body, but I am not free to use it to strike you or steal from you or to hurt an innocent child. The key question is whether what is done with one person's body brings significant harm to others. Clearly, abortion does.

11c. Prolifers consistently affirm true reproductive rights.

Reproduction takes place at conception, not at birth. The only people I have heard argue against the right to reproduce are radical prochoice advocates who believe in sterilizing the mentally disabled and the poor with large families, who are often minorities. Prolifers do not oppose the right to reproduce. What they oppose is the right to kill a child after reproduction has taken place. "Abortion rights" are not reproductive rights, but child-killing rights.

11d. Even prochoicers must acknowledge that the "right to control one's body" argument has no validity if the unborn is a human being.

Prochoice philosopher Mary Anne Warren admits:

> The fact that restricting access to abortion has tragic side effects does not, in itself, show that the restrictions are unjustified, since murder is wrong regardless of the consequences of prohibiting it; and the appeal to the right to control one's body, which is generally construed as a property right, is at best a rather feeble argument for the permissibility of abortion. Mere ownership does not give me the right to kill innocent people whom I find on my property, and indeed I am apt to be held responsible if such people injure themselves while on my property. It is

equally unclear that I have any moral right to expel an innocent person from my property when I know that doing so will result in his death.[196]

11e. Too often "the right to control my life" becomes the right to hurt and oppress others for my own advantage.

Whenever one group of human beings affirms its rights to determine the fate of other human beings, it is the beginning of oppression. Whites used blacks to enhance their own quality of life but did so at the expense of blacks. Men have often used women to live their lives as they wanted but at the expense of the women.

Ironically, the same oppression that women have sometimes endured from men is inflicted upon unborn children in abortion. Some men have used their greater size and strength to justify their mistreatment of women, as if his size gives him the right to control another. Today some women use their greater size and strength to justify taking away the rights and lives of unborn children.

11f. Control over the body can be exercised to prevent pregnancy in the first place.

Except in the rare case of pregnancy by rape, a child-carrying woman has made choices of control over her body that have resulted in the pregnancy. She has chosen whether to have sex and whether to use birth control. She has the full right to make these choices, and I would not want to see those rights taken from her. But these control-choices she has already made have ushered in a whole new scenario in which not simply her personal preferences, but also the life of another human being is now at stake.

The mother's first two matters of control—sex and birth control—were personal and private. The issue of abortion is not personal and private. It directly involves the life of another person and therefore becomes the concern of a decent society. As society would protect the life of the mother if someone tried to kill her, so it must protect the life of the child if someone tries to kill him.

11g. It is demeaning to a woman's body and self-esteem to regard pregnancy as an unnatural, negative, and "out of control" condition.

One feminist group states:

> When women feel that a pregnant body is a body out of control, deviant, diseased, they are internalizing attitudes of low self-esteem toward the female body. These attitudes contradict the rightful feminist affirmation of pregnancy as a natural bodily function which deserves societal respect and accommodation.[197]

12. "Abortion is a decision between a woman and her doctor. It's no one else's business. Everyone has a constitutional right to privacy."

12a. The Constitution does not contain a right to privacy.

There is nothing constitutional about the right to privacy, because that right is nowhere to be found in the United States Constitution. It was declared by the Supreme Court in 1973 as a right higher than an unborn child's right to live. Those who wrote the Constitution would be shocked to learn that their document, which was dedicated to ensure justice and compassion for all people, has been claimed by some to guarantee a right to kill preborn children.

Is privacy a right? Of course, but society recognizes that some rights are higher than others. Does one person's right to privacy outweigh another person's right to live? Of course not.

12b. Privacy is never an absolute right, but is always governed by other rights.

What would we think of a man who defended wife-beating on the grounds that "what I do in the privacy of my home is no one's business but mine." The question is, "Does abortion kill babies?" Killing done in private is no more acceptable nor less destructive than killing done in public.

An undated fund-raising letter from Planned Parenthood, signed by Faye Wattleton, attacks the prolife movement by saying, "We thought that what we did in our bedrooms was nobody else's business." Her primary argument for abortion is the right to privacy. The rest of the letter portrays prolifers as hateful, antisex, and a serious threat to society.

As I have written elsewhere, sex is a wonderful gift of God, a positive dimension of life that he intended a husband and wife to enjoy together.[198] Many prolifers believe that sex outside of marriage is destructive to individuals and society. Others do not share this belief, but still oppose the killing of children, since that is not the same issue. Though Wattleton's claim may generate both hostility and money, neither I nor the vast majority of prolifers I know have ever tried to monitor or regulate what goes on in other people's bedrooms. Those who oppose abortion are prochoice about choices before a baby is conceived, and prolife about choices thereafter.

The truth is, abortion isn't done in the bedroom. And even if it were, child-killing in a bedroom would be no different than child-killing in the streets. The issue isn't sex. The issue is whether an innocent child deserves to live or die.

12c. The encouragement or assistance of a doctor does not change the nature, consequences, or morality of abortion.

A physician's advice is authoritative when it comes to tonsils, gall bladders, and cancers. These are questions of physiology and pathology, not morality. Doctors are trained in medicine and sometimes in surgery, but their moral opinions are not always as reliable as their medical diagnoses (which themselves are sometimes flawed). Many doctors are conscientious people who place human welfare above expedience and money. Others, unfortunately, do not. Still others are sincere, but have embraced the prochoice party line without having thought the matter through scientifically, logically, or morally.

That physicians are capable of profoundly incompetent moral judgments was decisively demonstrated by many German doctors during World War II. Robert Jay Lifton, in his powerful book *The Nazi Doctors: Medical Killing and the Psychology of Genocide*, documents how normal and intelligent medical professionals endorsed and participated in cruel and deadly surgeries with shocking ease.[199] They were the best-trained medical personnel in Europe, but they were poor sources of moral guidance.

Doctors who perform abortions are surely the least objective people to discuss abortion with. Their personal and monetary interests in abortion disqualify them. One does not go to a tobacco company executive for guidance on whether to smoke cigarettes.

12d. The father of the child is also responsible for the child and should have a part in this decision.

On the one hand, a man is told he should take responsibility for an unwanted pregnancy and give the mother financial help and emotional support. He should take ownership of a situation he helped cause by regarding the baby not just as the woman's, but as his own. On the other hand, the same man is told that abortion is none of his business, only the mother's and doctor's. Given this mixed message, how can we expect a man to act responsibly toward the mother and child?

Ironically, abortion allows and even encourages men to sexually exploit women without the fear of having to take responsibility for any children that are conceived. If the woman does get pregnant, the man can hand over three hundred dollars and buy a dead child. When the man is long gone, with no child to have to support, the woman is left with the burden of having killed her child. "Abortion rights" bring out not the best, but the worst in men.

12e. The father will often face serious grief and guilt as a result of abortion. Since his life will be significantly affected, shouldn't he have something to say about it?

The implication of the "just between a mother and her doctor" argument is that no one else will have to deal with the consequences of the decision. On the contrary, abortion has powerful long-term effects on men. In an article in *Esquire* magazine, twelve men speak candidly on the price they have paid because of abortion.[200] Some agreed to the decision to abort, some didn't. Some pushed the decision to abort, but now desperately wish they hadn't:

> It's her body, but I had her brainwashed. I made all the decisions. Once it was over, we never talked about it again. We kept our mouths shut. She did have some real prophetic words, though. She said, "Wagner, you're going to regret this all your life." I told her, "No, no." But inside

me something would spark and cling to that. She was right. I'll never forget it. I'll never forgive myself.

Reflecting on his experience, one man simply said, "An abortion is a terrible thing." Many of the men commented on the disastrous effects on their relationship with their wife or girlfriend. One says, "Everything just dissolved after she had the abortion." A married man reflects:

> We tried to figure out why we weren't getting along so well. It occurred to one of us that it was a year since the abortion. That was the first time we realized that we felt we had killed something that we had made together and that it would have been alive and might have been our child.... We talked and shared how disturbed about it we both had been.... We hadn't known that we were angry and upset and hadn't been willing to face the facts.

One man reluctantly agreed to an abortion he did not feel good about. Years later he said:

> I've got to think of the pain and the damage it did to her, because I know about the pain that it does to me, and it wasn't my decision. I was part of the cause and I certainly didn't resist in any way. I can't help but think, am I guilty of being an accomplice in the taking of a life, or at least in not bringing it to fruition? There's guilt, but more than anything, there's just sadness.

One man demonstrates an understanding that not only women, but many men come to years after an abortion. In light of such testimonies, surely we should consider not only the welfare of the children and mothers, but also of fathers.

> I've had a hell of a time dealing with it, actually. To this day I still think about it. I'll go to bed and I'll think about it and say to myself, "Man, what a terrible thing to do. What a cop-out. You don't trade human life for material niceties." Which is what I was doing, because I was hoping for a better future, more goods I could buy.
>
> I don't have a good rationalization for it either. I'm not one of those people who believe that it's only potential life. I've come to believe more

PROLIFE ANSWERS TO PROCHOICE ARGUMENTS

and more that the baby in the womb is just that—a human life. I wish I didn't. I wish I could make myself believe differently, but I can't. It would make it easier to deal with mentally. When you have the opposite view and you go through with the abortion anyway, well, that's worse than anything.

So, you see, I'm kind of stuck. She did it for me. I feel like I murdered somebody. I wish I could do it over again, if I could just go back in time and relive those years. If she'd had the child, even if we'd got married and everything, it wouldn't have been that bad. I've seen other people do it. Reality's such a bitch sometimes, you know?

---

13. "It's unfair for an unmarried woman to have to face the embarrassment of pregnancy or the pain of giving up a child for adoption."

13a. Pregnancy is not a sin. Society should not condemn and pressure an unmarried mother into abortion, but should help and support her.

No matter what one's view of sex outside of marriage, clearly pregnancy per se is not wrong. It is not a moral, but a biological reality. Society should not treat the mother as a "bad girl" or pressure her to "solve her problem" by aborting her child. Rather, it should love her and help her through the pregnancy and the postbirth options available to her.

Society should affirm a woman for not taking the "easy out" of abortion to preserve her image and avoid some inconvenience, but at the cost of someone's life. Whenever I see an unmarried woman carrying a child, my first response is one of respect. I know she could have taken the quick fix without anyone knowing, but she chose instead to let an innocent child live.

13b. The poor choice of premarital sex is never compensated for by the far worse choice of killing an innocent human being.

Abortion may cover up a problem, but it never solves it. The poor choice of premarital sex can be learned from, reconsidered, and not repeated. The poor choice of killing an innocent human being by abortion is more serious, more permanent, and more unfair. It causes one person to pay for another's mistake. Furthermore, it forces the young woman to live with the guilt of her decision and gives her an even worse mistake to cover up. Not only the young woman, but all society suffers from the attitudes fostered by the abortion alternative. We send the message to her and to everyone, "The individual's comfort and happiness come first—even if you have to disregard the rights of an innocent person to get it." This attitude emerges in a thousand arenas, big and small, which cumulatively tear apart the moral fabric of society.

13c. One person's unfair or embarrassing circumstances do not justify violating the rights of another person.

It is unfortunate to lose one's job, and it may also be unfair and embarrassing. But this difficult situation does not justify armed robbery in order to pay one's bills. We must commit ourselves to finding workable solutions that treat a pregnant, unmarried woman with dignity and do not require others to suffer or die.

13d. Adoption is a fine alternative that avoids the burden of child raising, while saving a life and making a family happy; it is tragic that adoption is so infrequently chosen as an alternative to abortion.

In her outstanding book *Real Choices*, Frederica Mathewes-Green, past president of Feminists for Life, says that research with pregnancy care centers indicates emotional resistance to adoption as the most common barrier that surfaces among abortion-bound women.[201]

I am amazed at the negative light in which adoption is often portrayed in prochoice literature. Prochoice advocates Carole Anderson and Lee Campbell say of adoption, "The unnecessary separation of mothers and children is a cruel, but regrettably usual, punishment that can last a lifetime."[202]

It is not adoption that is cruel: What is cruel is an innocent child's death and a woman's lifelong guilt when she realizes that she has killed her child. Adoption

121

is hardly a punishment to a woman carrying a child. It is a heaven-sent alternative to raising a child she is unprepared to raise, or to killing that same child.

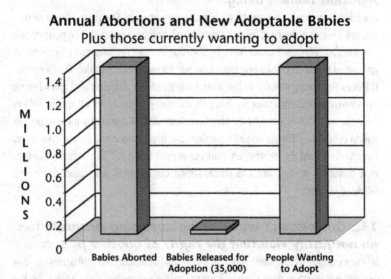

Annual Abortions and New Adoptable Babies
Plus those currently wanting to adopt

The National Council for Adoption estimates that 1.3 million couples are waiting to adopt a child.[203] With proper education and a positive portrayal of adoption, even this number could be increased. Yet each year, while 1.3 million children are being killed by abortion, less than 50,000 new children are made available for adoption. This means that for every new adoptable child, thirty others are killed. For every couple that adopts, another forty wait in line.[204] See two of the many web sites available to find profiles of prospective parents wanting desperately to adopt: www.parentprofiles.com; www.adopting.org/private.html. Tragically, most women with unwanted pregnancies are not given accurate information about the adoption alternative:

A 1984 study by Edmund Mech showed that nearly 40 percent of pregnancy counselors did not include adoption as an option in their counseling. Another 40 percent were uncertain or provided inaccurate information on adoption. Conversely, 68 percent could provide accurate information on abortion clinic locations.[205]

The adoption option is much healthier for everyone involved, not only for the child, but also for the adoptive parents, society, and the pregnant woman herself. By carrying a child to term, a young woman accepts responsibility for her choices and grows and matures. She can then look back with pride and satisfaction that she did the right thing by allowing her child both life and a good family. (Of course, adoption is only one alternative. The young woman may choose to keep the baby and raise him herself. Either alternative is viable. The one that isn't is the one that kills a baby.)

13e. The reason that adoption may be painful is the same reason that abortion is wrong—a human life is involved.

I have talked with several women considering abortions who had identical reactions to the suggestion of adoption: "What kind of mother would I be to give up a child for adoption?" The irony is that a mother who would not give away her child because he is too precious will instead kill that same child. The question she should ask herself is not, "How could I give up my baby for adoption?" but, "How could I kill my baby by abortion?" Even if she cannot care for her child herself, she will want to allow him to live so that another mother can love and raise him.

Because she has not yet bonded with the child, the abortion might seem like an easy solution, while parting with her child after birth might be emotionally difficult. But the child's life is just as real before bonding as after. The woman has three choices—have her child and raise him, have her child and allow another family to raise him, or kill her child. Two of these options are reasonable. One is not.

We took a pregnant teenage girl into our home. Though she'd had two abortions, this time she chose to have her baby and give him up for adoption. It was not easy, but this wonderful woman (ten years, a husband, and three more children later) told me: "I look back at the three babies I no longer have, but with very different feelings. The two I aborted filled me with grief and regret. But when I think of the one I gave up for adoption, I'm filled with joy, because I know he's being raised by a wonderful family that wanted him."

14. "Abortion rights are fundamental for the advancement of women. They are essential to having equal rights with men."

14a. Early feminists were prolife, not prochoice.

Susan B. Anthony was a radical feminist at a time when women were not even allowed to vote. She referred to abortion as "child murder" and viewed it as a means of exploiting both women and children:

> I deplore the horrible crime of child murder.... No matter what the motive, love of ease, or a desire to save from suffering the unborn innocent, the woman is awfully guilty who commits the deed...but oh! thrice guilty is he who drove her to the desperation which impelled her to the crime.[206]

Anthony's newspaper, *Revolution*, made this claim: "When a woman destroys the life of her unborn child, it is a sign that, by education or circumstances, she has been greatly wronged."[207]

Another leading feminist, Elizabeth Cady Stanton, said, "When we consider that women are treated as property, it is degrading to women that we should treat our children as property to be disposed of as we wish."[208]

These women were later followed by a new breed of feminists. Most prominent of these was Margaret Sanger, founder of Planned Parenthood, who advocated abortion as a means of sexual freedom, birth control, and eugenics (see answer 19d).

Sanger and others who followed her tried to tie the abortion agenda to the legitimate issues of women's rights. The same thing happened in the sixties. Dr. Bernard Nathanson says he and his fellow abortion-rights strategists deliberately linked the abortion issue to the women's issue so it could be furthered not on its own merits, but on the merits of women's rights.[209] Because of the legitimate concerns for women's rights, the abortion issue was pulled along on its coattails.

Early feminists such as Susan Anthony would have been appalled and angered to think that abortion—which they deplored as the killing of innocent children—would one day be linked in people's minds with the cause of women's rights!

14b. Some active feminists still vigorously oppose abortion.

Alice Paul drafted the original version of the Equal Rights Amendment. She also referred to abortion as "the ultimate exploitation of women."[210]

Feminists for Life of America (FFL) was started in the early 1970s. FFL supported the Equal Rights Amendment and has labored for other feminist goals, but is adamantly prolife.[211] One FFL member, Mary Ann Schaefer, has labeled the attempt to marry feminism to abortion as "terrorist feminism." In her words, it forces the feminist to be "willing to kill for the cause you believe in."[212]

Both men and women should be free to affirm certain platforms of the feminist movement without affirming others. One may support some or most feminist ideals, while wholeheartedly opposing abortion because it kills children.

14c. Women's rights are not inherently linked to the right to abortion.

Kate Michelman, president of NARAL, says: "We have to remind people that abortion is the guarantor of a woman's right to choose and her right to participate fully in the social and political life of society."[213] But a pregnant woman *can* fully participate in society. And if she can't, the solution is changing society, not killing babies. (Notice that abortion is called "*the* guarantor" of women's rights. Are there no women's rights unless there is license to kill unborn children?)

"How can women achieve equality without control of their reproductive lives?" Feminists for Life responds:

> How can women ever lose second-class status as long as they are seen as requiring surgery in order to avoid it? The premise of the question is the premise of male domination throughout the millennia—that it was nature which made men superior and women inferior. Medical technology is offered as a solution to achieve equality; but the premise is wrong.... It's an insult to women to say women must change their biology in order to fit into society.[214]

14d. The basic premises of the abortion-rights movement are demeaning to women.

Rosemary Bottcher, an analytical chemist and environmentalist, wrote an essay titled, "Feminism: Bewitched by Abortion."[215] Bottcher thinks women are much different than the way the feminist movement portrays them. If women can't handle the stress and pressures of pregnancy, Bottcher wonders how they could ever handle the stress and pressures of the presidency. Here is the crux of her argument, as summarized by D. James Kennedy:

> A man is expected to be mature when he fathers a child; he is expected to endure inconvenience and hardship, if necessary, to provide the means to bring a child up and go through college, even if this requires taking an extra job or working late at night. He is expected to do this because he is supposedly mature.
>
> But the woman, according to feminists, is so selfish, immature, irrational and hysterical that she cannot stand the fact of nine months of inconvenience in order to bring life to another person or to bring happiness, perhaps, to some other family who might adopt that child.[216]

In response to pictures of aborted babies, Naomi Wolf says,

> If these images *are* often the facts of the matter, and if we then claim that it is offensive for prochoice women to be confronted by them, then we are making the judgment that women are too inherently weak to face a truth about which they have to make a grave decision. This view of women *is* unworthy of feminism. Free women must be strong women, too; and strong women, presumably, do not seek to cloak their most important decisions in euphemism.[217]

14e. Many of the assumptions that connect women's welfare with abortion, the pill, and free sex have proven faulty.

Writing for the *Chicago Tribune* in 2000, Dr. Jose A. Bufill said:

> We can only hope that the physical harm done to women does not equal the social ills ascribed to contraceptives. Since birth control has become socially acceptable, the rates of teen pregnancy, sexually transmitted diseases, infant abandonment, illegitimate births and divorce have reached epidemic proportions.
>
> The "age of the Pill" has in fact become the "age of the ill": sick families, wounded women, fatherless children. This is the sobering re-

ality that statistics do show: the Pill has caused far more pathology than its advocates could ever dream of preventing.[218]

14f. Some of the abortion-rights strategies assume female incompetence and subject women to ignorance and exploitation.

Watchdog groups tracking abuses of women have leveled serious charges:

> The Peruvian government is using U.S. aid money to force poor Peruvian women to undergo sterilization or abortions.... PRI investigators cited numerous examples of native women who alleged they were verbally abused, falsely diagnosed, mistreated, threatened, and otherwise coerced into allowing themselves to be sterilized. Many women agreed to family planning methods because they were afraid of angering officials who controlled other programs they needed, PRI officials reported.[219]

Whenever such allegations arise anywhere in the world, they are usually denied or ignored by major feminist and proabortion groups. Even in the United States women's rights are taking the backseat to the abortion agenda. For instance, prochoice groups consistently oppose efforts to require by law that abortion be treated like every other surgery when it comes to informing the patient of its nature and risks. They do not seem to believe that women are capable of making intelligent choices after being presented with the facts.

The Supreme Court ruled against the legality of states requiring information to be given to a woman considering an abortion because, the Court argued, such information "may serve only to confuse her and heighten her anxiety."[220] The message is, "Don't tell women the whole truth; they can't handle it." Instead, abortion clinics are free to tell women whatever they want in order to sell abortions. As Feminists for Life points out, "This attitude is patronizing to women's decision-making abilities, and essentially establishes for women a constitutional 'right' to ignorance."[221]

It is remarkable that prochoice advocates oppose having even the most common-sense health and disclosure regulations at abortion clinics. Are they concerned about women or simply that women will have abortions? Why did a Virginia House committee defeat a 2000 bill that would have required abortion facilities and abortion practitioners to comply with hospital guidelines where surgeries of comparable magnitude are done? Why was it decided not to impose any regulations on abortion facilities? Feminists for Life comments,

> Those seriously concerned about women's rights should at the very least support consumer protection regulations. Abortion is the most remarkably unregulated medical procedure in the country. Why are abortionists given such free reign in a procedure which, after all, involves only women? Women are deserving of better protection.[222]

14g. Abortion has become the most effective means of sexism ever devised, ridding the world of multitudes of unwanted females.

One of the great ironies of the women's movement is that by its advocacy of abortion, it has endorsed the single greatest tool to rob women of their most basic right—the right to live. Abortion has become the primary means of eliminating unwanted females across the globe. A survey of a dozen villages in India uncovered a frightening statistic: Out of a total population of ten thousand, only fifty were girls.[223] The other girls, thousands of them, had been killed by abortion after prenatal tests revealed they were females, who are considered an economic liability. *Newsweek* reported that in six clinics in Bombay, of eight thousand amniocentesis tests indicating the babies were female, all but one were killed by abortion.[224] *Time* gives this alarming report:

> In South Korea, where fetal testing to determine sex is common, male births exceed female births by 14%, in contrast to a worldwide average of 5%. In Guangdong province, the China news agency Xinhua reported, 500,000 bachelors are approaching middle age without hopes of marrying, because they outnumber women ages 30 to 45 by more than 10 to 1.[225]

Because of the use of amniocentesis in sex selection abortions, two-thirds of children born in China are now males. In 2000, Beijing demographers issued warnings that China's population is headed for upheaval. The one-child "family planning" regime initiated twenty years ago has led to a critical situation. The problems will become severe over the next ten years as alarming numbers of men reach marriageable age with a severe shortage of possible partners. Chinese officials are especially concerned about the countryside where the ratio of boys to girls is currently four to one.[226]

Already seventy million Chinese men aged twenty-five to forty-nine must remain bachelors. The phenomenon has led to the selling of wives. Nonetheless, China's government is vowing to continue the draconian one-child policy, in which people are motivated to abort girls since if they can have only one child, they want it to be a boy.

Amniocentesis is also being used to detect a child's gender in America. If you want a boy, you don't have to go through months of inconvenience till you can get a reliable ultrasound. You can tell within a month or two, then kill your little girl by abortion and start over again. *Medical World News* reported a study in which ninety-nine mothers were informed of the sex of their children. Fifty-three of these preborns were boys and forty-six were girls. Of this number, only one mother elected to kill her boy, while *twenty-nine* elected to kill their girls.[227]

As the husband of a wonderful woman and the father of two precious girls, I cannot understand why anyone would not want to have a daughter. But for reasons that reflect some irrational bias against women, females are being targeted for extinction. And the tool for this destruction of women is staunchly defended by those who call themselves prowoman.

Since many more girls than boys are being killed by the amniocentesis-abortion connection, some outraged feminists have labeled the practice "femicide."[228] Ironically, the term betrays what those who use it deny: The unborn are people, and to kill an unborn female is to kill a young woman. There can be no equal rights for all women until there are equal rights for unborn women.

---

15. "The circumstances of many women leave them no choice but to have an abortion."

15a. Saying they have no choice is not being prochoice, but proabortion.

One of the great ironies of the prochoice movement is that it has left many women feeling that they have no choice but abortion. This is because abortion is constantly portrayed as the preferred choice. Having been taught that abortion is the easiest way out of a difficulty, fathers, mothers, boyfriends, husbands, teachers, school counselors, doctors, nurses, media, and peers often pressure the pregnant woman into making a choice that is more theirs than hers. One young woman reflects back on her own pregnancy:

> There were plans racing through my mind of where we would live, what we'd name it, what it would look like.... But, on his father's advice of "it'll ruin your life" [my boyfriend] opted for an abortion. I was in shock, so I went along with him when he said that there was no way I could have it alone and that I'd be kicked out of the family.
>
> Reality set in, and the choice was not mine. That's the heartache— the choice was not *mine*—it was his, my family's, society's. It was his choice because he would have been the only financial support. It was my family's because of the rejection of me and the unborn. And it was society's because of the poverty cycle I would enter as a teenage mother.[229]

Studies confirm that many women feel pressured into abortions:

> Altogether, fully 64 percent of the aborted women surveyed described themselves as "forced into abortion because of their particular circumstances at that time."... Abortion was simply the most obvious and fastest way to escape from their dilemmas. Over 84 percent state that they would have kept their babies "under better circumstances."[230]

15b. Those who are truly prochoice must present a woman with a number of possible choices instead of just selling the choice of abortion.

If we are prochoice, why are doctors, schools, family planning clinics, and abortion clinics not required to present women with facts about available choices, including adoption? A friend of mine who was formerly an abortion clinic counselor said this:

> I was totally uninformed of available alternatives to abortion. I never recommended adoption or keeping the child. Furthermore, I was completely unaware of the medical facts, including the development of the

fetus. I received no training in factual matters—my job was just to keep women happy and make sure they went through with an abortion.

With this kind of "counseling," how many women will choose anything other than abortion? Former owners and employees of abortion clinics have stated it was their job to "sell abortions" to pregnant women. Some clinics even hire professional marketing experts to train their staff in abortion sales[231] (see answer 28c).

Feminists for Life maintains, "If we could limit abortion to only those women who truly decided to have one, with adequate information without unfair and unjust pressures, we could cut the abortion rate dramatically."[232]

15c. "Abortion or misery" is a false portrayal of the options; it keeps women from pursuing—and society from providing—positive alternatives.

It is a terrible thing to present pregnant women with inadequate choices, leaving them in an apparent no-win situation.

This is not a choice between vanilla and chocolate. This is a choice like "Do you want me to break your arm, or your leg?" This is a choice that says, "Do you want to see your life derailed, see your dreams turn to ashes—or do you want to undergo a humiliating, invasive operation and have your own child die?" "Do you want to sacrifice your life plans, or would you rather sacrifice your offspring?" It's a lousy choice. Women should not be forced into making such a choice. We should be able to keep both mother and child's lives and bodies intact.[233]

We must reject this trap of presenting the choice between abortion and misery, as if there were no misery in abortion, and as if there were no alternatives. Why does Planned Parenthood, with all its hundreds of millions of dollars from tax revenues and foundations, not devote itself to a third alternative, such as adoption? Instead of helping with adoptions, why is Planned Parenthood the largest abortion provider in the country?[234] And because it makes millions of dollars from abortions every year, giving it huge vested interests in abortion, how can Planned Parenthood be expected to offer real and objective choices to pregnant women in need?

We cannot improve the abortion alternative; it will always result in the death of an innocent child. But we can surely work to promote adoption and to free adoption agencies from the red tape that sometimes clogs the process. We can work to improve the quality of children's services and aid to unmarried mothers. We can open our homes to women in crisis pregnancies. To not do so is to leave women with the tragic perception that abortion is their only choice.

16. "I'm personally against abortion, but I'm still prochoice. It's a legal alternative, and we don't have the right to keep it from anyone. Everyone's free to believe what they want, but we shouldn't try to impose it on others."

16a. To be prochoice about abortion is to be proabortion.

Suppose drug-dealing were legalized, as some have advocated. Then suppose you heard someone argue this way for selling cocaine:

> I'm personally not in favor of drug dealing, but this is a matter for a drug dealer to decide between himself and his attorney. Lots of religious people are against drug dealing, but they have no right to force the anticocaine morality on others. We don't want to go back to the days when drug dealing was done in back alleys and people died from poorly mixed cocaine, and when only rich people could get drugs and poor people couldn't. It's better now that qualified drug dealers can safely give cocaine to our children. I personally wouldn't buy drugs, so I'm not prodrugs, you understand, I'm just prochoice about drug dealing.

In terms of moral impact, there is no significant difference between people who are in favor of drug dealing and people who don't like it personally but believe it should be legal. Someone who is prochoice about rape might argue that this is not the same as being prorape. But what is the real difference? Wouldn't being prochoice about rape allow and effectively promote the legitimacy of rape?

Those who were prochoice about slavery fancied that their moral position was sound if they didn't own slaves. Yet it was not just the proslavery position, but the prochoice about slavery position, that resulted in the exploitation, beatings, and deaths of innocent people in this country. Similarly, most people in Germany did not favor the killing of Jews, but they did nothing to stop that killing.

In ancient Rome it was legal for fathers to kill their newborn children by setting them out to die of exposure or to be eaten by wild beasts. While many people would not do this to their own children, they recognized the rights of others to do so. The early Christians saw this "right" as a wrong, and when they found such children, they took them into their homes to care for them.

Some people have the illusion that being personally opposed to abortion while believing others should be free to choose it is some kind of compromise between the proabortion and prolife positions. It isn't. Prochoice people vote the same as proabortion people. Both oppose legal protection for the innocent unborn. Both are willing for children to die by abortion and must take responsibility for the killing of those babies even if they do not participate directly. To the baby who dies it makes no difference whether those who refused to protect her were proabortion or merely prochoice.

16b. The only good reason for being personally against abortion is a reason that demands we be against other people choosing to have abortions.

If abortion doesn't kill children, why would someone be opposed to it? If it does kill children, why would someone defend another's right to do it? Being personally against abortion but favoring another's right to abortion is self-contradictory and morally baffling. It's exactly like saying, "I'm personally against child abuse, but I defend my neighbor's right to abuse his child if that is his choice." Or "I'm personally against genocide, but if others want to kill off an entire race, that's none of my business."

I've often heard people say, "Don't call me proabortion. I'm not proabortion; I'm prochoice." My response to this statement is always the same: "*Why* are you opposed to being called proabortion? Is there something wrong with abortion?"

A radio talk show host interviewing me was saying what terrible people prolifers are. She was offended that they would call people like her proabortion instead of prochoice. So I asked her, "Why don't you want to be called proabortion? Is there something wrong with abortion?"

She responded, "Abortion is tough. It's not like anybody really wants one." I then asked, "What makes it tough? Why wouldn't someone want one?" She said, in an emotional flurry, "Well, it's a tough thing to kill your baby." The moment she said it, she caught herself and tried to backtrack. But it was too late. In an unguarded moment she had used the "B-word"—baby. She revealed the true reason why in her conscience she knew what everyone knows if they allow themselves to come to terms with it—abortion is wrong because it is always the killing of a child. And no reason to kill a child is good enough.

The "I personally oppose abortion, but..." position is popular among politicians who want to make prolifers like them because they don't feel good about abortion and prochoicers like them because they won't do anything to restrict abortion. My point is not simply that this position is cowardly, though certainly it is. My point is that it is utterly illogical.

The only good reason for feeling bad about abortion is that it kills an innocent child. If it doesn't, there's no need to feel bad. But if it does, then you should not just refrain from it yourself, you should oppose *others* doing it also. You should favor laws to restrict it, for exactly the same reason you favor laws to restrict rape, child molesting, and murder.

A Gallup poll of American adults answered the following question:
When do you think abortions should be considered legal?

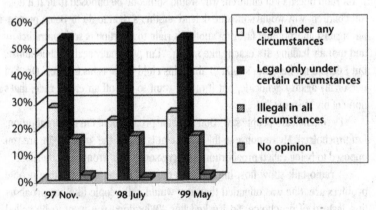

16c. What is legal is not always right.

One of the weakest arguments for the legitimacy of abortion is that it is legal. Civil law does not determine morality. Rather, the law should reflect a morality that exists independently of the law. Can anyone seriously believe that abortion was immoral on January 21, 1973, and moral on January 23, 1973? If abortion killed children before the law changed, it continues to kill children since the law changed. Law or no law, either abortion has always been right and always will be, or it has always been wrong and always will be.

For hundreds of years, slaveowners argued that the slaves were theirs and that they had the right to do with them as they wished. They claimed that their personal rights and freedom of choice were at stake. They said slaves were not fully persons. They said they would experience economic hardship if they were not allowed to have slaves, and they developed slogans to gain sympathy for their cause. They maintained that others could choose not to have slaves, but that they had no right to impose their antislavery morality on them. Above all, they argued, slavery was perfectly legal, so no one had the right to oppose it.

This point of view was given further legal support in the Dred Scott decision of 1857. The Supreme Court determined in a seven-to-two decision that slaves were not legal persons and were therefore not protected under the Constitution. In 1973, the Supreme Court, by another seven-to-two decision, determined that unborn children also were not legal persons and therefore not protected under the Constitution. In 1857 the chief justice of the Supreme Court said, "A black man has no right which the white man is bound to respect."[235] Despite slavery's legality, Abraham Lincoln challenged its morality. "If slavery is not wrong," he said, "then nothing is wrong."[236]

In the 1940s a German doctor could legally kill Jews, while in America he would have been prosecuted for murder. In the 1970s an American doctor could legally kill unborn babies, while in Germany he would have been prosecuted for murder. Laws change. Truth and justice don't.

16d. How can we tell people that they are perfectly free to believe abortion is the killing of children but that they are not free to act as if what they believe is really true?

If *you* believed that a class of persons were being murdered by methods that included dismemberment, suffocation, and burning, resulting in excruciating pain in many cases, wouldn't you be perplexed if someone tried to ease your outrage by telling you that you didn't have to participate in the murders if you didn't want to? That's exactly what prolifers hear when abortion-rights supporters tell them, "Don't like abortion, don't have one" or "I'm prochoice, but personally opposed." In the mind of the prolifer, this is like telling an abolitionist, "Don't like slavery, don't own a slave," or telling Dietrich Bonhoeffer, "Don't like the Holocaust, don't kill a Jew." Consequently, to request that prolifers "shouldn't force their prolife belief on others," while claiming that "they have a right to believe what they want to believe," is to reveal an incredible ignorance of their position.[237]

Part Three

∞

Arguments Concerning

Social Issues

17.

"'Every child a wanted child.' It's unfair to children to bring them into a world where they're not wanted."

17a. Every child is wanted by someone; there is no such thing as an unwanted child.

One and a half million American families want to adopt, some so badly that the scarcity of adoptable babies is a source of major depression. There is such a demand for babies that a black market has developed where babies have been sold for as much as $35,000.[238] Not just "normal" babies are wanted—many people request babies with Down syndrome, and there have been lists of over a hundred couples waiting to adopt babies with spina bifida.[239]

Would the demand for babies keep up with the supply if abortion were made illegal? The National Committee for Adoption (NCA) maintains that most women would choose to keep their babies, but 11 percent of the children that would have been aborted would instead be given up for adoption. The NCA's president says, "If abortion were totally outlawed, we would guess the numbers to be 68,400 more white infants and 3,960 nonwhite infants needing adoptive homes."[240] Those waiting to adopt would still have to wait in line, but the wait would be shorter and less agonizing.

It's important to clarify that this has no direct bearing on the moral issue of abortion. Even if no one wanted to adopt a baby, it would still not be right to kill him. The point is simply that if someone does not want a baby, there are others who do.

17b. There is a difference between an unwanted pregnancy and an unwanted child.

Many children who are at first unwanted by their mothers are very much wanted later in the pregnancy, and even more so at birth. Unfortunately, many women who would have bonded with and wanted the child by their six month of pregnancy get an abortion in their third month.

Furthermore, many children wanted at birth are *not* wanted when they are crying at 2:00 A.M. six weeks later. Shall whether or not the parents want the baby

139

still determine whether she deserves to live? If that is a legitimate standard before birth, why not after?

17c. "Unwanted" describes not a condition of the child, but an attitude of adults.

The problem is not unwanted children, but unwanting adults. "Wanting" is simply one person's subjective and changeable feeling toward another. The unwanted child is a real person regardless of anyone else's feelings toward her. For years women were degraded when their value was judged by whether or not they were wanted by men. Just as a woman's value is real whether or not a man recognizes it, so a baby's value is real whether or not his mother or father recognizes it. "Every woman or child a wanted woman or child" is a good goal, but if a woman or child is not wanted, it does not justify killing her.

17d. The problem of unwantedness is a good argument for wanting children, but a poor argument for eliminating them.

Planned Parenthood argues that unwanted children "get lower grades, particularly in language skills." It says unwanted adolescents "perform increasingly poorly in school" and are "less likely to excel under increased school pressure." And, "they are less than half as likely as wanted children to pursue higher education."[241]

I do not question the accuracy of these findings. They tell us what we should already know—the importance of wanting our children. Instead, prochoice advocates use such research to justify aborting the unwanted. They say the solution to having unwanted children who don't perform well in school is to eliminate them. But isn't this a backwards approach? Aren't there better ways to cure the disease than killing the patient?

In another Planned Parenthood publication, abortion is defended on the basis that "children need love and families who want and will care for them."[242] This is a fine argument for providing prenatal care for women in need. But according to its own 1999 annual report, Planned Parenthood performed 167,928 abortions while managing, out of its over half a billion dollar annual budget, to provide prenatal care for only 16,065 women.[243] This is about ten abortions for every one woman helped to have or care for a child. Saying children need love and families is also a great argument for adoption. But Planned Parenthood and other prochoice groups don't promote adoption. They promote abortion.

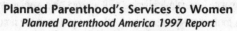

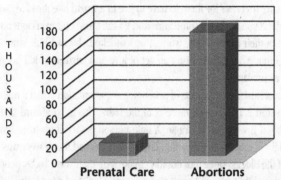

Planned Parenthood's slogan, "Every child a wanted child," is something we can all agree with. Where we disagree is in the proper way to finish the sentence. Check the box that indicates how you think the sentence should be finished:

☐ Every child a wanted child, so let's place children for adoption in homes where they are wanted, and let's learn to want children more. (Eliminate the "unwanted" in "unwanted children.")

☐ Every child a wanted child, so let's identify unwanted children before they're born and kill them by abortion. (Eliminate the "children" in "unwanted children.")

Everyone agrees that children should be wanted. The question is whether we should eliminate the adjective "unwanted" or the noun "children." When it comes to the unborn, the prochoice position is captured in a different slogan: "Every unwanted child a dead child."

17e. What is most unfair to unwanted children is to kill them.

In 1995 Jocelyn Elders, then surgeon general of the United States, said, "America needs to get over its love affair with the fetus." The callousness of this remark—accentuated by the fact it was spoken by the leading health defender in the nation—demonstrates the extent to which it has become popular to depersonalize the unborn.

One day my wife was calmly sharing with a prochoice woman why she is prolife. The woman looked at Nanci and said, "Haven't you seen the homeless kids on the streets of our city? It's *cruel* for them to have to live in a world like this!" My wife said, "Okay, why don't you and I get some guns and go kill those children right now. Let's put them out of their misery." The woman was shocked (I was a little stunned myself), but Nanci made her point. It isn't an act of love and fairness to kill people just because they're unwanted.

One of the most misleading aspects of prochoice argumentation is that it makes it appear that abortion is in the best interests of the baby. This is so absurd that it would be laughable if it were not so tragic. A little person is torn limb from limb, never to see the light of day, for her benefit? Slave owners argued that slavery was in the best interest of the blacks, since they couldn't make it on their own. Today people say, "I can't have this child because I can't give it a good life." And what is the solution to not being able to give him a good life? To take from him the only life he has. Exploiting people and stripping them of their rights is always easier when we tell ourselves we're doing it for *their* good rather than our own.

18. "Having more unwanted children results in more child abuse."

18a. Most abused children were wanted by their parents.

A landmark study of 674 abused children was conducted by University of Southern California professor Edward Lenoski. He discovered that 91 percent were from planned pregnancies; they were wanted by their parents. What is startling is that, in society in general, 63 percent of pregnancies are planned. Hence, *among abused children, a significantly higher percentage were wanted children compared to the percentage of wanted children in society at large.*[244]

Dr. Lenoski also discovered, again to his surprise, that the mothers of abused children had begun wearing maternity clothes at 114 days gestation, compared to 171 days in the control group, suggesting that mothers of abused children looked forward to having the child more than most women. Furthermore, fathers named later-to-be-abused boys after themselves 24 percent of the time, compared to only 4 percent in the control group. However we explain these findings, the best study done to date indicates that many more "wanted" children are abused than are "unwanted" children! The prochoice argument that more unwanted children are destined for abuse may sound logical, but solid research demonstrates it is not true.

18b. Child abuse has not decreased since abortion was legalized, but has dramatically increased.

Statistics reveal a sharp rise in child abuse in countries that legalize abortion. In 1973, when abortion was legalized, child abuse cases in the United States were estimated at 167,000.[245] By 1982 the number had risen to 929,000.[246] *In the first ten years after the legalization of abortion in America, child abuse increased over 500 percent.*[247] By 1991 there were 2.5 million reported child abuse cases, fifteen times more than in 1973. Overall, child abuse increased 63 percent between 1985 and 1994.[248] In 1997, over 3 million (3,195,000) children were reported as being abused, and over 1 million of these were confirmed as definite abuse cases.[249]

While the increased attention on child abuse in the mideighties no doubt accounted for the reporting of abuse that was already happening, the rise was extraordinary prior to this point. The experts agree that child abuse—not just the reporting of it—has dramatically increased since the early seventies. About 47 out of every 1,000 children are reported as victims of child maltreatment.[250] While some of those reported are not truly abused, many who are abused are not reported.

The actual increase in child abuse is even more dramatic than it appears, however, since surgical abortion alone (not counting chemical abortion) has left us 40 million fewer children in America to abuse. Since these children were abused to death by abortion, they too should be counted as victims of child abuse.

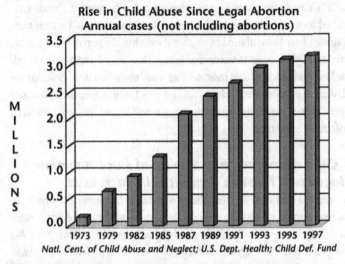

Rise in Child Abuse Since Legal Abortion
Annual cases (not including abortions)

Natl. Cent. of Child Abuse and Neglect; U.S. Dept. Health; Child Def. Fund

18c. If children are viewed as expendable before birth, they will be viewed as expendable after birth.

Princeton bioethics professor Peter Singer draws a logical but frightening conclusion from the reasoning used to justify abortion: "Human babies are not born self-aware, or capable of grasping that they exist over time. They are not persons. Hence their lives would seem to be no more worthy of protection than the life of a fetus."[251] Once we assume the fetus isn't worthy of protection, we must logically conclude other human beings aren't either.

"Studies indicate that child abuse is more frequent among mothers who have previously had an abortion."[252] Dr. Philip G. Ney's studies indicate that this is partially due to the guilt and depression caused by abortion and its hindering of the mother's ability to bond with future children.[253] Writing in a psychiatric journal, Dr. Ney documents that having an abortion may decrease a parent's natural restraint against feelings of rage felt toward small children.[254]

A parent overcomes her natural impulse to care for a child's helplessness when she chooses abortion. Having suppressed the preserving instinct once before, that instinct may become less effective in holding back rage against the helplessness of a newborn or the crying of a toddler or the defiance of a preschooler.[255]

The attitude that results in abortion is exactly the same attitude that results in child abuse. The pressure to abort is a pressure to reject the child. Even if she doesn't abort, the mother can look at her baby and think, "I could have aborted you," or even, "I *should* have aborted you." The child owes her everything; she owes the child nothing. This can cause resentment for any demands or needs of the child that require parental sacrifice. The logic, whether conscious or unconscious, is inescapable—if it was all right to kill the same baby before birth, is it really so bad to slap him around once in a while now?

Of the five thousand "born children" in this country murdered every year, 95 percent are killed by one or both of their parents.[256] The horror stories of young people discarding newborns in trashcans, fields, or hotels, and even at the prom, have been spawned by the notion that children belong to their parents, who believe they have the same right to dispose of them that society told them they had before the child was born. Once the child-abuse mentality grips a society, it does not restrict itself to abusing only one group of children. If preborn children aren't safe, neither are born children.

Peter Singer says,

> There remains, however, the problem of the lack of any clear boundary between the newborn infant, who is clearly not a person in the ethically relevant sense, and the young child who is. In our book, *Should the Baby Live?* my colleague Helga Kuhse and I suggested that a period of twenty-eight days after birth might be allowed before an infant is accepted as having the same right to life as others.[257]

Children have the right to live at twenty-eight days after birth? Why not three months? Three years? Should everyone just choose the figure they're comfortable with?

18d. It is illogical to argue that a child is protected from abuse through abortion since abortion is child abuse.

The solution to battered children outside the womb is not butchered children inside the womb. More babies already dead means fewer babies to abuse now, but this is hardly cause for encouragement. The solution to child abuse isn't doing the abusing earlier. It's not abusing at all. Abortion is the earliest form of child abuse, and there is no other more deadly.

19. "Restricting abortion would be unfair to the poor and minorities, who need it most."

19a. It is not unfair for some people to have less opportunity than others to kill the innocent.

Planned Parenthood claims that "laws restricting abortion discriminate against low-income women and minority women."[258] Because rich white people can afford something and others can't makes it neither right nor advantageous. Rich people have greater access to cocaine and can more easily hire a hit man or commit any crime. Is the solution to subsidize a harmful activity so all can have equal opportunity to do it? Shall we make burglary legal so it would be a more viable alternative for the poor and minorities?

The question is whether or not abortion kills children. Neither economics nor race have anything to do with it. If the rich kill their children, it does not make child-killing a virtue that should be available to all. Equal rights does not mean equal opportunity to destroy the innocent.

19b. The rich and white, not the poor and minorities, are most committed to unrestricted abortion.

While white women obtain 60 percent of all abortions, their abortion rate is well below that of minority women. Black women are more than three times as likely as white women to have an abortion, and Hispanic women are roughly two times as likely.[259] The fact that abortion rates are higher among minority groups leads many to conclude that minorities are generally proabortion. The truth is, however, they feel trapped into abortion because it is the only alternative they know. As Frederica Matthews-Green puts it, "No one wants an abortion as she wants an ice-cream cone or a Porsche. She wants an abortion as an animal, caught in a trap, wants to gnaw off its own leg. Abortion is a tragic attempt to escape a desperate situation by an act of violence and self-loss."[260]

Studies show that "abortion finds its heaviest support not among lower or lower-middle class women, but among white upper-middle class women for whom child-bearing may conflict with career goals."[261] Women with family incomes less than $15,000 obtain 28.7 percent of all abortions; women with family incomes between $15,000 and $29,999 obtain 19.5 percent; women with family incomes between $30,000 and $59,999 obtain 38.0 percent; women with family incomes over $60,000 obtain 13.8 percent.[262] Appealing to the "poor and minority" issue diverts attention from the actual reasons most prochoice advocates favor convenience abortions.

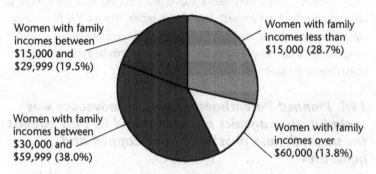

Who is having abortions?
(Divided by income)

Women with family incomes between $15,000 and $29,999 (19.5%)

Women with family incomes less than $15,000 (28.7%)

Women with family incomes between $30,000 and $59,999 (38.0%)

Women with family incomes over $60,000 (13.8%)

It is the poor and minorities—not the rich and white—who foot the physical and psychological bill for their abortions. What may sometimes be behind prochoice arguments is not concern *for* the poor and minorities but concern *about* them. What better way to control the numbers of African-Americans, Hispanics, and other minorities than by providing the means for them to eliminate their preborn children? The poor and minorities do not want abortion for themselves nearly as much as the rich and white want abortions for them.

19c. Prochoice advocates want the poor and minorities to have abortions, but oppose requirements that abortion risks and alternatives be explained to them.

Regulations requiring the giving of complete and accurate information to women getting abortions are consistently opposed by prochoice groups. Since minorities have many more abortions, they suffer most from misinformation. Prochoice groups do not favor the poor and minorities making informed choices; they favor the poor and minorities having abortions.

A classic indication of this surfaces in the issue of the relationship between abortion and breast cancer. A U.S. woman has a 12 percent risk of contracting breast cancer during her lifetime. The *Journal of the National Medical Association* (*JNMA*) reported in 1993 that black women age fifty and above who had at least one induced abortion have an increased risk of breast cancer of 370 percent.[263] This means they have a 56 percent lifetime risk of contracting breast cancer.

JNMA is a publication of black medical professionals concerned with black health problems. Yet not once have I read in prochoice literature any warning to black women about this dramatic risk to their health. Why not give this information to women and let them decide? Is it because Planned Parenthood and other prochoice advocates simply prefer that minority children be aborted, regardless of the risks to the mothers?

19d. Planned Parenthood's abortion advocacy was rooted in the eugenics movement and its bias against the mentally and physically handicapped and minorities.

Margaret Sanger was the direction-setter and first president of Planned Parenthood, the world's largest abortion promoter and provider. Although in her earlier writings she condemned abortion, ultimately her organization ended up viewing abortion as just one more means of controlling the birthrate of those considered inferior. I have in front of me a stack of Sanger's original writings, as well as copies of her magazine, *Birth Control Review*. I encourage readers to review these writings and decide for themselves the beliefs and attitudes that gave birth to Planned Parenthood and the American abortion movement.[264]

Margaret Sanger spoke of the poor and handicapped as the "sinister forces of the hordes of irresponsibility and imbecility," claiming their existence constituted an "attack upon the stocks of intelligence and racial health."[265] She warned of "indiscriminate breeding" among the less fit that would bring into the world future voters "who may destroy our liberties, and who may thus be the most far-reaching peril to the future of civilization."[266] She called the less privileged members of society "a dead weight of human waste."[267]

In a chapter called the "Cruelty of Charity," Sanger argued that groups dedicated to helping pregnant women decide to give birth to their children were "positively injurious to the community and the future of the race."[268] She claimed, "the effect of maternity endowments and maternity centers supported by private philanthropy would have, perhaps already have had, exactly the most dysgenic tendency."[269] Her use of the technical term *dysgenic* clearly indicates her belief that these woman-helping efforts violated Darwin's doctrine of the survival of the fittest, by which the weaker were naturally eliminated by virtue of their inferiority.

This same spirit permeates Sanger's magazine, *Birth Control Review*. It is full of articles with titles such as "The World's Racial Problem," "Toward Race Betterment," and "Eugenic Sterilization: An Urgent Need."[270] The latter article was written in 1933 by Dr. Ernst Rudin, a leader in the German eugenics movement that was at the time busily laying the foundation for the Nazi's acts of "racial improvement" and "ethnic cleansing." Elsewhere in that issue an article titled "Defective Families" calls the "American Gypsies" a "family of degenerates" started by a man and "a half-breed woman," and warns that "their germ plasm has been traced throughout seven middle-western states."[271] Also in the same issue, in his article "Birth Control and Sterilization," Sanger's companion and lover, Dr. Havelock Ellis, stated, "sterilization would be…helpful, although it could not be possible in this way to eliminate the mentally unfit element in the population. It would only be a beginning."[272] Students of history know where that "beginning" ended only a decade later, under the leadership of a eugenic devotee name Adolf Hitler. (Though Sanger did not write these specific articles herself, as founder and director she was responsible for the ideas promoted by the magazine.)

In fact, the international eugenics movement, of which Margaret Sanger was inarguably a part, was openly praising Nazi racial policies at least as late as 1938.[273] Sanger gave the welcoming address to a 1925 international eugenics conference.[274] According to Marvin Olasky, Margaret Sanger's "Negro Project" of the 1930s was "hailed for its work in spreading contraception among those whom eugenicists most deeply feared."[275] When it became evident that contraceptives were not sufficiently curtailing the black population and other target groups, the eugenicists turned to abortion as a solution to the spread of unwanted races and families.[276]

In Margaret Sanger's own words, to help the weaker and less privileged survive and to allow them to reproduce was to take a step backward in human evolution: "Instead of decreasing and aiming to eliminate the stocks that are most detrimental to the future of the race and the world, it tends to render them to a menacing degree dominant."[277] These "stocks" were the poor and uneducated, a large portion of whom were ethnic minorities. Sanger was more interested in "aiming to eliminate" these "stocks" (read *people*) than in helping them.

This history helps to explain why to this day Planned Parenthood does virtually nothing to promote adoption or help poor and minority women who choose to give their children life rather than abort them. Planned Parenthood has even brought legal action to shut down alternative pregnancy centers that give women other choices besides abortion. Though I have read many Planned Parenthood materials, I have never seen any that renounce or apologize for Sanger's blatant eugenicism, her bias against the poor and the mentally and physically handicapped, and her implicit racism, all of which characterized Planned Parenthood's philosophy from its inception. The fact that there are some highly visible blacks and other minority leaders in Planned Parenthood does not change its heritage or philosophy. It simply makes it easier to carry out its policies among target groups.

I do not believe Margaret Sanger was insincere or incorrect in everything she said and did. Nor do I believe most people who support abortion rights are racists, any more than I believe there are no racists among prolifers. I do believe that regardless of motives, a closer look at both the history and present strategies of the prochoice movement suggests that "abortion for the minorities" may not serve the cause of racial equality nearly as much as the cause of upper-class white supremacy.

20. "Abortion helps solve the problem of overpopulation and raises the quality of life."

20a. The current birthrate in America is less than what is needed to maintain our population level.

In 1957 the average American woman in her reproductive years bore 3.7 children. Taking into account all causes of death and the increases in average life span, zero population growth requires that the average woman bear 2.1 children. Since 1972 the average in America has been 1.8 children.[278] For two decades we have been below zero population growth. Every day more people die in America than are born. Any increases in population since 1972 have been due to immigration. The sociological perils we face are not those of population explosion, but population reduction.

In April of 2000 the Russian State Statistics Committee issued a monthly report stating that the country's death rate is twice as high as its birth rate. The country literally shrinks by 2500 people each day. The decreasing number of people, especially young and productive workers, will only increase the economic and security problems in Russia.

If the current birth and death rates stabilize, in 2050 Russia will have 116 million people compared to 147 million today. Since 1994 approximately 70 percent of all pregnancies ended in abortion. One in five Russian couples are infertile, partly because of the lasting health effects abortions can have on a woman's body.[279]

Prochoice advocates warn the American people that the prolife movement is trying to outlaw contraceptives. This is untrue. Some confusion may stem from the opposition to some forms of contraception, specifically the intrauterine device (IUD),[280] Norplant, Depo-Provera and oral contraceptives which often or at least sometimes do not prevent conception but prevent implantation of an already fertilized ovum.[281] The result is an early abortion, the killing of an already conceived individual. Tragically, many women are not told this by their physicians, and therefore do not make an informed choice about which contraceptive to use. (After extensive research, in 1997 I authored a small book titled *Does the Birth Control Pill Cause Abortions?*[282] Currently in its fifth revision, this book presents the available evidence on this subject. Appendix E is a summary of this evidence.) Opposition to specific abortion-causing agents is not the same as opposition to true contraceptives, which do not cause abortions. It is certainly true that among prolifers there is honest debate about contraceptive use and the degree to which people should strive to control the size of their families.[283] But on the matter of controlling family size by killing a family member, we all ought to agree. Solutions based on killing people are not viable.

20b. The dramatic decline in our birthrate will have a disturbing economic effect on America.

A declining population is a serious threat to social and economic prosperity. Most western European countries are now experiencing economic problems that their governments attribute to population reduction. France offers childbearing incentives that include monthly financial payments to families with more than a certain number of children. Why would a government pay its people to have children? Because it recognizes that all societies need a continuous influx of the young in order to remain healthy.

The problem of a shrinking population propagates itself. Because today's women have fewer children, there will be fewer parents tomorrow, resulting in still fewer children. Fewer and fewer people having fewer and fewer children adds up to a dying society.

The legalization of abortion resulted in a drastic reduction of the number of children in this country. By 1980 there were 6.5 million fewer school-age children in America than just a decade earlier. This required the closing of nine thousand elementary schools.[284]

Legalized abortion has resulted in over 20 million fewer taxpayers in America to support the elderly. "Population loss from abortion on demand is already responsible for past and future economic, employment and tax revenue losses and is eroding the solvency of Social Security."[285] The imbalance of older and younger is shaping into a generational civil war. By 2025 there will be twice as many grandparents as young children.[286] Some experts predict Social Security taxes will rise from 25 to 40 percent of total income.[287] In 1980 there were over four people of wage-earning age for each retired person; in 2020 there will be only two. By 2040 there will be one and a half.[288] (Abortion would be morally wrong even if it were financially profitable for the country, which ultimately it will not be.)

Having endorsed abortion as a means of decreasing the number of young, will society be compelled to use euthanasia as a means of reducing the old?[289] If back in the 1980s the governor of Colorado could tell old people they have a duty to "step aside" (die), what will happen in the 2010s? If the elderly don't step aside, will society begin setting them aside?

Former Surgeon General C. Everett Koop publicly stated his fear that mandatory euthanasia would eventually result from the unwillingness of the younger generation to support the elderly. He said, "My fear is that one day for every Baby Doe in America, there will be ten thousand Grandma Does."

20c. Overpopulation is frequently blamed for problems with other causes.

In the sixties there was a widespread fear that the world was swarming with people and that we were quickly running out of space. Yet the truth is that in 1992 Marilyn vos Savant calculated that the entire world population of 5.4 billion people, standing several feet apart, would cover an area of less then eight hundred square miles—the size of Jacksonville, Florida.[290] Every single global inhabitant could be placed in one gigantic city within the borders of the state of Texas, with a smaller population density than many cities around the world.[291] The rest of the globe would be completely empty of people.

> There are now almost three million fewer Russians than there were when the Soviet Union collapsed. Most experts see the population decline continuing due to a low birth rate, which is exacerbated by widespread abortion, and a far higher death rate blamed on formidable alcohol abuse, a failing public health system, and a shockingly high suicide rate. "Russia is on the verge of a demographic crisis because we don't have very many children being born," said Valentin Pokrovsky, head of Russia's Academy of Medical Sciences.[292]

Does this mean that there is no overcrowding and that our resources are infinite? Of course not. The world is full of problems, including poverty and starvation. But studies consistently show that enough food is presently produced to feed every person on the planet. The problem of starvation is a combination of many factors, including natural disasters, wars, lack of technology, misuse of resources, waste, greed, government inefficiency, and failure to distribute food properly. None of these has a direct cause and effect link to overpopulation. It is simplistic and inaccurate to attribute most of our global problems to overpopulation. Having fewer people alive to experience social problems is not a solution to those problems.

Christian relief and development agencies—whose outstanding work I not only applaud, but support and encourage others to support—should take every care to avoid advocating or taking part in programs that result in abortions. We cannot expect God to bless and honor our efforts to help the needy if part of our "help" includes distributing chemicals and devices that may kill children who belong not to us, but to them, and above all to God.

20d. If there is a population problem that threatens our standard of living, the solution is not to kill off part of the population.

Suppose there *is* a severe overpopulation problem. Suppose it could be demonstrated that the standard of living is higher in America because 1.3 million children are killed each year. Hitler's philosophy might have increased the standard of living—for those, that is, who were allowed to live. We must ask ourselves whether we want to live in a society where the standard of living was bought with the blood of the innocent.

20e. Sterilization and abortion as cures to overpopulation could eventually lead to mandatory sterilization and abortion.

China's one-child policy places extreme pressure on women pregnant with a second child to get abortions. Not only are they punished economically, but in some cases they are physically forced to get abortions. Abortion "posses" have rounded up expectant mothers and taken them to abortion clinics. In a single town, nineteen thousand abortions were performed in fifty days, all in the name of population control.[293]

If we imagine that this could not happen in America, a closer look at the direction of the prochoice movement should cause us to think again. The president of a scientific affiliation looks forward to the day when the government will require "that no parents will in the future have a right to burden society with a malformed or mentally incompetent child."[294] Molly Yard, past president of the National Organization for Women (NOW), has said, "We are going to have to face, as China has faced, the policy of controlling the size of families."[295] As George Grant points out, Planned Parenthood has been supportive of China's abortion policy:

> The truth is that from its very inception, Planned Parenthood has sought mandatory population control measures—measures carefully designed to *deny* the freedom to choose. Over the years it has proposed that our government implement such things as "compulsory abortion for out-of-wedlock pregnancies," federal entitlement "payments to encourage abortion," "compulsory sterilization for those who have already had two children," and "tax penalties" for existing large families.[296]

20f. The "quality of life" concept is breeding a sense of human expendability that has far-reaching social implications.

The slippery slope starts with the concept that some lives have more quality than others. Historically, this has always slid society into further human exploitation. Dr.

Leo Alexander was a consultant to the secretary of war at the Nuremberg Trials. Writing in the *New England Journal of Medicine*, he says that the Holocaust began with a subtle shift in medical ethics:

> Whatever proportions these crimes finally assumed, it became evident to all who investigated them that they had started from small beginnings. The beginnings at first were merely a subtle shift in emphasis in the basic attitude of the physicians. It started with the acceptance of the attitude…that there is such a thing as life not worthy to be lived. This attitude in its early stages concerned itself merely with the severely and chronically sick. Gradually the sphere of those to be included in this category was enlarged to encompass the socially unproductive, the ideologically unwanted, the racially unwanted and finally all non-Germans.[297]

"Quality of life" is a euphemism when applied to those not allowed to live. There is no quality of life for those whose lives are taken. For those allowed to live, life becomes more precarious. Variables such as age, health, or handicap may take one out of the position of privilege, making him a potential victim of others' quality of life.

In 1994 at the National Prayer Breakfast, Mother Teresa made the following powerful remarks to a U.S. president, first lady, many members of congress, and other luminaries who were decidedly proabortion:

> I feel that the greatest destroyer of peace today is abortion, because it is a war against the child, a direct killing of the innocent child, murder by the mother herself. And if we accept that a mother can kill even her own child, how can we tell other people not to kill one another?…
>
> Any country that accepts abortion is not teaching its people to love, but to use any violence to get what they want. This is why the greatest destroyer of love and peace is abortion.
>
> Many people are very, very concerned with the children of India, with the children of Africa where quite a few die of hunger, and so on. Many people are also concerned about all the violence in this great country of the United States. These concerns are very good. But often these same people are not concerned with the millions who are being killed by the deliberate decision of their own mothers. And this is what

is the greatest destroyer of peace today—abortion which brings people to such blindness.

And for this I appeal in India and I appeal everywhere—"Let us bring the child back." The child is God's gift to the family. Each child is created in the special image and likeness of God for greater things—to love and to be loved. In this year of the family we must bring the child back to the center of our care and concern. This is the only way that our world can survive because our children are the only hope for the future. . . .

Jesus said, "Anyone who receives a child in my name, receives me." By adopting a child, these couples receive Jesus but, by aborting a child, a couple refuses to receive Jesus.

Please don't kill the child. I want the child. Please give me the child. I am willing to accept any child who would be aborted and to give that child to a married couple who will love the child and be loved by the child. From our children's home in Calcutta alone, we have saved over 3000 children from abortion. These children have brought such love and joy to their adopting parents and have grown up so full of love and joy. . . .

We can keep the joy of loving Jesus in our hearts, and share that joy with all we come in contact with. Let us make that one point—that no child will be unwanted, unloved, uncared for, or killed and thrown away. . . .

If we remember that God loves us, and that we can love others as He loves us, then America can become a sign of peace for the world. From here, a sign of care for the weakest of the weak—the unborn child—must go out to the world. If you become a burning light of justice and peace in the world, then really you will be true to what the founders of this country stood for. God bless you![298]

21. "Even if abortion were made illegal, there would still be many abortions."

21a. That harmful acts against the innocent will take place regardless of the law is a poor argument for having no law.

There are laws against burglary, rape, and armed robbery, yet every one of these crimes continues to happen in our society. That these things still happen should not convince us to make them legal. Laws should discourage bad things from happening, not conform to them simply because they happen.

21b. The law can guide and educate people to choose better alternatives.

In her 1998 study of abortion laws and attitudes around the world, Rita J. Simon said:

> Abortions are permitted on request in forty-one nations. Tunisia is the only country in Africa to do so and across the Atlantic, a rather strange trio, Canada, the United States, and Cuba do so. In Asia and Europe, almost all of the communist and former communist bloc countries do so along with the Scandinavian countries and Austria, the Netherlands, and Greece.
>
> Public attitudes toward abortion were found to be positively and significantly correlated with abortion statutes. Those countries that had the most restrictive statutes vis-à-vis abortion reported the lowest approval ratings for abortion and those countries that permitted abortion on demand reported the highest approval ratings for abortion.[299]

This study shows that most people do not seriously contemplate abortion as an ethical issue, but simply buy into the beliefs about abortion implied by the existing laws of their country.

It is true that hearts and minds—not just laws—need to change in relation to abortion. Yet, we often underestimate the power of law to mold thought as well as action. When slavery was abolished, people gradually began to think differently.

The civil rights movement brought about further changes in law, and further changes in people's thinking. The law is a moral guide, a tutor that helps shape the conscience of society.

Even when law doesn't change attitudes right away, it does affect the actions of many. Martin Luther King Jr., said, "Morality cannot be legislated, but behavior can be regulated. Judicial decrees may not change the heart, but they can restrain the heartless."[300]

21c. Laws concerning abortion have significantly influenced whether women choose to have abortions.

Marvin Olasky's *Abortion Rites: A Social History of Abortion in America*, is an insightful study that documents the historical emergence of American abortion.[301] Olasky recounts how various groups in the nineteenth and early twentieth century provided abortion alternatives without dealing with the issue of laws and demonstrates that it is inaccurate to suppose abortion cannot be fought, and alternatives to it effectively offered, without changing the law. However, this is only one part of the picture.

There were abortions in this country before abortion was legal, but the number skyrocketed once it was legalized. There are now fifteen times more abortions annually in this country than there were the year prior to *Roe* v. *Wade*.[302] The laws that once restrained abortion now encourage it.

> A change in abortion laws, from restrictive to permissive, appears— from *all data* and in *every country*—to bring forward a whole class of women who would otherwise not have wanted an abortion or felt the need for one.... Women can be conditioned (and are in many places) to want and feel the need for abortions. Evidence from those countries where abortion-on-request has been long available (Russia, Japan, Hungary, for instance) shows that the subjectively felt stress that leads women to seek an abortion is socially influenced.[303]

In one survey of women who had abortions, 72 percent said they would definitely not have sought an abortion if doing so were illegal.[304] Though making abortion illegal again would not stop all abortions, it would encourage the larger number of women to pursue available alternatives.

22. "The antiabortion beliefs of the minority shouldn't be imposed on the majority."

22a. Major polls clearly indicate that the majority, not the minority, believes that there should be greater restrictions on abortion.

The *Boston Globe,* a proabortion newspaper, reported the results of its own survey: "Most Americans would ban the vast majority of abortions performed in this country."[305] The *Globe* found that "while 78 percent of the nation would keep abortion legal in limited circumstances, those circumstances account for only a tiny percentage of the reasons cited by women having abortions."[306] The "limited circumstances" were rape, incest, danger to the mother's life, and deformity of the child. But in cases where pregnancy poses financial or emotional strain, or when the woman is alone or a teenager—in other words, in 97 percent of actual situations—an overwhelming majority of Americans believe abortion should be illegal.

Should Abortion Be Legal or Illegal?

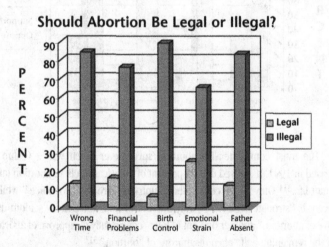

A *Los Angeles Times* poll indicated that 61 percent believe abortion is immoral, and 57 percent believe it is murder.[307] A *New York Times* poll indicated that 79 percent of the population opposes the current policy of unrestricted

159

abortion.[308] A *USA Today* poll showed that 63 percent believe that laws should be changed to allow greater restrictions on abortion.[309]

A *Newsweek* poll indicated strong support for legislation restricting abortion.[310] The question was asked, "Would you support or oppose the following restrictions that may come before state legislatures?" Nearly two out of three supported the restriction, "No public funds for abortion, except to save a woman's life." Three out of four supported the restriction, "Teenagers must have parent's permission to get an abortion." And an overwhelming nine out of ten affirmed support for a law saying, "Women seeking abortions must be counseled on the dangers and on alternatives to abortion." Significantly, many of these restrictions are still not in place in most states, even though the overwhelming majority of Americans supports them.

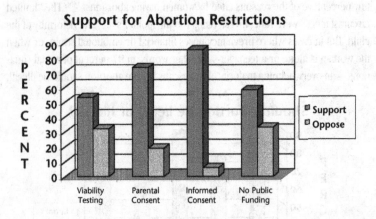

Support for Abortion Restrictions

The most comprehensive abortion survey ever taken was a Gallup poll released in 1991. It showed that 77 percent of Americans believe abortion takes a human life.[311] Only 17 percent of the country is "strongly prochoice," while 26 percent is "strongly prolife."[312] Only one out of four Americans "seldom disapprove of abortion," another one out of four "consistently disapprove of abortion," and the remaining half "often disapprove of abortion."[313]

When asked when the child's right to life outweighs the woman's right to choose, a full 50 percent said at conception. Only 7 percent said at birth, the position that most closely corresponds to current law.[314] A clear majority of Americans approves of almost every kind of legislative proposal restricting abortions.[315] For instance, 73 percent support the banning of all abortions in the second and third trimester; 69 percent support parental consent laws; an overwhelming 84 percent believe that health and safety standards should be imposed on abortion clinics; and 86 percent believe that the law should require that a

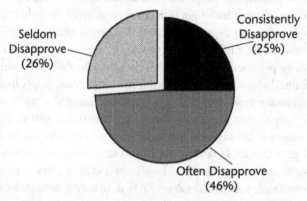

U.S. Disapproval of Abortion

Seldom Disapprove (26%)

Consistently Disapprove (25%)

Often Disapprove (46%)

woman receive information regarding fetal development and alternatives to abortion before she may obtain one.[316]

In summary, "The survey data yield the unmistakable conclusion: Americans generally disapprove of abortion in most circumstances under which it is currently performed."[317]

A 1999 Gallup poll worded the questions differently, but found somewhat of a tilt to the prochoice side. Those calling themselves "strongly prochoice" moved from 17 percent to 26 percent, while those calling themselves "strongly prolife" increased from 26 percent to 29 percent, a less significant gain. "The public is almost evenly split on the issue, with 48% currently calling themselves 'prochoice' and 42% identifying themselves as 'prolife.'"[318] Given the margin of error, and the fact that prolifers indicated they felt more strongly about their viewpoint, Gallup called it a tie between the prolife and prochoice positions. Still, many who say they are prochoice continue to favor what they consider reasonable restrictions on abortion.

22b. Many people's apparent agreement with abortion law stems from their ignorance of what the law really is.

In reference to the 1991 Gallup poll, the *Washington Times* asked and answered a critical question: "So why has there been no tidal wave of opposition to the legal status quo of abortion-on-demand? Simply this: Americans don't know what the abortion laws say."[319]

The most startling discovery of the Gallup poll was that *only 11 percent of Americans have an accurate understanding that abortion is available throughout all nine months of pregnancy.*[320] Interestingly, the one in four who "seldom disapprove" of abortion were the most likely to say they were "very familiar" with *Roe* v. *Wade* and abortion law.[321] But of those who considered themselves "very familiar" with the law, only 24 percent accurately understood what the law is![322]

In the words of Victor Rosenblum, past president of the Association of American Law Schools, the poll revealed that "an overwhelming majority of Americans simply do not understand what is allowed under current law. In many cases, it appears that people who consider themselves 'prochoice' simply don't know what they're supporting."[323] The poll shows that if they did know, many would not support it.

It is common to talk to people who honestly believe that under current law you cannot get an abortion for birth control, failed contraception, or sex selection. They cannot be more wrong. The law is loose enough to allow abortion for any and every conceivable reason. Under *Roe* v. *Wade*, there is virtually no such thing as an illegal abortion.

What Americans Think about Abortion
When it's legal and when it isn't (under *Roe* v. *Wade*)

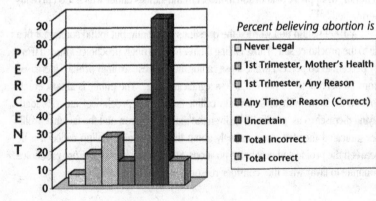

Percent believing abortion is

- ☐ Never Legal
- ▦ 1st Trimester, Mother's Health
- ▨ 1st Trimester, Any Reason
- ▩ Any Time or Reason (Correct)
- ▤ Uncertain
- ■ Total incorrect
- ☐ Total correct

22c. Beliefs that abortion should be restricted are embraced by a majority in each major political party.

The 1991 Gallup poll also categorized abortion beliefs according to political party. The differences were much less significant than most would anticipate. For instance, 55 percent of Republicans believed that the unborn's right to be born outweighed the mother's right to choose at the point of conception. Among Democrats, 51 percent said the same, as did 43 percent of Independents and 57 percent of "other parties."[324] Only 17 percent of Republicans believe abortion is acceptable when pregnancy would interrupt a professional career, and only 20 percent of Democrats believe the same. Only 26 percent of Republicans believe abortion is acceptable because of low income and financial burden, and only 31 percent of Democrats believe the same. Only 26 percent of Republicans, 28 percent of Democrats, and 29 percent of Independents believe abortion is acceptable when a woman is abandoned by her partner.[325]

Among voters who identified themselves as either "strongly prolife" or "strongly prochoice" (those who would "withhold their vote from a political candidate with whom they largely agree, but with whom they disagree on abortion"), the "strongly prolife" outnumber the "strongly prochoice" among Democrats, Republicans, and Independents.[326]

22d. In 1973 the Supreme Court imposed a minority morality on the nation, ignoring the votes of citizens and the decisions of state legislatures.

Abortion was illegal in every state in America until 1967, when some abortions became legal in Colorado. Fourteen other states followed, permitting abortion under very restricted conditions. In 1970 New York became the first state to have abortion-on-demand, though even that was limited to twenty-four weeks. In the following two years, *thirty-three states debated the issue in their legislatures and all thirty-three voted against legal abortion.* New York even repealed its own abortion law, but because of a veto by Governor Nelson Rockefeller, the law remained in force.[327]

After being stopped in legislatures and in state courts, proabortion advocates proposed ballot measures in Michigan and North Dakota in the November 1972 election. It had been claimed that Michigan was 60 percent proabortion, yet 63 percent voted against legalizing abortion. Prochoice leaders claimed that the Catholic church was behind antiabortion sentiments, so North Dakota, with only 12 percent

Catholics, seemed an ideal place to pass a referendum legalizing abortion. But an overwhelming 78 percent of the state's citizens voted against the measure.[328]

Only two months later, the Supreme Court imposed abortion-on-demand upon every state, making it illegal for states to restrict abortion in any meaningful way. The opinions of seven men imposed a radical new morality on the entire nation.

Bob Woodward and Scott Armstrong's *The Brethren* is a well-researched and compelling account of the inner workings of the Supreme Court from 1969 to 1975. It discusses the subjective and arbitrary rulings of the court, most notably *Roe* v. *Wade*. Judge Harry Blackmun, the author of *Roe*, was heavily influenced by his wife, who actually told her husband's proabortion clerk that while he was lobbying Blackmun in the office, she was working on the judge at home.[329] Such influence helps explain the fact that the decision had no basis in law but merely reflected personal preference in a changing moral climate. Speaking of *Roe*, Woodward and Armstrong say, "As a constitutional matter, it was absurd."[330] Even with its prochoice bias, *Newsweek* summarizes *Roe* this way: "With a wave of the judicial wand, abortion had become a constitutional right, without an accounting of why."[331]

The Supreme Court determined in *Roe* v. *Wade* that no state could put any legal restrictions on abortion in the first three months of pregnancy. It said that abortion was allowed until birth provided only that one physician considered it necessary for the mother's health. In an adjoining case, *Doe* v. *Bolton*, health was defined to embrace almost any consideration. Abortions were legal "in the light of all factors—physical, emotional, psychological, familial, and the woman's age—relevant to the well-being of the patient. All these factors may relate to health."[332]

Hence, *what was imposed on America was not only legalized abortion, but the most liberalized abortion policy conceivable*. The first major step in correcting this policy was the 1989 *Webster* decision, which gave back to the states some of the power abruptly taken from them sixteen years earlier.[333]

Ronald Reagan summarized the issue this way: "Our nationwide policy of abortion-on-demand through all nine months of pregnancy was neither voted for by our people nor enacted by our legislators—not a single state had such unrestricted abortion before the Supreme Court decreed it to be national policy in 1973."[334] According to dissenting Justice White, the *Roe* v. *Wade* decision was nothing but "an act of raw judicial power."[335]

Not only the Constitution, but also the beliefs of the majority of citizens and the laws and votes of the states and their legislatures have never been more blatantly disregarded. *The prochoice position was forcibly imposed upon the largely unwilling citizens of America.* Any change in that law is not the imposition of a new minority morality, but the restoration of an old majority morality.

23. "The antiabortion position is a religious belief that threatens the vital separation of church and state."

23a. Many nonreligious people believe that abortion kills children and that it is wrong.

The polls cited under the previous argument show that an antiabortion position, at least to a certain extent, is held by a majority of citizens. Many of these citizens are not religious, and those that are belong to a wide variety of religious groups that transcend political parties. As the *Washington Times* states, "Women and men and people of varying religious faiths and races tend to support the right to life in equal measure."[336]

A study of thirty women who considered their abortions highly stressful yielded this revealing insight: "Though 72% of the subjects reported no identifiable religious beliefs at the time of the abortion, 96% regarded abortion as the taking of a life or as murder subsequent to their abortion."[337] One does not have to subscribe to a particular religion to have a conscience or an innate sense that killing the innocent is wrong.

Nat Hentoff is the creator and editor of New York's ultraliberal *Village Voice*. He is a self-described "atheist, a lifelong leftist, and a card-carrying member of the ACLU."[338] He detests most of the policies of conservative administrations. He is also an outspoken prolife advocate who takes constant heat for publicly calling abortion the killing of children.[339]

In the most widely listened to radio talk show in history, host Rush Limbaugh regularly argues against abortion. He appeals not to religious beliefs, but to scientific, historical, and common sense realities. And to many listeners—nonreligious and religious—he makes a lot of sense.

Dr. Bernard Nathanson was an atheist until his firsthand involvement in abortion made him realize that it was the killing of the innocent. He argued that abortion falls far short of the most profound tenet of human morality, spoken by Jesus Christ: "Do unto others as you would have them do unto you."[340] Responding to the charge that this was some sectarian religious tenet, Nathanson said:

> On the contrary, it is simply a statement of innate human wisdom. Unless this principle is cherished by a society and widely honored by its individual members, the end result is anarchy and the violent dissolution of the society. This is why life is always an overriding value in the great ethical systems of world history. If we do not protect innocent, nonaggressive elements in the human community, the alternative is too horrible to contemplate. Looked at this way, the "sanctity of life" is not a theological but a secular concept, which should be perfectly acceptable to my fellow atheists.[341]

Writing in another context, Nathanson said:

> I think that abortion policy ought not be beholden to a sectarian creed, but that obviously the law can and does encompass moral convictions shared by a variety of religious interests. In the case of abortion, however, we can and must decide on the biological evidence and on fundamental humanitarian grounds without resorting to scriptures, revelations, creeds, hierarchical decrees, or belief in God. Even if God does not exist, the fetus does.[342]

The abortion issue is really a human life issue, a civil rights issue. It is not simply a religious issue, any more than the rights of Jews and blacks is simply a religious issue. Though most governments are secular, there is hardly a nation in the world where abortion was legal prior to World War II. You do not need to be a Christian, nor to subscribe to any religion, to believe that the unborn are children and that it should not be legal to kill them.

23b. Morality must not be rejected just because it is supported by religion.

William Carey, known as the "father of Christian missions," faced the terrible practice of widow burning in India. He labored long and hard to make this killing illegal and finally succeeded. While trying to be sensitive to the Indian culture, Carey didn't think it inappropriate to bring his Christian morality to bear when the lives of innocent people were at stake.

Lord Melbourne said, "Things have come to a pretty pass when religion is allowed to invade public life." What he was objecting to was the Christian efforts to abolish the slave trade. Some people want religion to stay out of public life because they want morality to stay out of public life.

Every law establishes a certain moral position as a social norm. Every society can and must implement legislation that defines what is right and wrong and what citizens should and should not do. Whether it is from the Bible or elsewhere, all law must come from somewhere. Most of our laws are rooted in the Judeo-Christian religion.

The Bible says, "You shall not steal." Should we get rid of our laws against stealing because they impose a Judeo-Christian morality? Shall we invalidate all moral standards that are founded on religious principles? If we did, what moral standards would be left?

Some who are eager to remove religious people from the public forum are quick to make exceptions when religious people hold viewpoints they agree with. Should we also dismiss out of hand the opinions of various religious leaders who support animal rights and environmental protection and oppose nuclear testing?

Abortion-rights advocate Laurence Tribe argues that religious Americans have just as much right to enter the public arena as other citizens:

> But as a matter of constitutional law, a question such as [abortion], having an irreducibly moral dimension, cannot properly be kept out of the political realm merely because many religions and organized religious groups inevitably take strong positions on it.... The participation of religious groups in political dialogue has never been constitutional anathema in the United States. Quite the contrary. The values reflected in the constitutional guarantees of freedom of religion and political expression argue strongly for the inclusion of church and religious beliefs and arguments in public life.[343]

23c. America was founded on a moral base dependent upon principles of the Bible and the Christian religion.

If our goal is to keep religion from dictating the moral principles and laws of our country, we are hundreds of years too late. Virtually every significant document that defines the values of the United States of America—including the Declaration of Independence, the Constitution, and the Bill of Rights—leans heavily on a belief in God and the moral authority of the Bible.[344]

George Washington said, "It is impossible to rightly govern the world without God and the Bible."[345] In his farewell address, Washington reminded the country that religion and morality are inseparable: "Let us with caution indulge the supposition that morality can be maintained without religion.... Reason and experience both forbid us to expect that national morality can prevail in exclusion of religious principles."

Noah Webster warned, "The moral principles and precepts contained in the Scriptures form the basis of all our civil constitution and laws. All the miseries and evils which other nations suffer from vice, crime, ambition, injustice, oppression, slavery, and war, proceed from their despising or neglecting the precepts contained in the Bible."[346]

It is impossible to reject the moral framework of the Scriptures, including the sanctity of human life, and to simultaneously affirm the values of freedom and human rights that distinguish the United States of America.

23d. Laws related to church and state were intended to assure freedom for religion, not freedom from religion.

Neither the words "separation of church and state" nor the concept as we now know it are found in the Constitution. The First Amendment's establishment of religion clause was devised to protect religious liberty, not to banish religion's influence on society. But even if we adopt the later meaning of the separation of church and state, the "church" that was to be separate from the state was a single denomination or sectarian group, not religion in general. The founders of our country did not want one church or denomination to control the state. They definitely *did* want religion, specifically the Christian religion, to influence the moral principles and laws of the state.[347] America's colonists came here to have freedom *of* religion, not freedom *from* religion. Their intention was that the moral principles founded in religious beliefs should permeate the social order.

23e. Religion's waning influence on our society directly accounts for the moral deterioration threatening our future.

In their book, *The Day America Told the Truth*, James Patterson and Peter Kim put their fingers on the moral pulse of the nation. By their own testimony, many of the results were alarming.[348]

Three out of four Americans say, "I will steal from those who won't really miss it." Two-thirds say, "I will lie when it suits me, so long as it doesn't cause any real damage." Over half say, "I will cheat on my spouse—after all, given the chance, he or she will do the same." One-third acknowledge, "I will put my lover at risk of disease. I sleep around a bit, but who doesn't?"

Only one-third of Americans agree with the statement "Honesty is the best policy." When asked what they would do for ten million dollars, 25 percent said they would abandon their entire family, 23 percent said they would become prostitutes for a week or more, and 7 percent—one out of fourteen—said they would murder a stranger. "Americans believe that our country has become a colder, greedier, meaner, more selfish and less caring place."

To what can we attribute this startling unraveling of the moral fiber of our nation? Patterson and Kim say, "In the 1950s, 75% of Americans believed that religion was very important. Today the figure is 54%." They say Americans now live in a moral vacuum:

> Americans of the 1990s stand alone in a way unknown to any previous generation. When we want to answer a question of right and wrong, we ask ourselves.... The overwhelming majority of people [93%] said that they—and nobody else—determine what is and what isn't moral in their lives. They base their decisions on their own experience, even on their daily whims....
>
> We are a law unto ourselves.... What's right? What's wrong? When you are making up your own rules, your own moral codes, it can make the world a confusing place. Most Americans are very confused about their personal morals right now.[349]

And Patterson and Kim say this about the relationship between religion and morality in this country:

> People describing themselves as "very religious" [14%] definitely make better citizens.... Religion appears to play a strong role in building moral character. We found that people who defined themselves as religious showed a much stronger commitment to moral values and social institutions than did nonreligious people.[350]

Based on their interviews Patterson and Kim maintain, "A letdown in moral values is now considered the number one problem facing our country. Eighty percent of us believe that morals and ethics should be taught in our schools again." But no suggestion is made as to what these morals and ethics could be based upon if not what they always were in our past—the Judeo-Christian morality rooted in the Scriptures.

When traveling in the Soviet Union in 1991, I had the opportunity to talk with two public school principals. Both were Communists who had followed the strict practice of keeping religion out of the classrooms. They now realized that there was a moral crisis in the Soviet Union. One of them said, "Our children have nothing to believe in, no morality, no reason to be honest, good citizens. We want to bring the Christian religion back to our young people, back to our classrooms, so we can have a moral society again." Though these men had no strong religious faith, they recognized what we in America have forgotten—the essential connection between a society's morality and its religious beliefs.

Part Four

∞

Arguments Concerning

Health
& Safety

24.

> ## "If abortion is made illegal, tens of thousands of women will again die from back-alley and clothes-hanger abortions."

24a. For decades prior to its legalization, 90 percent of abortions were done by physicians in their offices, not in back alleys.

Fifteen years before abortion was legal in America, around 85 percent of illegal abortions were done by "reputable physicians in good standing in their local medical associations."[351] In 1960, Planned Parenthood stated that "90% of all illegal abortions are presently done by physicians."[352] The vast majority of abortions were not done in back alleys, but in the back offices of licensed physicians.

Were these doctors "butchers," as prochoice advocates claim? The majority of physicians performing abortions *after* legalization were the same ones doing it *before* legalization. Neither their training nor their equipment improved when abortion was decriminalized. Either they were not butchers before legalization, or they continued to be butchers after legalization. It cannot be argued both ways.

24b. It is not true that tens of thousands of women were dying from illegal abortions before abortion was legalized.

Former abortion-rights activist Bernard Nathanson admits that he and his cofounders of NARAL fabricated the figure that a million women were getting illegal abortions in America each year. The average, he says, was actually ninety-eight thousand per year. Nonetheless, the abortion advocates fed their concocted figures to the media, who eagerly disseminated the false information. Nathanson says that he and his associates also invented the "nice, round shocking figure" for the number of deaths from illegal abortions:

> It was always "5,000 to 10,000 deaths a year." I confess that I knew the figures were totally false, and I suppose the others did too if they

173

stopped to think of it. But in the "morality" of our revolution, it was a useful figure, widely accepted, so why go out of our way to correct it with honest statistics? The overriding concern was to get the laws [against abortion] eliminated, and anything within reason that had to be done was permissible.[353]

Research confirms that the actual number of abortion deaths in the twenty-five years prior to 1973 averaged 250 a year, with a high of 388 in 1948.[354] In 1966, before the first state legalized abortion, 120 mothers died from abortion.[355] By 1972 abortion was still illegal in 80 percent of the country, but the use of antibiotics had greatly reduced the risk. Hence, the number dropped to 39 maternal deaths from abortion that year.[356] Dr. Christopher Tietze, a prominent statistician associated with Planned Parenthood, maintained that these are accurate figures, with a margin of error no greater than 10 percent.[357]

However, suppose that only one out of ten deaths from illegal abortion was properly identified. This would mean that the number of women dying the year before abortion was legalized would be less than four hundred, still only a fraction of the five to ten thousand claimed by prochoice advocates.

24c. The history of abortion in Poland invalidates claims that making abortion illegal would bring harm to women.

Dr. John Willke writes,

> Poland, along with the rest of the Iron Curtain, Eastern Europe countries, was occupied for 44 years by Russia. Russia legalized state-paid abortion in the first three months of pregnancy. What are the official figures of the numbers of abortions performed annually during those years in Poland? In 1960, it was 150,400—in 1965, 168,600—in 1970, 148,200—in 1975, 138,600—in 1980, 138,000—in 1985, 135,500. By 1990, with the advent of the Solidarity independence movement and the influence of Pope John Paul II, the number of abortions had declined to 59,417. This was a spontaneous movement.

It was at this time that abortion was made illegal in Poland except in the most exceptional cases. What was the result? Willke continues,

In 1998 the total number of induced abortions in Poland was 253. What were the reasons given for these? To save the "life and health" of the woman—199; for "fetal impairment"—45, for rape or incest—9.

In summary, then, here we have a large nation that, for four and a half decades, had abortion-on-request, paid for by the state. Certainly, the practice of abortion in Poland had become deeply ingrained. Then came independence and a law that took the total number of abortions down to 0.004% of what they had been, and this contrary to all predictions by government agencies, the media, the UN and Planned Parenthood. To perhaps everyone's surprise, there have been 25% fewer miscarriages and 30% fewer women dying compared with what it had been while abortion was legal. In the latest annual report, 21 women died from pregnancy-related problems, with none listed as dying from illegal abortions.

These are firm statistics. The facts above have been annually reported and heatedly discussed by the Polish parliament, its ministries of health, labor, social welfare and education, as well as by mass media, nongovernmental organizations and anyone else interested in the problem.

If abortions are again forbidden, will illegal abortions, with all of their alleged tragic consequences, take their place? Certainly in Poland the answer is in—it is a resounding *no*. In fact, the women in Poland are clearly healthier now, from a gynecologic and obstetric standpoint, than they were when abortions were legal.[358]

24d. Women still die from legal abortions in America.

Abortion is normally not life threatening to the mother. However, the fatality rate is much higher than many prochoice advocates admit. For instance, a widely disseminated prochoice video produced in the late 1980s states, "By 1979 the Federal government could not identify a single woman anywhere in this country who died of abortion."[359]

This is an amazing statement, since many sources document a number of deaths from legal abortion. According to the *American Journal of Obstetrics and Gynecology,* "the New York City Department of Health reported seven legal abortion-related deaths that occurred between 1980 and 1985. The cause of death in all cases was attributed directly to general anesthesia."[360] (These were seven deaths in a single city.) There were four abortion-caused deaths in a single Florida clinic between 1979 and 1983.[361] In 1986, four doctors and researchers presented a study of no less than 193 deaths by legal abortion between 1972 and 1985.[362] One researcher has uncovered the tragic cases of some 300 women who have died as a result of legal abortion.[363]

Since public health officials stopped looking for abortion-caused deaths after abortion became legal, the opportunity to overlook or cover up abortion-caused deaths is now much greater. A former abortion clinic owner says, "A woman died because of an abortion at our clinic, but the public never heard about it, and it wasn't reported to the authorities as abortion related."[364] When the *Chicago Sun-Times* investigated Chicago-area abortion clinics in 1978, it uncovered the cases of twelve women who died of legal abortion but whose deaths had not been reported as abortion-related. Twelve unreported deaths from abortion in one small part of the country is a revealing number when the official statistics indicated twenty-one deaths from abortion *in the entire country* the previous year![365]

Statistics on death by abortion are dependent on the voluntary reporting of abortion clinics, who have much to lose and nothing to gain by doing so.[366] What makes abortion-related deaths hard to trace is that the majority of the deaths do not occur during the surgery but afterward. Hence, any number of secondary reasons are routinely identified as the cause of death:

Consider the mother who hemorrhaged, was transfused, got hepatitis, and died months later. Official cause of death? Hepatitis. Actual cause? Abortion. A perforated uterus leads to pelvic abscess, sepsis [blood poisoning], and death. The official report of the cause of death may list pelvic abscess and septicemia. Abortion will not be listed. Abortion causes tubal pathology. She has an ectopic pregnancy years later and dies. The cause listed will be ectopic pregnancy. The actual cause? Abortion.[367]

In his novel *Prophet*, Frank Peretti masterfully portrays the web of deception and complicity surrounding legal abortion and its dangers.[368] Family members, doctors, the media, and political figures all have vested interests in this cover-up. Six weeks after finishing the first edition of *ProLife Answers*, I attended the funeral of a woman who died in a hospital after "treatment" at a Portland abortion clinic. There was no media coverage indicating the place of her surgery or her cause of death.

Legalized abortion has resulted in fifteen times more women having abortions. This means that if it is fifteen times safer than illegal abortion, the number of women dying remains the same. Writing in the *American Journal of Obstetrics and Gynecology*, Dr. Dennis Cavanaugh stated that since abortion has been legalized, "there has been no major impact on the number of women dying from abortion in the U.S.... After all, it really makes no difference whether a woman dies from legal or illegal abortion, she is dead nonetheless. I find no comfort in the fact that legal abortion is now the leading cause of abortion-related maternal deaths in the U.S."[369]

24e. If abortion became illegal, abortions would be done with medical equipment, not clothes hangers.

One woman told me, "People must think women are stupid. If abortion were illegal and I wanted one, I sure wouldn't use a clothes hanger." Since 90 percent of pre-1973 illegal abortions were done by doctors, it's safe to assume many physicians would continue to give abortions. "Self-help" abortion kits are being widely promoted and distributed by proabortion groups who have vowed they will step up their efforts if abortion is made illegal again.[370] Sadly, many women would continue to have abortions. But the "many" might be a quarter of a million rather than one and a half million. The result would be over a million mothers and babies annually saved from abortion.

Clothes hangers make effective propaganda pieces at prochoice rallies, but they do not accurately reflect what would happen if abortion were made illegal again. Clothes hangers would be used for baby clothes, not abortions.

24f. We must not legalize procedures that kill the innocent just to make the killing process less hazardous.

The coat-hanger argument is valid only if the unborn are not human beings, with commensurate human rights. Typically those appealing to the emotions through use of this argument completely avoid the real issue, since it is easier to talk about coat hangers than dead children.

From the child's point of view, there is no such thing as a safe, legal abortion. It is always deadly. For every two people who enter an abortion clinic, only one comes out alive.

Rape is a horrible attack on an innocent human being, so we do not attempt to make rape safe and legal. We do not try to make kidnapping or child abuse safe and legal. If abortion kills children, our goal should not be to make it as safe and legal as possible, but to provide alternatives and legal restrictions that help avoid it in the first place.

24g. The central horror of illegal abortion remains the central horror of legal abortion.

Unfortunately, every horror that was true of illegal abortion is also true about legalized abortion. Many veterans of illegal abortion, however, do not realize this. Instead, they cling to the belief that all the pain and problems they suffered could have been avoided if only abortion had been legal. They imagine that if their abortions had been legal, their lives would somehow be better today. Instead of recognizing that it is the very nature of abortion itself which caused their problems, they blame their suffering on the illegality of abortion at that time.[371]

Abortion is horrible primarily because it is a process in which instruments of death invade a woman's body and kill her innocent child. Neither laws nor slogans nor attractive waiting rooms nor advanced medical equipment can change the nature of abortion. What it is it will always be—the killing of children.

25. "Abortion is a safe medical procedure—safer than full-term pregnancy and childbirth."

25a. Abortion is not safer than full-term pregnancy and childbirth.

Less than one in ten thousand pregnancies results in the mother's death.[372] Government statistics indicate that the chances of death by abortion are even less. But while deaths from childbirth are accurately reported, many deaths by legal abortion are not. This completely skews the statistics. Furthermore, "abortion actually increases the chance of maternal death in later pregnancies."[373]

This means that some maternal deaths in full-term pregnancies are actually caused by earlier abortions, which creates a double inaccuracy.

But even if abortion did result in fewer maternal deaths, that wouldn't make it safer. The nonfatal but significant complications of abortion are much more frequent and serious than those of full-term pregnancy. One researcher states, "The evidence overwhelmingly proves that the morbidity and mortality rates of legal abortion are several times higher than that for carrying a pregnancy to term."[374]

A year 2000 government-funded study in Finland revealed that women who abort are four times more likely to die in the year following the abortion than women who carry their pregnancies to term. Women who carry to term are only half as likely to die as women who are not pregnant.

> Researchers from the statistical analysis unit of Finland's National Research and Development Center for Welfare and Health examined death certificate records for all women of reproductive age (fifteen to forty-nine) who died between 1987 and 1994, a total of 9,129 women. Then they examined the national health care database to identify pregnancy-related events for the women in the twelve months prior to their deaths.
>
> The researchers found that, compared to women who carried to term, women who had aborted in the year prior to their deaths were 60 percent more likely to die from natural causes, seven times more likely to die from suicide, four times more likely to die of injuries related to accidents and fourteen times more likely to die from homicide. Researchers believe that the higher rate of deaths related to accidents and homicide may be linked to higher rates of suicidal or risk-taking behavior.[375]

25b. Though the chances of a woman's safe abortion are now greater, the number of suffering women is also greater because of the huge increase in abortions.

> No one doubts that legal abortion is marginally safer than illegal abortion, but neither is there any doubt that decriminalization has encouraged more women to undergo abortions than ever before. Risk goes down, but numbers go up.... This combination means that though the

odds of any particular woman suffering ill effects from an abortion have dropped, the total number of women who suffer...from abortion is far greater than ever before.[376]

25c. Even if abortion were safer for the mother than childbirth, it would still remain fatal for the innocent child.

Having a baby is a low-risk undertaking, but suppose the risk were much higher. When an innocent life is at stake, isn't there a moral obligation to take risk? Childbirth is much safer than trying to rescue a drowning child in the ocean or trying to rescue a woman who is being beaten or raped. An adult swimming to shore from a capsized boat has a much greater chance of survival if he doesn't try to save a child. But does that mean he shouldn't?

25d. Abortion can produce many serious medical problems.

Ectopic pregnancies occur when gestation takes place outside the uterus, commonly in a fallopian tube. Though usually not fatal, such pregnancies are nonetheless responsible for 12 percent of all pregnancy-related maternal deaths.[377] Studies show that the risk of an ectopic pregnancy is twice as high for women who have had one abortion, and up to four times as high for women with two or more previous abortions.[378] There has been a 300 percent increase of ectopic pregnancies since abortion was legalized. In 1970 the incidence was 4.8 per 1,000 births; by 1980 it had risen to 14.5 per 1,000 births.[379]

Pelvic Inflammatory Disease is an infection that leads to fever and infertility. Researchers state, "Pelvic infection is a common and serious complication of induced abortion and has been reported in up to 30% of all cases."[380] A study of women having first-trimester abortions demonstrated that "women with postabortal pelvic inflammatory disease had significantly higher rates of...spontaneous abortion, secondary infertility, dyspareunia, and chronic pelvic pain."[381] Other infectious complications, as well as endometriosis, follow approximately 5 percent of abortion procedures.[382]

Internal bleeding is normal following abortions, but in some cases it is severe due to a perforated uterus. This can cause sterility and other serious and permanent problems. A perforated uterus was the cause of at least twenty-four deaths among U.S. women having abortions between 1972 and 1979.[383] Numerous scientific studies demonstrate that the chance of miscarriages significantly increases with abortion, as much as tenfold.[384] Tragically, some women are unable to conceive after having abortions. Tubal infertility has been found to be up to 30 percent more common among women who have had abortions.[385] Having taken the life of a child they did not want, they will never be able to carry a child they do want.

The health of future children is also at risk, as both premature births and low birth weights are more common among women who have had abortions.[386] Malformations, both major and minor, of later children are increased by abortion.[387] For various reasons, the frequency of early death for infants born after their mothers have had abortions is between two and four times the normal rate.[388]

The Elliot Institute has published data indicating that women who abort are twice as likely to have preterm or postterm deliveries.[389] Placenta previa is a condition occurring when the placenta covers the cervix, preventing the baby from passing through the birth canal. It usually requires a caesarian section and can threaten the life of both mother and child. Placenta previa is seven to fifteen times more common among women who have had abortions than among those who have not.[390]

Calculations of abortion complication rates vary considerably, but even the lower estimates are significant: "The reported immediate complication rate, alone, of abortion is no less than 10 percent. In addition, studies of long-range complications show rates no less than 17 percent and frequently report complication rates in the range of 25 to 40 percent."[391] After carefully studying the vast body of the world's medical literature on the subject, Dr. Thomas W. Hilgers concluded, "The medical hazards of legally induced abortion are very significant and should be conscientiously weighed."[392]

25e. Abortion significantly raises the rate of breast cancer.

Because of the rapid growth of breast tissue in early pregnancy, a premature cessation of pregnancy (such as that caused by abortion) creates an unnatural condition. Consequently, women who have first trimester abortions face twice the risk of contracting breast cancer as those who complete their pregnancies and give birth.[393]

The leading authority on the connection of abortion and breast cancer is Dr. Joel Brind, Professor of Endocrinology, Department of Natural Sciences, Baruch College of the City University of New York. He is the author of the *Comprehensive Review and Meta-Analysis of the Abortion/Breast Cancer Link*. Dr. Brind says "the single most avoidable risk factor for breast cancer is induced abortion."[394]

In his testimony before the Reproductive Health Drugs Advisory Committee of the Food and Drug Administration, Dr. Brind said,

Only induced abortion—not spontaneous abortion—is consistently linked to the incidence of breast cancer. The biological basis of this difference is also clear: Most spontaneous abortions are characterized by subnormal ovarian estradiol secretion. It is the surge of estradiol early in a normal pregnancy which provides an estrogen overexposure by which most known risk factors increase breast cancer risk.

Induced abortion increases breast cancer risk independently of its effect in delaying first full-term pregnancy. An early full-term pregnancy decreases breast cancer risk. Since induced abortion also abrogates this protective effect, it raises breast cancer risk in two ways for young nulliparous women.[395]

A 1997 *New England Journal of Medicine* article by Mads Melbye and others claimed that the abortion breast cancer connection wasn't valid.[396] "There is no increased risk of breast cancer for the average woman who has had an abortion," the author told the *Wall Street Journal*.[397]

The *New York Times* echoed the reassuring counsel that women "need not worry about the risk of breast cancer" when considering abortion.[398] But why had the same sources not reported the results of ten out of the eleven previous studies on the subject, nearly all of them more significant than Dr. Melbye's, which had found a significant increase of breast cancer among women who had had abortions?[399] Dr. Brind has demonstrated fatal flaws in the Melbye study.[400] But the most haunting question is why any study that makes abortion look bad is ignored and any that makes it look good is trumpeted.

According to Dr. Brind, the scientific community has known for over twenty years that early abortion is a risk factor for breast cancer. Dozens of studies have been published confirming this.[401] Yet this information has not even been acknowledged in the literature of the American Cancer Society. These studies show that aborting a first pregnancy during the first trimester can double a woman's risk of breast cancer. Multiple abortions can triple or quadruple the risk. In a *National Review* article, Dr. Brind asks what seems to be a reasonable question: "If there is a way to reduce the incidence of breast cancer, shouldn't American women be told about it?"[402]

25f. The statistics on abortion complications and risks are often understated due to the inadequate means of gathering data.

It is not only abortion deaths that go unreported. Researchers warn that studies are likely to underestimate the risks and complications of abortion because of the reluctance of women to report prior abortions and the difficulty of following up women who may have been injured through abortions.[403] A former director of several abortion clinics told me, "Most abortion complications are never made known to the public, because abortion has a built-in cover-up. Women want to deny it and forget it, not talk about it."[404]

Furthermore, the accuracy of reported complications is largely dependent upon the willingness of abortion clinics to give out this information.[405] An abortion clinic director told me of a young woman at her clinic whose uterus was perforated during her abortion. The abortionist proceeded to accidentally pull out her bowel with the abortion instrument. No ambulance was called, because the clinic didn't want the bad publicity. The girl was driven to the hospital in a clinic worker's car. The damage was permanent, and she had to have a colostomy. Yet this was not reported as an abortion-related incident.[406]

25g. The true risks of abortion are rarely explained to women by those who perform abortions.

It is common to talk to women physically or psychologically damaged by abortions, who say, "I had no idea this could happen; no one told me about the risks." Many people do not realize the privileged status of abortion clinics:

> Abortion is the only surgery for which the surgeon is not obligated to inform the patient of the possible risks of the procedure, or even the exact nature of the procedure. Indeed, abortion providers are the only medical personnel who have a "constitutional right" to withhold information, even when directly questioned by the patient.[407]

The large body of evidence indicating significant abortion risks has been suppressed and ignored. This suppression is made possible by prochoice advocates who zealously oppose any requirements for abortion clinics to provide information. The "immunity to stating the facts" enjoyed by abortion clinics increases their profits, but only at the expense of women who are not allowed to make an informed choice.

The Court guarantees "freedom of choice" but denies the right to "informed choice." Abortionists can legally withhold information, or even avoid their clients' direct questions, in order to ensure that the patient will agree to an abortion which will be, they assume, "in her best interests."

Why is there such widespread silence about the dangers of legal abortion? Wasn't abortion legalized in order to *improve* health care for women rather than to encourage them to take unnecessary risks?[408]

Some abortion clinics may object that they voluntarily offer consent forms which patients must sign. Yet many patients testify that they did not read these forms, that the forms did not give specific information, or that they did not understand what they signed. The few who do ask questions are assured by clinic workers that any references to possible complications are just a formality, and there is nothing to worry about. Because of the nervous anxiety associated with an abortion, and the desire to get it over with, signing such a form is no different than not signing a form at all—except that it absolves the clinic of legal responsibility for the health problems the woman may suffer later.

The evidence indicates that the only way to avoid the risks of abortion is not to have one.

---

26. "Abortion is an easy and painless procedure."

26a. The various abortion procedures are often both difficult and painful for women.

There are several different kinds of abortion procedures, each creating its own kind of pain and difficulty. In a D & C, a tiny hoe-like instrument is inserted into the womb. The abortionist then scrapes the wall of the uterus, cutting the baby's body to pieces, which are pulled out piece by piece through the cervix. The scraping of the uterus typically involves some bleeding and other possible side effects that some women find quite painful.

In a suction abortion, a powerful suction tube is inserted through the cervix into the womb. The baby and the placenta are torn to pieces and sucked out into a jar. Sometimes this method follows a D & C. Infections, damage, and pain in the cervix and uterus can result.

In a saline abortion, a long needle is inserted through the mother's abdomen and a strong salt solution is injected directly into the amniotic fluid which surrounds the child. The salt is swallowed and absorbed into the baby, burning his skin and resulting in his death some hours later. The baby's death causes the mother to go into labor and expel a shriveled and visibly burnt baby.[409] (See photograph #5 at the center of this book.) The baby's thrashing, caused by his trauma, can be physically painful to his mother, and is often psychologically devastating. Sometimes the baby is born alive, writhing in pain because of severe burns. In such cases, the emotional consequences to the mother are considerable.

In a prostaglandin or chemical abortion, hormone-like compounds are injected or applied to the muscle of the uterus, causing it to contract and force the baby out. "This injection results in a very painful abortion for the mother."[410] In D & E, dilatation and evacuation, a forceps is used to crush the head of the unborn, and to pull out body parts from the uterus. This places a stress on the woman's body that can create various complications.[411]

A hysterotomy or C-section abortion is used in the last trimester. The womb is entered by surgery through the wall of the abdomen. It is the same as a live delivery except the baby is killed in the uterus, or is allowed to die from neglect if he is not yet dead upon removal. This is a major surgery with inherent difficulties, possible complications, and a potentially painful recovery.

The D & X abortion (see diagram on page 213[412]), also known as the partial-birth abortion, is not as frequently done and it is difficult to find information about its consequences on the mother. The nature of the abortion itself, however, would suggest considerable potential for physical and emotional trauma not only for the child but for the mother (see answer 28e).

A biologist states, "Unnatural abortions are violent and abusive to the human body."[413] Each of the abortion methods is unnatural and invasive; any of them can cause acute anxiety. One clinic manager told me she has seen a distraught woman getting an abortion who had to be held to the table by six people.[414] While this is not the norm, it demonstrates the extent of abortion's potential difficulty.

A woman interviewed in the *Journal of the American Medical Association* said, "Doctors shouldn't say it is easy for people to have an abortion. Because it's not an easy thing. People like my friends get pregnant, get an abortion, get pregnant, get an abortion, get pregnant, get an abortion. You know what I mean? All my friends that I've called say, 'Oh, it's a piece of cake.' For me, it wasn't a piece of cake."[415]

26b. Abortion is often difficult and painful for fathers, grandparents, and siblings of the aborted child.

One man who decided to abort his child has this to say:

> Abortion is presented to you as something that is easy to do. It doesn't take very long. It doesn't cost very much money nowadays, for a middle-class person. You say, "Well, it's okay." But it wasn't okay. It left a scar, and that scar had to be treated tenderly and worked on in order for us to get on with our lives. I don't think abortion is easy for anybody. The people who say it's easy either don't want to face the pain of it or haven't been through it, because it's really a tough experience.[416]

A schoolteacher in her forties says, "Advising my daughter to have an abortion led me into a long, suicidal siege. I'm not over it yet. I can picture a baby who never even existed."[417] (Or does the guilt stem from the knowledge that a baby *did* exist, but was killed by the abortion?)

Imagine this conversation between a six-year-old girl and her mother, who aborted one of the child's siblings or who the child knows to be prochoice:

Daughter: Mom? Why didn't you abort me?

Mother: Darling, how can you say such a thing? I wanted you! You're my little girl!

Daughter: But what if you hadn't wanted me?

Mother: But I did!

Daughter: But what if you stopped wanting me?

Mother: But I won't!

Daughter: But how can you be sure? What if you *do* stop wanting me?[418]

Whether on the conscious or subconscious level, these questions have to be asked by any child aware of his mother's choice to abort a sibling or of his parents' support of abortion. This cuts to the core of the child's sense of security in his parents' love. Such questions cannot be painless or inconsequential to the child.

26c. Abortion is often difficult and painful for clinic workers.

A veteran abortionist and his nurse assistant presented to the Association of Planned Parenthood Physicians a troubling report on reactions to the dilation and evacuation abortion procedure. They stated that the dismemberment of the fetus is "more traumatic for the operator and assistants than for the patient."[419] (Unlike the staff, the patient is not allowed to see the baby's body parts.) They followed up a questionnaire with in-depth interviews of twenty-three present and former staff members of their abortion clinic:

> Many subjects reported serious emotional reactions which produced physiological symptoms, sleep disturbances, effects on personal relationships, and moral anguish.... Reactions to viewing the fetus ranged from "I haven't looked" to shock, dismay, amazement, disgust, fear and sadness.... Two felt that it must eventually damage [the doctor] psychologically....
>
> Two respondents described dreams which they had had related to the procedure. Both described dreams of vomiting fetuses along with a sense of horror. Other dreams revolved around a need to protect others from viewing fetal parts, dreaming that she herself was pregnant and needed an abortion or was having a baby.... The more direct the physical and visual involvement [i.e. nurses, doctors], the more stress experienced.[420]

Because of their lack of understanding of what abortion really is, it is hard for many people to understand such reactions. This firsthand description of an abortion facility's saline unit, written by a prochoice advocate, should shed some light:

> I am drawn to the unit, irresistibly, by my reactions of disbelief, sorrow, horror, compassion, guilt. The place depresses me, yet I hang around after working hours. When I leave, I behave outside with the expansiveness of one who has just escaped a disaster. I have bad dreams. My sense of complicity in something nameless grows and festers. I consider giving up the research....
>
> I remove with one hand the lid of a bucket.... I look inside the bucket in front of me. There is a small naked person there floating in a bloody liquid—plainly the tragic victim of a drowning accident. But

then perhaps this was no accident, because the body is purple with bruises and the face has the agonized tautness of one forced to die too soon. Death overtakes me in a rush of madness.[421]

When the same woman watched an abortion for the first time from the surgeon's end of the table her shock went even deeper:

[The doctor] pulls out something, which he slaps on the instrument table. "There," he says. "A leg."... I turn to Mr. Smith. "What did he say?" "He pulled a leg off," Mr. Smith says. "Right here." He points to the instrument table, where there is a perfectly formed, slightly bent leg, about three inches long. It consists of a ripped thigh, a knee, a lower leg, a foot, and five toes. I start to shake very badly, but otherwise, I feel nothing. Total shock is passionless....

"There, I've got the head out now."... There lies a head. It is the smallest human head I have ever seen, but it is unmistakably part of a person. My vision and my hearing though disengaged, continue, I note, to function with exceptional clarity. The rest of me is mercifully gone.[422]

Abortionist David Zbaraz told the *Washington Post*, "It's a nasty, dirty, yucky thing and I always come home angry." The article says, "On those days when he performs an abortion, his wife can tell as soon as he walks in the door."[423]

Sallie Tisdale, an abortion clinic nurse says,

There are weary, grim moments when I think I cannot bear another basin of bloody remains, utter another kind phrase of reassurance.... "How can you stand it" even the clients ask. They see the machine, the strange instruments, the blood, the final stroke that wipes away the promise of pregnancy. Sometimes I see that too: I watch a woman's swollen abdomen sink to softness in a few stuttering moments and my own belly flip-flops with sorrow.[424]

In a *New York Times* editorial, Dr. Susan Conde said, "I observed during my medical training as an Australian physician many abortions by experienced practitioners. They experienced, without exception, physical revulsion and moral bewilderment."[425] One clinic worker says, "You know that there is something alive in there that you're killing."[426]

Judith Fetrow, a former abortion clinic employee from San Francisco, says this:

> Clinic workers have very mixed emotions about abortion...clinic workers may say they support a woman's right to choose, but they will also say that they do not want to see tiny hands and tiny feet. They do not want to be faced with the consequences of their actions.... There is a great difference between the intellectual support of a woman's right to choose and the actual participation in the carnage of abortion. Because seeing body parts bothers the workers.[427]

Abortion clinic workers may cover twinges of conscience with flippancy, apparent indifference, or morbid joking about their profession. Beneath this veneer, however, they often suffer guilt, which manifests itself in destructive behavior. Bernard Nathanson says doctors in his own clinic suffered from nightmares, alcoholism, drug abuse, and family problems leading to divorce.[428] Carol Everett says the same was true in her clinics.[429]

Dr. George Flesh confessed, "Extracting a fetus, piece by piece, was bad for my sleep.... I stared at the sad face in the mirror and wondered how all those awards and diplomas had produced an angel of death."[430] Dr. David Brewer states, "My heart got callous against the fact that I was a murderer, but that baby lying in a cold bowl educated me to what abortion really was."[431] Dr. McArthur Hill confesses, "I am a murderer. I have taken the lives of innocent babies and I have ripped them from their mothers' wombs with a powerful vacuum machine."[432]

26d. Abortion is difficult and painful for the unborn child.

Surgeon Robert P. N. Shearin says,

> As early as eight to ten weeks after conception, and definitely by thirteen-and-a-half weeks, the unborn experiences organic pain.... First, the unborn child's mouth, at eight weeks, then her hands at ten weeks, then her face, arms, and legs at eleven weeks become sensitive to touch. By thirteen-and-a-half weeks, she responds to pain at all levels of her nervous system in an integrated response which cannot be termed a mere reflex. She can now experience pain.[433]

When President Ronald Reagan stated in 1984 that during an abortion "the fetus feels pain which is long and agonizing," it set off a furious reaction by prochoice advocates. They did not want to believe this, nor did they want the public to believe it. But twenty-six medical authorities, including two past presidents of the American College of Obstetricians and Gynecologists, stepped forward with a letter documenting that *the unborn does in fact feel pain during an abortion*. Their letter says in part:

> Mr. President, in drawing attention to the capability of the human fetus to feel pain, you stand on firmly established ground.... That the unborn, the prematurely born, and the new-born of the human species is a highly complex, sentient, functioning, individual organism is established scientific fact.... Over the last eighteen years, real time ultrasonography, fetoscopy, study of the fetal EKG [electrocardiogram] and the fetal EEG [electroencephalogram] have demonstrated the remarkable responsiveness of the human fetus to pain, touch, and sound.[434]

Pioneer fetologist Albert Liley, of the University of Auckland, says that by the fifty-sixth day after conception, the baby's spinal reflexes are sufficiently developed to feel pain. He adds, "When doctors first began invading the sanctuary of the womb, they did not know that the unborn baby would react to pain in the same fashion as a child would. But they soon learned he did."[435]

Dr. Liley's observation is graphically demonstrated in Dr. Bernard Nathanson's classic film, *The Silent Scream*, the first widely circulated ultrasound of an actual abortion.[436] It shows a child serenely resting in her mother's womb. Suddenly the child is alarmed because of the intruding abortion device. She moves as far away as she can, trying desperately to save her life. Just before her body is torn to pieces and sucked out through the vacuum tube, her tiny mouth opens in an unheard scream of terror. After the abortion the doctor who performed it was invited to view the ultrasound. He was so upset with what he saw that he left the room. Though he had performed over ten thousand abortions, he never performed another one.[437]

Dilation and evacuation (D & E), saline, and prostaglandin abortions can all cause pain for the unborn.[438] Many babies now undergo fetal surgery, including Sarah Marie Switzer, whose extended arm at twenty-four weeks gestation is shown on the back cover. These babies are routinely given anesthesia to prevent pain during the procedure.

Because of the obvious fact that late-term abortions cause pain for preborn children, a California assemblyman introduced the Fetal Pain Prevention Act of 1998, which would have required that babies be sedated to reduce their suffering in third trimester abortions. (The Center for Disease Control indicates thirty-nine hundred of these are performed annually in California alone.) Planned Parenthood strongly opposed the bill, which subsequently failed.

Of course, the solution is not to inflict less suffering while killing babies, but to stop killing babies in the first place. But what does it say about our society, or about Planned Parenthood or the prochoice movement, that people would not only insist upon the killing, but refuse to require measures to reduce human suffering? These are measures that would be required by any veterinary clinic in putting to sleep a dog.

The Royal College of Obstetricians and Gynecologists, a British panel of medical and scientific experts, affirmed in October 1997 that fetal pain does exist and recommends that "practitioners who undertake termination of pregnancy at 24 weeks or later should consider the requirements for feticide analgesia and sedation."[439]

American medical experts also indicate that unborn children beyond 20 weeks are capable of experiencing pain, or at least react to stimuli in a manner that could be interpreted as reaction to pain. One expert, in congressional testimony, characterized the pain experienced in a partial-birth abortion procedure as a "dreadfully painful experience." Apparently fetal surgeons agree that their patients feel pain, since anesthesia is given not only to the mother but to her child. Despite the prochoice rhetoric, the patients/victims would not likely agree that abortion is easy or painless.[440]

Registered nurse Brenda Pratt Shafer recounts her experience of watching a partial-birth abortion:

> I stood at a doctor's side as he performed the partial-birth abortion procedure, and what I saw is branded forever on my mind. On the ultrasound screen, I could see the heart beating.... Dr. Haskell went in with forceps and grabbed the baby's legs and pulled them down into the birth canal. Then he delivered the baby's body and the arms—everything but the head. The doctor kept the baby's head just inside the uterus. The baby's little fingers were clasping and unclasping, and his feet were kicking. Then the doctor stuck the scissors through the back of his head, and the

baby's arms jerked out in a flinch, a startle reaction, like a baby does when he thinks that he might fall. The doctor opened up the scissors, stuck a high-powered suction tube into the opening and sucked the baby's brains out. Now the baby was completely limp. Dr. Haskell delivered the baby's head. He cut the umbilical cord and delivered the placenta. He threw that baby in a pan, along with the placenta and the instruments he'd used. I saw the baby move in the pan. I asked another nurse and she said it was just 'reflexes.' I have been a nurse for a long time and I have seen a lot of death—people maimed in auto accidents, gunshot wounds, you name it. I have seen surgical procedures of every sort. But in all my professional years, I had never witnessed anything like this.[441]

26e. Even if abortion were made easy or painless for everyone, it wouldn't change the bottom-line problem that abortion kills children.

If in the future, "improved" procedures make abortion painless—or at least less painful—for both mother and child, this will do nothing to change the moral issue. While it is more horrible for a man to torture his wife before killing her, no jury would be impressed by his decision to kill her painlessly while she slept. Improving the ease and efficiency of killing does nothing to lessen the reality and the tragedy of the lost life.

27. "Abortion relieves women of stress and responsibility, and thereby enhances their psychological well-being."

We've never talked about it since. Never. It was only mentioned once. Just before our first child was born, out of the blue she said, "If I hadn't had the abortion, that child would be five years old now." We both let it drop.... For all I know there is a lot of psychological damage hidden behind the silence.[442]

These words speak for many men, women, and married couples. Until it is dealt with honestly and forthrightly, the shadow of abortion hangs over them the rest of their lives.

27a. Research demonstrates abortion's adverse psychological effects on women.

Dozens of studies tie abortion to a rise in sexual dysfunction, impotency, aversion to sex, loss of intimacy, unexpected guilt and extramarital affairs, traumatic stress syndrome, personality fragmentation, grief responses, child abuse and neglect, and increase in alcohol and drug abuse.[443]

An Elliot Institute study indicates that women who abort are five times more likely to abuse drugs.[444] The study was authored by the Institute director, Dr. David Reardon, and Dr. Philip Ney, a psychiatrist who specializes in postabortion counseling:

> According to the authors, while the connection between abortion and substance abuse has never been widely publicized, this is at least the 16th published study connecting a history of abortion to subsequent drug or alcohol abuse....
>
> According to Reardon, the increase in accidental or homicide-related deaths among post-abortive women is most likely due to risk-taking behavior that is an expression of self-destructive or suicidal tendencies.
>
> It is still unclear whether abortion causes self-destructive behavior or whether it simply aggravates previously existing self-destructive tendencies.[445]

27b. The many postabortion therapy and support groups testify to the reality of abortion's potentially harmful psychological effects.

Women Exploited by Abortion (WEBA) has over thirty thousand members in more than two hundred chapters across the United States, with chapters in Canada, Germany, Ireland, Japan, Australia, New Zealand, and Africa.[446] Other post-abortion support and recovery groups include Victims of Choice, Healing Encouragement for Abortion Related Trauma (HEART), Healing Visions Network, Counseling for Abortion-Related Experiences (CARE), Women of Ramah, Project Rachel, Open

Arms, Abortion Trauma Services, and American Victims of Abortion. (For further information on these and other groups, see Appendix K, "Prolife Resources.") The existence of such groups testifies to the mental and emotional needs of women who have had abortions.

I read an editorial comparing abortion to a root canal or to having one's tonsils or appendix removed. But why are there no ongoing support groups for those who have had tonsillectomies, appendectomies, and root canals? Because abortion takes a toll on women that normal surgeries do not. And no wonder—normal surgeries do not take a life.

27c. The suicide rate is significantly higher among women who have had abortions than among those who haven't.

Feelings of rejection, low self-esteem, guilt and depression are all ingredients for suicide, and the rate of suicide attempts among aborted women is phenomenally high. According to one study, women who have had abortions are nine times more likely to attempt suicide than women in the general population.[447]

Women's World reports a study of aborted women in which 45 percent said they had thoughts of suicide following their abortions.[448] The article quotes women who describe the aftermath of abortion as "devastating," "insidious," "misery," and "prolonged anguish." One woman says, "I was completely overwhelmed with grief." Another says, "I was so depressed, nothing mattered," and "I wished I were dead."

27d. Postabortion syndrome is a diagnosable psychological affliction.

In 1981 Nancy Jo Mann came to terms with her abortion of seven years earlier, then went public and established Women Exploited by Abortion. After hearing the stories of thousands of women, she was the first to identify consistent psychological consequences of abortion. Terry Selby runs a residential treatment program for those suffering from postabortion syndrome (PAS). Dr. Vincent Rue and Dr. Susan Stanford-Rue head the nonprofit Institute for Abortion Recovery and

Research, which was founded to provide accurate information on the psychological effects of abortion.[449]

Though the American Psychiatric Association (APA) has not taken a position on PAS (doing so would be highly unpopular in a field dominated by prochoice thinking), it nevertheless lists abortion as a stressor event that can trigger post-traumatic stress disorder (PTSD).[450] Hence, in this indirect way, it recognizes the reality of PAS.

The woman who suffers heavily from PAS becomes severely depressed and loses pleasure in almost everything in life. She is likely to experience poor appetite, sleep disturbance, agitation of behavior, loss of pleasure in usual activities, such as her sexual relationship[s], loss of energy, inappropriate guilt, a diminished ability to concentrate, and recurrent thoughts of suicide ["I just want to sleep" or "I wish to join my baby"].[451]

Dr. Vincent Rue offers this list of identified consequences of induced abortion, keeping in mind that some women experience fewer of these than others:

Guilt, depression, grief, anxiety, sadness, shame, helplessness and hopelessness, lowered self-esteem, distrust, hostility toward self and others, regret, sleep disorders, recurring dreams, nightmares, anniversary reactions, psychophysiological symptoms, suicidal ideation and behavior, alcohol and/or chemical dependencies, sexual dysfunction, insecurity, numbness, painful re-experiencing of the abortion, relationship disruption, communication impairment and/or restriction, isolation, fetal fantasies, self-condemnation, flashbacks, uncontrollable weeping, eating disorders, preoccupation, confused and/or distorted thinking, bitterness, and a sense of loss and emptiness.[452]

27e. Many professional studies document the reality of abortion's adverse psychological consequences on a large number of women.

Prochoice advocates often claim that former Surgeon General C. Everett Koop issued a report that there were no adverse psychological effects of abortion on women. This is not true. Dr. Koop stated after the report that as a physician he *knows* abortions are dangerous to a woman's mental health. "There is no doubt about it," he commented."[453]

What Dr. Koop actually said, in a three-page letter to the president, was that the available studies were flawed because they did not examine the problem of psychological consequences over a sufficiently long period. Based on his own experience and knowledge he says, "Any long-term studies will add more credibility to those people who say there are serious detrimental health effects of abortion."[454]

Because abortion has been legal for less than thirty years, it is difficult to prove its long-term effects. But many studies and expert observations indicate serious short- and mid-term effects on some women. Furthermore, other significant studies have been done since Dr. Koop's letter to the president. A study by clinical psychologist Catherine Barnard, released in 1991, indicated that 18.8 percent of post-aborted women interviewed showed diagnosable post-traumatic stress disorder. Another 39 to 45 percent had sleep disorders, hypervigilance, flashbacks, and other high stress reactions. Dr. Barnard concluded that nearly half of women who have had an abortion may be suffering some type of emotional trauma as a result.[455]

Although prochoice advocates often cite a 1977 study by Brewer which concluded that childbirth creates more psychiatric problems than abortion, the study was seriously flawed. Dr. James L. Rogers says, "Brewer's study is riddled with severe methodological pitfalls."[456] He compares a 1981 study done by David, Rasmussen, and Holst, which is based on much sounder research, including the careful use and comparison of a control group. Rogers concludes, "The best study to date indicates that women who undergo abortion are at greater psychiatric risk than women who deliver at term."[457]

From a survey of psychiatric and psychological studies, the Royal College of Obstetricians and Gynecologists concluded, "The incidence of serious, permanent psychiatric aftermath [of abortion] is variously reported as between 9 and 59%."[458] Even taking a low figure, if one out of ten women getting abortions faced such "serious" and "permanent" psychiatric effects, this would be 160,000 women *per year*.

Columnist John Leo cites a researcher who says that only 1 percent of women who abort are "so severely scarred by post-abortion trauma that they become unable to function normally." Leo noted that given the number of abortions that year, this 1 percent came to sixteen thousand "severely scarred" women per year[459] and over a quarter of a million women "severely scarred and unable to function normally" since abortion was legalized. The percentage may be low, but the total numbers are staggering.

27f. Abortion can produce both short- and longer-term psychological damage, especially a sense of personal guilt.

The *British Medical Journal*, after reviewing psychological research on abortion, concluded that "almost all those terminated feel guilt and depression" for at least a brief period.[460] Research has indicated that "about half of all abortion patients" experience psychological disturbances lasting at least eight weeks, including guilt feelings, nervous symptoms, sleeplessness, and feelings of regret.[461]

Longer-term studies have found that 10 to 30 percent of abortion patients experience serious ongoing psychiatric problems.[462] In one five-year study, 25 percent of women who had undergone abortion surgery sought out psychiatric care, as opposed to 3 percent of women with no prior abortions.[463] Another study found that psychiatric disorders were 40 percent more common among women who had abortions than among those who hadn't.[464] This is not definitive proof that abortion is a direct cause of such problems, but its relationship to some cases of psychological disorders is evident.

Interviews with women within a year of their abortions might indicate that they are still glad they had an abortion because of the relief it gave to their life situation. Often it is much later that reality sinks in and identifiable depression emerges:

> A woman that a six-month post-abortion survey declares "well-adjusted" may experience severe trauma on the anniversary of the abortion date, or even many years later. This fact is attested to in psychiatric textbooks which affirm that…"the psychiatrist frequently hears expressions of remorse and guilt concerning abortions that occurred twenty or more years earlier." In one study, the number of women who expressed "serious self-reproach" increased fivefold over the period of time covered by the study.[465]

Dr. C. Everett Koop tells this story of later emerging consequences of abortion:

> A woman had a pregnancy at about 38 or 39. Her kids were teenagers. And without letting either her family or her husband know,

she had an abortion. At the moment, she said, "[The abortion was] the best thing that ever happened to me—clean slate, no one knows. I am all fine." Ten years later, she had a psychiatric break when one of those teenage daughters who had grown up, got married, gotten pregnant, delivered a baby, and presented it to her grandmother.... Unless you studied that one for ten years, you would say, "Perfectly fine result of an abortion."[466]

A *Los Angeles Times* poll found that 56 percent of aborted women had "a sense of guilt about having an abortion." The same poll found that almost two-thirds of men whose children are killed by abortion felt guilt.[467] Guilt and grief over abortion are sometimes more severe on the anniversary of the due date or the date of the abortion.[468] One study demonstrates that teenagers who have had an abortion sometimes attempt to kill themselves on the day corresponding to the birth date if the baby had been allowed to live.[469] (Appendix A, "Finding Forgiveness after an Abortion," is written for women who have had abortions— and men who have made abortion-related decisions—and shares the good news of how they can experience real and lasting forgiveness.)

27g. Most women have not been warned about and are completely unprepared for the psychological consequences of abortion.

A woman getting an abortion at three months relays her conversation with an abortion clinic counselor:

"Are there psychological problems?" I continued.

"Hardly ever. Don't worry," I was told.

"What does a three-month-old fetus look like?"

"Just a clump of cells," she answered matter-of-factly.[470]

Later this same woman, by then sterile as a result of her abortion, saw some pictures of fetal development. She said, "When I saw that a three-month-old 'clump of cells' had fingers and toes and was a tiny perfectly formed baby, I became really hysterical. I'd been lied to and misled, and I'm sure thousands of other women are being just as poorly informed and badly served."[471]

Psychologist Vincent Rue confirms that this kind of misinformation is common:

I have seen hundreds of patients in my office who have had abortions who were just lied to by the abortion counselor. Namely: "This is less painful than having a tooth removed. It is not a baby." Afterwards the woman sees *Life* magazine and she breaks down and goes into a major depression.[472]

In recent years, more abortion alternative centers have been offering free ultrasound examinations, performed by licensed personnel. A friend of mine performs ultrasounds at their center in Marietta, Georgia. Audrey wrote me a letter telling this story:

Barb came to Cobb Pregnancy Services Tuesday wanting a verification of pregnancy so she could get an abortion. She was sixteen weeks pregnant. Janet, her counselor, put in a video *[The Eclipse of Reason]* that showed the abortion procedure for a baby of this age. When Janet returned to the room, Barb was looking down and said, "I can't have no baby."

Janet shared her regret concerning an abortion she's lived with for more than 25 years. She then got permission to call me to do an ultrasound and show Barb her baby. The little girl was most cooperative to show even her mom's untrained eye that she was alive, very active and doing well inside her. She opened and closed her mouth, had the hiccups, laid back as if in a beach chair, stretching her little legs. She even held up hands so Barb could count her fingers.

Barb was visibly touched. When the scan was over I asked Barb what her plans were. She replied, "I am going to have my baby." I asked if the scan had made a difference; she said, "Big time. I just came in here to get a pregnancy verification so I could go have an abortion."[473]

The fact that prochoice advocates oppose the showing of ultrasounds to pregnant women considering abortion suggests they are more interested in women having abortions than in them making informed choices based on factual data.

At age thirteen Kathy Walker, who later became president of Women Exploited by Abortion, had an abortion that was supposed to solve her problems. But Planned Parenthood misled her, and she paid a terrible psychological price that would haunt her for years:

As soon as the needle went through my abdomen, I hated myself. I wanted to scream out, "Please don't do this to me!" I wanted to run as far away as I possibly could...I felt my baby thrash around violently while he was being choked, poisoned, burned, and suffocated to death. I wasn't told any of that was going to happen.

I remember talking to my baby and telling him I didn't want to do this, and that I wished he could live and that his mommy loved him and that I was so sorry. I prayed that he understood and that someday, if he could, he would learn to forgive me. He was dying, and there was nothing I could do to save him. I remember his very last kick. He had no strength left to fight.[474]

Karen Sullivan Ables also says she wasn't told the truth of what her abortion might do to her:

I could feel the baby being torn from my insides. It was really painful.... Three-quarters of the way through the operation I sat up.... In the cylinder I saw the bits and pieces of my little child floating in a pool of blood. I screamed and jumped up off the table. They took me into another room and I started vomiting.... I just couldn't stop throwing up....

I had nightmares and recurring dreams about my baby. I couldn't work my job. I just laid in my bed and cried. Once, I wept so hard I sprained my ribs. Another time while crying, I was unable to breathe and I passed out. I was unable to walk on the beach because the playing children would make me cry. Even Pampers commercials would set me into fits of uncontrollable crying.[475]

An in-depth study of thirty women experiencing turmoil over abortion revealed this:

Eighty-five percent of the subjects were surprised at the intensity of their emotional reaction. In other words, these women were not anticipating or expecting significant personal response to their abortion.... Eighty-one percent of the subjects reported feeling victimized by the abortion process. Feelings of victimization were generally associated with either feeling coerced into the abortion or a belief that significant information regarding the pregnancy resolution and abortion procedure had been withheld.[476]

One researcher concludes, "For most women, abortion is not just an assault on their womb; it is an assault on their psyche."[477] It is a tragedy that the mental health of women is considered expendable by the prochoice movement, which opposes laws requiring that women considering abortions be given accurate information on the risks of abortion.

Abortion may relieve a woman of some immediate stress and responsibility, but it often creates much more than it relieves. Ironically, those women who do not experience psychological consequences as a result of their abortion can maintain their mental health only through denial. By choosing not to acknowledge it, they escape the emotional trauma that invariably comes with realizing you've killed a baby. This is a tenuous situation, requiring a lifetime of running from reality. And reality has a way of pursuing and catching us.

Many women will testify that it is much easier to scrape a baby from a mother's uterus than to scrape him from her mind.

28. "Abortion providers are respected medical professionals working in the woman's best interests."

28a. Abortion clinics do not have to maintain the high standards of health, safety, and professionalism required of hospitals.

According to Planned Parenthood, "Most abortions are performed in specialized clinics, and only 10 percent are performed in hospitals...4 percent in physicians' offices."[478] To understand the abortion business in America, we must understand what goes on inside abortion clinics.

The *Miami Herald* found abominable conditions in abortion clinics, including mold growing on a suction machine.[479] Florida's Department of Health secretary examined four abortion clinics, finding no restrooms or hot water at one of the clinics, stirrups covered with blood, an oxygen mask with smeared lipstick from a previous patient, and disposable tubes used with bodily fluid being reused on patient after patient. There wasn't any soap in one abortion clinic, so inspectors had to go to a building next door to wash their hands. One official stated, "It is hard to believe that places like this can exist in this age of modern medicine."[480]

The *Chicago Sun-Times* exposé of Illinois abortion clinics described an abortionist dashing from one woman to the next, "without washing his hands or donning sterile gloves."[481] *Sun-Times* reporters also discovered dirty and rusty instruments, instruments encrusted with "dried matter," and recovery room beds made with dirty linens. Surgical equipment, including the suction machine, were being cleaned with nothing more than plain water.[482] Abortionists were described as "cold," "mechanical," and even "sadistic" in their behavior.[483]

These are not stories of back-alley abortions, but of legal clinics that have been doing legal abortions since 1973. Neither were they located in "sleazy" areas—the *Sun-Times* investigation centered on abortion clinics in Chicago's high-rent district, where one-third of all Illinois abortions are done. Abortion clinics can get away with such substandard conditions because they are not carefully regulated or monitored like hospitals.

Many people assumed that the *Sun-Times* exposé would clean up the abortion industry in that state. Six years later, however, a spokesperson for the Illinois Department of Public Health was unable to identify any lasting reform in abortion clinics.[484]

For those who believe such things don't happen anymore, in February 2000 the *New York Times* told the story of Dr. Allan Zarkin, an obstetrician who carved his initials into a woman's abdomen at New York's Beth Israel Medical Center after delivering her first baby. After being dismissed from the hospital and his former practice, he was hired to perform abortions at the Choices Women's Medical Center in Long Island City, Queens.[485]

In March 2000 a New York appellate court reversed a lower court ruling and required the Board of Regents to reconsider restoring the license of Dr. Andre Nehorayoff, who practiced in Manhattan. He lost his medical license in 1991 based on negligence and incompetence, after an eighteen-year-old girl died at his hands from a botched abortion at the Manhattan Women's Health Center. Court records also document Dr. Nehorayoff's abortion on a thirty-six-year-old woman who had an emergency hysterectomy after suffering a lacerated uterus, as well as another incident in which an eighteen-year-old woman's bowel was delivered through her cervix during the abortion. The Regents revoked his license for "negligent treatment of five patients" and poor record keeping, court records stated.[486] Because of the appellate court ruling, however, his license can now be restored at any time.

Ohio state law requires that abortion clinics be licensed like other medical clinics. In 2000 several Ohio state lawmakers called for the closing of eighteen unlicensed, freestanding abortion facilities, including four in Akron. The abortion businesses were found to be without outpatient surgery center licenses after Cleveland Right to Life requested a probe. State law requires that all outpatient surgery centers pass health and safety inspections. At the time of the report, only four of the twenty-two abortion businesses in Ohio were licensed.[487]

Mark Crutcher's *Lime 5* is a startling exposé of the abortion industry. It's especially sobering when we consider that many Americans who are uncomfortable with abortion reluctantly accede to its necessity in order to protect the safety of women. A closer look at these clinics will quickly dispel these myths.

In his 300-page book Crutcher documents hundreds of cases that would be cause for alarm at any reputable hospital. But these incidents are startlingly common in abortion clinics. He describes cases of injuries to the uterus, cervix, intestines, and urinary tract. He deals with incomplete abortion and retained fetal tissue, complications from anesthesia and other drugs, infection, and hemorrhage. He covers the masking of ectopic pregnancies, misdiagnosis of fetal age, ignoring preexisting conditions, hysterectomies, heart failure, embolism, abscess, coma, incapacitation, amputation, aspirated vomitus, disease contraction, and "abortions" on women who were not pregnant. He documents unauthorized sterilizations, unsought abortions, disseminated intravascular coagulation, fetal hemograph, psychological injury, and suicide.[488]

Equally frightening is Crutcher's documentation of cases of rape and sexual assault in abortion clinics. He also deals with the myth that the abortion industry polices itself and with the common occurrence of financial improprieties and disaster cover-up, in which government organizations and the media routinely look the other way in the interests of doing nothing to change the perception that abortion is "safe" and abortionists are dependable medical professionals.[489]

I have personally spoken with a number of former abortion clinic employees. This is a partial list of abuses they have described to me: falsified records, unreported injuries, unsanitary conditions, invalid licenses, no lab work, inadequate supervision of patients in recovery, illegal disposal of fetal remains and biohazardous wastes (e.g., body parts, needles, and bloody material in trash cans), unprofessional behavior of doctors toward patients, insurance fraud, medical advice and drugs dispensed by untrained and unlicensed employees, and use of illegal drugs and alcohol by clinic staff while on duty.

The contrast between abortion clinics and hospitals doing legitimate surgeries is conspicuous.[490] Abortions seldom include pathologic exams, while normal surgeries do. Abortion clinics aggressively advertise their services, while real hospitals seldom do. The patient's informed consent is always required at hospitals, while abortion clinics almost never explain to women the full risks of abortion or the physiological development of the unborn. The consent of the parents of a minor is always required for an ethical surgery, but not for abortion (except in states with parental consent laws). Abortion clinics sometimes give kickbacks to family planning clinics that send them business, something ethical hospitals would not do.[491] Hospitals require detailed record keeping, abortion clinics records are often sketchy. The great majority of ethical surgeries are for true medical reasons, whereas 99 percent of abortions are for nonmedical reasons.[492]

28b. Many clinics are in the abortion industry because of the vast amounts of money involved.

According to the *Wall Street Journal*, abortion is a 450 million dollar a year industry in America alone.[493] In 1992, when the average annual income for a physician in Portland, Oregon, was just under $100,000, a local abortionist testified in court that in the previous year his income had been $345,000. One physician says, "An abortionist, working only twenty or thirty hours a week, with no overhead, can earn from three to ten times as much as an ethical surgeon."[494] Doctors who do abortions not only make more money, but they are not on call and usually don't have to worry much about malpractice lawsuits. Most women don't want others to know that they've had an abortion and won't come forward, no matter how badly they've been hurt. Performing abortions is a doctor's dream job—unless it bothers him to kill babies.

In its "Abortion Profiteers" investigative series, *Chicago Sun-Times* reporters spoke of "counselors who are paid not to counsel but to sell abortion with sophisticated pitches and deceptive practices." One clinic owner admitted, "No matter how you put it, we're in the business of selling abortions. Use a positive approach. It's not, 'Do you want a termination, but *when?'*"[495]

Dr. Beverly McMillan, who described herself as "a radical feminist," opened the first abortion clinic in Mississippi. She states that not only is there a lot of money in doing abortions, but many clinics don't report a significant amount of incoming funds to the government. Dr. McMillan says, "Why the IRS doesn't go after those guys, I don't know."[496]

Abortion clinic worker Nita Whitten says, "Every single transaction that we did was cash money. We wouldn't take a check, or even a credit card. If you didn't have the money, *forget it*. It wasn't unusual at all for me to take $10,000 to $15,000 a day to the bank—in cash." Whitten adds, "It's a lie when they tell you they're doing it to help women because they're not. They're doing it for the money."[497]

In her autobiography, *Blood Money: Getting Rich Off a Woman's Right to Choose*, former abortion clinic owner Carol Everett testifies that the motive of financial profit pervades the business of abortion, belying the noble-sounding rhetoric of "helping women in need."[498]

28c. Clinic workers commonly prey on fear, pain, and confusion to manipulate women into getting abortions.

Nita Whitten says:

> I was trained by a professional marketing director in how to sell abortions over the telephone. He took every one of our receptionists, nurses, and anyone else who would deal with people over the phone, through an extensive training period. The object was, when the girl called, to hook the sale so she wouldn't get an abortion somewhere else, or adopt out her baby, or change her mind.[499]

Abortion clinic staffer Debra Henry confesses, "We were told to find the woman's weakness and work on it. The women were never given any alternatives. They were told how much trouble it was to have a baby."[500]

From her inside experience in several abortion clinics, Carol Everett says:

> Those kids, when they find out that they are pregnant, may not want an abortion; they may want information, but when they call that number, which is paid for by abortion money, what kind of information do you think they're going to get? Remember, they sell abortions—they don't

sell keeping the baby, or giving the baby up for adoption, or delivering that baby. They only sell abortions.[501]

Sometimes clinics sell abortions to women who aren't even pregnant. The caption in one of the *Sun-Times* articles said, "Some are pregnant, some are not. Most will be sold abortions." Everett says that her clinics, too, gave false pregnancy test results, told women they were pregnant, then did fake abortions just for the money.[502]

28d. Clinic workers regularly mislead or deceive women about the nature and development of their babies.

Former clinic workers have told me that they used euphemisms to suggest that the unborn was not a baby. Among these were "cluster of cells," "product of conception," "blood clot," and "piece of tissue." Dr. Anthony Levatino, who performed abortions for years, claims that doctors doing abortions are less than forthright: "I want the general public to know that the doctors know that this is a person; this is a baby. That this is not some kind of blob of tissue."[503]

Dr. Joseph Randall says, "The picture of the baby on the ultrasound bothered me more than anything else. The staff couldn't take it. Women who were having abortions were never allowed to see the ultrasound."[504]

Dr. Warren Hern, a Colorado abortionist stated, "We have reached a point in this particular technology where there is no possibility of denial of an act of destruction by the operator. It is before one's eyes. The sensations of dismemberment flow through the forceps like an electric current."[505]

Dr. Hern states in his handbook for abortionists, "The advantages of the D & E [dilation and evacuation] procedure for the patient are significant.... She does not have to experience the expulsion of the fetus, which may or may not have signs of life."[506] Note that the goal is to keep the patient unaware of what's really happening—the death of her child.

Dr. Hern says a "disadvantage of the D & E procedure is that it is objectionable to physicians and their assistants."[507] (Are patients told that the doctors find the procedure objectionable?) Referring to clinic employees who witness and participate, Hern says the abortion procedure "is an emotionally stressful experience for many."[508] Why is this abortion so stressful? Dr. Hern's description sheds light:

As the calvaria is grasped, a sensation that it is collapsing is almost always accompanied by the extrusion of white cerebral material from the external os. This calvaria sign may not be much in evidence with the 13-week procedure, but it is more likely to appear at 14 weeks. Prior to 14 weeks, the calvaria may enter the suction cannula and may not be noticed.[509]

The *calvaria* is the skull or head. The technical term allows a little professional distance from the atrocity that's being committed. Dr. Hern is talking about the crushing of a skull and the leaking of the child's brains. (This would explain why it could be stressful to those participating or watching.) Dr. Hern continues:

At 16 to 17 weeks, fetal tissue is much more easily identifiable with the forceps and in some ways is easier to grasp and remove than in earlier gestations. The calvaria is about the size of a ping-pong ball and usually can be grasped readily with the Bierer. Collapsing it gives a definite sensation, which can be identified simultaneously with the appearance of calvaria sign.

[At 20 weeks fetal age] grasping and collapsing the calvaria are often difficult. Stripping the calvaria of soft tissue is sometimes the first step in successful delivery of this part, followed by dislocation of parietal bones.

The procedure changes significantly at 21 weeks because the fetal tissues become much more cohesive and difficult to dismember. This problem is accentuated by the fact that the fetal pelvis may be as much as 5 cm in width. The calvaria is no longer the principal problem; it can be collapsed. Other structures, such as the pelvis, present more difficulty.... A long Mayo scissors may be necessary to decapitate and dismember the fetus.[510]

How many women are told by their doctors or abortion clinic employees that their baby will be decapitated and dismembered?

My wife often used to do sidewalk counseling outside abortion clinics. She offered accurate medical information as well as financial and practical support for women who felt they had no choice but abortion. Routinely clinic workers would take this information out of the women's hands or tell them, "It's a bunch of lies."

Nanci has watched clinic employees tear the literature to pieces so the patient cannot read it later. (So much for "freedom to choose.") It is the clinic employees, not prolife volunteers, who have vested financial interests in persuading the woman to make one particular choice and no other.

A 2000 Supreme Court ruling further restricted the opportunity for women to get accurate information about their developing babies. The Court upheld Colorado's limits on sidewalk counseling at abortion clinics, where a bubble zone prohibits people from counseling, passing out literature, or displaying signs within eight feet of others without their consent whenever they are within one hundred feet of the clinic entrance.

The Court's argument was that "the right to avoid 'unwanted communication' sometimes outweighs free-speech rights."[511]

In other words, when it comes to abortion the Supreme Court is saying, "If one person or business doesn't want to hear it, another person doesn't have the right to say it, even on public property." The U.S. government has joined hands with abortion advocates in preventing women from hearing or having the chance to hear vital information before having an abortion.

28e. Abortionists engage in acts so offensive to the public that most media outlets refuse to describe them even in the abortionist's own words.

In 1999 it was discovered that the University of Nebraska Medical Center was conducting experiments using brain tissue from children aborted by Dr. Leroy Carhart, a specialist in the D & X abortion technique. In December the Nebraska University Regents board met to discuss the situation. When a board member tried to prevent someone from reading Dr. Carhart's testimony, it was decided that since Carhart was a specialist in an area perfectly suited for collecting live brain tissue, his testimony concerning his specialty was relevant to the discussion.

Someone then read to the board Dr. Carhart's court statement, given in July 1997. Testifying under oath, Carhart spoke of procedures which, had they been described by a prolife advocate, would have been considered outrageous. Significantly, very few newspapers and television stations reported any substantial contents from the testimony.[512] However, the reading of the testimony was taped and played on a local radio program the following Monday, introducing it into the public arena.

What follows are excerpts from that testimony, with questions from an attorney and judge. I will let the testimony stand on its own, without further comment, so the reader can judge for herself the significance of what abortion really is and why most of the public was never given the opportunity to hear this testimony:

Are there times when you don't remove the fetus intact?

Carhart: Yes, sir.

Can you tell me about that—when that occurs?

Carhart: That occurs when the tissue fragments, or frequently when you rupture the membranes. An arm will spontaneously prolapse through the os...we talk about the forehead or the skull being first. We talked about the feet being first, but I think in probably the great majority of terminations, it's what they would call a transverse lie; so really you're looking at a side profile of a curved fetus. When the patient's uterus is already starting to contract, and they are starting to miscarry, when you rupture the waters, usually something prolapses through the uterine, through the cervical os, not always, but very often an extremity will.

What do you do then?

Carhart: My normal course would be to dismember that extremity and then go back and try to take the fetus out either foot or skull first, whatever end I can get to first.

How do you go about dismembering that extremity?

Carhart: Just traction and rotation, grasping the portion that you can get ahold of which would be usually somewhere up the shaft of the exposed portion of the fetus, pulling down on it through the os, using the internal os as your countertraction and rotating to dismember the shoulder or the hip or whatever it would be. Sometimes you will get one leg and you can't get the other leg out.

In that situation...are you...when you pull on the arm and remove it, is the fetus still alive?

Carhart: Yes.

Do you consider an arm, for example, to be a substantial portion of the fetus?

Carhart: In the way I read it, I think if I lost my arm, that would be a substantial loss to me. I think I would have to interpret it that way.

And then what happens next after you remove the arm? You then try to remove the rest of the fetus?

Carhart: Then I would go back and attempt to either bring the feet down or bring the skull down, or even sometimes you bring the other arm down and remove that also and then get the feet down.

At what point is the fetus...does the fetus die during that process?

Carhart: I don't really know. I know that the fetus is alive during the process most of the time because I can see fetal heartbeat on the ultrasound.

The Court: Counsel, for what it's worth, it still is unclear to me with regard to the intact D & E when fetal demise occurs.

Okay, I will try to clarify that. In the procedure of an intact D & E where you would start foot first, with the situation where the fetus is presented feet first, tell me how you are able to get the feet out first.

Carhart: Under ultrasound, you can see the extremities. You know what is what. You know what the foot is, you know what the arm is, you know what the skull is. By grabbing the feet and pulling down on it, or by grabbing a knee and pulling down on it, usually you can get one leg out, get the other leg out, and bring the fetus out. I don't know where this...all the controversy about rotating the fetus comes from. I don't attempt to do that—just attempt to bring out whatever is the proximal portion of the fetus.

At the time that you bring out the feet, in this example, is the fetus still alive?

Carhart: Yes.

Then what's the next step you do?

Carhart: I didn't mention it. I should. I usually attempt to grasp the cord first and divide the cord, if I can do that.

What is the cord?

Carhart: The cord is the structure that transports the blood, both arterial and venous, from the fetus to the back of the fetus, and it gives the fetus its only source of oxygen, so that if you can divide the cord, the fetus will eventually die, but whether this takes five minutes or fifteen minutes and when that occurs, I don't think anyone really knows.

Are there situations where you don't divide the cord?

Carhart: There are situations when I can't.

What are those?

Carhart: I just can't get to the cord. It's either high above the fetus and structures where you can't reach up that far. The instruments are only eleven inches long.

Let's take the situation where you haven't divided the cord because you couldn't, and you have begun to remove a living fetus feet first. What happens next after you have gotten the feet removed?

Carhart: We remove the feet and continue with traction on the feet until the abdomen and the thorax come through the cavity. At that point, I would try...you have to bring the shoulders down, but you can get enough of them outside, you can do this with your finger outside of the uterus, and then at that point the fetal...the base of the fetal skull is usually in the cervical canal.

What do you do next?

Carhart: And you can reach that, and that's where you would rupture the fetal skull to some extent and aspirate the contents out.

At what point in that process does fetal demise occur between initial remove...removal of the feet or legs and the crushing of the skull, or—I'm sorry—the decompressing of the skull?

Carhart: Well, you know, again, this is where I'm not sure what fetal demise is. I mean, I honestly have to share your concern, your Honor. You can remove the cranial contents and the fetus will still have a heartbeat for several seconds or several minutes; so is the fetus alive? I would have to say probably, although I don't think it has any brain function, so it's brain-dead at that point.

So the brain death might occur when you begin suctioning out of the cranium?

Carhart: I think brain death would occur because the suctioning to remove contents is only two or three seconds, so somewhere in that period of time, obviously not when you penetrate the skull, because people get shot in the head and they don't die immediately from that, if they are going to die at all, so that probably is not sufficient to kill the fetus, but I think removing the brain contents eventually will.[513]

28f. Abortionists, feminists, a past president of the United States, many congressmen, and the Supreme Court have defended partial-birth abortion, one of the most chilling medical atrocities in human history.

President Clinton vetoed a 1995 bill that would have banned partial-birth abortions.[514] Some in Congress vowed to override the veto. In September 1996, they finally failed to gain the necessary votes to do so. At that point the U.S. government became an accessory to a procedure so gruesome it would horrify most people living in the most primitive cultures. While killing children has been legal since the judicial branch's *Roe* v. *Wade* decision in 1973, this was the first direct endorsement of the United States government's executive and legislative branches of what is, without question, infanticide.

On June 28, 2000, in *Carhart* v. *Nebraska*, the U.S. Supreme Court struck down a state law preventing late term abortions.[515] The Nebraska law required that viable babies be delivered alive rather than deliberately and violently killed just before birth. Dr. Leroy Carhart, the late-term abortionist cited in the previous section, challenged Nebraska's right to keep him from performing partial-birth abortions. The Supreme Court sided with Carhart.

In his dissent, Justice Anthony Scalia compared this historic decision to the 1857 Dred Scott ruling, which declared that blacks could not be citizens and were not worthy to have judicial protection of their lives.[516] The most chilling aspect of the decision is that, in the face of thirty states that had passed laws restricting partial-birth abortion, the Supreme Court implied that states have no right to protect the lives of children who are in the process of being born.

The accompanying illustration[517] accurately depicts the process of partial-birth abortion. Keep in mind that the child pictured here is no more nor less valuable than smaller children who die in earlier abortions.

In a partial-birth (also called D & X) abortion, the child is delivered live until only the head remains in the birth canal. The abortionist then uses a pair of scissors to rip a wound in the base of the living child's skull. He inserts a tube into the wound and sucks the helpless child's brain out with a vacuum pump. The now dead infant's skull collapses, and the body is removed the rest of the way from the mother. Dr. Carhart's testimony was about this kind of procedure.

If a veterinarian performed a partial-birth abortion on a dog at his clinic, not only animal rights activists, but the media and general public would be outraged. The fact that it is being done on human beings—and that Congress could not muster enough votes to overturn the president's veto on their efforts to make it illegal—documents the moral slippery slope of abortion. It also demonstrates the shadow of evil that hangs over not only the abortion industry, but our political leaders and our nation.

Syndicated columnist Linda Bowles wrote of this episode,

When the history of the rise and fall of our nation is finally written, it may well be recorded that the single event which signaled the beginning of the end was the countenance of mass infanticide by the president of the United States and the subsequent failure of the people to rise up in righteous anger.[518]

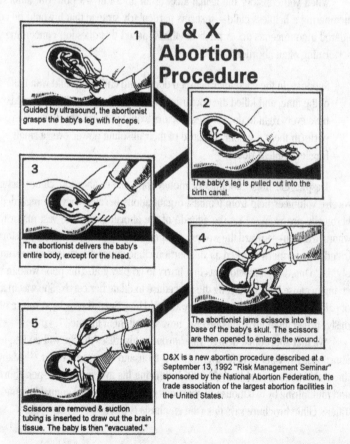

D & X Abortion Procedure

1 Guided by ultrasound, the abortionist grasps the baby's leg with forceps.

2 The baby's leg is pulled out into the birth canal.

3 The abortionist delivers the baby's entire body, except for the head.

4 The abortionist jams scissors into the base of the baby's skull. The scissors are then opened to enlarge the wound.

5 Scissors are removed & suction tubing is inserted to draw out the brain tissue. The baby is then "evacuated."

D&X is a new abortion procedure described at a September 13, 1992 "Risk Management Seminar" sponsored by the National Abortion Federation, the trade association of the largest abortion facilities in the United States.

28g. Abortion clinics often exploit the feminist connection, making it appear that their motive is to stand up for women.

Those performing the partial-birth abortion procedure have been applauded by many feminists as heroes in the cause of women's rights. An April 2000 column by feminist Ellen Goodman spoke of the hardships endured by Dr. Leroy Carhart, whose testimony on D & X abortion I cited above. Goodman quoted Carhart as saying "Women's health became my life."[519] The article makes no mention of Carhart's own admission of what is involved in his "life's work," nor does it mention how much he is paid to do it. (He does not volunteer.)

When you consider the actual facts of an abortion—a powerful adult dismembering a helpless child—it seems particularly strange that it would be considered a courageous act. A medical ethicist posed this question concerning the performing of an abortion:

> Suppose, in the encounter between doctor and child, the child won half of the time, and killed the doctor in self-defense—something he would have every right to do. Very few doctors would perform abortions. They perform them now only because of their absolute power over a small, fragile, helpless victim.[520]

Despite the huge amounts of money they make, abortion clinics actually receive volunteer help from feminist organizations because they are regarded as heroically pro-woman. Yet the attitude of the abortionists—the vast majority of whom are men—toward the women coming for abortions tells a different story. A friend who formerly worked as an abortion clinic counselor shared one example of this. "One day the doctor was in a hurry to go play golf. This poor woman was crying because he was rushing the procedure to dilate her cervix. She was in a lot of pain and really afraid. He got angry and told her, 'Spread your legs! You've obviously spread them for someone else, now spread them for me.'"

Wichita abortionist George Tiller proudly advertises that he will do late-term abortions. Dr. Tiller says he averages two thousand abortions a year.[521] Many of these abortions cost at least $2,000. Estimating his average charge per abortion and multiplying by two thousand abortions gives an idea of his annual income. Dr. Tiller's clinic brochure says this (the emphasis is his):

Our purpose at Women's Health Care Services is to guide and support women through an experience which will allow them the opportunity to change the rest of their lives. We are here to help our patients make their DREAMS COME TRUE by maximizing their assets and minimizing their shortcomings. We are dedicated to providing the chance for women to live joyous, productive and free lives.

The brochure offers package deals that include a night in a nice Wichita hotel, with language that suggests an unforgettable getaway vacation rather than a traumatic life-taking procedure that will haunt women the rest of their lives. Tiller sells late-term abortion as something beautiful. Surely it should be offensive to true feminists that a man could grow rich by killing children and crassly manipulating and exploiting women. But he does, and prochoice feminists hail him as a hero.

28h. Doctors doing abortions violate the fundamental oaths of the medical profession.

The fifth-century B.C. Hippocratic Oath was a resolution intended to forever separate killing and healing in the medical profession. Previously killing and healing had been incongruously wedded together in the practices of pagan "doctors," who were more like witchdoctors. In the Hippocratic Oath, routinely taken by doctors for centuries, physicians swore they would never participate in inducing an abortion:

I swear by Apollo the physician and…all the gods and goddesses, that, according to my ability and judgment, I will keep this Oath….

I will follow that system of regimen which, according to my ability and judgment, I consider for the benefit of my patients, and abstain from whatever is deleterious and mischievous.

I will give no deadly medicine to anyone if asked, nor suggest any such counsel; in like manner I will not give to a woman a pessary to produce abortion….

I will abstain from every voluntary act of mischief and corruption; and, further, from the seduction of females or males, of freemen and slaves….

While I continue to keep this Oath unviolated, may it be granted to me to enjoy life and the practice of the art, respected by all men, in all times. But should I trespass and violate this Oath, may the reverse be my lot. [522]

Two physicians conducted research to determine which medical schools were still using this Oath. This is what they discovered:

There has been a progressive and marked increase in percentage of schools administering an oath over the past 65 years. The graduates of 98% of the 150 responding schools took an oath in 1993 while only 26% of schools administered an oath in 1928.

We determined that only one school used the text of the classical Hippocratic Oath, but 68 reported they used other "versions" of the traditional oath.

When we examined the contents of all oaths in current use, we discovered that all still pledge a commitment to patients, only 43% vow to be accountable for their actions, only 14% include a prohibition against euthanasia, only 11% invoke a deity, only 8% forbid abortion, and only 3% retain a proscription against sexual contact with patients.[523]

The Nazi doctors, with their program of euthanasia and cruel experiments on "undesirable" people, cast a dark shadow over the medical profession. Dr. Josef Mengele, the notorious "butcher of Auschwitz," who epitomized the Nazi ideal of fastidious devotion to research and medicine, killed innocent people in the name of bettering humanity.[524] Argentine files opened in the 1990s reveal that Dr. Mengele spent his postwar years performing abortions.[525]

In 1948, the Holocaust still fresh in its memory, the World Medical Association adopted the Declaration of Geneva that said, "I will maintain the utmost respect for human life, from the time of conception; even under threat, I will not use my medical knowledge contrary to the laws of humanity."[526] In 1949 the World Medical Association also adopted the International Code of Medical Ethics, which said, "A doctor must always bear in mind the importance of preserving human life from the time of conception until death."[527]

The strongest statements of condemnation for doctors who perform abortions were made not by a religious group or a prolife organization, but by the American Medical Association. In the last century the AMA publicly called abortionists "monsters" and men of "corrupt souls," a "blight" on society and a "shame" to the medical profession.

What follows is a portion of the AMA's official position on abortionists, issued in 1871. Keep in mind that though abortion has been made legal, the nature of abortion—which the medical community found so repugnant—has not changed in any way:

> There we shall discover an enemy in the camp; there we shall witness as hideous a view of moral deformity as the evil spirit could present.... Men who seek not to save, but to destroy; men known not only to the profession, but to the public, as abortionists....
>
> "Thou shalt not kill." This commandment is given to all, and applies to all without exception.... Notwithstanding all this, we see in our midst a class of men, regardless of all principle, regardless of all honor, who daily destroy that fair fabric of God's creation; who daily pull down what he has built up; who act in antagonism to that profession of which they claim to be members....
>
> It matters not at what state of development his victim may have arrived—it matters not how small or how apparently insignificant it may be—it is a murder, a foul, unprovoked murder; and its blood, like the blood of Abel, will cry from earth to Heaven for vengeance....
>
> Every practicing physician in the land (as well as every good man) has a certain amount of interest at stake in this matter.... The members of the profession should form themselves into a special police to watch, and to detect, and bring to justice these characters. They should shrink with horror from all intercourse with them, professionally or otherwise. These men should be marked as Cain was marked; they should be made the outcasts of society.[528]

Part Five

∞

Arguments Concerning

The Hard Cases

29. "What about a woman whose life is threatened by pregnancy or childbirth?"

29a. It is an extremely rare case when abortion is required to save the mother's life.

While he was United States Surgeon General, Dr. C. Everett Koop stated publicly that in his thirty-eight years as a pediatric surgeon, *he was never aware of a single situation in which a preborn child's life had to be taken in order to save the life of the mother.* He said the use of this argument to justify abortion in general was a "smoke screen."

Due to significant medical advances, the danger of pregnancy to the mother has declined considerably since 1967. Yet even at that time Dr. Alan Guttmacher of Planned Parenthood acknowledged, "Today it is possible for almost any patient to be brought through pregnancy alive, unless she suffers from a fatal illness such as cancer or leukemia, and, if so, abortion would be unlikely to prolong, much less save, life."[529] Dr. Landrum Shettles says that less than 1 percent of all abortions are performed to save the mother's life.[530]

29b. When two lives are threatened and only one can be saved, doctors must always save that life.

If the mother has a fast-spreading uterine cancer, the surgery to remove the cancer may result in the loss of the child's life. In an ectopic pregnancy the child is developing outside the uterus. He has no hope of survival, and may have to be removed to save his mother's life. These are tragic situations, but even if one life must be lost, the life that can be saved should be. More often than not, that life is the mother's, not the child's. There are rare cases in later stages of pregnancy when the mother can't be saved, but the baby can. Again, one life saved is better than two lives lost.

Friends of ours were faced with a situation in which removing the mother's life-threatening and rapidly spreading cancer would result in the unborn child's death. It was heartbreaking, but they and we were confident that the decision to save the mother's life was right. The pregnancy was still so early that there wasn't time for the child to become viable before both mother and child would die from the cancer. But it is critical to understand that this was in no sense an abortion. The purpose of the surgery was not to kill the child, but to save the life of the mother. The death of the child was a tragic and unintended secondary effect of life-saving efforts. This was a consistently prolife act, since to be prolife does not mean being prolife just about babies. It also means being prolife about women, who are just as valuable as babies.

29c. Abortion for the mother's life and abortion for the mother's health are usually not the same issue.

The mother's *life* and the mother's *health* are usually two distinct considerations. A woman with toxemia will have adverse health reactions and considerable inconvenience, including probably needing to lie down for much of her pregnancy. This is a difficulty, but not normally a threat to her life. Hence, an abortion for the sake of "health" would not be lifesaving, but life-taking, since her life is not in jeopardy in the first place.

There are other situations where an expectant mother has a serious or even terminal medical condition. Her pregnancy may cause complications, but will not cause her death. If she is receiving radiation therapy, she may be told that the child could have handicaps as a result. It may be possible to postpone or reduce such treatment, but if it is essential to continue the treatment to save the mother's life, this is preferable to allowing her death or killing the child. Efforts can and should be made that value the lives of both mother and child.

29d. Abortion to save the mother's life was legal before convenience abortion was legalized and would continue to be if abortion were made illegal again.

Even under restrictive abortion laws, the mother's right to life is never disregarded. Contrary to what some prochoice advocates have said, there is no danger whatsoever that women whose lives are in jeopardy will be unable to get treatment, even if such treatment tragically results in the death of an unborn child. Even prochoice *USA Today* acknowledges, "The National Right to Life Committee consistently has maintained that while abortion should be banned, there should be exceptions if an abortion is needed to save a woman's life."[531]

30. "What about a woman whose unborn baby is diagnosed as deformed or handicapped?"

30a. The doctor's diagnosis is sometimes wrong.

Many parents have aborted their babies because doctors told them that their children would be severely handicapped. Others I have met were told the same thing, but chose to let their babies live. These parents were then amazed to give birth to normal children.

A few years ago I saw on the television news a woman who was diagnosed as having a growing tumor. The "tumor" turned out to be a child. The woman, who did have cancer, had been under extensive chemotherapy for two years. Had her doctors known she was pregnant, she almost certainly would have been advised to get an abortion on the assumption the child would be deformed. Yet the child was perfectly normal.

In 1997 an Oregon resident, Mary Shaidaee LaDu, went to a Portland medical clinic to have doctors review a CT scan. Doctors interpreted the scan as revealing a large pelvic mass that appeared to be sitting on top of the woman's uterus. The woman underwent surgery for a hysterectomy to remove the presumed tumor. It turned out she did not have cancer, but was sixteen weeks pregnant. In 1998 she filed a $3.5 million lawsuit for the loss of her uterus and an additional $500,000 on behalf of her unborn child in a wrongful death claim. In 2000 the Oregon Court of Appeals concluded that applicable definitions of "person" under Oregon law do not include a nonviable fetus.[532] Not only was this woman faced with the reality of never being able to bear another child, but according to the state, the baby she was carrying was not really a person.

Some doctors suggest "terminating the pregnancy" if a couple's genetic history suggests a probable or even possible risk of abnormality. Ironically, "Of all eugenic abortions prescribed on the basis of genetic history, one-half to three-quarters of the unborn children destroyed are not affected by the disease. More "normal" children are killed than 'handicapped' children."[533]

30b. The child's deformity is often minor.

Planned Parenthood's Guttmacher Institute says that 1 percent of women who have abortions have been advised by their doctors that the unborn has a defect.[534] But what are called deformities are sometimes easily correctable conditions, such as cleft lips and cleft palates. After reading in London's *Sunday Times* about these common cosmetic abortions, a mother of a five-year-old girl with a cleft lip and palate wrote to the editor:

> I was horrified to read that many couples now opt for abortion rather than risk having a baby with such a minor physical imperfection. My daughter is not some subnormal freak…she can, and does, lead a happy, fulfilled life…. What sort of society do we live in when a minor facial deformity, correctable by surgery, is viewed as so abnormal as to merit abortion?[535]

30c. Medical tests for deformity may cause as many problems as they detect.

The standard test for possible deformities is done by amniocentesis. One study found a 1.5 percent rate of spontaneous miscarriage after amniocentesis.[536] This means that "a forty-year-old woman undergoing amniocentesis faces a greater risk of miscarrying a healthy child because of the procedure than she faces for having a Down syndrome baby in the first place."[537]

Dr. Hymie Gordon, chairman of the Department of Medical Genetics at Minnesota's Mayo Clinic, says that in amniocentesis "a conservative estimate is that there is a 2 percent risk of either damaging the baby, tearing the uterus, introducing infection, or precipitating a miscarriage."[538] Furthermore, Dr. Gordon states that the procedure is not always effective even when it is safe. In his extensive experience, most women are not told of the risks and limitations of amniocentesis, and when they are, the great majority of them elect not to have the procedure done.[539]

30d. Handicapped children are often happy, always precious, and usually delighted to be alive.

Often medical tests or doctors' predictions are accurate, and the child *is* born with a serious deformity. To be sure, it is hard to raise a handicapped child. He requires extra attention and effort. What makes this a hard case, however, is not whether the child deserves to live or die. What is hard is the difficult responsibilities that letting him live will require of his parents.

The film, *The Elephant Man*, depicts the true story of John Merick. He was a terribly deformed young man, rejected and ridiculed, until someone took the time to know him and discover that he was a wonderful human being. Merick said, "My life is full because I know that I am loved."

A young man born without a left leg and without arms below the elbows says, "When I was born, the first thing my dad said to my mom was that 'this one needs our love more.'"[540] Not only were these parents just what their son needed, he was just what they needed. Many families have drawn together and found joy and strength in having a child with mental or physical handicaps. It is significant that "there has not been a single organization of parents of mentally retarded children that has ever endorsed abortion."[541] Some argue that it's unfair to bring a handicapped child into the world, because he will be unhappy. Yet studies show that suicide rates are no higher for the handicapped. Experience confirms that many people with severe handicaps are happy and well adjusted, often more so than "normal" people. Dr. C. Everett Koop dealt with innumerable "deformed children" in his role as a pediatric surgeon. He says:

> I am frequently told by people who have never had the experience of working with children who are being rehabilitated into our society after the correction of a congenital defect that infants with such defects should be allowed to die, or even "encouraged" to die, because their lives could obviously be nothing but unhappy and miserable. Yet it has been my constant experience that disability and unhappiness do not necessarily go together. Some of the most unhappy children whom I have known have all of the physical and mental faculties and on the other hand some of the happiest youngsters have borne burdens which I myself would find very difficult to bear.[542]

According to *World* magazine, January 18, 1997, the current population of Americans with Down syndrome is more than 250,000. People with this condition generally score in the "mild to moderate" range of mental retardation. Most can learn to read, hold jobs, and live independently.[543]

Some years ago, the television series "Life Goes On" portrayed a teenager named Corky who had Down syndrome. The starring role was played by a young man with Down syndrome, and many people were touched by his winsome performance. Critics raved. But many of the same critics favor the killing of Down syndrome children, just like Corky, before they are born.

In 1982, "Infant Doe" was born in Bloomington, Indiana. A routine operation could have corrected the birth defect that would not allow food to pass into his stomach. But his parents and their doctors decided to let him starve to death because he had Down syndrome. When word got out that the baby was dying, a dozen families came forward and said they would gladly adopt him. His parents said no. Some in the media labeled them "courageous." Though it would cost them no money, time, or effort to allow someone else to raise their child, the parents, their doctors, and the Supreme Court of Indiana said they had the right to allow the child to starve to death. Seven agonizing days after birth, he died.

A survey of pediatricians and pediatric surgeons revealed that more than two out of three would go along with parents' wishes to deny lifesaving surgery to a child with Down syndrome. Nearly three out of four said that if they had a Down syndrome child, they would choose to let him starve to death.[544] This is not only horrible, but baffling, for many Down children are the happiest you will ever meet. We have good friends who have adopted three Down children. Each is delightful. One of them sang "Jesus Loves Me" in church one morning, and the applause was thunderous. These children require special care, of course, but surely they deserve to be born and to live as much as any of us.

Some argue: "It's cruel to let a handicapped child be born to a miserable and meaningless life." We may define a meaningful life one way, but we should ask ourselves what is meaningful to the handicapped themselves. A number of spina bifida patients were asked whether their handicaps made life meaningless and if they should have been allowed to die after birth. "Their unanimous response was forceful. Of course they wanted to live! In fact, they thought the question was ridiculous."[545]

Let's not kid ourselves. When adults kill a handicapped child, preborn or born, we aren't doing it for his good, but for what we think is our own. We aren't preventing cruelty to the child; we're committing cruelty to the child in order to prevent difficulty for ourselves.

30e. Handicapped children are not social liabilities, and bright and "normal" people are not always social assets.

The Bible is one of the oldest sources of moral guidance in the world. It asks and answers these questions about the handicapped: "Who gave man his mouth? Who makes him deaf or mute? Who gives him sight or makes him blind? Is it not I, the LORD?" (Exodus 4:11). Jesus Christ said that a certain man was born blind "so that the work of God might be displayed in his life" (John 9:3). He also said, "When you give a banquet, invite the poor, the crippled, the lame, the blind, and you will be blessed. Although they cannot repay you, you will be repaid at the resurrection of the righteous" (Luke 14:13–14). The message is this: When it comes to the handicapped, ignore the bottom-line cost; take care of them, and God will take care of you.

A geneticist tells this thought-provoking story that challenges society's assumptions about the relative worth of the handicapped, as opposed to "normal" people:

> Many years ago, my father was a Jewish physician in Braunau, Austria. On one particular day, two babies had been delivered by one of his colleagues. One was a fine, healthy boy with a strong cry. His parents were extremely proud and happy. The other was a little girl, but her parents were extremely sad, for she was a [Down syndrome] baby. I followed them both for almost fifty years. The girl grew up, living at home, and was finally destined to be the one who nursed her mother through a very long and lingering illness after a stroke. I do not remember her name. I do, however, remember the boy's name. He died in a bunker in Berlin. His name was Adolf Hitler.[546]

30f. Using dehumanizing language may change our thinking, but not the child's nature or value.

I heard a prochoice advocate say with disgust, "Should a woman be forced to bring a *monster* into the world?" Only by using such words long enough can we deceive ourselves into believing them. The term *vegetable* is another popular word for disadvantaged humans. This kind of terminology dehumanizes people in our eyes but does not change their true nature.

A bruised apple is still an apple. A blind dog is still a dog. A senile woman is still a woman. A handicapped child is still a child. A person's nature and worth are not changed by a handicap. Hitler called the Jews "useless eaters." This made it easier to kill them, but no less terrible.

30g. Our society is hypocritical in its attitude toward handicapped children.

On the one hand, we provide special parking and elevators for the handicapped. We talk tenderly about those poster children with MS, spina bifida, and leukemia. We are touched when we see the telethons, the March of Dimes, and the United Way ads. We sponsor the Special Olympics and cheer on the Down syndrome competitors, speaking of the joy and inspiration they bring us. We watch with admiration a television series that stars a Down syndrome young man. But when we hear that a woman is carrying one of these very children, we say, "Kill it before it is born."

30h. The adverse psychological effects of abortion are significantly more traumatic for those who abort because of deformity.

One study showed that of forty-eight women who terminated their pregnancies for genetic reasons, 77 percent demonstrated acute grief reactions, and 45 percent continued in this grief six months after the abortion.[547] Another study showed a higher rate of depression for genetic abortion than for other kinds, and demonstrated postabortion family disharmony and flashbacks.[548]

Still another study analyzed the reactions of children in families where the mother aborted after fetal abnormalities were detected. Even very young children—and children sheltered from knowledge of the event—showed negative reactions.[549] This may relate also to the finding that children who have siblings killed by abortion have psychological conflicts similar to those of children who survive disasters or have siblings who die of accidents or illness.[550]

30i. The arguments for killing a handicapped unborn child are valid only if they also apply to killing born people who are handicapped.

Aborting children on the basis of their handicaps jeopardizes the rights of born people who are handicapped.

People with disabilities have rightly been working hard to achieve recognition for their needs. To justify abortion on the grounds that the baby is or might be disabled is to express a bigotry against people with disabilities which should not be countenanced in an egalitarian, democratic society.[551]

Suppose your six-year-old becomes blind or paraplegic. He is now a burden to his parents and society. Raising him is expensive, inconvenient, and hard on your psychological health. Some would say that he does not have a significant "quality of life." Should you put him to death? If a law were passed that made it legal to put him to death, would you do it then? If not, why not?

You would not kill your handicapped child, because you know him. But killing an unborn child just because you have not held him in your arms and can't hear his cry does not change his value or mitigate his loss when he is killed.

What about the anencephalic child who doesn't have a fully developed brain? Since he will die anyway, his parents often decide to have an abortion or allow his life to be taken in order to harvest his organs. It is one thing to know a child will probably die and another thing to choose to take his life. Many families have had precious and enriching experiences naming and bonding with an anencephalic baby. Then they experience healthy grief at the natural death of this family member. This is in stark contrast to the unhealthy grief and guilt that comes from denying a baby's place in the family and actually taking his life.

The quality of a society is largely defined by how it treats its weakest and most vulnerable members. Killing the innocent is never justified because it relieves others of a burden. It is not a solution to inflict suffering on one person in order that another may avoid it. What defined Nazi Germany as an evil society was its wanton disregard for human life. That disregard surfaced in Hitler's killing of 275,000 handicapped people before he began killing the Jews. If abortion is wrong because it is killing a child, then whether or not the child is normal has no bearing on the matter—unless, of course, it is wrong to kill "normal" people, but right to kill handicapped people.

30j. Abortions due to probable handicaps rob the world of unique human beings who would significantly contribute to society.

A medical school professor gave his students a case study in whether or not to advise an abortion. He laid out the facts like this: "The father had syphilis and the mother had tuberculosis. Of four previous children, the first was blind, the second died, the third was both deaf and dumb, and the fourth had tuberculosis. What would you advise the woman to do when she finds she is pregnant again?"

One student gave what seemed the obvious answer: "I would advise an abortion." The professor responded, "Congratulations...you have just killed Beethoven."

30k. Abortions due to imperfections have no logical stopping place; they will lead to designer babies, commercial products to be bred and marketed, leaving other people to be regarded as inferior and disposable.

In his testimony before Congress in 2000, Dr. Bernard Nathanson said, "The geneticists are running wild." He updated the nation's leaders on what is happening in our brave new world:

> There's something known as genetic enhancement that is being carried out on a large scale.... For example, if you want a child to be in the NBA and 6 feet 10 inches tall, at the embryo stage you'd ask that extra genes be put in for tallness. Or if you wanted extra memory so that you forget nothing, you put in more memory genes at the embryo stage....
>
> All sorts of human mapping has been carried out. The entire human genome will be mapped out by the end of this year.
>
> At the University of Utah, an artificial chromosome has been created that self-destructs on command if it is faulty or if it looks primitive to some future generation. I leave you to imagine what this could do and what the possibilities of such technologies are.[552]

Ron Harris, a fashion photographer, recently began offering eggs from models for a fee of up to $150,000. Mr. Harris claims that his egg sale is an outgrowth of humans' natural urge to mate with genetically superior people and produce babies with "evolutionary advantages."[553]

31. "What about a woman who is pregnant due to rape or incest?"

31a. Pregnancy due to rape is extremely rare, and with proper treatment can be prevented.

Studies conducted by Planned Parenthood's Guttmacher Institute indicate that two consenting and fertile adults have only a 3 percent chance of pregnancy from an act of intercourse. They also indicate that there are factors involved in a rape that further reduce the chance that rape victims will become pregnant.[554] The Guttmacher Institute says that fourteen thousand abortions per year are due to rape or incest, [555] which amounts to just over 1 percent of all abortions.[556] Other studies show that pregnancies due to rape are much rarer than is generally thought, perhaps as few as one in a thousand cases.[557] Statistics are often self-serving. Starting in 2002, the Centers for Disease Control formulated guidelines for gathering data more accurately, including reporting loss of pregnancy due to rape. There are no published studies using the new criteria.[558]

So where does the misconception come from that many pregnancies are due to rape? Fearful young women will sometimes attribute their pregnancies to rape, since doing so gains sympathy and avoids condemnation. The young woman called "Roe" in the famous *Roe* v. *Wade* case—who elicited sympathy in the court and media because she claimed to be a rape victim—years later admitted that she had lied and that she had not been raped at all.[559]

Prochoice advocates often divert attention from the vast majority of abortions by focusing on rape because of its inherent (and well-deserved) sympathy factor. Their frequent references to rape during discussions of the abortion issue leaves the false impression that pregnancy due to rape is common.

31b. Rape is never the fault of the child; the guilty party, not an innocent party, should be punished.

In those rare cases when a pregnancy is the result of rape, we must be careful who gets the blame. What is hard about this hard case is not whether an innocent child deserves to die for what his father did. What is hard is that an innocent woman has to take on childbearing and possibly mothering—if she decides to keep the child rather than choose adoption—for which she was not willing or ready. This is a very hard situation, calling for family, friends, and church to do all they can to support her. But the fact remains that none of this is the fault of the child.

Why should Person A be killed because Person B raped Person A's mother? If your father committed a crime, should you go to jail for it? If you found out today that your biological father had raped your mother, would you feel you no longer had a right to live?

Biblical law put it this way: "The soul who sins is the one who will die. The son will not share the guilt of the father" (Ezekiel 18:20). And, "Fathers shall not be put to death for their children, nor children put to death for their fathers; each is to die for his own sin" (Deuteronomy 24:16). Civilized people do not put children to death for what their fathers have done. Yet aborting a child conceived by rape is doing that exact thing. He is as innocent of the crime as his mother. Neither she nor he deserves to die.

Rape is so horrible that we easily transfer our horror to the wrong object. We must not impose the ugliness of rape or incest upon either the innocent woman or the innocent child. The woman is not "spoiled goods"—she is not goods at all, but a precious human being with value and dignity that not even the vilest act can take from her. Likewise, the child is not a cancer to be removed, but a living human being. By all means, let's punish the rapist. (I favor stricter punishment of the rapist than do the prochoice advocates I know.) But let's not punish the wrong person by inflicting upon the innocent child our rage against the rapist.

31c. The violence of abortion parallels the violence of rape.

One woman says, "When a woman exercises her right to control her own body in total disregard of the body of another human being, it is called abortion. When a man acts out the same philosophy, it is called rape."[560]

There is a close parallel between the violent attack on an innocent woman that happens in a rape and the violent attack on a innocent child that happens in an abortion. Both are done in response to a subjective and misguided sense of need, and both are done at the expense of an innocent person. The woman might not hate her child the way the rapist might hate his victim, but this is no consolation to the child. Regardless of the motives or disposition of his mother, he is just as brutally killed.

The violence of abortion is no solution to the violence of rape. The killing of the innocent by abortion is no solution to the hurting of the innocent by rape.

31d. Abortion does not bring healing to a rape victim.

Imposing capital punishment on the innocent child of a sex offender does nothing bad to the rapist and nothing good for the woman. Creating a second victim doesn't undue the damage to the first.

In February 2000 presidential candidate Alan Keyes addressed 120 middle school students in Detroit. A thirteen-year-old girl asked if his position on abortion included making an exception for rape. He spoke of the pain of rape, then said, "But I don't believe it is right to take that pain and actually make it worse. And to the burden of that rape down through the years, if that abortion takes place, do you know what I'm adding if I let you have an abortion? I'm adding the burden of that abortion. And at some point, the truth of God that is written on your heart comes back to you. And you're wounded by that truth."[561]

One feminist group says, "Some women have reported suffering from the trauma of abortion long after the rape trauma has faded."[562] It is hard to imagine a worse therapy for a woman who has been raped than to add the guilt and turmoil of having her child killed. Even if we convince ourselves and her that it isn't a real child or even *her* child, some day she will realize that it was. Those who advised abortion will not be there then to help carry her pain and guilt.

I have a dear friend who was raped and became pregnant as a result. Because of her circumstances, it wasn't best for her to raise the child, but she gave birth, and the baby was adopted into a wonderful Christian family. She periodically has contact with them and her child.

It has not been an easy road, and I would say nothing to minimize her pain. The hardest part is not being able to raise her child, not hearing the footsteps in her home. Yet there is a bittersweet joy—the joy of knowing that God brought this beautiful little girl into the world through her and brought an immense happiness to the family who adopted her baby.

When I look at my friend, I find great comfort in knowing how she has brought joy to our Father in heaven, who has been pleased by her decisions and has brought character and beauty and life out of her suffering. Hers is not the suffering that comes with regret over having done the wrong thing to an innocent child. It is a suffering accompanied by the hand of God who comforts and sustains her and brings present waves of joy and contentment that are a foretaste of the fullness of joy in the heaven to come. But even now, the wonder she knows when she sees this delightful child overshadows the suffering she has gone through.

Francine Rivers's novel, *The Atonement Child*, deals with this subject in a powerful way.

31e. A child is a child regardless of the circumstances of his conception.

On a television program about abortion, I heard a man argue, "Anything of this nature has no rights because it's the product of rape." But how is the nature of this preborn child different from that of any other preborn child? Are some children more worthy of living because their fathers were better people? And why is it that prochoice advocates are always saying that the unborn child is really the mother's, not the father's, until she is raped—then suddenly the child is viewed as the father's, not the mother's?

A child conceived by rape is as precious as a child conceived by love, because a child is a child. The point is not *how* he was conceived but *that* he was conceived. He is not a despicable "product of rape," but a unique and wonderful creation of God.

Women often think that a child conceived by such a vile act will be a constant reminder of their pain. On the contrary, the innocence of the child often has a healing effect. But in any case, the woman is free to give up the child for adoption, which may be the best alternative. Aborting the child is an attempt to deny what happened, and denial is never good therapy.

One woman told me, "A baby is the only beautiful thing that can come out of a rape." Having and holding an innocent child can do much more good for a victimized woman than the knowledge that an innocent child died in an attempt to deny or reduce her trauma.

31f. What about already-born people who are "products of rape"?

What if you found that your spouse or adopted child was fathered by a rapist? Would it change your view of their worth? Would you love them any less? If not, why should we view the innocent unborn child any differently?

After I shared similar thoughts in a lecture, a dear woman in her midtwenties came up to me in tears. I'll never forget what she said:

> Thank you. I've never heard anyone say that a child conceived by rape deserved to live. My mother was raped when she was twelve years old. She gave birth to me and gave me up for adoption to a wonderful family. I'll probably never meet her, but every day I thank God for her and her parents. If they hadn't let me live, I wouldn't be here to have my own husband and children and my own life. I'm just so thankful to be alive.

Singer Ethel Waters was conceived after her twelve-year-old mother was raped. Waters touched millions through her life and music. Many other people, perhaps some of our dearest friends whose stories we'll never know, are what some disdainfully call "the product of rape."

31g. All that is true of children conceived in rape is true of those conceived in incest.

Incest is a horrible crime. Offenders should be punished, and young girls should be carefully protected from further abuse. Decisive personal and legal intervention should be taken to remove a girl from the presence of a relative who has sexually abused her. The abuser—not the girl or her child—is the problem. Intervention, protection, and ongoing personal help for the girl—not the death of an innocent child—is the solution. Despite popular beliefs, fetal deformity is rare in such cases. Even if the child has handicaps, however, he still deserves to live.

Final Thoughts on the Hard Cases

---

1. No adverse circumstance for one human being changes the nature and worth of another human being.

The hard cases are also sometimes called the exceptional cases. But the fundamental question remains, "Is there any exception to the fact that a preborn child is a human being?" As we demonstrated in the responses to arguments 1 through 8, the scientific facts and commonsense evidence conclusively demonstrate that the answer to this question is *no*. What is exceptional is the difficult situation of the mother, not the nature of the child.

Compassion for the mother is extremely important, but is never served through destroying the innocent. One person must not be killed under the guise of compassion for another. An alternative must be sought that is compassionate to both mother and child. Furthermore, true compassion to the mother considers her psychological well-being, which is not served by abortion. Instead of encouraging her to kill her child, we should do something that requires much more compassion and sacrifice. We should offer tangible support and sacrificial help.

Giving up the child for adoption to eagerly waiting families is often the answer in cases where the mother is too young and immature. The same is true if the baby's handicap is so great that it takes a special person to raise him. (But willing parents often find they become just such special people.)

In cases of rape and incest, family and friends need to offer compassionate support and help find counseling that can assist in personal healing. Society needs to protect the innocent by stiffer sentences and enforced restraining orders for sex offenders. Exposing the woman to further abuse is unjustifiable. So is making an unborn child the scapegoat for a crime he or she didn't commit.

2. Laws must not be built on exceptional cases.

Research shows that only 1 to 3 percent of abortions are performed for the reasons of rape, incest, deformity, or threat to the life of the mother.[563] If a building is burning, it is permissible for someone to break in to save lives or property. However, recognizing the legitimacy of this exception does not mean that we shouldn't have laws against the usual cases of forcible entry and trespassing. That an exception may exist does not invalidate the normal standard of behavior.

Suppose you disagree with my firm conviction that a handicapped child or a child conceived by rape or incest deserves to live and should be protected by law just like every other child. Nevertheless, surely you must recognize that even if there *were* legitimate grounds for abortion in the exceptional cases, it would in no way justify legal abortion for the vast majority of cases, which are matters of personal and economic convenience. These cases account for over 97 percent of abortions, while the "hard cases" account for less than 3 percent. (Of course, the deaths of those 3 percent are equally tragic.)

Some believe that laws restricting convenience abortions could go a long way in protecting the lives of 1.5 million innocent children each year in America alone. Others believe that legislation allowing exceptions for rape and deformity are an unjustifiable compromise and would be badly abused, encouraging false claims to cover convenience abortions. In any case we must seek to find ways—personal, educational, and political—to save as many innocent lives as possible.

Part Six

❧

Arguments Against

The Character
of Prolifers

Even if it were true that prolifers are undesirable and offensive people, this is not a logical argument against their position. Tiresome and offensive people can be right, just as winsome and likeable people can be wrong. This cuts both ways—a bothersome prochoice advocate is not automatically wrong, any more than a warm sympathetic prochoice person is automatically right. Truth should be determined by an objective evaluation of the evidence, not on the basis of personality or likability.

32. "Antiabortionists are so cruel that they insist on showing hideous pictures of dead babies."

32a. What is hideous is not the pictures themselves, but the reality they depict.

Pictures of aborted babies are not invented by prolifers. Anyone who thinks they are is simply ignorant of the medical facts about the development of the unborn and the nature of abortion procedures. The pictures are authentic. What people object to is their content. No one wants to look at dead babies. Feminist Naomi Wolf acknowledges:

To many prochoice advocates, the imagery is revolting propaganda. There is a sense among us, let us be frank, that the gruesomeness of the imagery *belongs* to the prolifers: that it emerges from the dark, frightening minds of fanatics: that it represents the violence of imaginations that would, given half a chance, turn our world into a scary, repressive place. "People like us" see such material as the pornography of the prolife movement.

But feminism at its best is based on what is simply true. While prolifers have not been beyond dishonesty, distortion and the doctoring of images (preferring, for example, to highlight the results of very late, very rare abortions), many of those photographs are in fact photographs of actual D & Cs; those footprints are in fact the footprints of a 10-week-old fetus; the prolife slogan, "Abortion stops a beating heart," is incontrovertibly true. While images of violent fetal death work magnificently for prolifers as political polemic, the pictures are not polemical in themselves: they are biological facts. We know this.[564]

When a prolife candidate ran television ads showing aborted babies, people were outraged. A reporter on the *CBS Evening News* declared that the abortion debate had reached a "new low in tastelessness." I found it fascinating that there was no outrage that babies were being killed, only that someone had the audacity to *show* they were being killed. This was a classic case of "shooting the messenger"—attacking the one who points out an evil as if he were responsible for doing it.

What is it that makes a picture beautiful or hideous? Not the picture itself but what is *in* the picture. The pictures document that babies are being killed. Proabortionists are against the pictures of killed babies. Prolifers are against the killing of the babies in the pictures.

The question we should ask is not "Why are these people showing these pictures?" but "Why would anyone defend as legitimate what is shown in these pictures?" When a prochoice person looks at the pictures and says, "This is sick; it's horrible," the prolifer responds, "Exactly. That's why we are opposed to doing such a horribly sick thing to a baby."

A radio talk show host expressed outrage that this book, *ProLife Answers*, is "filled" with "horrible " pictures of aborted babies. (In fact, it contains three pictures of live preborn babies, three of miscarried babies, and only two of aborted babies.) I asked her "Why are you angry at me? Who do you think killed these babies? Me?" Her reply was revealing: "No, I guess it was the doctor." In other words, it was someone holding the host's own prochoice position, one of those doctors she considered heroic, who did the killing she described as "horrible."

32b. Pictures challenge our denial of the horrors of abortion. If something is too horrible to look at, perhaps it is too horrible to condone.

Some prolifers choose to show pictures of the developing child and rarely or never show pictures of aborted babies. Others believe that the pictures of aborted babies are essential to wake up society to the reality of butchered children. The Holocaust was something so evil that words alone could not describe it. The descriptions of Nazi death camps had long been fed to western newspapers. But it was the pictures of slaughtered people that communicated the reality of what was happening.

Most of us would neither understand nor believe the extent of the Holocaust were it not for the pictures.

The solution to the Holocaust was not to ban the disgusting pictures of the death camps. The only solution was to end the killing. Similarly, the solution to our current situation is not to get rid of the pictures of dead babies. The solution is to end what is making the babies dead. Like the Holocaust, abortion is an evil so great that words fall short of describing it. Prolife people hope that showing pictures of aborted babies will help end the killing.

Gregg Cunningham, director of the Center for Bio-Ethical Reform, argues for the vital need to show pictures of aborted babies: "Pictures state the hideous truth so forcefully that lies and deception are robbed of their power to distort reality. Words alone will never change the way a person feels about abortion when they are in denial; and most Americans are deeply in denial over this issue."[565]

Cunningham spearheaded the Genocide Awareness Project (GAP), a remarkable visual display of aborted babies alongside the victims of the Nazi death camps, the Killing Fields, American slavery, and other historical atrocities. The GAP project has gone to twenty-three university campuses in ten different states. The stated purpose of GAP is "to make it as difficult as possible for people to continue to maintain that an unborn baby is not a baby and abortion is not an act of violence which kills that baby."[566] By placing abortion images alongside traditionally recognized forms of genocide, they have attempted to expand the context in which people think about abortion. Signs with warnings concerning the graphic photographs are posted clearly where people approach the display, so all those who look do so by choice. Staff members are there to interact with students, answer questions, and engage in dialogue.

I went to a college campus to observe this display and witnessed the profound effect on students and faculty, including many who did not want to deal with the issue. But even by choosing to look away, they were forced, if just for a few seconds, to come to terms with why they would not want to look.

Eleven babies lives were confirmed saved as a direct result of this project. This doesn't account for all those not reported and those saved from future abortion decisions. According to a report written by a Kent State University professor, in the four months following the GAP project at the University of Akron, three of the six Crisis Pregnancy Centers in the Akron area reported an increase in traffic over the same period in the previous year. One Crisis Pregnancy Center near Penn State reported a 60 percent increase in traffic in the four to five months following the project.[567]

On some university campuses, students have gathered to hold up sheets and other barriers to keep students from looking at the pictures. This causes thoughtful students to ask, "Why are people who call themselves prochoice not allowing us to see what's behind those sheets? Why are they not allowing us to make our own choice about what we will look at? What is it about these pictures that could possibly compel people to so aggressively censor them?"

The answer to these questions is simple: If people actually looked at these pictures and allowed the truth to settle in, it would essentially end the debate about abortion. Once you see that abortion is nothing but the killing of children, it is impossible for most people—though unfortunately not for all—to imagine they are assuming the moral high ground in defending it.

32c. Nothing could be more relevant to the discussion of something than that which shows what it really is.

I was on a television program where prochoice and prolife advocates were discussing abortion. After we'd been talking a few minutes, one of the prolifers tried to illustrate his point by showing a picture of an aborted baby. As soon as he did, there were audible gasps, people started waving their arms, and the prochoice activist next to me cried out, "God, don't let them show that." The cameras turned quickly away, and there was momentary panic and confusion in the studio.

Had the issue not been so serious, the response would have been humorous. The picture was no more gruesome than pictures of Holocaust victims that appear in countless documentaries. And it was just as authentic. It simply showed what abortion is and what is left of the unborn baby afterward. What could be a more relevant piece of evidence when discussing abortion than a picture of an abortion?

I received a phone call from a college professor who was invited to participate in a debate in which he would defend the prolife position and a colleague the prochoice position. The only stipulation was this: "Neither side can show any pictures." It sounded very fair to the professor who called me, who hadn't publicly addressed the issue before. "After all," he said, "both sides have to abide by the same rule." My question was, "What pictures would someone taking the prochoice position *want* to show?"

Imagine a debate about whether the Holocaust really happened. The Holocaust believer and the Holocaust denier are both given the same rule: "Neither of you can show pictures." The result of this is that one side is deprived of what may be its most persuasive proof, while the other side is spared from having to explain away pictures that would cut through the fog of his Holocaust denial.

Anyone who has participated in debates about abortion knows that it's very typical to be told you cannot exercise a free choice to show pictures of aborted babies. (I've even been told that I couldn't show live intrauterine photographs of the unborn—as if people shouldn't be burdened with factual information that could complicate their decision!) This attempt at censorship is never reciprocated; I would never dream of attempting to censor my opponent's presentation. Prolife advocates invite their opponents to present their best case and ask only that they be allowed to do the same. When one side in a debate insists on not allowing the other side to present critical evidence, what does it suggest about their interest in the truth or in letting the audience choose for themselves? What does it suggest about the weakness of their position?

Banning such pictures from the abortion debate is like banning x-rays of smoke-damaged lungs from the smoking debate or saying that we cannot show pictures of harpooned whales or clubbed seals when discussing animal rights. If the fetus is simply a lump of tissue, then fine—let the public see the pictures of the lump of tissue. Let them be treated like adults and allowed to choose for themselves what they believe. If this is not a baby, what could be the harm in looking at the pictures? The truth will surely serve the position that is true.

The success of the prochoice position is dependent on the public's denial that abortion kills children. The pictures are a devastating challenge to this denial. Yet the denial itself has become an accepted part of not just public opinion, but of medical practice. Consider this advice in a national publication for obstetricians and gynecologists:

> Sonography in connection with induced abortion may have psychological hazards. Seeing a blown-up, moving image of the embryo she is carrying can be distressing to a woman who is about to undergo an abortion, Dr. Dorfman noted. She stressed that the screen should be turned away from the patient.[568]

The doctor's job is to not allow the woman to see the truth, thereby perpetuating the fiction that this is not a baby. This is the extent of our social commitment to denial. This denial is so extreme and widespread that the prolife movement has no choice but to continue to point to the pictures of unborn babies, both dead and alive, even though those in the deepest denial will be outraged.

32d. It is the prochoice position, not the prolife position, that is cruel.

The prochoice position has made it open season on the unborn, and the result has been cruelty beyond imagination. The saline abortion, which is agonizingly painful to the child and emotionally devastating to the mother, was originally developed in the concentration camps of Nazi Germany.[569] That alone should tell us something. (See photograph #5 at the center of this book.)

Live fetuses have been subjected to grisly experiments—bodies have been dissected, chests sliced open to observe heart action, heads cut off for bizarre purposes.[570] In Arizona, the E. R. Squibb Drug Company offered $10,000 to fourteen pregnant women if they would take a certain drug before having abortions and let their baby's blood be tested after they were killed.[571] Babies have been conceived and aborted for the purpose of using their cells to treat adults with diabetes, Alzheimer's, and Parkinson's disease.[572]

Though nine out of ten Americans support a ban on abortion for purposes of choosing a preferred gender, Planned Parenthood and other prochoice groups favor keeping sex selection abortions legal.[573] How can anyone defend such cruelty to young females?

Gianna Jessen's biological mother had a saline abortion in a Southern California abortion clinic. Gianna was severely burned and traumatized, but managed to survive.[574] Babies surviving abortions—estimated at more than five hundred a year—are typically suffocated, drowned, or left to die of exposure. But someone had mercy on Gianna and smuggled her out to a nearby hospital. Her medical records read, "Saline Abortion Survivor."

Gianna was adopted by a caring prolife family. As a result of her abortion trauma she suffers from cerebral palsy. She is now a vivacious young woman and a gifted singer. She is also an articulate prolife spokesperson who speaks with an authority like that of survivors of the Nazi Holocaust. Gianna Jessen has been affected by both sides in the abortion debate. Ask *her* which side is the cruel one.

Aborted babies are dumped into plastic bags for disposal, yet it is fashionable to be more concerned whether the plastic sacks are recyclable than to be concerned about the lives of the babies. The killing of 100,000 dolphins is an "ecological holocaust," while the killing of thirteen times that many babies every year is an accepted way of life.

Isn't it ironic that those who endorse this killing label those who oppose it as "cruel"?

In 1999 an Illinois nurse blew the whistle on "Christ," a Chicago-area hospital where, she claims, abortions are being performed in which "problem" infants are born—and then just left to die. Jill Stanek is a labor and delivery nurse at Christ Hospital, located in the Chicago suburb of Oak Lawn. She says the "therapeutic abortion" procedure involves inducing premature births of babies with deformities, including Down syndrome and spina bifida:

> "The babies are fully delivered, often resulting in live births, and then die outside the mother's body. Attending medical personnel do not provide life support, and the babies oftentimes die in the arms of nurses.... When a nurse or parent isn't holding one of these babies, often they're put in a soiled utility room. They're left there to die alone," the nurse said. The procedures—called "medically indicated pregnancy terminations"—are done at Christ Hospital between 10 and 20 times a year, hospital spokeswoman Sue Reimbold said. They are performed between the 16th and 23rd weeks of pregnancy.[575]

It's hard to fathom this level of prochoice cruelty toward precious children. We need not speculate as to what the person who this hospital was named after thinks about this practice.

---

33. "Prolifers don't care about women, and they don't care about babies once they're born. They have no right to speak against abortion unless they are willing to care for these children."

A publication of the National Abortion Rights Action League states, "The 'prolife' concerns of abortion foes are only for fetal lives, not the lives of women or unwanted babies."[576]

33a. Prolifers are actively involved in caring for women in crisis pregnancies and difficult child-raising situations.

A "Dear Abby" letter, signed "Hates Hypocrites," angrily challenges people opposing abortion: "Why aren't you volunteering to baby-sit a child born to a single mother so she can work? Why haven't you opened your door to a pregnant teenager whose parents have kicked her out when she took your advice and decided not to have an abortion?" The writer rails against prolifers, calling them hypocrites. Abby responds, "I couldn't have said it better."[577]

This approach has two basic flaws. First, it is possible to point out an injustice even when one does not provide the solution. People could say slavery was wrong even if they did not open their homes to a slave. A man can say it is wrong for his neighbor to beat his wife, even if he isn't in a position to give her a home. If a woman chooses not to volunteer to adopt her neighbor's three children, does this disqualify her from saying she thinks it would be wrong for her neighbor to kill them?

Francis Beckwith comments on this common but rather bizarre line of pro-choice argumentation:

> This bit of rhetoric can be distilled into the following assertion: unless the prolifer is willing to help bring up the children he does not want aborted, he has no right to prevent a woman from having an abortion. As a principle of moral action, this seems to be a rather bizarre assertion. Think of all the unusual precepts that would result: unless I am willing to marry my neighbor's wife, I cannot prevent her husband from beating her; unless I am willing to adopt my neighbor's daughter, I cannot prevent her mother from abusing her; unless I am willing to hire ex-slaves for my business, I cannot say that the slave owner should not own slaves. By illegitimately shifting the discussion from the morality of abortion to whether one has a "solution" to certain social problems, the abortion-rights advocate avoids the point under question. Although a clever move, it has nothing to do with whether or not abortion results in the death of human beings who have a full right to life or whether or not abortion is immoral.[578]

I do agree, however, that people who point out injustices should seek to be part of the solution. This raises the second and most important flaw in the argument of the one writing to Abby: No evidence whatsoever is offered for the damning assumption made, which Abby buys into as well. Who says prolifers are not doing the things they are assumed not to be doing? The truth is, they are!

In virtually every part of the United States there are abortion alternative centers that provide free pregnancy tests, free counseling, and free material and human resources to pregnant women. There are more prolife help-giving centers, well over three thousand of them, than there are prolife education and political action centers.[579] Most of these centers have dozens of volunteers, some of them hundreds, donating not only time spent with clients, but everything from clothing to maintenance to service to office supplies and computer support. I have served on the board of one such center, on the steering committee to get another started, and have visited dozens of them across the country. Though their services cost them a great deal of money—as opposed to making them a great deal of money— there are more abortion alternative centers in the United States than there are abortion clinics.[580]

Since these clinics draw business away from abortion clinics, they have come under fire from the prochoice movement and its representatives in the media.[581] When a U.S. House committee, chaired by Oregon's Ron Wyden, investigated so-called "fake" abortion clinics, its members did not allow a single prolife representative from any of the centers in question to testify. Had they done so, they would have found that the great majority of Pregnancy Resource Centers require that their clinics advertise themselves as offering "Abortion Alternatives" and train their workers to give accurate medical information.[582]

Throughout 1999 abortion advocates launched a fresh barrage of attacks on pregnancy centers. According to *World* magazine, this was triggered when word got out that a California Crisis Pregnancy Center network had established a system of referrals with HMO giant Kaiser-Permanente. Fearing this could start a dangerous trend, the National Abortion Rights Action League (NARAL) posted on its web site a document titled "Deceptive Anti-Abortion Crisis Pregnancy Centers."

It cites Planned Parenthood materials that refer to the tactics in the mid-eighties of a small group of pregnancy centers, unaffiliated with the vast majority of pregnancy clinics. Planned Parenthood "crafted a far-ranging media campaign that painted all CPCs as deceptive, anti-choice terrorist cells populated by religious extremists." The attack worked for a while and "left CPCs reeling in a backlash of negative public opinion."[583]

Congressional hearings, court battles, and new advertising regulations forced those few prolife clinics using deceptive measures to change their methods. But NARAL keeps bringing up charges from the past as if they were current or representative of pregnancy resource centers. In fact, Planned Parenthood web sites still have pages devoted to "The Deceptive Practices of Crisis Pregnancy Centers,"[584] when in fact "Crisis Pregnancy Centers" is the name historically used for the clinics under CareNet,[585] which has always required its clinics to be aboveboard in their advertising and counseling. Attempts by Planned Parenthood to discredit abortion alternative centers suggests that they do not want women to have the alternative information or services offered by those centers. They simply want them to have abortions.

A Planned Parenthood web site says,

> In their zeal to stop women from having abortions, anti-abortion activists have set up "counseling centers" in hundreds of communities around the country. Far from true counseling, these centers are designed to misinform and intimidate women; some will go to any lengths necessary to dissuade women from ending their pregnancies.
>
> Increasingly, women complain about their unwitting encounters with anti-abortion centers. Women describe being harassed, intimidated, and given blatantly false information. They complain that confidential information they provided was used against them. In some cases, they describe instances of medical malpractice which threatened their lives.[586]

The Brooklyn Prochoice Network's web site has much to say about "fake clinics," including,

> Phony clinics perform *no* medical services. Their entire purpose is to lure in women and bombard them with antiabortion propaganda. Most fake clinics have no doctors or other medical staff. A woman who visits one of these phony facilities is merely given a home pregnancy test of the kind available in drug stores, then told to wait for her results. While she waits, she is shown graphic, medically inaccurate antiabortion videos.[587]

I have seen firsthand the provision of free prenatal care, free clothing, baby clothes, furnishings, and other help to needy women. Prolife families give free room and board as well as love and support to women who need it. Often prolife doctors volunteer no-cost medical help, and prolife lawyers donate legal aid to help with adoptions when this is the woman's choice. When women choose to keep their children, single mother support groups and child care are offered. Like tens of thousands of prolife families, my family opened our home to a pregnant teenage girl and helped her financially and legally. The royalties from this book and others are partly used to help such women in need.

I believe prolifers can and should do more and more to help women in crisis pregnancies. But what they are already doing, free of charge, is substantial. It amounts to what may be the single largest volunteer effort in our nation's history and certainly one of the most effective. While there are hypocrites in any group, to label prolifers in general as hypocrites is a position unsupported by the facts.

33b. Prolifers are actively involved in caring for unwanted children and the other "disposable people" in society.

When I was on a radio talk show one irate caller asked, "Once you people 'save the lives of the unborn,' where are you for the next eighteen years?" I said, "At this very moment, one of my prolife friends is picking up his eighteenth adopted child, a hard-to-place handicapped minority. Three of his other adopted children have Down syndrome." I told of many prolife families waiting to adopt and many others involved in foster care with "drug babies" and other children with special needs. The claim that prolife people don't help with unwanted children makes inflammatory rhetoric, but it is simply false.

Many prolifers are also on the cutting edge of care for the poor, elderly, and handicapped. There are hundreds of organizations across the country that specialize in helping such people. The organization I am part of is committed not only to meeting spiritual needs, but to feeding the hungry and providing education and resources for the poor. Helping women and children who are victims of abortion is only one aspect of our focus on helping people.

33c. It is abortion providers who do not provide support for women choosing anything other than abortion.

When you hear abortion providers talk about the help they offer women, ask them: "If a fifteen-year-old girl comes into your clinic with no money, no one to help her, no home to go to, and no desire to have an abortion, what services does your facility provide for her?"[588] The answer is always the same—none. Abortion advocates don't offer help. They offer only abortion, and then only to those who can pay their price. Many former abortion providers have come forward to tell their stories and admit to their patterns of indifference, materialism, and deceit.[589]

I challenge anyone to do his or her research and find out who is doing the most, at the lowest cost and in the most caring way, to help pregnant women. If you don't just listen to what both sides say about the other, but actually investigate what both sides are doing, I don't have the slightest doubt what you will discover.

34. "The antiabortionists are a bunch of men telling women what to do."

34a. There is no substantial difference between men and women's views of abortion.

In 1999 the Gallup News Service reported,

> The latest Gallup poll finds few gender differences in public opinion or voting behavior on [abortion]. There is no significant difference in the percentage of men and women identifying with the two abortion labels. The prochoice label is preferred by a plurality of both groups, including 49% of women and 47% of men. The percentage calling themselves prolife is also very similar: 42% among women and 43% among men.
>
> In terms of their specific views about the legality of abortion, women tend to be slightly more liberal, with 41% of women compared to 35% of men saying abortion should be legal under all or most circumstances. However, the majority of both groups favor the more conservative set of positions, with 57% of women and 60% of men saying abortion should be restricted to few or no circumstances.
>
> While their basic attitudes toward abortion are similar, women do express somewhat greater intensity about the issue than do men. Overall, 60% of women—compared with 47% of men—say they feel very

strongly about their abortion views. (Interestingly, women are equally divided—at 30% each—between those who are very strongly prochoice and those who are very strongly prolife.) However, women are only slightly more likely than are men—21% versus 17%—to say they would vote only for candidates who share their views on the issue.[590]

34b. Some polls suggest that more women than men oppose abortion.

A poll conducted by the University of Cincinnati indicated that 59 percent of women opposed abortion, while only 46 percent of men opposed it.[591] A *New York Times* poll found that 67 percent of women agreed that America "continues to need a strong women's movement to push for changes that benefit women."[592] Significantly, about half of this same group of women favored stricter limitations on abortions.

A Gallup poll asked, "At what point in the pregnancy do you personally feel that the unborn child's right to be born outweighs the woman's right to choose whether she wants to have a child?" 52.6 percent of women and 47.3 percent of men answered "conception." Only 5.5 percent of women compared to 9.6 percent of men answered "birth."[593] More women than men affirmed the rights of unborn children.

According to the polls, "the most pro-abortion category in the United States (and also in other nations) is white males between the ages of twenty and forty-five."[594] More specifically, "the group that is most consistently prochoice is actually single men."[595]

34c. The great majority of prolife workers are women.

The largest prolife affiliation in America is National Right to Life. Nearly two-thirds of Right to Life's members are women.[596] Nine out of ten volunteers at Birthright, another large prolife organization, are women. The national office of CareNet, a network of Pregnancy Resource Centers, estimates that 80 to 90 percent of their workers are women. Of the Right to Life delegates elected by each of the fifty states and the District of Columbia, thirty-eight were women, and only thirteen were men.[597]

At prolife gatherings I have attended and spoken at, typically there are many more women than men, often twice as many. My experience is confirmed by the past president of National Right to Life, who says, "Look at who is at prolife rallies.

You will find the composition of the crowd is consistently better than 2 to 1 women, with a heavy sprinkling of young people and some children."[598]

34d. If men are disqualified from the abortion issue, they should be disqualified on both sides.

It is common for men to pressure women into abortion. The vast majority of doctors who perform abortions are men, as are most prochoice congressmen. Why do prochoice advocates continuously quote from Dr. Alan Guttmacher and other male authorities? Why do they embrace the judgment of the all-male Supreme Court that legalized abortion in 1973? And why do prochoice groups donate sizable campaign funds to male legislators who endorse abortion? If men should be eliminated from the abortion debate, shouldn't they be eliminated from both sides?

34e. Men are entitled to take a position on abortion.

Abolitionist Samuel May once said to feminist Susan B. Anthony that because she was single she had no business talking about the institution of marriage. Anthony pointed out that the same logic demanded that May should quit speaking about slavery since he had never been a slave.[599] Should stock brokers and investors be the only ones allowed to discuss stock market ethics? Should debates about war be restricted to those in the military?

Abortion is a human issue, not a gender issue. Facts, logic, reason, and compassion have no anatomy. Whether they are espoused by men or women is no more relevant than whether they are espoused by black or white. The point is not the gender of those advancing arguments, but whether or not the arguments are accurate. To believe otherwise is simply sexism.

34f. There are many more women in prolife organizations than there are in proabortion organizations.

In 1992, the National Women's Coalition for Life made its debut in Washington, D.C.[600] Its membership was an impressive 1.3 million women, far bigger than N.O.W. and the National Abortion Rights Action League, with no abortion advocacy group anywhere near its size. The coalition consisted only of prolife women's groups; it didn't include organizations such as National Right to Life, which are made up of both women and men.

Despite the fact that many more women belong to prolife groups than to proabortion ones, when the media wish to hear someone speak up for American women, they routinely approach women in prochoice organizations, not prolife organizations. This appears to say something about women, but in fact it simply says something about the media.

34g. Of women who have had abortions, far more are prolife activists than prochoice activists.

The arguments against male involvement in prolife activities are often based on the idea that only those who have had abortions can know firsthand how important it is to have abortion rights. Leaving men completely out of the picture, then, which movement has more women who have had abortions—the prochoice movement or the prolife movement?

An article in Planned Parenthood's *Family Planning Perspectives* gives the results of sociologist Donald Granberg's study of the nation's two largest groups supporting and opposing abortion.[601] Of National Right to Life's female membership of 7.5 million members, about 245,000 have had abortions. Of NARAL's 125,000 women about 39,000 have had abortions.[602] While the percentage of women who have had abortions in NARAL is, as you would expect, much higher than in National Right to Life, it is not the percentages, but the total numbers that tell the story. Planned Parenthood's figures suggest that *women who have had abortions are six times more likely to be prolife activists than prochoice activists.*

35. "Antiabortionists talk about the sanctity of human life, yet they favor capital punishment."

A prochoice newspaper claims, "Almost all legislators who oppose abortion rights also support the death penalty. One might ask if they think people who are convicted of murder are no longer human.[603]

35a. Not all prolifers favor capital punishment.

Prolifers are a diverse constituency with a wide variety of personal and political convictions. In fact, many prolife leaders oppose capital punishment.[604] Many others, no doubt, favor it.

35b. Capital punishment is rooted in a respect for innocent human life.

History's earliest argument for capital punishment is found in the Bible (Genesis 9:5–6). Capital punishment was to be imposed in cases of premeditated murder. The rationale is simple: Human life, which is made in God's image, is so highly valued that if a person deliberately takes such a life, he forfeits his own right to live. Justice demands that the murderer receives the ultimate punishment.

Capital punishment is prolife in that it affirms the value of innocent human lives. Furthermore, it assures protection for the lives of other innocent people. Those who claim that capital punishment is not a deterrent to crime forget that those who are executed for murder do not reenter society to murder again.

I believe that it isn't inconsistent to oppose abortion and to favor capital punishment. Both positions affirm the sanctity of human life created in the image of God. However, even if you oppose capital punishment and believe prolifers are inconsistent to favor it, it's not logical to conclude that those who favor putting murderers to death must therefore be wrong if they say unborn children should not be put to death.

35c. There is a vast difference between punishing a convicted murderer and killing an innocent child.

It is twisted logic to say that if one believes that innocent children should not be put to death, he is a hypocrite to believe that a convicted murderer should be put to death. Unlike the murderer, the child has committed no crime, no jury has found him guilty, and he is not being executed by the state. He is innocent and is being put to death by a private and subjective decision.

The real inconsistency lies with many prochoice advocates. They oppose the death penalty for men who rape, torture, and murder women and children, yet support the killing of innocent unborn children.

Capital punishment and abortion are radically different issues. That these differences are not obvious to many prochoice advocates raises the question of whether they are thinking clearly about moral issues.

36. "Antiabortion fanatics break the law, are violent, and bomb abortion clinics."

In April 2000, while the Supreme Court deliberated, prolife demonstrators gathered outside. They had applied for and received permits months in advance, allowing them to show their signs and stand in peaceful protest in front of the Supreme Court building. They were informed that despite their permits, they would no longer be able to hold their signs. Many people were arrested for this, including a number in their early twenties. They spent ten hours in jail, then faced a $1000 fine and/or six months in jail.[605]

While the rescue movement has been largely curtailed since the mid-1990s—when the FACE (Freedom to Access Clinic Entrance) bill made peaceful civil disobedience at abortion clinics a felony—many prolifers each year are engaged in civil disobedience to draw attention to the plight of the unborn and the unequal treatment of people under the law.

Under FACE a person would have to use force or threat of force or physical obstruction to injure, intimidate, or interfere with a person who is seeking or providing reproductive health services. In defending FACE, the attorneys for the National Organization for Women redefined terms to condemn peaceful prolife protesters. Although they claimed that they were only objecting to physical blockades of abortion clinics, the definitions both they and their witnesses used have been applied to sidewalk counselors and to prayer teams in front of abortion facilities.[606]

While the incidents of picketing declined slightly, 1999 was still the second highest year for picketing after 1998. Incidents of picketing (the vast majority of which are peaceful) have steadily increased throughout the years from hundreds per year throughout the 1980s to thousands per year by the end of the 1990s.[607]

36a. Media coverage of prolife civil disobedience often bears little resemblance to what actually happens.

The proabortion bias of the media is well documented, but it has never been more blatant than in its coverage of prolife rescues over the period of 1988 to 1995. The media's opposition to the prolife position, coupled with extreme resentment at any

255

interference with someone's free choice, resulted in subjective and selective reporting. (Though civil disobedience at abortion clinics is rarer now, it still happens. The public's impressions of prolifers were deeply affected through media coverage of the rescue movement.)

After attending and observing the peaceful behavior of the participants in a prolife rescue, my daughters were shocked to read the account in the next day's newspaper that described the rescue as "violent." They had a clear view of the events and had not seen anything remotely violent. The newspaper was full of inaccuracies, leading my then ten-year-old to ask through tears, "Daddy, how can they lie like that?" Unfortunately, most Americans have never been to an abortion clinic to see the behavior of prolifers firsthand and so are wholly dependent on the media for their impressions.

A classic example of such media distortions was the coverage of the Wichita rescues in the summer of 1991.[608] After ignoring the situation for the first week, the media consistently distorted the nature of the events. They spoke of "violence," while those present said there was no violence. They said that the protesters were unwelcome by the citizens of Wichita, but did not mention that some local hotels, restaurants, and other businesses provided free or low-cost services for these protesters because they believed in what they were doing. They falsely stated that most of the protesters were from out of town, when the majority was from Wichita itself.

The Associated Press printed a story that was picked up by many newspapers, including *USA Today,* which said, "Prosecutors are weighing charges against a man, 36, suspected of beating his three kids with a board because they refused to wear red ribbons in support of abortion foes."[609] Yet the district attorney's office in Wichita, which was never contacted for confirmation, said this report was "erroneous."[610] But the 6.6 million readers of *USA Today,* outraged that anyone would do such a thing, will never know that, in fact, no one did.

Newspapers around the world printed another Associated Press report quoting a proabortion spokesperson: "Who could have ever assumed that people would push two-year-old children in front of moving vehicles? To use children like that is just so appalling." It *would* have indeed been appalling, but it never happened. This report was also totally false.[611] Furthermore, AP failed to mention that the woman who made this claim was an employee of the abortionist whose clinic the protesters were surrounding. When asked why he didn't check to see if the charge was true, the reporter said he was under a deadline and didn't have time.[612] There was no retraction.

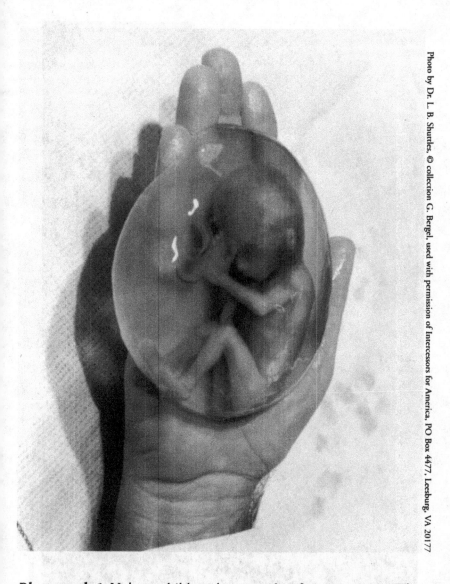

Photograph 1: Unborn child at eleven weeks after conception. This miscarried baby, still in its amniotic sac, is held in a doctor's hand. The heart was beating since three weeks, brain waves measurable since six weeks.

Photograph 2: Feet of miscarried child at ten weeks after conception. Note the perfectly formed toes, weeks before the end of the first trimester of pregnancy.

Dr. Russell Sacco, Portland, OR

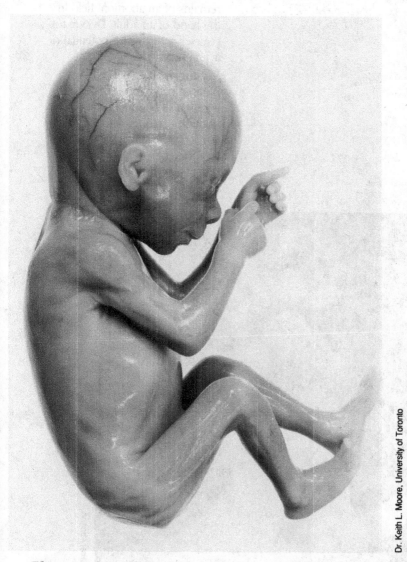

Dr. Keith L. Moore, University of Toronto

Photograph 3: Unborn child at seventeen weeks after conception. This is early in the second trimester.

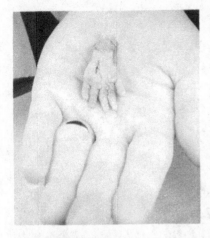

Photograph 4 (left): A hand taken from the discarded remains of an abortion, held in the hand of an adult. Decide for yourself if this was a potential or actual human life.

Photograph 5 (below): A preborn baby killed by saline abortion. A poisonous salt solution is injected into the amniotic sac, killing the child over a process of several hours, then bringing on the mother's labor and delivery of the dead baby.

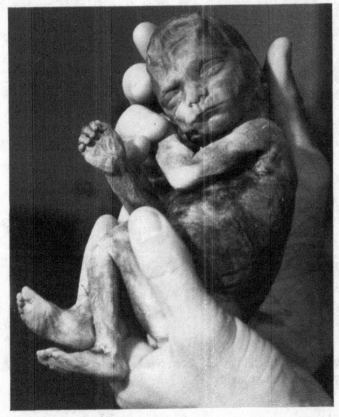

Some news sources did not report a rally of thirty thousand people, mostly Wichitans, who gathered to support the prolife efforts. Thousands of peaceful protesters were arrested, again most of them locals. The protesters had the support of many community leaders. Even the governor of Kansas, Joan Finney, said, "It is the character and courage of our state which is at risk. We shall not achieve the ideals for which this state is founded as long as Kansas turns its back on the powerless, the helpless, the unborn."[613] Most Americans didn't hear this quote, but instead heard from proabortion advocates, selected according to the political tastes of reporters.

During the 1992 rescues in Buffalo, New York, stations showed repeated footage of a man in a business suit angrily yelling at and shoving prochoice demonstrators. This man was called a "prolife activist," when, in fact, he was a passerby trying to walk down a blocked sidewalk. He had no connection with the rescuers, but millions of Americans were left with a very different impression.

Retired Brookline District Court Judge Henry P. Crowley, who presided over hundreds of Operation Rescue civil disobedience cases, offered this observation: "What I've seen in newspapers characterizing them as violent people is completely wrong."[614]

In a 2000 *Boston Globe* opinion article, William Cotter addressed cases where prolifers have been stripped of the rights granted citizens in virtually every other kind of public protest and sidewalk dialogue on every other subject but abortion. It has become common for courts to establish "bubble zones" outside abortion clinics where prolifers are prohibited from conversing with people approaching the clinic. Yet the bubble zones do not apply to prochoice escorts who come up to clients, talk them into handing over leaflets received from prolifers outside the bubble zone, and encourage the clients to enter the clinic and have their abortions. Outside of a competitive retail business, clinic escorts and prolife sidewalk counselors both exercise expressive behavior on the same sidewalk, but the court order protects the carriers of one message while it criminalizes the message of the other.

Cotter concluded, "It is no surprise that the prolife message is unwelcome in today's world; it may surprise some that communicating that message does not require forfeiting your First Amendment rights."[615]

The great majority of prolife groups and individuals have never practiced civil disobedience. There is honest disagreement among prolifers as to both the legitimacy and effectiveness of civil disobedience to save the lives of unborn children. In most cases, those groups that do practice civil disobedience have strict codes of conduct, and they require a commitment to peaceful nonviolence before they allow anyone to participate.[616]

36b. Prolife civil disobedience should not be condemned without understanding the reasons behind it.

The form of prolife civil disobedience called "rescuing" is a united action in which people peacefully place themselves in front of the entrances of an abortion clinic. The primary purpose of this civil disobedience is to keep the clinic closed for the day, and to thereby save the lives of unborn children. A secondary purpose is to make the statement to society that the unborn are human beings deserving the same protection afforded born people.

Of course, mothers denied entrance may reschedule an appointment, at the same clinic or a different one. But the rescue buys time for the unborn child. He does not die today, or at least not this hour. There is a good chance the child will not die at all, since the mother will now have opportunity to read the literature given to her by sidewalk counselors when she approached the clinic. There are any number of other reasons the child's mother might decide not to have an abortion, including the realization that people believed in the value of her child so much that they were willing to go to jail.[617] Regardless of the reasons, Planned Parenthood estimates that 20 percent of women who miss their initial appointment for an abortion end up not getting an abortion at all.

Those who participate in rescues cite many biblical references that advocate saving innocent people from imminent harm.[618] They also cite numerous examples from the Bible, church history, and secular history where civil disobedience was necessary to save lives and draw attention to social evils.[619] These people believe that just as it would be right to violate a no-swimming sign to save a drowning child or to violate a trespass law to rescue someone from a burning building, it is also right to break a trespass law for the higher purpose of saving a child about to die and a woman about to kill her child.

36c. Peaceful civil disobedience is consistent with the belief that the unborn are human beings.

Some people believe that there is an inherent contradiction in saying that unborn babies are human beings, but that one should never be willing to break the law to save their lives. Prochoice columnist B. D. Colen describes a scenario in which the reader is a Pole living near Auschwitz in 1943. He asks, "Are you morally obligated to save what lives you can? Of course you are." Though Colen does not believe abortion is murder, he goes on to say,

> How is the person who considers abortion to be murder any different from the Pole who knew what was going on at Auschwitz? If the Pole was morally obligated to attempt to save lives, isn't the person who opposes abortion under the same obligation?…
>
> No, the question being asked about Operation Rescue shouldn't be, "Why are these people doing this?" Rather, it should be, "Why has it taken them so long to get to this point? Where have they been?"[620]

Most rescuers have been given fines and jail sentences, and many have been sued. Occasionally, however, a court of law has allowed them to present the scientific and moral evidence and has recognized the legitimacy of their lifesaving activity. Missouri Judge George R. Gerhard came to this conclusion:

> The overwhelming credible evidence in this case is that life begins at conception.… The Court finds that the credible evidence in these cases established justification for the defendants' actions. Their violations of the ordinances involved here were necessary as emergency measures to avoid the imminent private injuries of death and maiming of unborn children.… The Court therefore finds the defendants…not guilty of the charges against them.[621]

36d. Prolife protests have been remarkably nonviolent, and even when there has been violence, it has often been committed by clinic employees and escorts.

Of the thousands of cases of organized prolife civil disobedience conducted in this country since 1987, the large majority have occurred without any violence. Most police have been gentle, and some have even supported and joined groups of rescuers.[622] Unfortunately, in some parts of the country police have used martial arts, weapons, and mace against peaceful and nonresistant rescuers. In our own area, militant prochoice activists have yelled obscenities and pushed and shoved peaceful prolifers, who with few exceptions have not retaliated. One local abortion clinic owner took a baseball bat and, as witnesses looked on, assaulted a woman who was standing peacefully outside a clinic door.

The Coalition Against Operation Rescue has published a guide specifically designed to make prolife activists look bad. *Clinic Defense: A Model* proudly points to the success of one of its many recommended tactics: "There are innumerable instances of clinic defenders neutralizing male ORs [Operation Rescuers] by shouting, 'Get your hands off me, don't you dare touch me,' all the while they are tugging or pushing OR out of line."[623]

The amount of violence has been very small, and most hostile acts have been inflicted on rescuers instead of by them. This stands in sharp contrast to many other protests for different causes. Nuclear protests, animal rights protests, antiwar protests, and homosexual protests have all involved destruction of property, yet none of the protesters has been given the lengthy jail sentences given prolife rescuers. Those arrested for participating in prolife civil disobedience far outnumber those arrested in the civil rights movement.[624] Yet prolife civil disobedience has involved less violence and property damage than the civil rights movement.

36e. Abortion clinic bombing and violence are rare, and are neither done nor endorsed by prolife organizations.

The vast majority of prolife groups oppose violence and the bombing of abortion clinics. There is a wide variety of peaceful prolife efforts that offers constructive alternatives that minimize such actions. In a number of cases the persons behind abortion clinic bombings have not been prolife advocates, but angry men whose girlfriends or wives have gotten an abortion. The number of abortion clinic bombings tied to prolife activists is extremely small. Though a television episode of *Law and Order* fictitiously portrayed a prolife leader masterminding an abortion clinic bombing that killed a woman and a child, I have been unable to find a single case of this sort where anyone has been injured.

The media portrayed the 1993 killing of a Florida abortionist as if it were typical prolife behavior, but the amazing fact is that it was actually the first incident of its kind in the twenty-year history of legal abortion. It was followed by a nonfatal shooting five months later; then in 1994 a Florida abortionist was shot and killed, as were two clinic workers in Massachusetts. In 1998 a New York abortionist was fatally shot. Also in 1998 a police officer, moonlighting as a security guard, was killed by a bomb at an Alabama abortion clinic. This brings the total number of fatalities to seven. The *Abortion Rights Activist* claims that an additional fifteen people have received abortion-related injuries from antiabortionists.[625] When you consider that well over a million abortions occur each year, this number of incidences is extremely small. The prolife movement has been considerably less violent than the civil rights movement, yet most people immediately see the illegitimacy of trying to discredit that movement because of the violence of some.

The National Abortion Federation (NAF) stated that in a six year period, there was a total of ten abortion clinic bombings and thirty-three arsons.[626] In 1999 there were eight arsons and one bombing.[627]

The cases where prolifers *have* bombed abortion clinics do not affect the issue of whether abortion is killing children at those clinics. Nor does it discredit the peaceful efforts of 99.99 percent of prolifers. To blame the prolife movement for such isolated events is like discrediting the antislavery movement because some zealous abolitionists burned the crops of slaveowners or like blaming all prochoice people for the personal threats received by some prolife advocates.

Arson and other property destruction for insurance fraud and other self-serving purposes does occur. The most effective way for abortion clinics to gain public sympathy and damage the reputation of prolifers is to portray themselves as the victims of prolife violence. A Concord, California, abortion clinic was burned to the ground, and local prolifers were blamed. Later the truth came out that a proabortion neighbor set the fire to discredit the prolifers he opposed.[628] I spoke with the police detective in charge of the arson investigation of an abortion clinic in our area. His official conclusion was that the fire was set by the abortion clinic owner. Nevertheless, till this day the fire is still blamed on antiabortionists.

---

37. "The antiabortionists distort the facts and resort to emotionalism to deceive the public."

37a. The facts themselves make abortion an emotional issue.

Every photograph of an aborted child, every testimony of women devastated by postabortion stress syndrome, every story of women being lied to and exploited by the abortion industry is emotional. No wonder, since all the facts point one direction—abortion kills children. Prolifers do not make this an emotional issue; it *is* an emotional issue. How could the killing of children be anything else?

37b. It is not the prolife position, but the prochoice position that relies on emotionalism more than truth and logic.

Philosophy professor Francis Beckwith is trained in the discipline of logic. He argues persuasively that the prochoice position is filled with logical flaws. In contrast, he finds prolife logic far more compelling and consistent with the facts.[629] Prochoice advocates compensate for their lack of factual foundations by appealing to the emotions through horror stories of back-alley abortions and pregnancies due to rape. Sometimes their treatment of the factual data is inaccurate in the extreme. If you listen carefully, the numbers just don't add up.

Robert Marshall and Charles Donovan cite the example of the New York City medical director of Planned Parenthood, who claimed "when it was illegal for a woman to end her pregnancy, one out of every forty women who had abortions died."[630] They match this claim with that of former Planned Parenthood president Faye Wattleton. In a speech before the American Bar Association, Wattleton said that in the 1960s the majority of women receiving abortions were "my poor African-American sisters." Wattleton claimed that there were 600,000 to 1,200,000 illegal abortions per year prior to *Roe*.[631] If her higher abortion figure (1.2 million) were correct, using the Planned Parenthood statistic of one death per forty women, this would mean that 15,300 black women aged fifteen to forty-four died each year from illegal abortion. The only problem is, that would be nearly 2,000 more black women than died from *all* causes in that age bracket during 1965, a typical year in that time period.[632]

Francis Beckwith says, "When abortion-rights supporters, such as Wattleton, start claiming that it is probable that more black women have died from illegal abortions than black women have died, it's time for the media, the medical community, and the legal system to start making abortion-rights proponents accountable for their claims."[633]

37c. The prolife position is based on documented facts and empirical evidence, which many prochoice advocates ignore or distort.

Though there are some unfortunate exceptions, prolife organizations usually disseminate documented scientific information, often obtained from secular research and sources that are not prolife. In contrast, many prochoice groups routinely ignore the scientific facts and do not tell the public what they privately know to be true.

For instance, in 1961, Dr. Alan Guttmacher, director of Planned Parenthood, wrote that when "fertilization has taken place; a baby has been conceived."[634] A 1963 Planned Parenthood publication stated, "An abortion kills the life of a baby after it has begun."[635] What Planned Parenthood knew four decades ago has been repeatedly proven since. Yet Planned Parenthood and other prochoice groups do not share this information with women because it does not serve their social agenda.

Prochoice advocates frequently misuse research and statistics. A Planned Parenthood Fact Sheet says, without qualification, "90 percent of Americans think abortion should be available under some or all circumstances."[636] Though it is technically true, this statement is completely misleading. Only one-fourth of Americans actually "seldom disapprove" of abortion, whereas three-fourths either "often disapprove" or "consistently disapprove."[637] Only 17 percent consider themselves "strongly prochoice," whereas 26 percent call themselves "strongly prolife."[638] By including in their 90 percent statistic those who believe abortion is acceptable to save a mother's life, which includes the vast majority of prolifers, Planned Parenthood misleads people into thinking it represents a point of view most Americans agree with.

Physician and novelist Walker Percy wrote:

> The onset of individual life is not a dogma of church, but a fact of science. How much more convenient if we lived in the thirteenth century when no one knew anything about microbiology, and arguments about the onset of life were legitimate. Nowadays, it is not some misguided ecclesiastics who are trying to suppress an embarrassing scientific fact. It is the secular juridical-journalistic establishment.[639]

A Fund for the Feminist Majority video asks: "Are we concerned about a one-inch tissue or a dead woman?"[640] Of course, the "tissue" is a perfectly formed human being, and the consequence of letting that human being live is not a "dead woman." It is deceptive to portray the issue of abortion as a forced choice between removing tissue or killing women. This appeal to the emotions is effective, as long as the audience does not realize it is simply not true.

37d. The prochoice movement consistently caricatures and misrepresents prolifers and their agenda.

A prochoice video refers to prolife information and activity in these terms: *hysteria, propaganda, immoral, almost obscene, medical McCarthyism,* and *domestic terrorism*. Prolifers are described as "antichoice," and are said to be "often opposed to sexuality in general." The video says, "The antichoice people really don't care about people, and they really don't care about children."[641] Planned Parenthood claims:

> The anti-abortion leaders really have a larger purpose. They oppose most ideas and programs which can help women achieve equality and freedom. They also oppose programs which protect the health and well-being of women and their children…. "Life" is not what they're fighting for. What they want is a return to the days when a woman had few choices in controlling her future.[642]

A NARAL publication says prolifers have a "vindictive, self-righteous attitude" which "stems from a belief that sex is bad and must be punished."[643]

Are some of these charges true of some prolifers? Of course. But these sources mislead by painting with a broad brush. Instead of dealing with facts, reason, and logic, prochoice material often resorts to highly charged emotional arguments without substance, misrepresenting the prolife position and attacking the character of prolifers.

37e. The prochoice movement, from its beginnings, has lied to and exploited women, including the "Roe" of Roe v. Wade and the "Doe" of Doe v. Bolton.

Norma McCorvey, the legendary Jane Roe of the 1973 U.S. Supreme Court *Roe* v. *Wade* ruling, converted to Christianity while working at an abortion clinic. Days later she appeared on Ted Koppel's *Nightline* on ABC. She recanted some of her earlier proabortion views, but said that she still thought a woman should have the freedom to choose abortion during the first trimester.

Not long after that, McCorvey was studying a human development chart closely and a light turned on. She said, "It really is a baby."[644] On April 1, 2000, as the keynote speaker at the Oregon Right to Life annual conference, she brought the crowd to its feet by declaring, "I am now prolife without exception, without compromise, and without apology."[645] Miss McCorvey acknowledges that she lied when she claimed to have been raped, which was the basis on which the urgency of her case had been argued before the Supreme Court. Because the court case took a great deal of time, McCorvey never got an abortion. Her daughter was born, and the two have since met. After many years of working in the abortion industry and serving as a national symbol of the right to abortion, McCorvey suddenly began proclaiming that abortion is wrong. She acknowledged that she had lived for years in shame, got involved in the occult, drugs, and lesbianism, and had come close to suicide. Norma McCorvey says that she was looking for a quick, quiet abortion, and was lied to in order to be made the center of a landmark legal case.[646]

Meanwhile, the truth came out about "Mary Doe" of *Doe* v. *Bolton,* the companion case that together with *Roe* assured the availability of abortion through all nine months of pregnancy (see answer 22d.). (It was the *Doe* v. *Bolton* ruling that defined "health" in such a way as to make abortion legal for physical, emotional, psychological, and familial reasons, and even a woman's concerns about her age.[647]) Mary Doe was actually Sandra Cano. Ms. Cano came forward in 1995 and stated she had never once sought an abortion. She had been lied to by proabortion attorneys, who used her for their ends without her understanding what they were doing. Her doctor and attorney sued to get her an abortion without ever consulting her, and when she found out, she believed she was going to be forced to have the abortion and fled.[648]

It should be understood that the validity of proabortion arguments cannot be disproven on the basis of acts demonstrating poor character, deceit, and abuse. Likewise, the validity of prolife arguments cannot be disproven based on the same sort of behavior by prolifers. The point is simply that since the ad hominem arguments against prolifers are often at the center of proabortion arguments, the public is entitled to view the dirty laundry of the proabortion movement as it weighs the evidence.

38.

"Antiabortion groups hide behind a profamily facade, while groups such as Planned Parenthood are truly profamily because they assist in family planning."

38a. The prochoice movement's imposition of "family planning" on teenagers has substantially contributed to the actual cause of teen pregnancy.

Though you would never know it from prochoice literature, the cause of unwanted pregnancies is *not* the absence of birth control. It is the presence of teenage sexual activity. Planned Parenthood has had a profound influence on the young people of America for two decades, yet the rate of teen pregnancy has skyrocketed in that time. Why? Largely because of the philosophy stated by former Planned Parenthood president Faye Wattleton: "We are not going to be an organization promoting celibacy or chastity."[649]

By their massive distribution of birth control and their advocacy of abortion as a "solution" to unwanted pregnancy, Planned Parenthood and other prochoice organizations have removed the traditional (and still valid) reasons for teenagers not to have sex. Consequently, the number of teenagers having sex has risen dramatically, resulting not only in increased pregnancies and sexually transmitted diseases, but in emotional and psychological scars.

Historically, Planned Parenthood has believed that it is naive to expect fifteen-year-olds to abstain from sex. This is no different than saying that teenagers cannot be taught to abstain from drugs. I suspect if Planned Parenthood were put in charge of children's traffic safety, it would devote its efforts to teaching children the art of dodging cars, rather than teaching them to stay off the freeway in the first place. The AIDS crisis has finally forced the term *abstinence* into Planned Parenthood's vocabulary. However, no moral foundation is laid, and discussions quickly move to how to use condoms. In spite of their efforts,

> the teenage abortion rate dropped from 1988 to 1996, from 43.5 per thousand to 29.2—a 33 percent decline. The overall teenage pregnancy rate has declined since 1991, falling 15 percent from 117 per 1,000 to 99 in 1996. The proportion of teen pregnancies ending in nonmarital

birth has increased sharply, rising from 25 percent of teen pregnancies in 1982 to 42 percent in 1995 and 1996. Changes in abortion rates at other ages were small.[650]

The evidence for a decline in abortion is, admittedly, incomplete. Many states don't collect the sort of data required to draw solid conclusions, such as annual figures for abortions, teen pregnancies, and illegitimate births. And whatever the decline in abortion, the descent has not been terribly steep.

There seem to be at least four reasons for this slight decline. Over the last several years, we have witnessed a social movement to encourage teenagers to postpone sexual relations until marriage, increased professionalism and sensitivity in the nation's prolife pregnancy care centers, growth in state laws fostering a fully informed abortion decision, and a decline in the number of doctors who perform abortions.

Part of the recent drop in abortions could be attributed more to a decline in teenage sexual activity than to a rise in contraceptive use. Studies by the Centers for Disease Control have shown the proportion of sexually experienced high schoolers dropping.

Abstinence-education programs across the country have found that telling kids not to have sex is surprisingly successful. A Title XX performance evaluation found that, two years after the Sex Respect program, nonparticipants were twice as likely as participants to have gotten pregnant.[651]

38b. Through its opposition to parental notification and consent, Planned Parenthood consistently undermines the value and authority of the family.

When Planned Parenthood comes to school classrooms, it typically passes out birth control samples and instructs students in how each is used. It tells students where the local clinic is located, its phone number, and hours of operation. Children are continuously reassured that their parents will never know. After thorough investigation, one magazine claims that "parental non-involvement is the cornerstone of PPFA's youth marketing strategy."[652]

In many states it is not legal for a girl to get her ears pierced or to go on a school field trip without parental consent. Yet in these same states junior high and high school girls are taken for abortions without their parents knowledge, much less their consent. Girls who cannot even be given an aspirin by the school nurse unless the nurse first gets permission from their parents, can be driven from the school by the same nurse to an abortion clinic without the parents ever being notified. In 1994 two Oregon women were charged with kidnapping an eighteen-year-old girl and taking her to get an abortion she didn't want. Two employees of the Amity School District in McMinnville allegedly took the girl out of school to get an abortion in Portland, then altered school attendance records to cover up the trip. Another woman faced charges of witness tampering in the case.[653] In

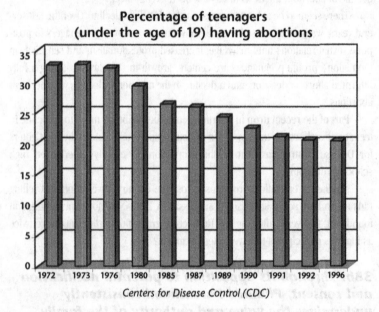

Percentage of teenagers (under the age of 19) having abortions

Centers for Disease Control (CDC)

some areas Planned Parenthood has actually provided an "abortion bus" to pick up students from local schools.[654]

According to Planned Parenthood, six out of ten teenagers tell one of their parents about the abortion,[655] but that means four out of ten don't. It's no wonder that a poll by NBC News and the *Wall Street Journal* indicated that three-fourths of Americans favor a law requiring parental notification of abortion.[656] Prior to 1981 teen pregnancy had skyrocketed in Minnesota, but after a parental notification law went into effect, teen pregnancies and teen abortions declined dramatically.[657] If Planned Parenthood's real goal is to reduce teen pregnancy, it would support such laws. But despite the undeniable reduction of teen pregnancies by Minnesota's law, Planned Parenthood vehemently opposes that law and all similar laws.[658]

How can this contradiction be explained? According to Planned Parenthood's own statistics, mandatory parental involvement provisions result in a 24 percent to 85 percent reduction in the teen caseloads of family planning clinics.[659] This means huge numbers of family planning employees would lose their jobs. Furthermore, every pregnancy test paid for by tax money brings in $57.51 to Planned Parenthood, as opposed to an average of $16.36 for those who pay for it themselves.[660] Planned Parenthood has become financially dependent on teen pregnancies and abortion. When teen pregnancies and abortions decrease, so does Planned Parenthood's cash flow and its ability to maintain its expensive programs and personnel.

Prochoice groups oppose not only parental consent legislation, but in Oregon they managed to defeat a bill that simply required that parents be *notified* of their child's abortion, even if they didn't consent to it. The whole situation defies belief. This very moment hundreds of parents across America are not even aware that their daughters are in pain, bleeding, and emotionally distraught because they had an abortion within the last few days. These parents don't know to look for such signs or to get immediate medical care if complications occur.

Distraught teenage girls often think, "My parents would disown me if they knew I was pregnant." Usually they are wrong. The majority of parents love their children and are in the best position to give them help and counsel. Yet by their opposition to parental consent laws, prochoice advocates teach girls they cannot trust their parents, while they *can* trust the abortion and family planning clinics.

Students at a California high school were told, "At Planned Parenthood you can also get birth control without the consent or knowledge of your parents. So, if you are 14, 15, or 16 and you come to Planned Parenthood, we won't tell your parents you've been there. *We swear we won't tell your parents.*"[661] A piece in the *Dallas Observer* read, "If your parents are stupid enough to deny you access to birth control and you are under 18, you can get it on your own without parental permission. Call Planned Parenthood."

Is it possible that parents are not as stupid as some people think—that they understand that providing birth control encourages sexual activity and that they wish to teach abstinence instead? Is it possible that a girl's parents love her even more than the abortion clinics that will take her $300 and never see her again?

38c. Planned Parenthood makes huge financial profits from persuading people to get abortions.

The 1997–1998 Planned Parenthood Revenue report shows income of $544 million. Planned Parenthood's February 2000 report showed that its profits nearly tripled during 1999. It generated profits of $125.8 million on gross income of $660 million, which included contributions and government funding. A third of their income came from clinic operations, and of that $58.8 million—more than one of every four dollars earned—came from performing abortions.[662]

Planned Parenthood has 850 clinics, in which the number of abortions increased from 139,000 in 1995 to nearly 168,000 in 1999. "During a time when the number of abortions nationally has steadily decreased, Planned Parenthood is performing more, not fewer abortions."[663] In fact, Planned Parenthood is by far the largest abortion provider in America.

Citizens, schools, and businesses who think of Planned Parenthood as an objective third party acting in the best interests of young people need to come to grips with the fact that this organization has tremendous vested interests in marketing abortions. Jobs and incomes are at stake.

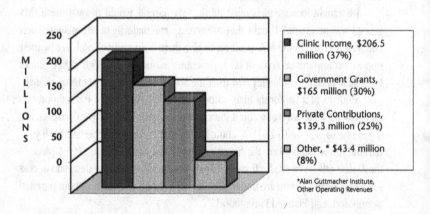

'97–'98 Planned Parenthood Revenues

- Clinic Income, $206.5 million (37%)
- Government Grants, $165 million (30%)
- Private Contributions, $139.3 million (25%)
- Other, * $43.4 million (8%)

*Alan Guttmacher Institute, Other Operating Revenues

38d. Planned Parenthood has been directly involved

in the scandals of trafficking baby body parts.

When ABC's *20/20* dealt with the marketing of fetal body parts, Planned Parenthood president Gloria Feldt sat before the camera condemning these activities. Life Dynamics, the group that brought the illegal activities to the attention of ABC, said:

> *20/20* was completely irresponsible in not making the viewer aware that all of the wrongdoing described in this broadcast occurred at Planned Parenthood facilities, and that Planned Parenthood is responsible for the national network that supports the trafficking of baby body parts. Ms. Feldt was clearly wanting to disguise this in her interview and *20/20*, by its silence, went right along with her. The result is that the viewer was left with the false impression that Planned Parenthood was outraged at these practices rather than a participant in them.[664]

38e. As demonstrated in the case of Becky Bell, the prochoice movement is willing to distort and exploit family tragedies to promote its agenda.

The most widely publicized prochoice case study in history is Becky Bell, a seventeen-year-old Indiana teenager who died in 1988 and is still frequently mentioned by prochoice activists. According to prochoice advocates, her death was the fault of a state law requiring her to get parental consent for an abortion. As *Ms.* magazine put it, "She Died Because of a Law."[665]

Prochoice groups have placed both of Becky's parents on their payrolls and have flown them around the country for political rallies and television interviews. They have been extremely effective in helping defeat parental consent legislation in states where polls show people actually favor it.

Major newspapers and magazines, using the language of prochoice press releases, contradict each other in their accounts of what actually happened to Becky Bell. Some say she had a botched abortion surgery, others that she took a "home remedy" abortion. None has bothered to investigate her actual cause of death.[666]

Becky Bell's autopsy report describes the tissue lining her uterus as "smooth and glistening," with no infection, discoloration, or any other indications of an induced abortion.[667] The doctor who performed the autopsy states that Becky died of pneumonia. He also says there had been a *spontaneous* abortion (a miscarriage) as opposed to an *induced* abortion. After he put *abortion* on the cover of the autopsy report, someone else added the word *septic* in front of it. This doctor stated flatly, "There is absolutely no evidence whatever of an induced abortion," and that Becky Bell's parents never talked to him about the autopsy or cause of death.[668] John Curry, former head of the Tissue Bank at Bethesda Naval Hospital, says that the pathology report clearly indicates massive infection in the lungs, but no infection whatsoever in or even near the uterus.[669] He maintains that the pneumonia was "unlikely to originate from a contaminated abortion procedure." He also says Becky's death could have been prevented by treatment of her pneumonia within the first six days. Dr. Bernard Nathanson studied Becky Bell's autopsy and concluded definitively, "Rebecca Bell did not die from a septic illegal abortion: there is not one shred of credible evidence to support this preposterous claim."[670]

Suppose, however, that Becky *did* die from an abortion. (It wouldn't be the first case or the last.) What would have happened if the Indiana parental consent law had been followed and the Bells had been told their daughter was pregnant and wanted an abortion? First, they could have expressed their support for keeping the child or giving him up for adoption. They could have warned her of the physical and psychological dangers of abortion. But even if they would have agreed to an abortion, they would have been alert to her recent surgery and would have taken her to a doctor when they first saw how ill she was days before her death.[671] The media failed to point out that Becky Bell desperately needed her parents' help in making decisions about her health and welfare. Her boyfriend was a drug supplier with a tendency toward violence, and she had recently been hospitalized for substance abuse. The coroner's report says that only days before she got sick she had been at a party where drugs were being used and that she "claimed that someone had put 'speed' in her drink."[672]

Columnist Cal Thomas stated, "The medical cause of Becky Bell's death may have been pneumonia, but the underlying cause remains unclear. One thing is clear: her death was *not* due to Indiana's parental consent law."[673]

38f. Planned Parenthood, the prochoice movement, and the media ignore family tragedies that do not support the prochoice agenda.

There may be other examples—past or future—of someone who does suffer or die because she chooses to get an illegal abortion rather than to consult her parents. But what prochoice advocates do not point out is that many more girls (not to mention babies) suffer as a result of the lack of parental notification laws.

In all the years parental notification and consent bills have been on the books, Becky's case is the only one that proabortionists have been able to find which—if misrepresented thoroughly enough—could lend even a semblance of credibility to their side of the debate. By contrast teenage girls have died and been crippled precisely *because* they were not required to involve their parents or because others maneuvered to get around telling the parents.[674]

Less than six months after Becky Bell's death, Erica Richardson, a Maryland sixteen-year-old, died from a legal abortion.[675] Only a few local newspapers covered her death. Erica underwent an abortion without her parents' knowledge or consent, since neither is required in Maryland. Had she been required to talk with her parents, they could have helped her make a more informed and careful decision. Had they done so, Erica Richardson would likely be alive today.

Most of the country knows the name of Becky Bell, whose death was unrelated to her state's parental consent law. Almost no one knows the names of girls such as Erica Richardson, who probably would not have died if their states required that parents be consulted or at least informed of their children's abortions.

It is mystifying that a movement can describe itself as profamily when it fights against the rights of parents to know that their child is undergoing a major surgery with significant physical and emotional risks—a surgery that will, among other things, kill their own grandchild.

39. "The last three decades of abortion rights have helped make our society a better place to live."

39a. Abortion has left terrible holes in our society.

Reader's Digest tells a heartwarming story involving a young Italian woman named Catuzza, living in New York. Back in the 1950s, Catuzza let an eleven-year-old neighbor boy and his three-year-old brother Joey touch her stomach when her unborn baby was kicking. Some thirty-five years later Joey was dying, but a skilled and dedicated surgeon saved his life. Recognizing the doctor's last name, Joey's older brother put the pieces together: "Only then did the realization hit me. The unborn baby who had kicked inside Catuzza all those years before on Irving Street had grown up to be the doctor who saved my brother's life."[676]

How different the story might have been if abortion had been legal in New York when Catuzza was pregnant. Her son would have had at least a one-in-three chance of being killed before he was born. How many lifesaving "connections" like that of Joey and Catuzza's son have failed to materialize because of legalized abortion?

The classic Jimmy Stewart movie, *It's a Wonderful Life,* captures this same mystery of connections. When George Bailey's life unravels, he wishes he had never been born. As he stands on a bridge contemplating suicide, an angel is sent by God to tell George how important his life has been. The angel shows George how the world would have been a much worse place without him. Then he says, "Strange, isn't it? Every man's life touches so many other lives, and when he isn't around he leaves an awful hole to fill, doesn't he?... You see what a mistake it would be to throw it away?"[677] Nearly forty million "awful holes" have been created by legal surgical abortion in this country. Every twenty-three seconds[678] a preborn child is killed in America. That is 3,700 a day, every day of the year, every year of the decade. The number is too great for us to possibly envision. Those who have stood before the national Vietnam Memorial with its 58,132 names may be helped by a comparison. Every two and a half weeks, year in and year out, there is an aborted child for each and every name on that memorial. How many miles would a memorial stretch if every aborted child were listed?

The total American casualties in all wars in our nation's history is less than 1.5 million people. This is comparable to the number of children killed *annually* in the war against our offspring. Ever since 1991, high school graduating classes have been missing up to a third of the members they would have had if they had not been killed by abortion.

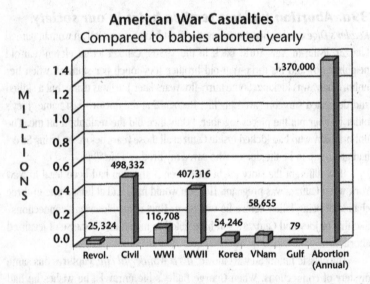

American War Casualties
Compared to babies aborted yearly

MILLIONS

Revol. 25,324	Civil 498,332	WWI 116,708	WWII 407,316	Korea 54,246	VNam 58,655	Gulf 79	Abortion (Annual) 1,370,000

39b. Abortion has made us a nation of schizophrenics concerning our children.

On the one hand, we value children as our greatest national resource. We are appalled at the dramatic rise in child abuse and the lack of care given many children. In the early 1990s the major newsmagazines devoted whole issues to the plight of children in America. A *Mother Jones* cover story, "America's Dirty Little Secret: We Hate Kids," called for a new commitment to the value of children's lives.[679] A feature article in *Parade* pleaded, "Save our Babies."[680] It decried

America's mortality rate of 9.1 infant deaths per 1000 live births.

Yet our infant mortality rate was actually about thirty-two times the official figure, due to abortion. Not one of the articles made the obvious connection between how we treat our unborn children and how we treat them when they are just a little older. Several of the articles emphasize the importance of prenatal care. None point out that the greatest violation of prenatal care is to kill the baby.

Our hospitals live daily in a state of extreme schizophrenia. Doctors and nurses feverishly attempt to save the life of a twenty-two-week "fetus" born prematurely, while in the very next room a child at twenty-four weeks is deliberately and legally killed. Some states require a medical team to back up late-term abortions in case the child survives. One medical team is trying to destroy the life, but if the job is botched and the child somehow survives, the other team takes over and tries to save his life.

An editorial in the *Oregonian,* a strongly prochoice newspaper, was titled, "Slaughtering Our Babies." It concerns an infant killed by a stray bullet in a war between drug gangs. The editorial asks:

> What hope is there for a community that slaughters its young? What in heaven's name is wrong with us?... No community—no civilized and caring community, at least—can allow this kind of slaughter to go by without comment.... Portlanders...must make clear again and again that this kind of activity is absolutely unacceptable and that they will help to choke it out in this city.[681]

Yet the same community and the same newspaper are indifferent to the vicious slaughter of infants that occurs daily in its four abortion clinics. More than indifferent, the newspaper and many in the community applaud and defend the right to kill thousands of infants annually, each just as human, just as alive, and just as valuable as the single infant the editorial laments. What else but a combination of blindness and schizophrenia can explain how we can abhor the death of one infant, while tolerating and even embracing the deaths of thousands of infants?

One prolife woman I know has taken photographs of aborted babies in abortion clinic dumpsters. Twice the photo developing lab has reported her to the police, who began a homicide investigation. When she explained the child was killed at an abortion clinic, the investigation was called off. Whether the woman or the clinic killed the child, in both cases a child was killed. *What's the difference?* To any rational person, there is no difference.

39c. Abortion is a modern holocaust which is breeding unparalleled violence and to which we are accomplices.

The unspeakable evil of child-killing has left a cloud over our country. We have immunized ourselves to this evil. Dr. Nathanson says:

> The abortion holocaust is beyond the ordinary discourse of morality and rational condemnation. It is not enough to pronounce it absolutely evil…. The abortion tragedy is a new event, severed from connections with traditional presuppositions of history, psychology, politics, and morality. It extends beyond the deliberations of reason, beyond the discernment of moral judgment, beyond meaning itself…. This is an evil torn free of its moorings in reason and causality, an ordinary secular corruption raised to unimaginable powers of magnification and limitless extremity.[682]

Many are alarmed at the level of violence among American young people, everything from gangs to school shootings to addiction to violent video games. With every act of violence, people are asking the same question: "Why are kids killing kids?" Maybe one of the reasons is that adults have been killing kids in America for nearly thirty years. Just because it's legal doesn't make it right. Perhaps the problem isn't that our children aren't listening to us. Perhaps it's that they're listening all too well. Or perhaps what we do speaks so loudly they can't hear a word we're saying.

39d. Abortion is taking us in a direction from which we might never return.

A NARAL publication states, "There is no evidence that respect for life has diminished or that legal abortion leads to killing of any persons."[683] On the contrary, there are unmistakable signs everywhere that abortion has desensitized us to the value of human life.

It is hard to believe that less than four decades have passed since the New

Jersey Supreme Court issued a decision that protected handicapped preborns. This decision was hailed by almost everyone at the time as the only conclusion a decent society could come to. It stated, "We are not talking here about the breeding of cattle. It may be easier or less expensive for the father to have terminated the life of his child, but these alleged deficits cannot stand against the preciousness of a single human life."[684]

Now over half of such children are routinely killed, and some have advocated legal requirements forcing the other half to be killed as well.[685] After a seventeen-year-old Florida girl smothered her newborn daughter, a judge sentenced her to two years in prison and to psychological counseling and birth control instruction.[686] Of course, the sentence for killing someone perceived as "a real person" would have been much more severe. As one social analyst points out, "A two-year sentence for the willful murder of an infant demonstrates beyond any shadow of doubt that the life of a child does not have the same value as the life of an adult."[687]

It appears that the courts, without officially saying so, are adopting Peter Singer's notion that children should not be granted the full right to life until sometime after they've been born.[688] University of Chicago biologist Dr. Leon Kass says that with the direction of modern science and medicine "we are already witnessing the erosion of our idea of man as something splendid or divine, as a creature with freedom and dignity. And clearly, if we come to see ourselves as meat, then meat we shall become."[689]

Doctors have revealed that a young woman in England was allowed to obtain two abortions because she did not like the physical features of the babies' fathers. In a case condemned as "abortion on demand," the woman obtained abortions because she did not like the height of one boyfriend and the eyes of another. The woman, who was nineteen when she had her first abortion, was about to undergo a third abortion on the grounds that she did not like the father's mouth, when she miscarried.

Doctors said the woman was able to convince her GP that she was "preoccupied" with the fear that her baby would share the father's characteristics. Calling for a crackdown on the availability of abortions on demand, a spokesman for the Society for the Protection of Unborn Children said, "Can it be that a life can be terminated because the baby might be too short?"[690]

279

Perhaps the most shocking development since the first edition of this book came out in 1992 has been the number of children committing violent crimes against each other and their parents. First it was gang killings, but many people considered the gang world far removed from their own. Then came school shootings. In response to school shooting after school shooting, people have been asking, "Why?" Perhaps the answer is really quite simple—our children are listening to what we tell them when we say it's fine for people to kill a small child. And if it's fine for them to kill a child before he's born, why isn't it fine for them or someone else to kill the same child after he's born?

If people are just animals, and if there is no Creator and therefore no moral Judge, what difference does it make? If diversity and tolerance and relativism mean that there are no moral absolutes, who are we to tell our children they shouldn't kill each other? Who are we to do this, especially when we provide them with all the rationalizations for killing our youngest and most vulnerable children?

We now have couples intentionally conceiving a child for no other purpose than to serve as an unconsenting bone marrow donor to help their older child. If it turns out that the bone marrow doesn't match, they are perfectly free to abort the child. Children could be conceived expressly to harvest their organs for a valued family member.

Abortion sets us on a dangerous slippery slope. We may come to our senses and back away, or we may continue down it until we completely lose control and go over the brink. As one feminist group points out, if unborn children are not safe, no one is safe:

> If we take any living member of the species Homo sapiens and put them outside the realm of legal protection, we undercut the case against discrimination for everyone else. The basis for equal treatment under the law is that being a member of the species is sufficient to be a member of the human community, without consideration for race, gender, disability, age, stage of development, state of dependency, place of residence or amount of property ownership. Abortion dynamites the foundation of feminism, and poisons the well against civil rights for African-Americans, the elderly, the disabled, and others.[691]

39e. Abortion has ushered in the brave new world of human pesticides.

What lies ahead in the war against our children? RU-486, the "abortion pill," has been sold in France since 1988. Fearing a boycott, the French manufacturer donated it's marketing rights in the U.S. to the nonprofit Population Council, a proabortion organization which licensed the pharmaceutical company Danco to bring the drug to market. As I write, RU-486 appears right on the verge of being legalized in America.

RU-486 induces an abortion without surgery using a two-drug process. The first drug kills the baby. A second drug, misoprostol (a prostaglandin) is given to induce uterine contractions which then expel the now-dead baby. The introduction of this abortifacient marks the first time in history that the FDA has deliberately approved a drug explicitly used to destroy human life. (They did this despite the many negative side effects described below.)

Similar "breakthroughs" that will make abortion appear cleaner and less disturbing are sure to come. But they will do nothing to change reality. Children will be killed with greater ease and efficiency, but *children will still be killed*. Abortion pills will not change the grisly reality of abortion any more than the Nazis' more efficient and sanitary killing procedures changed the reality of the Holocaust.

Not only children, but women will suffer from the new abortion drugs. RU-486 presents considerable medical risk.[692] Researcher George Grant documents the drug's serious and sometimes deadly side effects.[693] Common to most cases is prolonged bleeding, averaging nine to thirty days.[694] Well over half of women using RU-486 need pain medication, with about one-third needing narcotics. Nausea and vomiting occur in the majority of cases. At least one woman died, one had a cardiac arrest, and another ventricular fibrillation.[695] In France, severe cardiac complications occurred in one case in twenty thousand.[696] In Iowa, one woman almost died from hemorrhage after an RU-486 abortion.[697]

RU-486 and a prostaglandin will produce an abortion 95 percent of the time. In case of failure, a woman may opt for a surgical abortion, though some will choose to carry to term.[698] Fetal deformity is a significant possibility for these babies.[699] Although the drugs kill the baby in the uterus, they do not kill an embryo implanted in the fallopian tube. A woman could bleed and assume she had aborted, then the fallopian tube could rupture, which is a potentially fatal condition. The only preventative is to do an ultrasound exam on every woman, a test that costs as much as an entire surgical abortion.[700]

There are psychological ramifications as well. Three to four medical appointments are required. Dr. Edwardo Sakiz, then president of Roussel Uclaf, said, "The woman must live with this for a full week; this is an appalling psychological ordeal."[701] Postabortion syndrome is expected to be at least as common from this method as from surgical abortion.

Secular magazines ranging from the *American Druggist* to *Wall Street Journal* to *Vogue* have pointed out that RU-486 is a powerful steroid that causes heavy bleeding and other dangerous side effects.[702] Even the prochoice American Medical Association acknowledges that RU-486 has been proven neither safe nor effective.[703] RU-486 has been sharply criticized by three prochoice feminists, including a professor of Women's Studies and Medical Ethics at the University of Massachusetts.[704] The three claim that women are being treated as "guinea pigs" in experiments with this dangerous drug.

Despite all this, prochoice groups have portrayed RU-486 as a "wonder drug." Even if it remains illegal, they have promised to import or produce it. They claim that RU-486 will solve not only the problem of unwanted pregnancy, but may also cure breast cancer and AIDS. Ignoring its dangers to women, the Fund for the Feminist Majority (FFM) is waging an all-out campaign to legalize RU-486. One donor contributed ten million dollars to the FFM for this purpose.[705]

Does RU-486 really make abortion "safer"? Abortion proponents are disregarding the well-being of women and asking the FDA permission for women to take the drugs at home. Ingestion of this drug at home was not part of the FDA trials, and it is not practiced this way in France. Women would be put at greater risk in the multistep process without an overseeing physician.[706]

Even if a "safe" child-killing drug is developed, the tragedy will not be minimized. There is no clean way to kill innocent children, and there is no way that child-killing can leave any society unscarred. Abortion pills are nothing less than chemical warfare against our own species. They are, quite literally, human pesticides.

A nation determines its future by how it treats its children. We hold in our hands not only the fate of the unborn, but the fate of our nation. Will we remove our children as we would remove a wart? Will we take a medication to relieve ourselves of our children as we would take an antacid to relieve ourselves of indigestion? The abortion pill is one more test for America—perhaps one last test—of how inhumane we are willing to become.

39f. Abortion has led us into complete moral subjectivism in which we are prone to justify as ethical whatever it is we want to do.

I have frequently quoted bioethicist Peter Singer in this book. He has laid out definitions of personhood and decided who does and does not qualify to have time and money spent on them for care. In January 2000 an amazing fact surfaced concerning Singer and his mother:

> Mr. Singer, heralded in a recent interview with the *New Yorker* as the "greatest living philosopher," has a mother who suffers from Alzheimer's disease. She is, by his definition, no longer a "person." Yet he has, at great personal expense, hired round-the-clock health care workers to care for her. In a rather astounding fit of self-examination, Singer conceded in the same interview, that "I think this has made me see how the issues of someone with these kinds of problems are really very difficult. Perhaps it is more difficult than I thought before, because it is different when it's your mother."
>
> Dr. Peter Berkowitz, a professor at George Mason University Law School...says of Singer's revelation, "Although he strenuously denies that from the ethical point of view we ought to treat friends and family differently, Singer's actions seem to proclaim that what is right and what is rigorous applies only to other people's mothers.
>
> "Indeed, it is hard to imagine a more stunning rebuke to the well-heeled and well-ensconced academic discipline of practical ethics than that its most controversial and influential star, at the peak of his discipline, after an Oxford education, after twenty-five years as a university professor, and after the publication of thousands of pages laying down clear-cut rules on life-and-death issues, should reveal, only as the result of a reporter's prodding, and only in the battle with his own elderly mother's suffering, that he has just begun to appreciate that the moral life is complex."

And a final note on Mr. Singer's "solution": It is also different when it is your child![707]

283

Peter Singer has acted toward his mother in a way consistent with the traditional Christian morality he professes to despise. His actions are wholly inconsistent with the naturalistic utilitarian ethics he has devoted his life to teaching. The huge discrepancy between Singer's moral philosophy and his conscience, demonstrated in his actual behavior toward his mother, reflects the utter moral subjectivism of modern ethics and the need to return to a firm moral standard—the standard that in his heart Peter Singer, like all of us, knows to be right.

FINAL APPEALS

An Appeal to Men to Stand up for Women and Care for and Defend Their Children

The history of abortion in America should bring more shame to men than to anyone. No pregnancy happens without a man. Men should take the responsibility for their own purity and to protect that of women. When they fail to do this, they should be the first to accept full responsibility for the consequences of their actions, including the conception of a child.

As George Gilder argues in *Men and Marriage*,[708] when men exercise deep loyalties to women and children, when we take responsibility to protect and defend them, we are at our best; when we violate those loyalties, we are at our worst. We become abusers on the one hand, or passive cowards on the other. We place ourselves under the rightful scorn of women and under the judgment of God.

When I spoke on this subject at my church, a man in his sixties told me of a girl he got pregnant thirty-nine years ago. She gave him the choice of what to do, and he chose an abortion. He said it has haunted him since. He thinks about the woman he failed and the son or daughter he lost and wonders about the grandchildren he'd now be holding. He said to me, "Tell people about the consequences. Warn our young men—tell them God will hold them accountable for what they do with their children." Then he broke down in tears and said, "I don't want our young men to do what I did thirty-nine years ago."

One of our home Bible study leaders came to me, tears in his eyes. He told me of an abortion he paid for years ago and the devastating impact it had on his life. A quarter of a million babies are aborted each year by women who describe themselves as "evangelical" or "born again."[709] Most of these women no doubt have some church affiliation. In many cases the father of the child attends the same church. It is not only a moral crisis, but a matter of great shame that Christian men have been so weak that they not only commit sexual immorality, but allow a child to be killed to cover up their sin and make their lives easier (until their conscience takes revenge).

For the sake of women and children—and for our own sakes—it is time for men to stand up and make whatever sacrifices are necessary to care for children they have fathered. If this means begging the forgiveness of women, or standing in front of church leaders or a congregation and confessing their sin, so be it. If this were done more often, more young men in the church would be encouraged to pursue purity and discouraged from ever letting a child die for their sins.

Abortion isn't a women's issue. It's a human issue, and its effects are devastating to women and men alike. But it's high time for men to take personal responsibility, stand up for women and children, and exercise the kind of leadership God expects of us.

An Appeal to Women Considering Abortion

Be honest with yourself. Don't buy the prochoice rhetoric that would try to make you feel heroic by exercising your precious right to kill an innocent child. Naomi Wolf responds to a fellow feminist's claim that women get abortions in order to be better mothers. Wolf says this of her own chemical abortion:

> If what was going on in my mind had been mostly about the well-being of the possible baby, that pill would never have been swallowed. For that potential baby, brought to term, would have had two sets of loving middle-income grandparents, an adult mother with an education and even, as I discovered later, the beginning of diaper money for its first two years of life (the graduate fellowship I was on forbade marriage but, frozen in time before women were its beneficiaries, said nothing about unwed motherhood). Because of the baby's skin color, even if I chose not to rear the child, a roster of eager adoptive parents awaited him or her. If I had been thinking only or even primarily about the baby's life, I would have had to decide to bring the pregnancy, had there been one, to term.
>
> No: there were two columns in my mind—"Me" and "Baby"—and the first won out. And what was in it looked something like this: unwelcome intensity in the relationship with the father; desire to continue to "develop as a person" before "real" parenthood; wish to encounter my eventual life partner without the off-putting encumbrance of a child; resistance to curtailing the nature of the time remaining to me in Europe. Essentially, this column came down to: I am not done being responsive only to myself yet.
>
> At even the possibility that the cosmos was calling my name, I cowered and stepped aside. I was not so unlike those young louts who father children and run from the specter of responsibility.[710]

Don't succumb to the pressure to kill your baby. The testimony of one woman who gave in to that pressure echoes the feelings of hundreds of thousands of women:

My family would not support my decision to keep my baby. My boyfriend said he would give me no emotional or financial help whatsoever. All the people that mattered told me to abort. When I said I didn't want to, they started listing reasons why I should. They said it would be detrimental to my career, and my health, and that I would have no social life and no future. Could I actually keep it alone? I started feeling like maybe I was crazy to want to keep it.

I finally told everyone that I would have the abortion just to get them off my back. But inside I still didn't want to have the abortion. Unfortunately, when the abortion day came I shut off my inside feelings. I was scared to not do it because of how my family and boyfriend felt. I'm *so* angry at myself for giving in to the pressure of others. I just felt so alone in my feelings to have my baby.[711]

Every pregnant woman has an inner voice telling her not to abort her child and that she will regret this decision the rest of her life. Don't let the loud voices of society drown out this small voice. Listen to it. It's your conscience, and it's telling you the truth.

There are people who will gladly help you. Look up "Abortion Alternatives" in the Yellow Pages and call for help. Or go to www.abortionalternatives.com for a listing of people to call. Or call one of the toll free hotlines for women in crisis pregnancies (under the first listing in Appendix K). Instead of finding people who will kill your baby for a fee, you'll find people who will understand and help for free. If you don't know how to find help in your area, contact our organization listed on page 406, and we will gladly assist you at no cost. We will help both you and your baby any way we can.

An Appeal to the Abortion and Family Planning Clinics

I appeal to the clinics to take me up on a sincere offer. I promise to help them find an abortion alternative center in their area that will allow a prochoice clinic employee or volunteer to present to each client the best case for abortion. The client will then weigh the information given by the abortion alternative center against that given by the abortion clinic and make her own decision. This will assure true informed consent, leaving women to make their own choice about whether or not to abort.

All that we require in turn is that the abortion or Planned Parenthood clinic do the same thing—allow one employee or volunteer from an abortion alternative center to present to each client the facts about fetal development, visual aids showing what abortion is, psychological and physical risks of abortion, and the availability of abortion alternatives. The prolifer may also offer a free sonogram or ultrasound so she can see for herself who or what is inside her. The woman—not the counselors from either side—will make her choice.

Isn't that what the prochoice movement says it wants—women informed and free to choose? Isn't that a fair arrangement? I know lots of abortion alternative centers that would gladly agree to this. But in the eight years I've been making this offer, I have yet to hear of a single abortion clinic or Planned Parenthood clinic that would. I invite any of them to take me up on the offer.

An Appeal to the Media

I've been on over three hundred radio and television programs and have been interviewed by dozens of newspapers and magazines. I've had many very good experiences with people in the media. Most have been fair and reasonable. But while I have seen many subject matters handled fairly by the media, I have observed that coverage on the subject of abortion has been consistently biased. This has been true to the point that I have turned down interview requests on abortion while rarely refusing them on any other subject. (Too often what has been printed bears little resemblance to what I actually said.)

For too long journalists have rehearsed prochoice rhetoric rather than engage in objective reporting. Any journalist with integrity should be offended at the words of a former proabortion leader who confesses that the key to his group's success in misleading the public was its ability to manipulate the media: "We fed a line of deceit, of dishonesty, of fabrication of statistics and figures. We coddled, and caressed, and stroked the press."[712] It should further distress you to hear one of your own, a respected columnist, say:

> If the pro-abortionists were not in control of the press, I am convinced that not only would the debate on abortion be over by now (have we really even had a national debate?), but the prolife side would be victorious

because we would have seen the pictures every night on television of what is taking place behind the doors of the abortion clinics and hospitals.[713]

It should offend journalists, who of all people most abhor censorship, to learn that *in four cases the book you are reading was censored*. When I tried to obtain rights to use scientific photographs of unborn children, and was willing to pay the going rate for such usage, I was denied the use of them because this book takes a position against abortion. These are objective, scientific materials that were withheld from the readers of this book because they clearly demonstrate the humanity of the unborn.

Furthermore, both Chrysler and Volvo refused permission to reproduce two of their advertisements (from which I quoted in answer 8g) simply because this was a prolife book. I was told that Volvo has been under pressure from prochoice advocates because they used an actual ultrasound image of an unborn child in their ad. There is only one word for this: *censorship*.

But censorship has become routine in the abortion debate. For instance, a Bellingham, Washington, library has a display case for publicly contributed educational exhibits, which stay up for thirty days. One citizen set up an attractive exhibit using a series of plastic models and *Life* magazine photos. These showed, with scientific accuracy, the development of an unborn child from conception to birth. Because it was sending a prolife message (the message the facts inevitably send), the library director ordered the display taken down. Only the threat of legal action against the city kept it up.[714] Where is the media outcry when such attempts at censorship surface?

I appeal to all journalists who hate censorship to muster the courage to stop censoring the facts about abortion and to speak out boldly against those who do. I appeal to you to do exposés of the abortion industry with the same fervor you would apply to uncovering unethical practices in the White House or a religious organization. I appeal to you to tell the public that abortion clinics are immune to the informed consent, health, and safety requirements placed upon all legitimate hospitals.

I appeal to you to show the pictures of aborted babies the same way you showed the pictures of children killed in Viet Nam or Iran or Croatia. I appeal to you to convey the prolife position as it actually is, as presented in sources such as this book, and not as it is caricatured by prochoice advocates. Stop being ministers of propaganda for the politically correct position. Present the public with the facts, not your opinions, and let them make up their own minds.

An Appeal to Physicians

Dr. Bernard Nathanson accuses the medical community of "a willful and conscious disregard of the massive and still-growing data identifying the prenatal person as a living, valuable, and fully protectable human being."[715] He goes on to level these indictments against most of his fellow physicians:

> I accuse them of abandoning the canons and principles which lent legitimacy to their organizations, and caving in to the trendy political fashion of the moment. I accuse them of a heinous abuse of their professional trust in failing to protect this unborn patient in their charge. I accuse them of voluntary collaboration in an unprecedented surgical holocaust against these mute and defenseless victims, and I accuse all physician members of these organizations who fail to speak up against this unspeakable crime of complicity in that crime. History will not forgive them.[716]

I appeal to physicians to exonerate themselves by refusing to turn a deaf ear when they hear politically correct but scientifically absurd prochoice claims such as, "It's just a blob of tissue." You know better, or if you don't you should. Integrity demands that you correct the unscientific propaganda being served up to the public to make abortion palatable.

When you hear objections to showing pictures of aborted babies, integrity demands that you stand up and say, "Like it or not, these are real pictures of what happens in an abortion. Those who support abortion must face the fact that it dismembers unborn babies, stops beating hearts, and stops measurable human brain waves. This is not prolife rhetoric. It is established scientific fact."

I have many friends who are physicians, and I deeply respect them. I have no wish to place additional expectations on what is already such a demanding vocation. Still, I must appeal to prolife physicians to take a closer look at the issue of chemical abortions, including those caused not only by Norplant and Depo-Provera, but by the birth control pill. I ask you to read carefully Appendices D and E. If you doubt the evidence and conclusions, by all means research it yourself. But do not allow your personal or financial vested interests—or your inability to find time to do the research—to persuade you to keep prescribing or endorsing the use of chemical contraceptives that may result in the death of preborn children. If you do choose to keep prescribing them, please inform your patients that there is strong evidence suggesting that the Pill may cause abortions[717] and that they may wish to take a look at it before making their decision about whether to use or continue using it.

Counsel your patients to take a hard look at fertility drugs and in vitro fertilization as typically practiced, where embryos—children—are overproduced, resulting in 97% fatalities, and often frozen and later discarded as if they were trash (see 2f). Can you or your patients in good conscience participate in this?

I know it is unpopular for physicians to speak out against the practices of other physicians, but professional loyalty is misplaced when it comes to the killing of human beings. The whole medical profession lies under a shadow of dishonor and guilt for endorsing the practices of those who make their living killing unborn children. I appeal to all prolife doctors and nurses to state clearly your position among your colleagues and medical associations and to stand firmly on it. I appeal to you to band together as local groups and to take out full-page advertisements in local newspapers and make your position clear and unmistakable. I appeal to you to actively participate in prolife activities and to serve on the boards of prolife organizations, even if doing so subjects you to abuse from the politically correct elements of your profession. I appeal to you to remember your oaths and your commitment to human life and welfare.

I appeal to physicians sitting on the fence to get off it once and for all. The only way to come out of the abortion holocaust clean is to separate yourself from the practice of child killing. Refuse to acknowledge it as part of the medical profession, regardless of its current legal status. It is time not only to refuse to do abortions, but to refuse to practice medicine with or make referrals to those who kill children. Do not allow yourself to be remembered as we now remember those who collaborated with the Nazi doctors and became accomplices to their atrocities.

An Appeal to Representatives and Legislators

All those in political office must be painfully aware of the contempt with which many regard you. You are seen as people without integrity or moral courage, as chameleons who kowtow to special interest groups, as spineless bureaucrats more concerned about reelection than the welfare of people. *Show the public they are wrong about you.* Be different. Don't make your goal to keep your job, but to do your job. History condemns politicians who defended slavery because it was unpopular to oppose it. Don't let history condemn you for defending what all people will someday recognize to have been the killing of innocent children.

If you put popularity over morality, at least do so with common sense. The largest poll on abortion ever conducted showed that only 9.2 percent of Americans will withhold their vote from a prolife candidate with whom they largely agree in other areas, but 15.7 percent of Americans will withhold their vote from a candidate purely because he takes a prochoice position, even if they agree with him in other areas.[718] "Hardcore" prolifers outnumber their prochoice counterparts over three times among Republicans, but also outnumber them among Democrats and Independents.[719] The 1999 Gallup poll indicated that "24% of prolife Americans say abortion is a critical issue for them in supporting candidates, compared to only 16% of those in the prochoice camp."[720]

Poll after poll indicates that legislators favoring such measures as parental consent, informed consent, and restriction of all convenience abortions *have the support of most Americans*. Don't misunderstand: The reason you should adopt the prolife position is because of scientific, moral, and biblical reasons, not political ones. I am simply saying that in the majority of cases, holding consistently to the prolife position will gain you more votes than it will lose you. Even if you live in one of those regions where that is not true, of course, your moral responsibility remains the same. Far better to lose an election when standing up for what's right than to win one by compromising the truth.

An Appeal to Those Undecided on Abortion

Ironically, people who are not sure whether they should be prochoice or prolife often end up talking and voting as if they were prochoice. The benefit of their doubt goes to choice rather than life. This should be reevaluated.

If we are standing gun in hand, looking at movement in a bush, we must assume the movement is being made by a person, not a nonperson. Assuming that it's a nonperson will motivate us to shoot, whereas assuming that it's a person will motivate us not to shoot. What is good for hunter safety is good for social ethics. When we're unsure, let's not do something that could kill an innocent person.

The burden of proof is on the prochoice position. If you have read this book, I hope you agree that the evidence of the humanity of the unborn and the reasons against abortion are overwhelming. But even if you don't agree, if you have no more than a reasonable doubt about this matter, surely the benefit of your doubt should go to human life. You should oppose abortion in conversation and at the ballot box. If you don't, then you're shooting into the moving bush and one day, after it's too late, you'll be sorry you did.

An Appeal to Prochoice Christians

I appeal to you to come to grips with the impossibility of being prochoice about abortion without undermining the essence of what it means to be a Christian. A Christian can no more be prochoice about killing children before they are born than he can be prochoice about kidnapping or killing two-year-olds.

To endorse or even to be neutral about killing innocent children created in God's image is unthinkable in the Scriptures, was unthinkable to Christians in church history, and should be unthinkable to Christians today. (See Appendix B, "Abortion in the Bible and Church History.") True Christians do not mindlessly parrot whatever society happens to be saying. They go back to the Scriptures to see what God says, and they believe it even if it is unpopular. They realize that one day they will stand before the Audience of One, and in that day *God's* position on abortion will be the standard by which all others are judged.

An Appeal to Conservative Christians

An Oregon ballot measure proposed that convenience abortions be made illegal and that abortion be allowed only in the cases of rape, incest, and risk to the life of the mother. Though prolifers would want a measure to go even further, this one would have protected the lives of 98 percent of the babies dying in our state. Yet an exit poll found that among those identifying themselves as "fundamentalist Protestants," a full 40 percent *voted against* this measure.[721] Furthermore, on the same ballot, one out of four "fundamentalist Protestants" voted against a measure requiring parental *notification* (not even consent) when minors get abortions.[722] Needless to say, with that showing from the church, both ballot measures failed. (Surprisingly, Catholic voters polled were even more proabortion.)

The church's weak and half-hearted beliefs about abortion come to the surface when Christians face the hardship of a crisis pregnancy. Pregnancy Resource Center counselors confirm that many Christian girls seriously consider getting abortions, and many have been encouraged to do so by parents who profess to be Christians. Since 18 percent of women getting an abortion identify themselves as an evangelical or born again Christian, this means that if there are 1.3 million abortions in a year, 234,000 are performed on Christians.[723] Add chemical abortions and the figure would be much higher. This means that the church is killing its own children at an alarming rate. Our congregations are filled with single girls and boys, young couples, parents, grandparents, sympathetic friends, and even pastors, elders, and deacons who, through their counsel or lack of counsel, have innocent blood on their hands.

Prolife Christians have believed too long that our primary job is to convince the world of what we already know to be true about the unborn. In fact, *the church has failed to educate its own people about abortion.* If the church is to stop the killing in society, it must start by stopping the killing in its own midst. "For it is time for judgment to begin with the family of God" (1 Peter 4:17). If the church does not stand up for the unborn, surely the world never will. If *ProLife Answers* were nothing more than a tool for the church to use in teaching its own people these truths, it would be well worth all the painstaking months of research.

An Appeal to Pastors and Church Leaders

Church leaders should take responsibility for the sad state of the church just described. A bulletin insert or thirty-minute sermon once a year on Sanctity of Human Life Sunday is not nearly enough, though such a message is a great starting place. (See Appendix G for a sample sermon, Appendix H for a church position paper on abortion, and Appendix I for small group Bible studies.) We are dealing in our churches with people whose minds have been conformed to the world. It is our job to help transform the church's thinking according to God's Word (Romans 12:1–2). We must address the pervasive prochoice arguments that daily bombard Christians. (This book could be used with other resources as a text or training manual for this purpose.)

We must not hold back from speaking the truth just because there is no consensus about abortion in our church. It is our job, given to us by God, to teach and minister in such a way as to create that consensus. But if consensus never comes—and it may come only with great difficulty—our job is still to teach the truth.

Pastors should resist the temptation to decide for their people not to see pictures that show the reality of what abortion is. No one should be forced to view such pictures, but neither should others be deprived of the opportunity. By not showing actual pictures of abortion, we keep people from emotionally experiencing the children's humanity and the horrors of abortion. By sparing our churches some short-term discomfort, we leave them liable to consider abortion when they, their family, or friends face an unwanted pregnancy. Forcing such visuals on those who do not choose to see them creates anger, resentment, and resistance. We should carefully prepare our audience. The "Hard Truth" and the "Harder Truth" videos are ideal. They have a musical background without narration and are only eight to nine minutes long, allowing people to look away or close their eyes without having to leave or call attention to themselves.[724]

We must teach what the Bible says in no uncertain terms (see Appendices B and C). We must make use of the many fine prolife resources to educate our people and to equip them to educate the community (see Appendix K). We must participate in prolife strategies, programs, and activities that allow our people to do something for women and children being exploited by abortion (see Appendix F). And, knowing that when we address this subject many women who have had abortions will be touched, we must offer forgiveness and emotional support (see Appendix A).

We must not stay away from this subject for fear of "laying a guilt trip" on women in our churches who have had abortions. On the contrary, we must address it for their sake. There can be no healing without forgiveness, no forgiveness without confession and repentance, and no confession and repentance until abortion is clearly seen to be sin. If we don't speak out, our people will continue to suffer—and continue to kill their babies—without knowing the forgiveness and healing of Christ. The sorrow that comes in facing the reality of abortion is not to be avoided. It is a "godly sorrow" that leads to forgiveness and "leaves no regret" (2 Corinthians 7:10). Without it, there can be no healing and wholeness.

We must not be deceived into thinking that we need only wait for spiritual revival to come and solve the abortion problem. It is our responsibility to draw near to God by dealing with our sin and guilt, so that he is free to come near and bless us. Revival is likely not to precede, but to follow our coming to terms with child-killing:

> Come near to God and he will come near to you. Wash your hands, you sinners, and purify your hearts, you double-minded. Grieve, mourn and wail. Change your laughter to mourning and your joy to gloom. Humble yourselves before the Lord, and he will lift you up. (James 4:8–10)

As I develop in my novel *Lord Foulgrin's Letters,*[725] there are demonic forces behind child-killing. Abortion is Satan's attempt to kill God in effigy by destroying the little ones created in God's image. We are not dealing here with "one more social issue," but a unique and focused evil in which Satan has deeply vested interests.

Jesus said of the devil, "He was a murderer from the beginning.... When he lies he speaks his native language, for he is a liar and the father of lies" (John 8:44). It is no accident that Jesus speaks about Satan's murders and his lies in the same breath. Lies are the wheels that turn every holocaust. To pull off his murders, Satan tells us lies. He is so eloquent, so persuasive in his lies, and we are so gullible, that we fall for his schemes (2 Corinthians 2:11). He masquerades as an angel of light (2 Corinthians 11:14), calling right wrong and wrong right, making us think—as many prochoicers do—that they are taking the moral high ground even as they defend something unspeakably immoral.

If some of the prochoice arguments momentarily cloud and eclipse what you know to be right, realize it is simply because the devil is behind the persuasive rhetoric of the prochoice movement. He is fluent in the language of lies and uses the prevailing assumptions of culture, education, and media to draw us away from God's thoughts about children and abortion and toward his.

We are dealing here with a force of darkness that will bitterly resist every effort to combat it and that requires earnest and sustained prayer and alertness to the spiritual battle (Ephesians 6:10–20). The abortion battle is being fought in the realm of thoughts and ideas. Paul says, "We demolish arguments and every pretension that sets itself up against the knowledge of God, and we take captive every thought to make it obedient to Christ" (2 Corinthians 10:5).

As Christian leaders, we must realize that we will be held accountable, both in this life and in eternity, for how we deal with this issue. We must take deliberate and significant measures to stop the killing, to minister to our hurting women, and to make a difference in our community. The desire to be popular and avoid people's disapproval is a common reason for church leaders to hold back in prolife efforts. But for every reason we have, we must be ready to answer a question on the last day: "Was that reason more important than the lives of all those children I created in my image?"

Martin Luther addressed the pastor's role in facing the greatest evil of his day:

If I profess with the loudest voice and clearest exposition every portion of the truth of God except precisely that point which the world and the devil are at that moment attacking, I am not confessing Christ. Where the battle rages, there the loyalty of the soldier is proven, and to be steady on all the battle fronts besides is mere flight and disgrace if he flinches at that point.

An Appeal to Churches to Extend both Truth and Grace

The world is desperately hungry for two things—truth and grace. Jesus Christ is full of both grace and truth (John 1:14, 17). To see Christ through us, the world must see grace and truth in His followers.

Paradoxically, the church is simultaneously too hostile to the world and too friendly to it. Sinners wanted to be around Jesus, but today they don't want to be around the followers of Jesus. On the other hand, when the church tries to make itself a place where sinners are comfortable, the distinctives of Christianity are sacrificed. The church becomes one more social club that helps people feel good but fails to help them be good.

In the one case, Christians emphasize truth but neglect grace. In the other, they emphasize grace but neglect truth.

Some churches are strong on truth but weak on grace. Some are strong on grace but weak on truth. Truth is not complete without grace and grace is not complete without truth. Grace without truth deceives people. Truth without grace crushes people.

Martin Luther said that the devil doesn't care which side of the horse we fall off of as long as we don't stay in the saddle. To stay in the saddle, the church needs to mount the horse with one foot solidly in the stirrup of truth and the other solidly in the stirrup of grace.

Finding this balance isn't easy. In the past I've intervened on behalf of children at abortion clinics and been arrested and gone to jail for peaceful nonviolent civil disobedience. One of the consequences of that was having to step out of pastoral ministry when one of the clinics tried to garnish my wages from the church and another clinic sued us for 8.4 million dollars. I believed and still believe the truth that unborn children are created in the image of God. That truth has compelled me to say and do things that are not always popular, either in society or in the church. I've always tried to represent the truth in a spirit of grace, but not everyone interprets it that way.

In 1998 Good Shepherd Community Church, where I formerly served as a pastor and am still very active, was picketed by thirty protestors because some of our members do sidewalk counseling at a Portland abortion clinic. They offer women alternatives to abortion and share the gospel with them and pray and sometimes hold up signs encouraging them to let their babies live. So three proabortion groups decided to combine forces and give us a taste of our own medicine. (The groups were Radical Women for Choice, Rock for Choice, and Lesbian Avengers.)

We heard that they were coming, so we set out donuts and coffee for them and tried to strike up conversations with the thirty picketers who showed up. I spent an hour and a half talking with a man named Charles who was holding a sign saying "Keep Abortion Legal." I gave him coffee. When it started raining, I held an umbrella over him. We talked some about abortion, but most of the conversation was about Christ, whom I consider to be the central issue. I shared the gospel with Charles start to finish, he gave me his address, and since then I've sent him a couple of my books and some other gospel material.

Now, I really liked Charles. But when you believe as strongly as I do that abortion is the killing of a child, it's a bit awkward serving coffee and holding an umbrella for someone who is displaying a proabortion sign. Imagine if he were holding a sign saying "Legalize rape" or "Let's kill black people." To me, it's the same thing. Yet, because of the opportunity to share the love of Christ, His truth and His grace, I felt it was the right thing to do. As truth sometimes puts us in awkward situations, so does grace.

That morning we were picketed, having heard that we were going to be protested, some street preaching brothers showed up at our church wearing sandwich boards that talked about sin and hell. Their message was biblical, but there was a significant tactical difference. One of the street preachers barged between my then sixteen-year-old daughter and me and several of the Lesbian Avengers just as we had an opportunity to open a conversation with them. Some of us spoke with the street preachers, asking them to give us a chance to reach out to our visitors the way we thought God was leading us. Most cooperated, but a few of the brothers decided that we were compromisers waffling on the truth and that it was an abomination for us to be giving donuts to people who should be confronted with their sin.

The following Sunday two of the street preachers came back to our church and picketed us.

So, our church has been picketed only twice in our twenty-three year history, once by abortion and homosexual activists, and once by zealous Christians. When you stand for truth, you get picketed by non-Christians, and when you demonstrate grace, you get picketed by Christians.

The solution? You have to decide that you're not going to live for the applause of any particular group. You have to live out your life before the Audience of One, doing what you believe is right in the eyes of your only true Judge—a Savior who is full of both grace and truth.

If anything in the church today needs to be saturated in both grace and truth, it is our approach to the issue of abortion.

An Appeal to Prolife Churches Afraid of Being Distracted from the "Main Thing"

There are many hindrances to establishing a prolife emphasis in the church. One is the deeply held conviction of some members that prolife work distracts us from the main thing. To those who say the job of the church is evangelism, I would point out that prolife activities open great doors for evangelism. Students who make a speech on abortion have follow-up conversations that can lead to sharing the gospel. Those who work at Pregnancy Resource Centers have regular built-in opportunities they would otherwise not have to share Christ. Those who pass out literature at abortion clinics regularly share the love of Christ. People who open their homes to pregnant women can demonstrate a love that is more than words, then follow with the words of the gospel. My own family had the joy of seeing a pregnant young woman come to the Lord while living with us.

Many, both church leaders and members, still insist that it isn't the job of the church to get involved in prolife activities. But what *is* the job of the church? I appeal to you to come to grips with the fact that loving God cannot be separated from loving our neighbor (Matthew 22:34–40). To a man who wished to define "neighbor" in a way that excluded certain groups of needy people, Christ presented the Good Samaritan as a model for our behavior (Luke 10:25–37). He went out of his way to help the man lying in the ditch. In contrast, the religious hypocrites looked the other way because they had more "spiritual" things to do.

In Matthew 25:31–46 Christ makes a distinction of eternal significance based not merely on what people believe and preach, but on what they have *done* for the weak and needy. Can anyone read this passage and still believe that intervening for the needy is some peripheral issue that distracts the church from its main business? On the contrary, it is part and parcel of what the church is to be and do. It is at the heart of our main business.

In His Great Commission, Jesus didn't tell us only to evangelize. He told us to be "teaching them to obey everything I have commanded you" (Matthew 28:20). Jesus commanded us to be compassionate and to take sacrificial action for the weak and needy. If we fail to do this—and if we fail by our words and example to teach others to do this—*then we fail to fulfill the Great Commission.*[726] We show the world and the church that our words about the gospel are only that—words.

Finally, I appeal to you to look to the example of some of the most evangelistically oriented Christians in history. John Wesley actively opposed slavery and encouraged mine workers to unite in order to resist the inhuman treatment by their employers. Evangelist Charles Finney had a major role in the illegal Underground Railroad, saving the lives of many blacks, while under criticism from fellow Christians. D. L. Moody opened homes for underprivileged girls, rescuing them from hopelessness and exploitation. Charles Spurgeon built seventeen homes to help care for elderly women and a large school to provide education for hundreds of children. Spurgeon and his church built homes for orphans in London, rescuing them from starvation and vice on the streets. Amy Carmichael intervened for the sexually exploited girls of India, rescuing them from prostitution in the temples. She built them homes, a school, and a hospital.

We remember all of these Christians for their evangelism but forget their commitment to intervention for the weak, needy, and exploited. Perhaps they were effective in evangelism because, unlike many other Christians of their day—and this day—*they lived out the gospel they preached.* I appeal to churches today to do the same. Otherwise we may be prolife by belief, but prochoice by default.

An Appeal to Active Prolifers

Those of us already involved in prolife work need to be challenged to reexamine both our attitudes and our efforts. We must resist the turf-consciousness that inhibits cooperative action and therefore contributes to the very killing we are trying to stop. We must stop needless duplication of efforts in the same communities and learn from the experience and expertise of others. We must let go of our volunteers and donors and not fear losing them to other groups working for the same cause. We must set aside some of our personal agendas and realize that we can accomplish a great deal more if it doesn't matter who gets the credit.

We should be grateful for thousands of lives saved through informed consent, parental consent, waiting periods, and attempts to restrict partial-birth abortions. We should be grateful for the reduction in the rate of surgical abortions. But we must not smother ourselves in self-congratulation, for the fact is that over a million children are still killed every year. In that light our "victories" ring hollow.

We must not just seek to capture the minds and hearts of others. We must come to truly believe that the earliest surgical abortions and all chemical abortions, including those caused by hormonal "contraceptives," are just as bad as partial-birth abortions. As the battle shifts from surgical to chemical abortions, we must be sure we understand the distinctive nature of chemical abortions. We must not be lulled into thinking that they are somehow more acceptable and less tragic than surgical abortions because they are earlier, less visible, and more sanitized (see Appendices D and E).

We must realize that there are a variety of legitimate prolife activities. The Army, Air Force, Navy, Marines and their special forces all have their role in winning a war, but without strategy and cooperation, they would end up wasting resources and getting caught in each others' cross-fire. Likewise, there is an important place for abortion alternative centers, prolife education, literature distribution, sidewalk counseling, picketing, rescuing, boycotts, political action, Life Chain, and many other activities. But each of these is to serve the whole, not as "the" prolife effort but one working in concert with the others. If one of us wins, we all win; if one loses, we all lose. Without mutual respect and cooperation, prolife organizations will get caught in each other's cross fire, and we will end up fighting the wrong side.

We must work not only harder, but smarter, ever broadening the base of prolife activists, not just burning out a few. All our efforts need to be harnessed as part of a strategic long-term plan to save the most children and women from abortion. At the heart of this must be the mobilization of whole churches, not just individual Christians. *Only the churches can provide the numbers and resources needed to win the battle for children's lives.* Churches must be helped to form prolife task forces to educate and mobilize their own people and make community impact. (There are resources available for pastors, churches, and prolife groups wishing to develop a long-term prolife strategy.[727])

A Concluding Appeal from William Wilberforce

When my wife and I visited the Yad Vashim Holocaust Memorial in Jerusalem, we were most deeply touched by the children's memorial. It has 1500 candles, with mirrors designed to reflect each candle a thousand times, representing the 1.5 million children killed in the Holocaust. We stood in the darkness hearing the names of individual children read one by one.

I was struck by the number, because at the time it was the same number killed by abortion in America each of the previous few years. The fact that most of these children haven't been given names doesn't diminish their worth. I have stood at memorials for the unborn where parents have given names to their children and written them expressions of love and grief. If we could only hear the names of each of these children whispered to us in the darkness, perhaps we would wake up.

Abortion will not go away; it will long outlast *Roe* v. *Wade*. The changing of laws is important, but laws do not automatically change minds or hearts. States that prohibit abortion will be next to states with liberal abortion laws, which will become havens for abortion clinics. Abortion pills and do-it-yourself abortion kits may become increasingly popular. Those who look to the Supreme Court to grant us an abortion-free America will be disillusioned. Many lives can be saved through judicial reform and legislative action, and for that we should rejoice. But our work will not be done until our Lord returns. The jobs of personal intervention, education, and political action will continue for decades to come, requiring great perseverance.

Shortly after his conversion to Christ in 1784, British parliamentarian William Wilberforce began his battle for the black man's freedom. Relentlessly, year after year—in the face of apathy, scorn, and all the opposition the slave industry could offer—this one man reintroduced to Parliament the motion for the abolition of slavery. Rejected again and again, Wilberforce was encouraged by only a few, among them John Wesley and John Newton, former slaveship captain and writer of "Amazing Grace."

Stating that "we are all guilty" for tolerating the evil of slavery, Wilberforce said, "Never, never will we desist till we...extinguish every trace of this bloody traffic, of which our posterity, looking back to the history of these enlightened times will scarce believe that it has been suffered to exist so long a disgrace and dishonor to this country."[728]

Because his colleagues often refused to pay attention to what he said about the realities of slavery, Wilberforce would pull heavy chains from under his chair in Parliament and drape them over himself to symbolize the inhumanity of slavery. His fellow parliamentarians, who were prochoice about slavery, would roll their eyes, mock him, and call him a fool. But it is Wilberforce, not they, who is remembered—by God and men—as the one who stood for justice and mercy.

Year after year, while both non-Christians and Christians denied or ignored reality, Wilberforce suffered sleepless nights, plagued by dreams of the suffering black man. Finally, in 1807, against incredible odds, Wilberforce saw the slave trade outlawed. Even then, he had to fight eighteen more years for the emancipation of existing slaves. Wilberforce died in 1833—three days after the Bill for the Abolition of Slavery passed its second reading in the House of Commons, bringing slavery in England to its final end.

Wilberforce did not enjoy opposing slavery. And though my sacrifices do not begin to compare to Wilberforce's, I for one do not enjoy opposing abortion. It is draining, time consuming, and at times discouraging; it subjects me to frequent criticism. My life would be much easier, much more pleasant, if I could pretend that babies aren't dying. But I cannot. Much as I wish it were otherwise, *abortion kills children*.

Every prochoice argument requires that we pretend, that we play mind games, that we forget, ignore, or deny the humanity, worth, and dignity of unborn babies. The prochoice movement thrives on having a silent victim. It thrives on our ability to forget and ignore innocent victims as long as they are out of our sight. Tell a lie often enough and people will eventually believe it and end up reciting it. This is the story of the prochoice deception in America.

Not all of us are Wilberforces. But had England been filled with people of conviction who would have done what they could for the suffering slaves, Wilberforce's job would have been much easier and untold suffering could have been prevented. Isn't it time for all those who know the truth about abortion to speak up for those who cannot speak for themselves? And not only to speak up, but to show a better way, the way of love. May we reach out with truth and compassion to mothers feeling the pressure to abort. And may we show a morally disintegrating society the better way of mercy and justice for innocent children.

Appendices

Appendix A

FINDING FORGIVENESS
AFTER AN ABORTION

There are two victims in an abortion—one dead, one damaged. If you have been damaged by an abortion, this appendix is written for you. And if you are a man who has been involved in an abortion decision—whether it concerned your girlfriend, wife, daughter, sister, friend, counselee, or parishioner—it is also for you.

Naomi Wolf looks to her conscience in responding to the attempts of society to rationalize and justify her abortion:

> We don't have to lie to ourselves about what we are doing at such a moment. Let us at least look with clarity at what that means and not whitewash self-interest with the language of self-sacrifice. The landscape of many such decisions looks more like Marin County than Verdun. Let us certainly not be fools enough to present such spiritually limited moments to the world with a flourish of pride, pretending that we are somehow pioneers and heroines and even martyrs to have snatched the self, with its aims and pleasures, from the pressure of biology.
>
> That decision was not my finest moment. The least I can do, in honor of the being that might have been, is simply to know that.[729]

Sadly, Ms. Wolf ends her article by imagining a world more honest and forgiving than this one: "And in that world, passionate feminists might well hold candlelight vigils at abortion clinics, standing shoulder to shoulder with the doctors who work there, commemorating and saying goodbye to the dead."

My heart broke for Ms. Wolf as I read her article, and particularly at this ending. Though she makes a commendable attempt to be honest with herself and face the horrible truth of her abortion and her loss of a child, there is a part of her that holds onto abortion as the right decision. Unfortunately, by not fully confessing her sin, nor turning to the only One who can forgive her, she will inevitably remain haunted by her guilt feelings, which are rooted in actual moral guilt.

It is a mistake to try to eliminate feelings of guilt without dealing with the root cause of guilt. No matter how often someone may say to you, "You have nothing to feel guilty about," your guilt feelings will remain because you know better. Only by a denial of reality can you avoid guilt feelings, but such a denial is unhealthy. It sets you up for an emotional collapse whenever something reminds you of the child you once carried. You need a permanent solution to your guilt problem, a solution based on reality, not on denial or pretense.

Because the Bible offers such a solution to your guilt problem, I will quote from it, citing specific biblical books, chapters, and verses. I encourage you to look up these verses in a Bible and think about them on your own.

Because of Christ's death on our behalf, forgiveness is available to all.

The word *gospel* means "good news." The good news is that God loves you and desires to forgive you for your abortion, whether or not you knew what you were doing when you had it. But before the good news can be appreciated, we must know the bad news. The bad news is that there is true moral guilt, and all of us are guilty of many moral offenses against God, of which abortion is only one. "All have sinned and fall short of the glory of God" (Romans 3:23).

Sin is falling short of God's holy standards. Sin separates us from a relationship with God (Isaiah 59:2). Sin deceives us and makes us think that wrong is right and right is wrong (Proverbs 14:12). The Bible says, "The wages of sin is death, but the gift of God is eternal life in Christ Jesus our Lord" (Romans 6:23).

Jesus Christ is the Son of God who loved us so much that he became a member of the human race to deliver us from our sin problem (John 3:16). He came to identify with us in our humanity and our weakness, but did so without being tainted by our sin, self-deception, and moral failings (Hebrews 2:17–18; 4:15–16). Jesus died on the cross as the only one worthy to pay the penalty demanded by the holiness of God for our sins (2 Corinthians 5:21). Being God, and being all-powerful, he rose from the grave, defeating sin and conquering death (1 Corinthians 15:3–4, 54–57).

When Christ died on the cross for us, He said, "It is finished" (John 19:30). The Greek word translated "it is finished" was commonly written across certificates of debt when they were canceled. It meant "paid in full." Christ died so that the certificate of debt consisting of all our sins could once and for all be marked "paid in full."

The Bible is full of offers of forgiveness for every sin.

Because of the work of Jesus Christ on the cross on our behalf, God freely offers us
pardon and forgiveness. Here are just a few of those offers:

> He does not treat us as our sins deserve
> > or repay us according to our iniquities.
> For as high as the heavens are above the earth,
> > so great is his love for those who fear him;
> as far as the east is from the west,
> > so far has he removed our transgressions from us.
> As a father has compassion on his children,
> > so the LORD has compassion on those who fear him;
> for he knows how we are formed,
> > he remembers that we are dust. (Psalm 103:10–14)

> Who is a God like you,
> > who pardons sin and forgives the transgression
> > of the remnant of his inheritance?
> You do not stay angry forever
> > but delight to show mercy.
> You will again have compassion on us;
> > you will tread our sins underfoot
> > and hurl all our iniquities into the depths of the sea. (Micah 7:18–19)

> He who conceals his sins does not prosper,
> > but whoever confesses and
> > renounces them finds mercy. (Proverbs 28:13)

> If we confess our sins, he is faithful
> > and just and will forgive us our sins
> > and purify us from all unrighteousness. (1 John 1:9)

> Therefore, there is now no condemnation
> > for those who are in Christ Jesus. (Romans 8:1)

Forgiveness is a gift that must be received to take effect.

The Bible teaches that Christ died for every person, without exception (1 John 2:2). He offers the gift of forgiveness, salvation, and eternal life to everyone: "Whoever is thirsty, let him come; and whoever wishes, let him take the free gift of the water of life" (Revelation 22:17).

There is no righteous deed we can do that will earn us salvation (Titus 3:5). We come to Christ empty-handed. Salvation is described as a gift—"For it is by grace you have been saved, through faith—and this not from yourselves, it is the gift of God—not by works, so that no one can boast" (Ephesians 2:8–9). This gift cannot be worked for, earned, or achieved. It is not dependent on our merit or effort, but solely on Christ's generosity and sacrifice on our behalf.

Like any gift, the gift of forgiveness can be offered to you, but it is not yours until you choose to receive it. There are cases where convicted criminals have been offered pardon by governors but have actually rejected their pardons. Courts have determined that a pardon is valid only if the prisoner is willing to accept it. Likewise, Christ offers each of us the gift of forgiveness and eternal life, but just because the offer is made does not automatically make it ours. In order to have it, we must choose to accept it.

You may think, "But I don't deserve forgiveness after all I've done." That's exactly right. None of us deserves forgiveness. If we deserved it, we wouldn't need it. That's the point of grace. Christ got what we deserved on the cross so we could get what we don't deserve—forgiveness, a clean slate, a fresh start. Once forgiven, we can look forward to spending eternity in heaven with Christ and our spiritual family (John 14:1–3; Revelation 20:6, 11–15). And once forgiven, you can look forward to being reunited in heaven with all your loved ones covered by the blood of Christ, including the child you lost through abortion (1 Thessalonians 4:13–18).

Because of forgiveness, we need not dwell any longer on our past sins.

God does not want you to go through life punishing yourself for your abortion or for any other wrong you have done. Jesus said to a woman who had lived an immoral lifestyle, "Your sins are forgiven. Your faith has saved you; go in peace" (Luke 7:47–50). Jesus was surrounded by women who were rejected by society but who found compassion, forgiveness, and hope in His love.

No matter what you have done, no sin is beyond the reach of God's grace. God has seen us at our worst and still loves us. The apostle Paul was a murderer; he had participated in the killing of Christians. He called himself the "worst of sinners" (1 Timothy 1:15–16). Yet God not only forgave him, He elevated Paul to leadership in the church. *There are no limits to the forgiving grace of God.*

Having trusted God to forgive us, we must resist the temptation to wallow in our guilt, for we are no longer guilty. Accepting God's grace does not mean pretending we didn't do something wrong, but realizing that even though we did, we are now fully forgiven. Christ asks us to accept His atonement, not to repeat it.

Many women who have had abortions can identify with King David's description of the anguish that plagued him long after the sinful deed was done:

> When I kept silent [about sin], my bones wasted
>   away through my groaning all day long.
> For day and night your hand was heavy upon me;
>   my strength was sapped as in the heat of summer.
> Then I acknowledged my sin to you
>   and did not cover up my iniquity.
> I said, "I will confess my transgressions to the LORD"—
>   and you forgave the guilt of my sin. (Psalm 32:3–5)

You may feel immediately cleansed when you confess your sins, or you may need some help working through some of the things you've experienced. Either way, *you are forgiven*. You should try to forget what lies behind you and move on to a positive future made possible by Christ (Philippians 3:13–14). Whenever we start feeling unforgiven, it's time to go back to all those verses from the Bible and remind ourselves of the reality of our forgiveness.

Forgiveness for the past should be followed by right choices in the present.

Many women who have had abortions carry understandable bitterness toward men who used and abused them, toward parents who were insensitive to their situation, and toward those who misled them or pressured them into a choice that resulted in the death of their child. God expects us to take the forgiveness He has given us and extend it to others (Matthew 6:14–15). Among other things, this frees us from the terrible burden of resentment and bitterness. The warm light of forgiveness—both Christ's toward us and ours toward others—brightens the dark corners of our lives and gives us a whole new joy in living.

One of the most important things you need to do is become part of a therapeutic community, a family of Christians called a church. You may feel self-conscious around Christians because of your past. You shouldn't. A true Christ-centered church is not a showcase for saints, but a hospital for sinners. You will not be judged and condemned for a sin Christ has forgiven. The people you are joining are just as human, just as imperfect, just as needy as you are. Most people in the church aren't self-righteous, and those who are should be pitied because they don't understand God's grace.

There will be others in the church who have also had abortions. A good church will teach the truths of the Bible and will also provide love, acceptance, help, and support for you. If you are looking for such a church in your area, but cannot find one, contact our organization at the address on page 406, and we will gladly help you.

One very healthy thing you can do for others and yourself is to reach out to women in crisis pregnancies. God can use your experience to equip you to help others and to share with them the love and guidance He has given you. My wife and I have a number of good friends who've had abortions. Through their prolife efforts they have given to many other women the help they wish someone had given them when they were pregnant. This has not only saved children from dying and mothers from the pain and guilt of abortion, but it also has helped bring healing to them. It can do the same for you.

Appendix B

ABORTION IN THE BIBLE
AND CHURCH HISTORY

There is a small but influential circle of prochoice advocates who claim to base their beliefs on the Bible. They maintain that "nowhere does the Bible prohibit abortion."[730] Yet the Bible clearly prohibits the killing of innocent people (Exodus 20:13). All that is necessary to prove a biblical prohibition of abortion is to demonstrate that the Bible considers the unborn to be human beings.

Personhood in the Bible

A number of ancient societies opposed abortion,[731] but the ancient Hebrew society had the clearest reasons for doing so because of its foundations in the Scriptures. The Bible teaches that men and women are made in the image of God (Genesis 1:27). As the climax of God's creation mankind has an intrinsic worth far greater than that of the animal kingdom placed under His care. Throughout the Scriptures, personhood is never measured by age, stage of development, or mental, physical, or social skills. Personhood is endowed by God at the moment of creation—before which there was not a human being and after which there is. That moment of creation can be nothing other than the moment of conception (see arguments 1 through 8).

The Hebrew word used in the Old Testament to refer to the unborn (Exodus 21:22–25) is *yeled,* a word that "generally indicates young children, but may refer to teens or even young adults."[732] The Hebrews did not have or need a separate word for unborn children. They were just like any other children, only younger. In the Bible there are references to born children and unborn children, but there is no such thing as a potential, incipient, or "almost" child.

Job graphically described the way God created him before he was born (Job 10:8–12). The person in the womb was not some*thing* that might become Job, but some*one* who was Job, just a younger version of the same man. To Isaiah, God says, "This is what the LORD says—he who made you, who formed you in the womb"

(Isaiah 44:2). What each person is, not merely what he might become, was present in his mother's womb.

Psalm 139:13–16 paints a graphic picture of the intimate involvement of God with a preborn person. God created David's "inmost being," not at birth, but before birth. David says to his Creator, "You knit me together in my mother's womb." Each person, regardless of his parentage or handicap, has not been manufactured on a cosmic assembly line, but has been personally knitted together by God in the womb. All the days of his life have been planned out by God before any have come to be (Psalm 139:16).

As a member of the human race that has rejected God, each person sinned "in Adam," and is therefore a sinner from his very beginning (Romans 5:12–19). David says, "Surely I was sinful at birth." Then he goes back even further, back before birth to the actual beginning of his life, saying he was "sinful from the time my mother conceived me" (Psalm 51:5). *Each person has a sinful nature from the point of conception.* Who but an actual person can have a sinful nature? Rocks and trees and animals and human organs do not have moral natures, good or bad. Morality can be ascribed only to a person. That there is a sin nature at the point of conception demonstrates that there is a person present who is capable of having such a nature.

Jacob was given prominence over his twin Esau "though not yet born" (Romans 9:11). When Rebekah was pregnant with Jacob and Esau, Scripture says, "The *babies* jostled each other within her" (Genesis 25:22). The unborn are regarded as "babies" in the full sense of the term. God tells Jeremiah, "Before I formed you in the womb, I knew you" (Jeremiah 1:5). He could not know Jeremiah in his mother's womb unless Jeremiah, the person, was present in his mother's womb. The Creator is involved in an intimate knowing relationship not only with born people, but with unborn people.

In Luke 1:41, 44 there are references to the unborn John the Baptist, who was at the end of his second trimester in the womb. The word translated *baby* in these verses is the Greek word *brephos*. It is the same word used for the already born baby Jesus (Luke 2:12, 16) and for the babies brought to Jesus to receive His blessing (Luke 18:15–17). It is also the same word used in Acts 7:19 for the newborn babies killed by Pharaoh. To the writers of the New Testament, like the Old, whether born or unborn, a baby is simply a baby. It appears that the preborn John the Baptist responded to the presence of the preborn Jesus in His mother Mary, when Jesus was probably no more than ten days beyond His conception (Luke 1:41).

The angel Gabriel told Mary that she would be "with child and give birth to a son" (Luke 1:31). In the first century, and in every century, to be pregnant is to be *with child*, not with that which might become a child. The Scriptures teach the psychosomatic unity of the whole person, body, soul, and spirit (1 Thessalonians 5:23). Wherever there is a genetically distinct living human being, there is a living soul and spirit.

The Status of the Unborn

One scholar states: "Looking at Old Testament law from a proper cultural and historical context, it is evident that the life of the unborn is put on the same par as a person outside the womb."[733] When understood as a reference to miscarriage, Exodus 21:22–25 is sometimes used as evidence that the unborn is subhuman. But a proper understanding of the passage shows the reference is not to a miscarriage, but to a premature birth, and that the "injury" referred to, which is to be compensated for like all other injuries, applies to the child as well as to his mother. This means that, "far from justifying permissive abortion, it in fact grants the unborn child a status in the eyes of the law equal to the mother's."[734]

Meredith Cline observes, "The most significant thing about abortion legislation in Biblical law is that there is none. It was so unthinkable that an Israelite woman should desire an abortion that there was no need to mention this offense in the criminal code."[735] All that was necessary to prohibit an abortion was the command, "You shall not murder" (Exodus 20:13). Every Israelite knew that the preborn child was indeed a child. Therefore, miscarriage was always viewed as the loss of a child and abortion as the killing of a child.

Numbers 5:11–31 is an unusual passage of Scripture used to make a central argument in *A Prochoice Bible Study,* published by Episcopalians for Religious Freedom.[736] They cite the New English Bible's peculiar translation which makes it sound as if God brings a miscarriage on a woman if she is unfaithful to her husband. Other translations refer to a wasting of the thigh and a swelling of her abdomen, but do not take it to mean pregnancy, which would presumably simply be called that directly if it were in mind.

The woman could have been pregnant by her husband, assuming they had been having sex, which Hebrew married couples normally did. It appears that God was expected to do some kind of miracle related to the bitter water, creating a dramatic physical reaction if adultery had been committed. The text gives no indication of either pregnancy or abortion. Indeed, in the majority of cases of suspected adultery, there would be no pregnancy and therefore no child at risk.

The *Prochoice Bible Study* that cites the NEB's unique translation suggests if God indeed causes a miscarriage, it would therefore be an endorsement of people causing abortions. This is a huge stretch, since neither the wife, husband, nor priest made the decision to induce an abortion, nor would they have had the right to do so. The passage does not seem to refer to a miscarriage at all; but even if it did, there is certainly nothing to suggest any endorsement of human beings initiating an abortion.

Child Sacrifice

Child sacrifice is condemned throughout Scripture. Only the most degraded societies tolerated such evil, and the worst of these defended and celebrated it as if it were a virtue. Ancient dumping grounds have been found filled with the bones of hundreds of dismembered infants. This is strikingly similar to discoveries of thousands of dead babies discarded by modern abortion clinics. One scholar of the ancient Near East refers to infant sacrifice as "the Canaanite counterpart to abortion."[737] Unlike the pagan sacrifices, however, with abortion, child-killing need no longer be postponed till birth.

Scripture condemns the shedding of innocent blood (Deuteronomy 19:10; Proverbs 6:17; Isaiah 1:15; Jeremiah 22:17). While the killing of all innocent human beings is detestable, the Bible regards the killing of children as particularly heinous (Leviticus 18:21; 20:1–5; Deuteronomy 12:31). The prophets of Israel were outraged at the sacrifice of children by some of the Jews. They warned that it would result in the devastating judgment of God on their society (Jeremiah 7:30–34; Ezekiel 16:20–21, 36–38; 20:31; compare 2 Kings 21:2–6 and Jeremiah 15:3–4).

Abortion and Church History

Christians throughout church history have affirmed with a united voice the humanity of the preborn child.[738] The second-century *Epistle of Barnabas* speaks of "killers of the child, who abort the mold of God." It treats the unborn child as any other human "neighbor" by saying, "You shall love your neighbor more than your own life. You shall not slay a child by abortion. You shall not kill that which has already been generated" (*Epistle of Barnabas* 19.5).

The Didache, a second-century catechism for young converts, states, "Do not murder a child by abortion or kill a newborn infant" (*Didache* 2.2). Clement of Alexandria maintained that "those who use abortifacient medicines to hide their fornication cause not only the outright murder of the fetus, but of the whole human race as well" (*Paedogus,* 2:10.96.1).

Defending Christians before Marcus Aurelius in A.D. 177, Athenagoras argued, "What reason would we have to commit murder when we say that women who induce abortions are murderers, and will have to give account of it to God?... The fetus in the womb is a living being and therefore the object of God's care" (*A Plea for the Christians*, 35.6.)

Tertullian said, "It does not matter whether you take away a life that is born, or destroy one that is coming to the birth. In both instances, destruction is murder" (*Apology*, 9.4). Basil the Great affirmed, "Those who give abortifacients for the destruction of a child conceived in the womb are murderers themselves, along with those receiving the poisons" (*Canons*, 188.2). Jerome called abortion "the murder of an unborn child" (*Letter to Eustochium*, 22.13). Augustine warned against the terrible crime of "the murder of an unborn child" (*On Marriage*, 1.17.15). Origen, Cyprian, and Chrysostom were among the many other prominent theologians and church leaders who condemned abortion as the killing of children. New Testament scholar Bruce Metzger comments, "It is really remarkable how uniform and how pronounced was the early Christian opposition to abortion."[739]

Throughout the centuries, Roman Catholic leaders have consistently upheld the sanctity of human life. Likewise, Protestant reformer John Calvin followed both the Scriptures and the historical position of the church when he affirmed:

> The fetus, though enclosed in the womb of its mother, is already a human being and it is a most monstrous crime to rob it of the life which it has not yet begun to enjoy. If it seems more horrible to kill a man in his own house than in a field, because a man's house is his place of most secure refuge, it ought surely to be deemed more atrocious to destroy a fetus in the womb before it has come to light.[740]

Modern theologians with a strong biblical orientation agree that abortion is the killing of a child. Dietrich Bonhoeffer, who lost his life standing up against the murder of the innocent in Germany, argued that abortion is "nothing but murder."[741] Karl Barth stated, "The unborn child is from the very first a child...it is a man and not a thing, not a mere part of the mother's body.... Those who live by mercy will always be disposed to practice mercy, especially to a human being which is so dependent on the mercy of others as the unborn child."[742]

In the last few decades it has become popular for certain theologians and ministers to be proabortion. The Religious Coalition for Abortion Rights, for instance, has adopted the motto, "Prayerfully Prochoice," and prochoice advocates point to it as proof that conscientious Christians can be prochoice. Yet the arguments set forth by such advocates are shallow, inconsistent, and violate the most basic principles of biblical interpretation. Their arguments are clearly read into the biblical texts rather than derived from them.[743]

The "Christian" prochoice position is nothing more than an accommodation to modern secular beliefs, and it flies in the face of the Bible and the historical position of the church. If the church is to be the church, it must challenge and guide the morality of society, not mirror it.

Conclusion: The Bible and the Children

Even if church history were unclear on the matter, the Bible is very clear. Every child in the womb has been created by God, and He has laid out a plan for that child's life. Furthermore, Christ loves that child and proved it by becoming like him—He spent nine months in His mother's womb. Finally, Christ died for that child, showing how precious He considers him to be.

Christ's disciples failed to understand how valuable children were to Him, and they rebuked those who tried to bring them near Him (Luke 18:15–17). But Jesus called the children to Him and said, "Let the little children come to me, and do not hinder them, for the kingdom of God belongs to such as these." He did not consider attention to children a distraction from His kingdom business, but an integral part of it.

The biblical view of children is that they are a blessing and gift from the Lord (Psalm 127:3–5). Society is treating children more and more as liabilities. We must learn to see them as God does—"He defends the cause of the fatherless and the widow, and loves the alien, giving him food and clothing" (Deuteronomy 10:18). Furthermore, we must act toward them as God commands us to act:

> Defend the cause of the weak and fatherless;
> maintain the rights of the poor and oppressed.
> Rescue the weak and needy;
> deliver them from the hand of the wicked. (Psalm 82:3–4)

As we intervene on behalf of His littlest children, let's realize it is Christ Himself for whom we intervene (Matthew 25:40).

BIBLICAL PASSAGES
RELEVANT TO LIFE ISSUES

Note: Emphases are the author's.

1. Life begins in the womb.

"The **babies** [Jacob and Esau] jostled each other within her [Rebekah]" (Genesis 25:22).

"In the womb **he** [Jacob] grasped his brother's heel; as a man **he** struggled with God" (Hosea 12:3).

"**Your hands shaped me and made me.** Will you now turn and destroy me? Remember that **you molded me like clay.** Will you now turn me to dust again? Did you not pour me out like milk and curdle me like cheese, **clothe me with skin and flesh and knit me together with bones and sinews?** You gave me life and showed me kindness, and **in your providence watched over my spirit**" (Job 10:8–12).

"Did not he who made me in the womb make them? **Did not the same one form us both within our mothers?**" (Job 31:15).

"For you created my inmost being; **you knit me together in my mother's womb.** I praise you because I am fearfully and wonderfully made…. My frame was not hidden from you when I was made in the secret place. When I was woven together in the depths of the earth, **your eyes saw my unformed body.** All the days ordained for me were written in your book before one of them came to be" (Psalm 139:13–16).

"Surely I was sinful at birth; **sinful from the time my mother conceived me**" (Psalm 51:5). Note: Only a person can have a sin nature. David's statement clearly shows that he was a person at the point of conception.

"**Before I formed you in the womb I knew you,** before you were born I set you apart; I appointed you as a prophet to the nations" (Jeremiah 1:5).

"His mother Mary…was found to be **with child** through the Holy Spirit…[the angel said] '**what is conceived in her is from the Holy Spirit**'" (Matthew 1:18–20).

"But the angel said to Mary, 'You will be **with child** and give birth to a son, and you are to give him the name Jesus.... The Holy Spirit will come upon you, and the power of the Most High will overshadow you. So the holy one to be born will be called the Son of God'" (Luke 1:30–31, 35).

Summary of Luke 1:39–44: After the angel left, Mary "hurried" (v. 39) to get to Elizabeth. Unborn John the Baptist (in his sixth month after conception) responded to the presence of unborn Jesus inside Mary. Allowing for travel time, Jesus was no more than eight to ten days beyond conception when they arrived. Implantation doesn't begin until six days after conception and isn't complete until twelve. **Most likely Jesus was not yet fully implanted in his mother's womb when unborn John responded to his presence.**

"The Word became flesh and made his dwelling among us. We have seen his glory, the glory of the One and Only, who came from the Father, full of grace and truth" (John 1:14).

When did the Word (Christ) become flesh? When did He leave heaven and come to earth? Was there generic soulless flesh conceived in Mary waiting for Christ to inhabit it later in the pregnancy? No. It is basic Christian doctrine that Christ became flesh at the moment the Holy Spirit overshadowed Mary, at the moment of fertilization. He became human at the exact point all others become human, the point of conception. The "blastocyst" is an eternal human soul, literally "the least of these," Christ's brethren (Matthew 25:40).

2. God is Creator and Owner of all people—they belong to Him, not others.

"So God created man in his own image, in the image of God he created him; male and female he created them" (Genesis 1:27).

"Know that the LORD Himself is God: it is He who has made us, and not we ourselves; we are His people and the sheep of His pasture" (Psalm 100:3, NASB).

"For every living soul belongs to me, the father as well as the son" (Ezekiel 18:4).

"Yet, O LORD, you are our Father. We are the clay, you are the potter; we are all the work of your hand" (Isaiah 64:8).

"Do you not know that your body is a temple of the Holy Spirit, who is in you, whom you have received from God? You are not your own; you were bought at a price. Therefore honor God with your body" (1 Corinthians 6:19–20).

3. God has exclusive prerogatives over human life and death.

"See now that I myself am He! There is no god besides me. **I put to death and I bring to life,** I have wounded and I will heal, and no one can deliver out of my hand" (Deuteronomy 32:39).

"The LORD brings death and makes alive; he brings down to the grave and raises up" (1 Samuel 2:6).

"You shall not commit murder" (Exodus 20:13). *Note: Except when He specifically delegates that right to men (e.g., capital punishment, self-defense, just war), God alone has the right to take a human life.*

"And for your lifeblood I will surely demand an accounting.... And from each man, too, **I will demand an accounting for the life of his fellow man**" (Genesis 9:5).

"If men who are fighting hit a pregnant woman and she gives birth prematurely but there is no serious injury, the offender must be fined whatever the woman's husband demands and the court allows. But if there is serious injury, you are to take life for life, eye for eye, tooth for tooth, hand for hand, foot for foot, burn for burn, wound for wound, bruise for bruise" (Exodus 21:22–25).

"Nothing in all creation is hidden from God's sight. Everything is uncovered and laid bare before the eyes of him to whom we must give account" (Hebrews 4:13).

4. God hates the shedding of innocent blood.

"**Do not give any of your children to be sacrificed** to Molech, for you must not profane the name of your God. I am the LORD" (Leviticus 18:21).

"The LORD said...'Any Israelite or any alien living in Israel who gives any of his children to Molech must be put to death. The people of the community are to stone him.... **by giving his children to Molech, he has defiled my sanctuary and profaned my holy name....** If the people of the community **close their eyes** when that man gives one of his children to Molech...I will set my face against that man and his family and will cut off from their people both him and all who follow him'" (Leviticus 20:1–5).

"Do this **so that innocent blood will not be shed in your land**, which the LORD your God is giving you as your inheritance, and **so that you will not be guilty of bloodshed**" (Deuteronomy 19:10).

"The LORD sent Babylonian, Aramean, Moabite and Ammonite raiders against him. He sent them to destroy Judah, in accordance with the word of the

LORD proclaimed by his servants the prophets. Surely these things happened to Judah according to the LORD'S command, in order to remove them from his presence **because of the sins of Manasseh and all he had done, including the shedding of innocent blood.** For **he filled Jerusalem with innocent blood,** and the LORD was not willing to forgive" (2 Kings 24:2–4).

"The LORD said, 'What have you done? Listen! **Your brother's blood cries out to me from the ground'**" (Genesis 4:10).

"For God will deliver the needy who cry out, the afflicted who have no one to help. He will take pity on the weak and the needy and save the needy from death. He will rescue them from oppression and violence, for **precious is their blood in his sight**" (Psalm 72:12–14).

"There are six things the LORD hates, seven that are detestable to him: haughty eyes, a lying tongue, **hands that shed innocent blood**" (Proverbs 6:16–19).

"Therefore as surely as I live, declares the Sovereign LORD, I will give you over to bloodshed and it will pursue you. **Since you did not hate bloodshed, bloodshed will pursue you**" (Ezekiel 35:6).

5. God has a special love for children.

"See that you do not look down on one of these little ones. For I tell you that their angels in heaven always see the face of my Father in heaven" (Matthew 18:10).

"But Jesus called the children to him and said, 'Let the little children come to me, and do not hinder them, for the kingdom of God belongs to such as these'" (Luke 18:16).

"Your Father in heaven is not willing that any of these little ones should be lost" (Matthew 18:14).

"Sons are a heritage from the LORD, children a reward from him" (Psalm 127:3–4).

Appendix D

CHEMICAL ABORTIONS IN LIGHT
OF HISTORY AND SCRIPTURE

Many Christian women have surgical abortions—far more than most people realize. *Family Planning Perspectives* reports that nearly one out of five women getting surgical abortions claims to be a "born again" or an "evangelical" Christian.[744] While nonreligious women are four times more likely to get abortions than religious women, 68 percent of women getting abortions claim to be either Catholics or Protestants.[745] It is important for churches to teach on this subject, as well as related ones, such as abstinence.

In thousands of churches across the country there is at least *some* voice against surgical abortions. But in many of these same churches *chemical* abortions are going almost completely unchallenged. This is true even in some prolife organizations, which are strangely silent about chemical abortifacients or limit their concerns to Mifepristone (RU-486) and the morning-after pill.

Surgical abortions have begun to decrease, though unfortunately they'll still be around for a long time; chemical abortions are the future wave of abortion in America and around the world. It is essential that we understand their nature and impact.

The IUD, Norplant, Depo-Provera, ECP, and RU-486

Prolifers have long opposed using the intrauterine device (IUD) because it does not prevent conception, but keeps the already conceived child from implanting in his mother's womb. A 1995 paper by Irving Sivin challenges this understanding.[746] Since other evidence suggests that it is an abortifacient, the jury appears to still be out on the IUD.

RU-486 (Mifepristone), the antiprogestin abortion pill, is a human pesticide, causing a mother's womb to become hostile to her own child and resulting in an induced miscarriage.

Depo-Provera is a progestin (medroxyprogesterone) injected every three months. It sometimes suppresses ovulation, but it also thins the lining of the uterus, apparently preventing implantation.

Norplant is another progestin (levonorgestrel) enclosed in five or six flexible closed capsules or rods, which are surgically implanted beneath the skin. It often suppresses ovulation, but sometimes ovulation occurs; and when it does, an irritation to the uterine wall may often prevent implantation.

The Emergency Contraceptive Pill (ECP), also known as the "morning-after pill," can suppress ovulation, but its main function is to keep a fertilized egg from implanting in the uterus.

All of these birth control methods either sometimes or often alter the mother's womb in a way that causes it to reject the human life God designed it to nourish and sustain.

Christians properly reject these methods because they know that human life begins at conception, six days before implantation begins. Therefore, anything that interferes with implantation kills a person created in the image of God.

These birth control methods are routinely referred to as contraceptives, but they are *not* exclusively contraceptives. That is, they do not always prevent conception. Sometimes or often they result in the death of already conceived human beings.

The Minipill (Progestin-only)

Progestin-only pills, which have no estrogen, are often called minipills. Many people confuse minipills with the far more popular combination estrogen/progestin pills, which are the true birth control pill.

Drug Facts and Comparisons, a standard reference book for physicians, says:

> Oral contraceptives (OCs) include estrogen/progestin combos and progestin-only products. Progestin-only [pills]...alter the cervical mucus, exert a progestational effect on the endometrium, apparently producing cellular changes that render the endometrium hostile to implantation by a fertilized ovum (egg) and, in some patients, suppress ovulation.[747]

Note that a primary effect of progestin-only pills is to make the uterine lining, the endometrium, "hostile to implantation by a fertilized ovum." In other words, they cause an abortion of a human being roughly a week after his or her conception.

I have been told that many users of the minipill think their ovulations are being suppressed. But in his book *Gynecology: Principles and Practices,* Robert W. Kistner says, "Certainly the majority of women using the progestin-only pill continue to ovulate."[748]

A 1981 Searle leaflet, packaged with their progestin-only pill, says that the product "makes the womb less receptive to any fertilized egg that reaches it." Dr. Joseph W. Goldzieher states, "Endometrial resistance to implantation is an important mechanism of the minipill."[749] And *The Physician's Desk Reference* says progestogen-only oral contraceptives "are known to alter the cervical mucus and exert a progestational effect on the endometrium, interfering with implantation."[750]

Clearly the progestin-only pill, by its effects on the endometrium, causes abortions and must be added to the list of abortive birth control methods. Like all the aforementioned products, the changes the minipill creates in the mother's endometrium make the womb hostile to the newly conceived child, instead of hospitable to him, as God designed the mother's womb to be.

The New Morning-After Pill: Standard BCPs

In June 1996 the Food and Drug Administration announced a new use for standard combination birth control pills:

> Two high doses taken within two to three days of intercourse can prevent pregnancy, the FDA scientists said. Doctors think the pills probably work by preventing a fertilized egg from implanting in the lining of the uterus.[751]

On February 24, 1997, the FDA approved the use of high doses of combination birth control pills as "emergency contraception." The article explains,

> The morning-after pill refers to a regimen of standard birth control pills taken within 72 hours of unprotected sex to prevent an unwanted pregnancy. The pills prevent pregnancy by inhibiting a fertilized egg from implanting itself in the uterus and developing into a fetus.[752]

Of course, the pills do *not* "prevent pregnancy" since pregnancy begins at conception, not implantation. Acting as if pregnancy begins at implantation takes the emphasis off the baby's existence and puts it on the mother's endometrium's role in sustaining the child that has already been created within her. As *World* magazine points out, "In reality the pill regimen—designed to block a fertilized egg from implanting into the uterus—aborts a pregnancy that's already begun."[753]

It is significant that the morning-after pill is in fact nothing but a combination of several standard birth control pills taken in high dosages. When the announcement was made, the uninformed public probably assumed that the high dosage makes birth control pills do something that they were otherwise incapable of doing. But the truth is, it simply increases the chances of doing what it already sometimes does—causes an abortion.

A *USA Today* cover story stated,

> U.S. gynecologists are launching a major nationwide campaign to make sure women know about the best-kept morning-after contraceptive secret: common birth control pills.... Some oral contraceptives may be taken after intercourse—two in the first dose up to 72 hours after sex, then two more 12 hours later—and will prevent 75% of pregnancies.... Critics call the morning-after method de facto abortion, but Zinberg says the pills work before an embryo implants in the uterus so there's no abortion.[754]

This is another illustration of the role of semantics in minimizing our perception of the true nature of chemical abortions. The truth is that these pregnancies aren't prevented, they are *terminated*. It's semantic gymnastics to redefine abortion in such a way that killing the "fertilized egg" doesn't qualify.

There has been at least some backlash to the morning-after pill. Wal-Mart decided in 2000 not to sell the drug Preven presumably because it is commonly used as a "day after contraceptive," which means it is an abortifacient. Planned Parenthood initiated a boycott against Wal-Mart for choosing not to dispense this drug. Wal-Mart said that this was a business decision, not a moral one. A number of prolife pharmacists working for other drugstores have stated that they cannot in good conscience dispense chemical abortifacients. Some have been fired, while others have been allowed to exercise their consciences and keep their jobs.

Chemical Abortions: History and Scripture

It was in the face of chemical and device-caused abortions that Christian leaders in the first few centuries consistently denounced all abortions. For instance, in about A.D. 200, Minucius Felix wrote in *Octavius,* "There are women who swallow drugs to stifle in their own womb the beginnings of a man to be—committing infanticide before they even give birth to the infant." In the fourth century, Basil the Great wrote, "Those who give abortifacients for the destruction of a child conceived in the womb are murderers themselves, along with those receiving the poisons" (see Appendix B: "Abortion in the Bible and Church History").

In fact, a strong case can be made for understanding the Greek word translated "sorcery" in Galatians 5:20 as a reference to administering drugs to commit abortions. This word is *pharmakeia*, from which we get our word *pharmaceuticals*, or drugs. The administering of drugs and potions was common in sorcery, and hence the word sometimes took on that secondary connotation. But it is also used in the Greek literature of the day with its original primary meaning of drugs, chemicals, or medications. The most prevalent social example of the evil use of chemicals was administering them to induce abortions. *Pharmakeia* was used early in the second century by the physician Soranos of Ephesus in his book *Gynecology*, referring specifically to drugs that cause abortions.

Galatians 5:20 lists *pharmakeia*, translated "witchcraft" in the NIV, as one of the "acts of the sinful nature." Preceding it are sexual immorality, impurity, debauchery, and idolatry. All of these relate to the sexually immoral practices that led to many unwanted children and therefore many abortions, giving further credence to the idea that *pharmakeia* may refer to, or at least include, using chemicals to kill unborn children.

The same word is used three times in Revelation. Revelation 9:21 says: "Nor did they repent of their murders, their *pharmakeus*, their sexual immorality or their thefts." Revelation 21:8 states: "But the cowardly, the unbelieving, the vile, the murderers, the sexually immoral, the *pharmakeus*, the idolaters and all liars—their place will be in the fiery lake of burning sulfur." Revelation 22:15 says, "Outside are the dogs, the *pharmakeus*, the sexually immoral, the murderers, the idolaters and everyone who loves and practices falsehood."

Even if these scriptural passages do not refer to chemical abortions (we cannot be certain one way or the other), everything else we know of Scripture and church history tells us that we should oppose all forms of abortion with vigor and consistency.

As the devil loved the sacrifice of children in the ancient heathen cultures, so he loves the sacrifice of children in our modern culture. Whether children are sacrificed to a heathen god called Molech or to the god of our own convenience, he does not care. (See Appendix C for Scriptures on the shedding of innocent blood.) Whether these children are born or unborn does not matter to God's enemies, for each of them is equally created in the image of God, and by killing them Satan comes as close as he can to striking out at God Himself. In killing those created in God's image, Satan kills God in effigy.

The evil one's vested interests in our blindness to this issue cannot be overstated. The forces of darkness desperately do not want us to see these newly conceived children as their Creator sees them. If we are to come over to God's way of thinking about them, it will only be through searching the Scriptures, praying, examining the evidence, and openly and boldly addressing this issue in our churches and Christian organizations.

Will Chemical Abortions End the Debate?

Some abortion advocates and even some prolifers think that chemical abortifacients in general, and the abortion pill in particular, will at long last end the abortion debate. They suppose that the privatization of abortion procedures will mean that the prolife movement will not be able to effectively respond.

This is incorrect for several reasons. First, there will still be surgical abortions, as chemical abortions kill babies only in the early weeks of pregnancy. Some women will choose surgery because it seems less threatening to them than chemicals that could bring harm in unknown ways.

Furthermore, RU-486 requires multiple visits to an abortion center. It is not the private little measure it's portrayed as being. Father Frank Pavone says,

> If those who are pregnant can find out who administers chemical abortions, then so can the prolife movement, and the prolife movement will be there to protest the providers and provide alternatives for the mothers. Just as doctors who destroy babies and their mothers by surgical methods are increasingly brought to court to account for their malpractice, so will doctors who destroy babies and their mothers by chemical methods.
>
> Methods of injustice may change, but will we stop crying out for justice? What makes them imagine that by coming up with new ways to kill children, they can make us stop loving those children and working to save them?
>
> No matter the method of abortion, fundamental questions will still cry out for answers: Who are the unborn? Are they equal in dignity to the born? Who is responsible for them? Will they be protected and welcomed in a land which declares that all are created equal? Why should the rightful advancement of women—which we support—depend on providing them with license to kill their children?[755]

Appendix E

DOES THE BIRTH CONTROL
PILL CAUSE ABORTIONS?

"The pill" is the popular term for more than forty different commercially available oral contraceptives. In medicine, they are commonly referred to as BCPs (birth control pills) or OCs (oral contraceptives). They are also called "combination pills," because they contain a combination of estrogen and progestin.

The pill is used by about fourteen million American women in any given year. Across the globe it is used by about sixty million. The question of whether it causes abortions has a direct bearing on untold millions of Christians, many of them prolife, who use and recommend it. For those who believe that God is the Creator of each person and the giver and taker of human life, this is a question with profound moral implications.

In 1991, while researching the original edition of *ProLife Answers to ProChoice Arguments,* I heard someone suggest that birth control pills can cause abortions. This was brand new to me; in all my years as a pastor and a prolifer, I had never heard it before. I was immediately skeptical.

My vested interests were strong because Nanci and I used the pill in the early years of our marriage, as did many of our prolife friends. Why not? We believed that it simply prevented conception. We never suspected it had any potential for abortion. No one told us this was even a possibility. I confess I never read the fine print of the pill's package insert, nor am I sure I would have understood it if I had.

In fourteen years as a pastor, I did considerable premarital counseling. I always warned couples against the IUD because I'd read it could cause early abortions. I typically recommended that young couples use the pill because of its relative ease and effectiveness.

At the time I was researching *ProLife Answers,* I found only one person who could point me toward any documentation that connected the pill and abortion. She told me of just one primary source that supported this belief, and I found only one other. Still, these two sources were sufficient to compel me to include this warning in the book:

Some forms of contraception, specifically the intrauterine device (IUD), Norplant, and certain low-dose oral contraceptives, often do not prevent conception, but prevent implantation of an already fertilized ovum. The result is an early abortion, the killing of an already conceived individual. Tragically, many women are not told this by their physicians and therefore do not make an informed choice about which contraceptive to use.[756]

As it turns out, I made a critical error. At the time, I incorrectly believed that low-dose birth control pills were the exception, not the rule. I thought most people who took the pill were in no danger of having abortions. What I've found in more recent research is that *since 1988 virtually all oral contraceptives used in America are low-dose; that is, they contain much lower levels of estrogen than the earlier birth control pills.*

The standard amount of estrogen in the birth control pills of the 1960s and early 1970s was 150 micrograms. The use of estrogen-containing formulations with less than 50 micrograms of estrogen steadily increased to 75 percent of all prescriptions in the United States in 1987. In the same year, only 3 percent of the prescriptions were for formulations that contained more than 50 micrograms of estrogen. Because these higher-dose estrogen formulations have a greater incidence of adverse effects without greater efficacy, they are no longer marketed in the United States.[757]

After the pill had been on the market for fifteen years, many serious negative side effects of estrogen had been clearly proven. These included blurred vision, nausea, cramping, irregular menstrual bleeding, headaches, increased incidence of breast cancer, strokes, and heart attacks, some of which led to fatalities.[758]

In response to these concerns, beginning in the midseventies, manufacturers of the pill steadily decreased the content of estrogen and progestin in their products. The average dosage of estrogen in the pill declined from 150 micrograms in 1960 to 35 micrograms in 1988. These facts are directly stated in an advertisement by the Association of Reproductive Health Professionals and Ortho Pharmaceutical Corporation in *Hippocrates* magazine.[759]

Pharmacists for Life confirms: "As of October 1988, the newer lower dosage birth control pills are the only type available in the U.S., by mutual agreement of the Food and Drug Administration and the three major Pill manufacturers."[760]

What is now considered a "high dose" of estrogen is 50 micrograms, which is in fact a very low dose in comparison to the 150 micrograms once standard for the pill. The low-dose pills of today are mostly 20–35 micrograms. As far as I can tell, there are no birth control pills available today that have more than 50 micrograms of estrogen. An M.D. wrote to inform me that she had researched many pills by name and could confirm my findings. If such pills exist at all, they are certainly rare.

Not only was I wrong in thinking low-dose contraceptives were the exception rather than the rule, I didn't realize there was considerable documented medical information linking birth control pills and abortion. The evidence was there, I just didn't probe deeply enough to find it. Still more evidence has surfaced in subsequent years. I have presented this evidence in detail in my eighty-eight-page book *Does the Birth Control Pill Cause Abortions?* I will now summarize that research.

The Physician's Desk Reference (PDR)

The *Physician's Desk Reference* is the most frequently used reference book by physicians in America. The *PDR,* as it's often called, lists and explains the effects, benefits, and risks of every medical product that can be legally prescribed. The Food and Drug Administration requires that each manufacturer provide accurate information on its products, based on scientific research and laboratory tests. This information is included in the *PDR.*

As you read the following, keep in mind that the term *implantation,* by definition, *always* involves an already conceived human being. Therefore, any agent which serves to prevent implantation functions as an abortifacient.

This is the *PDR*'s product information for Ortho-Cept, as listed by Ortho, one of the largest manufacturers of the pill:

> Combination oral contraceptives act by suppression of gonadotropins. Although the primary mechanism of this action is inhibition of ovulation, other alterations include changes in the cervical mucus, which increase the difficulty of sperm entry into the uterus, and changes in the endometrium which reduce the likelihood of implantation.[761]

The FDA-required research information on the birth control pills Ortho-Cyclen and Ortho Tri-Cyclen also state that they cause "changes in. . .the endometrium [which reduce the likelihood of implantation]."[762]

Notice that these changes in the endometrium and the fact that they reduce the likelihood of implantation are not stated by the manufacturer as speculative or theoretical effects, but as actual ones. They consider this such a well-established fact that it requires no statement of qualification.

Similarly, as I document in my book, Syntex and Wyeth, the other two major pill manufacturers, say essentially the same thing about their oral contraceptives. (I also relate in the book the results of my phone calls to each of these manufacturers to discuss this issue.)

The inserts packaged with birth control pills are condensed versions of longer research papers detailing the pill's effects, mechanisms, and risks. Near the end, the insert typically says something like the following, which is taken directly from the Desogen pill insert:

> If you want more information about birth control pills, ask your doctor, clinic or pharmacist. They have a more technical leaflet called the Professional Labeling, which you may wish to read. The Professional Labeling is also published in a book entitled *Physician's Desk Reference*, available in many bookstores and public libraries.

Of the half dozen birth control pill package inserts I've read, only *one* included the information about the pill's abortive mechanism. This was a package insert dated July 12, 1994, found in the oral contraceptive Demulen, manufactured by Searle. Yet this abortive mechanism was *referred to in all cases* in the FDA-required manufacturer's Professional Labeling, as documented in the *Physician's Desk Reference*.

In summary, according to multiple references throughout the *Physician's Desk Reference*, which articulate the research findings of all the birth control pill manufacturers, there are *not one, but three mechanisms of birth control pills*:

1. inhibiting ovulation (the primary mechanism),
2. thickening the cervical mucus, thereby making it more difficult for sperm to travel to the egg,
3. thinning and shriveling the lining of the uterus to the point that it is unable or less able to facilitate the implantation of the newly fertilized egg.

The first two mechanisms are contraceptive. The third is abortive.

When a woman taking the pill discovers she is pregnant (according to the *Physician's Desk Reference*'s efficacy rate tables, this is 3 percent of pill takers *each year*), it means that all three of these mechanisms have failed. The third mechanism *sometimes* fails in its role as backup, just as the first and second mechanisms sometimes fail. Each and every time the third mechanism succeeds, however, it causes an abortion.

Medical Journals and Textbooks

The pill alters epithelial and stromal integrins, which appear to be related to endometrial receptivity. These integrins are considered markers of normal fertility. Significantly, they are conspicuously absent in patients with various conditions associated with infertility *and* in women taking the pill. Since normal implantation involves a precise synchronization of the zygote's development with the endometrium's window of maximum receptivity, the absence of these integrins logically indicates a higher failure rate of implantation for pill takers. According to Dr. Stephen G. Somkuti and his research colleagues, "These data suggest that the morphological changes observed in the endometrium of OC users have functional significance and provide evidence that reduced endometrial receptivity does indeed contribute to the contraceptive efficacy of OCs."[763]

In another research journal article, Drs. Chowdhury, Joshi, and associates state: "The data suggests that though missing of the low-dose combination pills may result in 'escape' ovulation in some women, however, the pharmacological effects of pills on the endometrium and cervical mucus may continue to provide them contraceptive protection."[764]

Note in some of these citations the word *contraceptive* is used of an agent which in fact prevents the implantation of an already conceived child. Those who believe each human life begins at conception would see this function not as a contraceptive, but an abortifacient.

In a study of oral contraceptives published in a major medical journal, Dr. G. Virginia Upton, Regional Director of Clinical Research for Wyeth, one of the major birth control pill manufacturers, says, "The graded increments in LNg in the triphasic OC serve to maximize contraceptive protection by increasing the viscosity of the cervical mucus (cervical barrier), by suppressing ovarian progesterone output, and by causing endometrial changes that will not support implantation."[765]

Drug Facts and Comparisons says this about birth control pills in its 1997 edition:

> Combination OCs inhibit ovulation by suppressing the gonadotropins, follicle-stimulating hormone [FSH] and lutenizing hormone [LH]. Additionally, alterations in the genital tract, including cervical mucus [which inhibits sperm penetration] and the endometrium [which reduces the likelihood of implantation], may contribute to contraceptive effectiveness. An independent clinical pharmaceutical reference also contains this assertion.[766]

Reproductive endocrinologists have demonstrated that changes induced by the pill cause the endometrium to appear "hostile" or "poorly receptive" to implantation.[767] Magnetic Resonance Imaging (MRI) reveals that the endometrial lining of pill users is consistently thinner than that of nonusers[768]—up to 58 percent thinner.[769] Recent and fairly sophisticated ultrasound studies[770] have all concluded that endometrial thickness is related to the "functional receptivity" of the endometrium. Others have shown that when the lining of the uterus becomes too thin, implantation of the preborn child (called the blastocyst or preembryo at this stage) does not occur.[771]

The minimal endometrial thickness required to maintain a pregnancy ranges from 5 to 13mm,[772] whereas the average endometrial thickness in women on the pill is only 1.1 mm.[773] These data lend credence to the FDA-approved statement that "changes in the endometrium reduce the likelihood of implantation."[774]

Dr. Kristine Severyn says:

The third effect of combined oral contraceptives is to alter the endometrium in such a way that implantation of the fertilized egg [new life] is made more difficult, if not impossible. In effect, the endometrium becomes atrophic and unable to support implantation of the fertilized egg.... The alteration of the endometrium, making it hostile to implantation by the fertilized egg, provides a backup abortifacient method to prevent pregnancy.[775]

Researchers have repeatedly and consistently pointed out this abortifacient effect of the pill. To date, no published studies have refuted these findings.

Dr. Walter Larimore is a clinical professor of family medicine who has written over 150 medical articles in a wide variety of journals. In two major medical journal articles, he has addressed the issue of the pill's capacity to cause early abortions.[776] In 2000 Dr. Larimore and I coauthored a chapter on this subject in *The Reproduction Revolution: A Christian Appraisal of Sexuality, Reproductive Technologies and the Family*.[777] In the same chapter, four Christian physicians present their belief that the pill does not result in early abortions. We respectfully suggest that their case is not based solidly on the medical evidence.

What Does This Mean?

As a woman's menstrual cycle progresses, her endometrium gradually gets richer and thicker in preparation for the arrival and implantation of any newly conceived child. In a natural cycle, unimpeded by the pill, the endometrium experiences an increase of blood vessels, which allow a greater blood supply to bring oxygen and nutrients to the child. There is also an increase in the endometrium's stores of glycogen, a sugar that serves as a food source for the blastocyst (child) as soon as he or she implants.

The pill keeps the woman's body from creating the most hospitable environment for a child, resulting instead in an endometrium that is deficient in both food (glycogen) and oxygen. The child may die because he lacks this nutrition and oxygen.

Typically, the new person attempts to implant at six days after conception. If implantation is unsuccessful, the child is flushed out of the womb in a miscarriage. When the miscarriage is the result of an environment created by a foreign device or chemical, it is in fact an abortion. This is true even if the mother does not intend it and is not aware of it happening.

Despite all the research, including much more presented in my full book, there are those who insist that these contentions are incorrect and should not be taken at face value by those concerned about early abortions. In the case of the pill manufacturers, those who say their FDA-approved assertions are false should, in my opinion, prevail upon the FDA to change their statements and not simply ask people to disregard them.

Confirming Evidence

When the pill thins the endometrium, it seems self-evident that a zygote attempting to implant has a smaller likelihood of survival. A woman taking the pill puts any conceived child at *greater* risk of being aborted than if the pill were not being taken.

Some argue that this evidence is indirect and theoretical. But we must ask: If this is a theory, how strong and credible is the theory? If the evidence is only indirect, how compelling is that indirect evidence? Once it was only a theory that plant life grows better in rich, fertile soil than in thin, eroded soil. But it was certainly a theory good farmers believed and acted on.

Some physicians have theorized that when ovulation occurs in women who take the pill, the subsequent hormone production "turns on" the endometrium, causing it to become receptive to implantation.[778] However, there is no direct evidence to support this theory, and there is at least some evidence against it. First, after a woman stops taking the pill, it usually takes several cycles for her menstrual flow to increase to the volume characteristic of women who are not on the pill. This suggests to most objective researchers that the endometrium is slow to recover from its pill-induced thinning.[779] Second, the one study that has looked at women who have ovulated on the pill showed that after ovulation the endometrium is not receptive to implantation.[780]

Intrauterine/Extrauterine Pregnancy Ratio

Another line of evidence of the pill's abortifacient effect is this: If the pill has no post-fertilization effect, then reductions in the rate of intrauterine pregnancies among women who take the pill should be identical to the reduction in the rate of extra-uterine (ectopic/tubal) pregnancies among them. Therefore, an increased extrauterine/intrauterine pregnancy ratio would constitute evidence for an abortifacient effect.

Two medical studies allow review of this association.[781] Conducted at seven maternity hospitals in Paris, France,[782] and three in Sweden,[783] the studies evaluated 484 women with ectopic pregnancies and control groups of 389 women with normal pregnancies who were admitted to the hospital for delivery during the same period. These studies were designed, in typical fashion for "case control" studies, to determine the risk factors for a particular condition (here, ectopic pregnancy) by comparing one group of individuals known to have the condition with another group of individuals not having the condition. Both of these studies showed an increase in the extrauterine/intrauterine pregnancy ratio for women taking the pill. Researchers who have reviewed these studies have therefore suggested that "some protection against intrauterine pregnancy is provided via the pill's post-fertilization abortifacient effect."[784]

What accounts for the pill inhibiting intrauterine pregnancies at a disproportionately greater ratio than it inhibits extrauterine pregnancies? The most likely explanation is that while the pill does nothing to prevent a newly conceived child from implanting in the *wrong* place (i.e., anywhere besides the endometrium), it may sometimes do something to prevent him from implanting in the *right* place (i.e., the endometrium).

Arguments against the Pill Causing Abortion

I have received a number of letters from readers, one of them a physician, who say something like this: "My sister got pregnant while taking the pill. This is proof that you are wrong in saying that the pill causes abortions—obviously it couldn't have, since she had her baby!"

Without a doubt, the pill's effects on the endometrium do not *always* make implantation impossible. I have never heard anyone claim that they do. To be an abortifacient does not require that something *always* cause an abortion, only that it sometimes does.

Whether it's RU-486, Norplant, Depo-Provera, the morning-after pill, the minipill, or the pill, there is no chemical that *always* causes an abortion. There are only those that do so never, sometimes, often, and usually.

Children who play on the freeway, climb on the roof, or are left alone by swimming pools don't *always* die, but this does not prove these practices are safe and never result in fatalities. We would immediately see this inconsistency of anyone who argued in favor of leaving children alone by swimming pools because they know of cases where this has been done without harm to the children. The point that the pill doesn't always prevent implantation is certainly true, but has no bearing on the question of whether it *sometimes* prevents implantation, which the data clearly suggests.

People also often argue, "The blastocyst is perfectly capable of implanting in various 'hostile' sites, e.g., the fallopian tube, the ovary, the peritoneum."

Their point is that the child sometimes implants in the wrong place. This is undeniably true. But again, the only relevant question is whether the pill sometimes hinders the child's ability to implant in the *right* place.

Imagine a farmer who has two places where he might plant seed. One is rich, brown soil that has been tilled, fertilized, and watered. The other is on hard, thin, dry, and rocky soil. If the farmer wants as much seed as possible to take hold and grow, where will he plant the seed? The answer is obvious—on the fertile ground.

Now, you could say to the farmer that his preference for the rich, tilled, moist soil is based on theoretical assumptions because he has probably never seen a scientific study that proves this soil is more hospitable to seed than the thin, hard, dry soil. Likely, such a study has never been done. In other words, there is no absolute proof.

But the farmer would likely reply, based on years of observation, "I know good soil when I see it. Sure, I've seen some plants grow in the hard, thin soil, too, but the chances of survival are much less there than in the good soil. Call it theoretical if you want to, but we all know it's true!"

Some newly conceived children manage to survive temporarily in hostile places. But this in no way changes the obvious fact that many *more* children will survive in a richer, thicker, more hospitable endometrium than in a thinner, more inhospitable one.

(In other publications and in a much more detailed fashion, we have discussed these and other lines of evidence, with hundreds of citations of many scientific studies, as well as researchers and experts in numerous fields. We encourage interested readers to look more deeply into these studies and arguments.[785])

Despite this evidence, some prolife physicians state that the likelihood of the pill having an abortifacient effect is "infinitesimally low, or nonexistent."[786] Though I would very much like to believe this, the scientific evidence does not permit me to do so.

Dr. Walt Larimore has told me that whenever he has presented this evidence to audiences of secular physicians, there has been little or no resistance to it. But when he has presented it to Christian physicians, there has been substantial resistance. Since secular physicians do not care whether the pill prevents implantation, they tend to be objective in interpreting the evidence. After all, they have little or nothing at stake either way. Christian physicians, however, very much do not want to believe the pill causes early abortions. Therefore, I believe, they tend to resist the evidence. This is certainly understandable. Nonetheless, we should not permit what we *want* to believe to distract us from what the evidence indicates we *should* believe.

I have mentioned my own vested interests in the pill that at first made me resist the evidence suggesting that it could cause abortions. Dr. Larimore came to this issue with even greater vested interests in believing the best about the birth control pill, having prescribed it for years. When he researched it intensively over an eighteen-month period, in what he described to me as a "gut wrenching" process that involved sleepless nights, he came to the conclusion that in good conscience he could no longer prescribe hormonal contraceptives, including the pill, the minipill, Depo-Provera, and Norplant.

Statement by Twenty Prolife Physicians

In January 1998, five months after the original printing of my book, a statement was issued opposing the idea that the pill can cause abortions. According to a January 30, 1998, e-mail sent me by one of its circulators, the statement "is a collaborative effort by several very active prolife OB-GYN specialists, and screened through about twenty additional OB-GYN specialists."

The statement is titled "Birth Control Pills: Contraceptive or Abortifacient?" Those wishing to read it in its entirety, which I recommend, can find it on our web page, at www.epm.org/doctors.html. I have posted it there because, while I disagree with its major premise and various statements in it, I believe it deserves a hearing.

The title is misleading in that it implies that there are only two possible ways to look at the pill: always a contraceptive or always an abortifacient. In fact, I know of no one who believes that it is always an abortifacient. There are only those who believe it is always a contraceptive and never an abortifacient and those who believe it is usually a contraceptive and *sometimes* an abortifacient.

The paper opens with this statement:

Currently the claim that hormonal contraceptives [birth control pills, implants (Norplant), injectables (Depo-Provera)] include an abortifacient mechanism of action is being widely disseminated in the prolife community. This theory is emerging with the assumed status of "scientific fact," and is causing significant confusion among both lay and medical prolife people. With this confusion in the ranks comes a significant weakening of both our credibility with the general public and our effectiveness against the tide of elective abortion.

The assertion that the presentation of research and medical opinions causes confusion is interesting. Does it cause confusion, or does it bring to light pertinent information in an already existing state of confusion? Would we be better off to uncritically embrace what we have always believed than to face evidence that may challenge it?

Is our credibility and effectiveness weakened through presenting evidence that indicates the pill can cause abortions? Or is it simply our duty to discover and share the truth regardless of whether it is well received by the general public or the Christian community?

The physicians' statement's major thesis is this: The idea that the pill causes a hostile endometrium is a myth.

Over time, the descriptive term "hostile endometrium" progressed to be an unchallenged assumption, then to be quasi-scientific fact, and now, for some in the prolife community, to be a proof text. And all with no demonstrated scientific validation.

When I showed this to one professor of family medicine he replied, "This is an amazing claim." What's so amazing is it requires that every physician who has directly observed the dramatic pill-induced changes in the endometrium, and every textbook that refers to these changes, has been wrong all along in believing what appears to be obvious: that when the zygote attaches itself to the endometrium, its chances of survival are greater if what it attaches to is thick and rich in nutrients and oxygen than if it is not.

This is akin to announcing to a group of farmers that all these years they have been wrong to believe the myth that rich fertilized soil is more likely to foster and maintain plant life than thin eroded soil.

It could be argued that if anything may cause prolifers to lose credibility, at least with those familiar with what the pill does to the endometrium, it is to claim that the pill does nothing to make implantation less likely.

The authors defend their position this way:

> [The blastocyst] has an invasive nature, with the demonstrated ability to invade, find a blood supply, and successfully implant on various kinds of tissue, whether "hostile," or even entirely "foreign" to its usual environment—decidualized [thinned] endometrium, tubal epithelium [lining], ovarian epithelium [covering], cervical epithelium [lining], even peritoneum [abdominal lining cells]…. The presumption that implantation of a blastocyst is thwarted by "hostile endometrium" is contradicted by the "pill pregnancies" we as physicians see.

This argument misses the point, since the question is not whether the zygote sometimes implants in the wrong place. Of course it does. The question, rather, is whether the newly conceived child's chances of survival are greater when it implants in the right place (endometrium) that is thick and rich and full of nutrients than in one which lacks these qualities because of the pill. To point out a blastocyst is capable of implanting in a fallopian tube or a thinned endometrium is akin to pointing to a seed that begins to grow on asphalt or springs up on the hard dry path. Yes, the seed is thereby shown to have an invasive nature. But surely no one believes its chances of survival are as great on asphalt as in cultivated fertilized soil.

According to the statement signed by the twenty physicians, "The entire 'abortifacient' presumption, therefore, depends on 'hostile endometrium.'"

In fact, one need not embrace the term "hostile endometrium" to believe that the pill can cause abortions. It does not take a hostile or even an inhospitable endometrium to account for an increase in abortions. It only takes a *less* hospitable endometrium. Even if they think that "hostile" is an overstatement, can anyone seriously argue that the endometrium transformed by the pill is not *less* hospitable to implantation than the endometrium at its rich thick nutrient-laden peak in a normal cycle uninfluenced by the pill?

One medical school professor told me that until reading this statement, he had never heard, in his decades in the field, *anyone* deny the radical changes in the endometrium caused by the pill and the obvious implications this has for reducing the likelihood of implantation. According to this physician, the fact that secular sources embrace this reality and only prolife Christians are now rejecting it (in light of the recent attention on the pill's connection to abortions) suggests that they may be swayed by vested interests in the legitimacy of the pill.

The paper states: "There are no scientific studies that we are aware of which substantiate this presumption [that the diminished endometrium is less conducive to implantation]." But it doesn't cite any studies, or other evidence, that suggest otherwise.

In fact, surprisingly, though this statement is five pages long, it contains not a single reference to any source that backs up any of its claims. If observation and common sense have led people in medicine to a particular conclusion over decades, should their conclusion be rejected out of hand without citing specific research indicating that it is incorrect?

On which side does the burden of proof fall—the one that claims the radically diminished endometrium inhibits implantation, or the one that claims it doesn't?

The most potentially significant point made in the paper is this:

> The ectopic rate in the USA is about 1% of all pregnancies. Since an ectopic pregnancy involves a pre-implantation blastocyst, both the "on-pill conception" and normal "non pill conception" ectopic rate should be the same—about 1% [unaffected by whether the endometrium is "hostile" or "friendly"]. Ectopic pregnancies in women on hormonal contraception [except for the minipill] are practically unreported. This would suggest conception on these agents is quite rare. If there are millions of "on-pill conceptions" yearly, producing millions of abortions, [as some "BC pill is abortifacient" groups allege], we would expect to see a huge increase in ectopics in women on hormonal birth control. We don't. Rather, as noted above, this is a rare occurrence.

The premise of this statement is right on target. It is exactly the premise proposed by Dr. Larimore, which I've already presented. While the statement's premise is correct, its account of the data, unfortunately, is not. The studies pointed to by Dr. Larimore, cited earlier, clearly demonstrate that the statement is incorrect when it claims ectopic pregnancies in women on hormonal contraception are "practically unreported" and "rare."

In fact, "a huge increase in ectopics" is exactly what we *do* see—an increase that five major studies put between 70% and 1390%. Ironically, when we remove the statement's incorrect data about the ectopic pregnancy rate and plug in the correct data, the statement supports the very thing it attempts to refute. It suggests that the pill may indeed cause early abortions, possibly a very large number of them.

Questions about This Problem

People raise many objections to the issues presented in this appendix, very few of which involve issues of evidential data or scientific fact. However, these objections deserve answers. These are some of the concerns I address in my book, *Does the Birth Control Pill Cause Abortions?*[787]

- "If this is true, why haven't we been told before?"
- "I don't trust this evidence."
- "If we don't know how often abortions happen, why shouldn't we take the pill?"
- "Spontaneous miscarriages are common; early abortions aren't that big a deal."
- "Taking the pill means fewer children die in spontaneous abortions."
- "Without the pill there would be more elective abortions."
- "Women who take the pill don't intend to have abortions."
- "Why not just use high-estrogen pills?"
- "You can't avoid every risk."
- "How can we practice birth control without the pill?"
- "I never knew this—should I feel guilty?"
- "We shouldn't lay guilt on people by talking about this."
- "We shouldn't tell people that the pill may cause abortions because they'll be held accountable."
- "We've prayed about it and we feel right about using the pill."
- "This issue will sidetrack us from fighting surgical abortions."
- "Prolifers will lose credibility if we oppose the pill."
- "This puts Christian physicians in a very difficult position."
- "Are there any good alternatives to the pill?"

Conclusion

The pill is used by about fourteen million American women each year and sixty million women internationally. Thus, even an infinitesimally low portion (say one-hundredth of one percent) of 780 million pill cycles per year globally could represent tens of thousands of unborn children lost to this form of chemical abortion annually. How many young lives have to be jeopardized for prolife believers to question the ethics of using the pill? This is an issue with profound moral implications for those believing that we are called to protect the lives of children.

Appendix F

FIFTY WAYS TO HELP UNBORN
BABIES AND THEIR MOTHERS

Direct Personal Involvement

1. *Open your home to a pregnant girl.* Help her financially, emotionally, and spiritually.

2. *Open your home to an "unwanted" child* for foster care or adoption.

3. *Volunteer time* with organizations helping pregnant women, newborns, drug babies, orphans, the handicapped, elderly, street people, and others in need. Personal care is the most basic prolife activity.

4. *Establish a pregnancy counseling and abortion alternative service* that offers free pregnancy tests, counseling, and support. You can often get the very first listing in the Yellow Pages as "Abortion Alternatives," which precedes "Abortion Services." (For help getting started, see "Abortion Alternatives and Support For Women" in Appendix K, "Prolife Resources.")

5. *Donate materials,* office equipment, furniture, baby clothes, professional skills and services, and money to pregnancy centers, Birthright, Bethany Christian Services, and other prolife groups. Mow their lawn, make them a web page, fix their computers.

6. *Teach your children and other young people how to say no* to premarital sex. Teenage sexual abstinence is not only spiritually and psychologically healthy, it is the only sure way to prevent teen pregnancies. (See the prochastity resources listed in Appendix K.)

Educating Yourself and Others

7. *Become thoroughly informed about the abortion issue.* Many fine books, tapes, and videos are available, as well as excellent (and usually free) prolife newsletters (see Appendix K). Know the facts so you can rehearse in advance the best responses to the prochoice arguments. Be prepared so no opportunities are missed.

8. *Talk to your friends, neighbors, and coworkers* about the abortion issue. Challenge them to rethink their assumptions and to be careful not to buy into an illogical or morally untenable position. Give them a copy of this book, with some pages marked for their attention. Refer women who have had abortions to Appendix A, "Finding Forgiveness after an Abortion." Read and discuss this book in a class or small group. Give away novels that have a prolife theme, such as *Deadline* by Randy Alcorn. Many people have reconsidered their prochoice position after reading this book. *The Atonement Child* by Francine Rivers gives a tremendous perspective on conception by rape.

9. *Volunteer your services as a prolife speaker* for schools and church groups. Use the arguments laid out in this book as your presentation outline. Approach a church or Christian school and offer to teach a course in "Prolife Logic and Action."

10. *Promote discussion of abortion in Internet chat rooms.* Take some perspectives from this book to stimulate interaction. Consider establishing your own prolife web site. Call in and speak up on talk shows and ask for equal time on television and radio stations that present the prochoice position. They often welcome a variety of positions. To say nothing is to endorse what is often an unchallenged prochoice bandwagon.

11. *Students: Write papers, make speeches, and start a campus prolife group.* (See "Organizing a Student Prolife Organization" under "Books on Prolife Strategies" in Appendix K. See "Communicating the Prolife Message," Appendix J.)

12. *Display attractive prolife posters and information* at your office or shop. You may lose a little business, but you'll probably gain some, too. More importantly, the truth will be served, children will be spoken up for, and some innocent human lives will likely be saved, which you probably won't hear about in this life.

Literature, Visuals, and Advertising

13. *Order and distribute prolife literature.* Have it displayed or available at your place of business. Leave it on your coffee table. Ask your doctor if you can leave it in the waiting room. Distribute literature door-to-door to influence opinion. An attractive piece left on each porch will be read by many. In some areas "every home" distribution has radically changed community sentiments about abortion. (See Appendix K for a literature list.)

14. *Donate prolife books and magazine subscriptions to public and school libraries.* They are usually well stocked with prochoice literature. Point out that

you just want to provide a little balance and make sure the other position isn't censored. We've had people give to libraries hundreds of copies of *ProLife Answers to ProChoice Arguments,* and nearly all of them have gratefully accepted them.

15. *Use a premade prolife slide presentation, assemble your own, or buy a video tape and offer to show it* in schools, churches, to your neighbors and government representatives (see Appendix K). Need guidelines for communicating the prolife message? (see Appendix J).

16. *Wear prolife symbols,* "precious feet" pins, buttons, and shirts. These often stimulate conversations. Use prolife bumper stickers or lawn signs. Place prolife stickers on letters—more than a dozen people see the average piece of mail (see Appendix K).

17. *Place newspaper ads, bench ads, and billboard posters.* Attractive premade ads and beautiful full-size billboard posters are available (see Appendix K).

Letter Writing

18. *Write letters to the editor.* Be courteous, concise, accurate, and memorable. Quote brief references cited in this book. Use the material in this book as you wish. Some local newspapers have a policy of printing every letter to the editor. *The opportunity for influence is enormous.* Letters to the editor in a major national magazine might be read by a million people.

19. *Compile a list of names, addresses, and phone numbers* of politicians, newspapers, television stations, hospitals, and others in your area that people can contact to express their prolife views. Distribute them widely.

20. *Select the most strategic measures and issues and host a prolife letter-writing party.* People can help each other compose informed and succinct letters to send to the right people and places. Since legislators and others assume that there are a hundred others who feel the same way for every one that writes, there is considerable impact from each letter.

21. *Write letters of encouragement* to the sometimes tired and discouraged prolife activists.

Personal Conversation

22. *Refuse any indirect or business support of abortion clinics and explain your refusal.* Boycott proabortion companies, landlords of abortion clinics, and businesses that share space with abortion clinics and abortion promoters

such as Planned Parenthood. Explain your reasons nicely, and they will often take you seriously. (Be an ethical investor. Are businesses and mutual funds you've put money into furthering the cause of abortion?)

23. *Contact physicians and hospitals that perform abortions*—and insurance companies that cover them—and express your convictions. Be polite but firm, stating that you, your family, and your business cannot in good conscience patronize those who contribute to the killing of innocent children. *Does your own physician perform abortions?* Ask him; you may be surprised to discover that he does. If so, tell him you must reluctantly change doctors. Is your doctor prolife? Encourage him to take a public stand and participate in local prolife events. Share this book with him and ask his opinion of it.

24. *Talk to journalists* about your concern that they accurately represent the prolife side in their reporting. Many have never heard an accurate presentation of the prolife position. Until we present it to them, how can we expect them to be fair? Highlight sections of this book for their interest. Many will read what you provide, and some may use the material in future articles.

25. *Talk to teachers,* especially junior high, high school, and college teachers. Express your desire that they understand and be able to represent the prolife position rather than ignore or distort it. Whatever a teacher believes is multiplied a hundred times over in his students and those they in turn influence. Give them a copy of this or other prolife books or videos (see Appendix K).

Political Action

26. *Write to representatives* and others in government at local, state, and national levels. Be respectful, legible, straightforward, brief, and nondefensive. Enclose attractive prolife literature. The more personal your letter, the better. Preprinted postcards are not as effective.

27. *Personally phone or set up a meeting with your representatives* to share your views on abortion. Groups of three are most effective. If possible include a prolife doctor or other professional. Be careful how you come across; show them that prolifers are intelligent and rational.

28. *Draft, circulate, and sign petitions* for prolife ballot measures, school board members, and so on.

29. *Run for political office,* school board, or precinct chairman. Or stand by other prolife candidates with your time and money. The only way there will be long-

term legal restrictions on abortion is if our state legislatures have a prolife majority. Churches and prolife groups should identify and support character-qualified, knowledgeable, and skilled candidates.

30. *Help a bright young prolifer through law school.* Challenge him or her to set a goal of becoming a judge. The legal and judicial arenas, as well as the medical and political, desperately need intelligent and skilled prolifers.

Prolife Events

31. *Picket abortion clinics, hospitals, and physicians who perform abortions.* Write a brochure or fact sheet documenting their performance of abortions. When abortions are only part of their practice, they are much more inclined to eliminate them to preserve their reputation in the community. But until they are exposed they usually won't stop.

32. *Make prolife signs for yourself and others.* Make them large and attractive, with concise messages. "Abortion Kills Babies." "Adoption, not Abortion." "Every Child Is Wanted by Someone." "Give Your Baby a Chance to Choose." "Please Let Your Baby Live." "Equal Rights for Unborn Women." "She's a Baby, not a Blob." "We Care—Talk to Us." "We'll Help Financially If You'll Let Your Baby Live."

33. *Organize or participate in a Life Chain,* where hundreds or thousands of pro-lifers stand on public sidewalks and display signs supporting the unborn and opposing abortion. Life Chain began in 1989 with twenty-five hundred partici-pants in a rural northern California area. In 1994 it grew to over one million par-ticipants across America and Canada combined, and in 1999 there were nine hundred Life Chains on the North American continent.[788] This is an effective means of mobilizing prolifers and making a clear statement for the children. Many who begin with Life Chain will solidify a prolife commitment and get involved in future prolife activities. (See "Life Chain" under "Prolife Event and Action Organizations" in Appendix K.)

34. *Join prolife rallies and marches* to galvanize prolife efforts. Have walk-a-thons and other projects to earn money for prolife groups. Get your children involved. They'll love it, and it's a great education as well as family activity.

35. *Attend prochoice rallies* as a counterdemonstrator. Be peaceful. The quiet pres-ence of your group and your signs will make others think and lead to conversa-tions with passersby.

36. *Participate in peaceful nonviolent civil disobedience* at the doorways of abortion clinics, or by standing and praying or distributing literature on public sidewalks where courts say the First Ammendment doesn't apply.... Or gather for prayer in conjunction with such civil disobedience.

Abortion Clinic Strategies

37. *Research and write a brochure on your local abortion clinic,* citing specific lawsuits and health code violations, which are a matter of public record. Write a leaflet or brochure asking, "What Do You Know about the Third Street Abortion Clinic?" Make it neat and attractive, perhaps with a photo of the clinic on the front. Give this brochure to women coming to the clinic, neighbors, nearby businesses, and passersby. Include information from this book on physical and psychological risks of abortion. Or use premade brochures specially designed for women entering abortion clinics (see Appendix K).

38. *Collect information and initiate lawsuits against abortion clinics.* Place newspaper or billboard ads asking, "Problems after an abortion?" Give a local or national phone number to call for medical, legal, or emotional help. (1-800-634-2224, the American Rights Coalition, is already set up for this purpose.) Many abortion clinics have been shut down by successful lawsuits.

39. *Hand out questionnaires and legal information to women* entering and leaving clinics. "Did you have a doctor-patient relationship? Did the doctor ask you for a complete medical history? Did he explain to you the possible complications of abortion? Did he show you a picture or explain to you the state of development of your unborn child?" This will encourage them to reconsider their decision, to seek other counsel, or—if the abortion is over—not to come back for another abortion, and possibly to initiate legal action against the clinic. Include the number of an alternative pregnancy center where they can get complete and accurate information the clinic won't give them.

40. *Keep new abortion clinics out of your community* by informing the public, writing letters to council members, and contacting potential landlords and real estate agents. Abortion clinics mean loss of business and declining property values due to public sentiment and frequent demonstrations. Those who do not respond to moral reasoning often do respond to public opinion and even more to financial loss. It is usually easier to keep a clinic out of an area than to shut it down once it's there.

41. *Rent space as close as possible to an abortion clinic or Planned Parenthood office* and establish a pregnancy counseling clinic or prolife information center.

Influencing Your Church

42. *Organize a prolife task force and approach key church leaders.* Identify pastors and other strategic leaders and speak with them one by one. Give them literature and ask them to watch a video. Recruit prolife activists—those who are positively supportive of the church's other ministries too—who will help you formulate and implement a plan of education and mobilization. Ask your church leaders to include prolife activities and literature in the budget.

43. *Set up a prolife table at church* with the best prolife literature and materials (see Appendix K). The presence of the table itself is a vital reminder of the prolife cause. Show in church services or classes prolife films and videos such as *The Abortion Providers, The Hard Truth,* and *The Eclipse of Reason.* Offer to pay the film rental yourself (see Appendix K).

44. *Construct a Memorial Rose Garden* on your church property, where people can place memorials to unborn children who died and whose memory they wish to preserve. (Sample plaque message: "Our precious Susie; We will hold you in heaven.") This can be a wonderful place to quietly meditate, which members of the community can also visit, and which members of the congregation see every time they drive onto church property; see www.epm.org/rosegard.html; call Grace Community Church in Marietta, Georgia, 770-425-0547.

45. *Place a prolife newspaper ad, bench ad, or billboard with your church's name and phone number,* offering your help to pregnant girls. (See Appendix K for premade ads.)

46. *Take your church bus to prolife activities.* Many people who won't go alone will go with a group. Some will discover an aptitude for regular prolife ministry they would otherwise never have realized.

47. *Have special prolife emphasis Sundays* with special music, speakers, films, and literature. This should include, but not be limited to, the Sanctity of Human Life Sunday in mid-January. (Special bulletin inserts and materials are available from CareNet and Right to Life of Michigan, listed in Appendix K.)

48. *Bring prolife issues and opportunities to the attention of your pastor, Sunday school class, Bible study, or men's, women's, or youth group.* Show them one of the videos listed in Appendix K, the sample sermon of Appendix G,

the church position paper on abortion in Appendix H, or the sample Bible study lesson in Appendix I. Provide relevant newspaper clippings and other information to inform your pastor and provide him with sermon ideas and illustrations. Give him this book as a resource. Instead of expecting him to fulfill your prolife agenda, help him out by offering to be a resource and facilitator for him.

49. *Start a group of sidewalk counselors from your church* that go once or twice a week to talk to women outside abortion clinics. This is hard but rewarding work, and you need the camaraderie of others by your side. Some excellent sidewalk counseling materials are listed in Appendix K.

50. *Pray daily for prolife ministries and victimized mothers and babies.* Organize your own prayer group, perhaps combining prolife concerns with other vital needs, such as missions. Go to prolife rallies, rescues, or sidewalk counseling and focus on the ministry of prayer. If the darkness of child-killing is to be overcome with the light of truth and compassion, it will require spiritual warfare, fought with humble and consistent prayer (Ephesians 6:10–20).

Appendix G

A SANCTITY OF LIFE MESSAGE

The following are my message notes from the Good Shepherd Community Church services of January 18 and 19, 1997. Pastors and all others communicating on this subject are welcome to use this material.

We who follow Christ sometimes have to face realities that make us uncomfortable. This is one of those times. We must not allow our discomfort to keep us from facing the truth—from coming to terms with God's Word. So let's give each other permission to be uncomfortable. The hurt we experience today will be the beginning of healing.

In a few moments we will do something we've never done in this church. People will come forward and cross the platform, carrying white roses that they'll put in the cradle. Each rose represents one million children—one million little boys and girls—who have died from abortion in America since it was legalized twenty-four years ago this week.

The people who will come forward are part of our church family at Good Shepherd, and each has a special connection to the unborn. Some of them are men and women who have lost their children to abortion. Some have lost grandchildren; some siblings. One used to work in Oregon's largest abortion clinic, the Lovejoy Surgicenter in Portland. One is a nurse who helped perform abortions. One, a few months ago on the fifth anniversary of her child's death, went down to place flowers at the Lovejoy abortion clinic where her baby died. While there, she met people from a Good Shepherd growth group who were praying and offering counsel on the sidewalk. Good Shepherd people meeting—one grieving, others ministering—and they embraced each other.

One is a teenage girl from our church who got pregnant, then made the right decision to have her baby. She lived at Bethany House, a home for unwed mothers, with house parents from our church. Another woman as a preborn child survived an attempt at abortion and was then carried to term and born.

One woman was strongly advised by two doctors to get an abortion and told that if she didn't, both she and her baby would have serious physical problems. She

351

rejected their advice and carried her baby, who was born prematurely but without complications. Her health *has* suffered, but she's glad she made that sacrifice.

One is a woman conceived when her thirteen-year-old mother was raped. One is a prolife physician who stands up for the unborn.

Several teenagers and adults are volunteers in prolife ministry. Many of these people are involved in sidewalk counseling at abortion clinics, CPCs, and other ministries.

Not all of these people have had abortions—about half of them have—but unless they've told you, you won't know which, because they choose today to walk in solidarity with each other, standing together as the Body of Christ. They willingly take the risk of someone judging or misjudging them.

I was with these people in a prayer meeting Monday night, one of the most powerful times I've ever been part of. There were tears of healing and gratitude to God for His grace. Many unforgettable prayers were offered through the tears. One of the teenage girls prayed, "Lord, I ask you speak to the adults this weekend because I know girls who haven't wanted to get abortions but were pressured into it by their parents at our church."

One rose for each million children killed by surgical abortion in America. Each rose carrier's life touched by abortion, through personal experience, through volunteer ministry, and many through both. One of the women who has had an abortion said, "Thanks for asking me to do this. It will be another step in my healing."

As the music plays and these dear sisters and brothers come, remember the children and the parents and ask God to speak to your heart.

As a soundtrack of Brahm's Lullaby played, fifty people (several came as couples and as parents with children) walked across the platform and placed the roses in the cradle. The cradle swung slightly from their touch. Some of the women kissed the roses before putting them in the cradle. The lights were dimmed, and a slide of a beautiful intrauterine child sucking his thumb was projected on the large front screen. Weeping could be heard throughout the auditorium in all five of the services. Before each service we had a powerful prayer time with the rose carriers. After each service many of them had great interactions with hurting people in the church body. After the last rose carrier I stood up to speak again.

Main Message

Today we are addressing something very close to the heart of God. The issue is not what we want to hear, but what God wants to say. If He is our Lord—if we are His people—we must listen to Him.

According to the Scriptures, there are spiritual beings present here, righteous angels and fallen angels, and we are under attack. There is a battle for our minds and a battle for our souls: It's not fiction, it's not imagination; it's revealed reality. There is great spiritual warfare associated with the issue of abortion.

God is the creator of children and a lover of children; Satan is a hater and destroyer of children, because they have been created in God's image and they are his weakest and most vulnerable victims. Killing children is his way of striking out at the very heart of God. If he cannot kill God, the next best thing to him is killing God's littlest children. By killing those created in God's image, he is killing God in effigy.

Every time this subject is brought up, some people get offended; but the alternative is not bringing it up, which offends God, whose approval is the one that really matters. He is the Audience of One. My prayer is that for every person offended today there will be three people deeply touched by the Holy Spirit. We're going to get to some very good news, but in order to be touched by the good news, first we're going to have to hear some very bad news.

Church is more than just a social club. We are not here simply to help each other *feel* good; we are here to help each other *be* good. And sometimes that means taking some medicine we'd rather not take in order to get well. I was asked by the elders to speak to you, and I will try to accurately convey God's perspective. That is an awesome task—one I am not up to—so I ask you to please pray with me.

PRAYER:

Lord, we come before You completely inadequate.
I lack the ability to communicate this message well,
and we as a people lack the ability to hear it well.
We are blinded by the relentless propaganda of this culture that
pretends to love children, while sacrificing our youngest, weakest,
and most vulnerable children on the altar of our convenience.

The evil one, the one our Lord called a murderer and liar,
has lied to cover his murders, and we have bought into his lies.
We ask you to break through the rationalizations to speak to each of us.
Father, protect us from the relentless lies of those evil
beings who love the shedding of innocent blood.

353

God, help us to put on spiritual armor and to use the sword of the
Spirit, Your Word, to fight the darkness that whispers lies into our ears.
We pray that by Your grace You would let us hear the truth
and that the truth would set us free—
free to experience Your forgiveness, Your grace, and Your blessing.
We pray this in the mighty name of Jesus. Amen.

There are 1.4 million children killed by abortion in this country every year. Over four thousand each day, twelve every five minutes, one every twenty-five seconds. One in every four pregnancies in America ends in abortion. Statistics show that a soldier's chances of survival in the front lines of combat are greater than the chances of an unborn child's avoiding abortion. What should be the safest place to live in America— a mother's womb—is now the most dangerous place.

I want to emphasize that every child has two parents and that God puts the biggest responsibility for protecting children on men. More instructions in Scripture are given to fathers than to mothers. If we men took our responsibility to be pure and to guard the purity of women rather than take advantage of them, there would be a fraction of the unwanted pregnancies. And if we took our responsibility to raise the children we have fathered, there would be a fraction of the abortions.

Men, we should be the first to accept the responsibility for our actions, the first to stand up for women who need help, and the first to stand up for weak, vulnerable children. When men exercise deep loyalties to women and children, we are at our best; when we violate those loyalties, we are at our worst. We become abusers or passive cowards. And God will surely judge us for it.

A man in his sixties here at Good Shepherd called me a few days ago and told me of a girl he got pregnant thirty-nine years ago. She gave him a choice of what to do; he chose an abortion. He said that it has haunted him since. He thinks about the son or daughter he lost and wonders about the grandchildren he'd now be holding. He said to me, "Tell people about the consequences. Warn our young men—tell them God will hold them accountable for what they do with their children." Then, he broke down in tears and said, "I don't want our young men to do what I did thirty-nine years ago."

Last week at church one of our growth group leaders came up to me, tears in his eyes. He told me of an abortion he had paid for years ago and what a terrible choice it was. Abortion isn't a women's issue. It's a human issue, and its effects are devastating to women and men alike. People, we are all in this together.

Transparency 1: (Picture of preborn child sucking his thumb) This isn't an issue; it's a baby. It's not a choice; it's a child. It's not politics; it's a human being created in the image of God. This child is as precious to God as my children and yours—as human, as important, as valuable to God as every child in our church nursery. We need to learn to look at this child through the eyes of God, not through the eyes of the world.

Transparency 2: (Picture) This is a child at eight weeks old, when the earliest abortions take place. Doesn't look like a blob of tissue, does it? It has a measurable heartbeat twenty-one days after conception and measurable brainwaves at forty-nine days after conception. That means that every surgical abortion stops a beating heart and stops brain waves. When I showed this picture on a college campus, a student said, "You're not fooling us with that trick photography."

What she was saying is, "Obviously that's a baby, but I want to believe that abortion doesn't kill children, therefore I will choose to believe this can't be a real picture." That's why people hate to see the pictures of aborted babies—if they were just blobs of tissue, they wouldn't be hard to look at, would they? What makes it hard is that we know these are babies.

I'm not going to show pictures of aborted babies today, but there's a tremendous irony here. It's not considered appropriate to show pictures of a baby killed by abortion, but it is considered appropriate to do nothing to stop the killing of those babies in the picture. The problem with the Holocaust wasn't the sickening *pictures* of bodies stacked like cord wood. The problem with the Holocaust was the evil the pictures simply pointed out. If something is too horrible to look at, shouldn't it be too horrible to defend and too horrible to ignore?

But the truth is: These are babies even before they look like babies. Science and Scripture tell us the same thing about when human life begins.

Transparency 3–4: Scientists—when human life begins (see *PLA* argument 1)

Transparency 5–7: Scripture—when human life begins (see *PLA* Appendices B and C)

Let me ask you a question. In what city did Christ's incarnation take place? In other words, where did God first "become flesh and dwell among us"? Ninety-nine out of a hundred Christians will say Bethlehem. But the answer is Nazareth. That's where Jesus was conceived.

Science and Scripture agree. There is a point of creation, where one moment there is only an egg with twenty-three chromosomes and a sperm with twenty-three chromosomes, neither of which has a life of its own. But when they are joined, there is a new human being with absolutely unique DNA, a distinct identity, with the equivalent of hundreds of volumes of detailed information down to hair thickness, eye color, height and thousands of other markers. That point of God's creation of the new individual is indisputably the point of conception.

This has tremendous implications, because no matter how soon after conception it happens, an abortion causes the death of a human being. Therefore using RU-486, the abortion pill, is absolutely wrong. So is the IUD, because it prevents implantation of a fertilized egg. So is the morning-after pill and the minipill. Often so are Depo-Provera and Norplant. These can cause early abortions.

Even the standard birth control pill states in its own manufacturers' literature, as indicated in the *Physician's Desk Reference,* that sometimes it can fail to stop ovulation and after conception takes place *can* prevent implantation of an already fertilized egg. No one seems to know how often this happens, and some think it is rare, but given this information, it is a risk I don't believe we should choose to take. Please, I am not trying to point the finger. Nanci and I used the pill for years, like many of us who are prolife, completely unaware of this possibility. If we believe that each life begins at conception, we need to take a careful look at what we might be doing to threaten the life of an already conceived child.

Transparency 8: Testimony of early church (see Appendix B)

The truth is, it doesn't take a theologian or a Bible scholar or a scientist to know when life begins.

Transparency 9: (See answer 8f) Have you seen this? Every establishment in Oregon that serves alcohol is required to prominently display it: "Pregnancy and alcohol do not mix." Notice the baby inside, with its human features. The message is, "what a pregnant woman does with her body may adversely affect another human being with his own body, and that's not right."

In Portland judges have put women in jail because they were taking drugs that endangered their unborn babies. But that same woman who is jailed for endangering her child is perfectly free to abort her child. In America today, *it is illegal to harm your preborn child, but it is perfectly legal to kill him.*

We wonder why child abuse has dramatically increased since 1973—that's when abortion was legalized. Not a coincidence. If it's okay to kill a child before he's born, what's so bad about slapping around the same child a year later? The first thing I thought when I heard the horrible story of Susan Smith in Carolina drowning her children was, "This is just a very late-term abortion—four years late." Same mother, same children. Other than timing, what's the difference?

Some of the lies sound so noble: "Every child a wanted child." This is the slogan of Planned Parenthood. I agree—"Every child a wanted child, so let's learn to want children more and get them into the hands of those who want them." But what they mean is, "Every child a wanted child, so let's kill unwanted children before they're born." Planned Parenthood's true slogan should be, "Every unwanted child a dead child." Doesn't sound quite as nice, does it?

I'm prochoice. Prochoice about what? Whether you have Mexican or Chinese food? Where you live? What kind of car you drive? Of course. But are you prochoice about rape? About burglary? About kidnapping? Are you prochoice about killing children? Of course not. Let's cut through the lies and identify what choice we're talking about—killing children.

I suppose it shouldn't surprise us that unbelievers would buy into these lies. Scripture says that Satan, the god of this world, has blinded the minds of unbelievers. But the greatest tragedy with abortion is that it isn't "out there" somewhere. It's right in here. Right inside the church. This isn't just about our nation or our community, people. It's about us.

Ten years ago the statistics indicated that those who call themselves evangelical Christians accounted for one out of six surgical abortions in America—a quarter of a million abortions per year. Statistics that came out in July 1996, published in *Family Planning Perspectives,* show that now 18 percent, or nearly one in five abortions, are done by evangelical Christians. That's 300,000 per year. And that doesn't count the chemical abortions.

There are hundreds of women and hundreds of men in this church who have made abortion decisions—some ten or twenty years ago, some two years ago, some last year, some last month. With the twenty-five hundred people in our combined services, I have no doubt that sitting in church this weekend are some who have made the decision and are planning abortions within the next few weeks. I ask you to pray that God would penetrate their hearts.

Scripture says it is time for judgment to begin with the house of God. We need to look to ourselves first. An unholy world will never be won to Christ by an unholy church. We have no moral authority to speak to the world in the realm of sexual morality or on the issue of abortion unless and until we deal with it in our midst. In order to help bring a solution, we must first deal with the fact that we ourselves are a large part of the problem.

Scripture teaches that God is the Creator and owner of all people and therefore has exclusive rights over them. It teaches that God alone is the giver and taker of human life. It tells us God has sole prerogatives over human life and death. He warns us, "You shall not commit murder."

Suppose you're told by your doctor, "The fetus is deformed. It probably won't survive more than a few weeks after birth, and if it does, it will never be able to walk, talk, see, or have a normal life. I recommend you terminate the pregnancy."

What do you do? Well, the last thing you should do is kill the child. If God chooses to take this child, that is His choice, just as if He would choose to take our five-year-old or ten- or fifteen- or thirty-year-old. Let God do what He wants. The decision is His, not yours. If you found out that your five-year-old was terminally ill, would you say, "Since he's probably going to die anyway, we'll just kill him." No? Then don't do it to your unborn child. Let God decide, not you and not the doctor.

"But what if the doctor says the child will have handicaps?" I'm glad you asked that question.

Transparencies 10–11: Children handicapped or conceived by rape (see Appendix C). Don't kill an unborn person because she is handicapped or conceived by rape any more than you would kill a *born* person because she is handicapped or was conceived by rape.

Of all the sins committed in the Old Testament, one stands out above the others in its utter abomination to God: the killing of children. Whether children offered to the demon god Molech then or the god of convenience and affluence today, God hates the killing of children. He says in Leviticus 20 that to kill children is "to defile my sanctuary and to profane my holy name." He says in Proverbs 7 there are seven things that are detestable to Him. One of those is "hands that shed innocent blood."

In 2 Kings 24, God says that He brought destruction on the nation Judah because of the evil of King Manasseh, for "he filled Jerusalem with innocent blood," the blood of children. I thought of that passage just a few months ago when the president of the United States officially approved partial-birth abortion. This is a practice in which children are delivered to the point that their whole body is out of the womb up to their neck; then the "doctor"—and I use the term loosely—inserts scissors into the base of the baby's skull and makes a hole. Next he inserts a suction catheter into the wound which pulls the baby's brains out. Then he crushes his skull.

I know we don't want to hear this any more than the German Christians wanted to hear what was happening to Jews. But it is happening and we must face it. If we can't face the truth in church, where can we face the truth? Don't get angry at me; get angry at the killing of innocent children and what legalized abortion has done to this country. I assure you, God is angry.

Our United States Congress couldn't even come up with enough votes to override the president's action. God help us. And where was the church? By our silence we consented to child-killing, as the people of Israel consented to the evil of their head of state by their failure to speak up. I confess I did not do enough to speak up against this horrible evil. God forgive me. God forgive us. We surely deserve every bit as severe a judgment as the destruction God brought upon the nation Judah. Don't think for a moment America is somehow immune to God's judgment. We are not.

God is a lover of children; Satan is a hater of children. When we care for little children, we do the work of God. When we destroy little children, we do the work of Satan.

These are hard words, but they are true. I wish they weren't. I debated whether to say some of these things, and last night I asked a dear friend her advice. She said, "Yes, you should say them."

I want to introduce that friend to you now. She is a sister whom my wife and I deeply love and respect. Fifteen years ago she lived in our home; now she works with our ministry. For all those fifteen years she's been a part of the Good Shepherd Community Church family. She is a true disciple of our Lord Jesus. The hand of God upon her has been powerful; many have been touched by her life. Please listen and pray as Diane shares her story with us.

When I was seventeen, I found myself apart from my family, involved in an unhealthy relationship with a man, and pregnant which was something I didn't want to think about or deal with.

Eventually, though, I did go down to Lovejoy abortion clinic in Portland to make an appointment to have an abortion. I made this decision because I had no desire to be a mother, and quite honestly, because I was terrified of going through the pain of labor. I just didn't think of it as being wrong.

When I was examined, I was found to be 24 weeks, or six months, pregnant. But I was assured that although I couldn't have a simple clinical abortion, I could still have one done at a nearby hospital. I agreed. I would have done anything to not be pregnant, and I showed up at the hospital on the scheduled day.

I was placed, along with about a dozen other young girls, in a large basement ward which was lined with cots. There, we received a saline injection in our abdomens which was designed to kill our unborn babies and expel their tiny bodies.

I will never be able to forget the sights or sound burned into my mind on that day. After a few hours of labor, we all began to lose our babies.

When the girl on my right lost hers, she began shrieking and screamed for the nurses to "get that away from me!" as she crawled backwards up her bed. The girl on my left cried quietly and asked the nurses if hers was a boy or a girl.

I felt a violent lurching sensation as the baby slid from my body. It is so sad to me that the only memory I have of my child is that of a small, still huddled form covered in blood laying on the white sheet of my cot.

When I left the hospital, I determined to put this horrible episode behind me—never thinking about it, never talking about it.

My relationship with my boyfriend, never strong, was now almost nonexistent. About this time, some friends of mine introduced me to the pastor of their church. His name was Randy Alcorn. When he saw my precarious living situation, he invited me to come and live with himself, his wife Nanci, and their daughter Karina. While living there, I sensed the extraordinary joy in their existence and I wanted that, too. So I accepted Christ as my Savior. Unfortunately, I was already pregnant again. Knowing that I would never go through a late-term abortion, I decided, with the full love and support of Randy and Nanci, to give my baby up for adoption. I had my baby just before Angela, the Alcorn's second daughter, was born.

I was completely unprepared for the feelings of awe that overwhelmed me when I give birth to a healthy baby boy. I was, however, content with my decision to give him up to a childless Christian couple.

Afterwards I moved out on my own, eager to begin my life as a new believer at Good Shepherd church. I became involved with the college-age group, attended a weekly Bible study and weekly functions, as well as church on Sundays. I met a lot of really neat people, including a guy named Rod, who became my boyfriend.

I wish I could end my story there, but I can't. Though I had accepted Jesus as my Savior, I hadn't put my sinful lifestyle behind me. I became deeply involved with Rod, and I became pregnant again. If anyone could die of shame, I would be dead. I was so scared everyone would find out and see what a phony Christian and failure I was. I was too scared to tell Rod. I knew he would marry me, but then he would have to tell his parents that I was pregnant. I was so ashamed. My only option seemed to be abortion. So I went down to Lovejoy and had it done, never giving a thought to our baby. I would never tell anyone what I had done. I would go to my grave with this secret.

Time passed and my secret remained deeply buried. Eventually Rod and I married, we had two kids, Josiah and Amy, we bought a house, attended Good Shepherd

Church and Growth Groups. But something was wrong.

My hidden sin held God at arm's length. I couldn't grow as a believer because I would never let God close to me, afraid He would see me as I really was, sinful and ugly.

One day when I had been married for eight years, God decided it was time for me to come to know Him better. I felt an intense, growing awareness of the Lord. I was totally overwhelmed by the incredible knowledge of His love. I felt chosen, special, humbled, and loved, not because of what I had or hadn't done, but simply because it was His pleasure to do so. For a week I was compelled to immerse myself in Scripture and constant prayer. And for the first time in my life I fell in love with my God.

At the end of the week I was praying in my room. I prayed, "Lord, I asked You into my life a long time ago but I never understood about wanting to give something back. I'm willing to die for You." No sooner had the words left my lips when my horrible sin rose up before me. I fell to my face on the carpet and wept as all the years of deceit and hypocrisy paraded before me. I cried even harder as the truth of having murdered my own children slammed into me.

When I went to Rod, I began by saying how sorry I was, over and over. I just couldn't say the words that would tell him that I had taken the life of his first child. If you know Rod, you know how he loves babies.

When I finally got the words out, Rod lay his head in his arms at the table. I remember looking at him suffering from this horrible loss, and all I wanted to do was reach out and comfort him. But I couldn't touch him. I felt so unclean. I was the one who had done this to him.

When he finally looked up, Rod tried to take my hand in his but I pulled away. He caught it and held on. Then he asked me to forgive him.

I was stunned. I couldn't say anything. He hadn't responded like I thought he would, like I deserved. Instead he accepted his responsibility in everything and asked *me* to forgive *him*. We cried and we asked each other and the Lord to forgive us.

The consequences to what I've done are great. I wonder about the children I lost to "choice" and see who they might have looked like in the smiles of Josiah and Amy. Sometimes I think I can almost hear them. But comforting me through it all is the awesome knowledge that Jesus' blood fully paid for my debt and that He loves me completely.

I want to thank both Diane and Rod. Without Rod's full support, Diane would not have been up here. They have given us a gift of honesty and transparency, at cost to themselves. It's a gift I believe will result in many saved lives—more children in our church nursery, fewer men and women suffering under the weight of guilt, more confession and repentance and healing, more effective kingdom work because of cleansed hearts.

As she spoke, you saw that children are not the only victims of abortion. Mothers and fathers and grandparents and uncles and aunts and many others are victims, too. You may think our children's classes are full, but they are missing many children. Maybe one of them would have been your child's best friend. Maybe several of them would be going on one of our summer missions projects.

If you have been damaged by an abortion, you are not alone. This room is full of damaged people. All of us have been damaged by the loss of those who should be here with us today.

Thirty-five million abortions—at least six million by those who profess to be evangelical Christians. But that's just the moms. Throw in an equal number of dads and you have twelve million. But that's not all. There are mothers who drove their daughters to an abortion clinic; fathers who gave them money to get an abortion. People who talked someone into an abortion or didn't try to talk them out of one. Health care professionals who have referred people for abortions. In some churches, there are pastors and lay leaders who've failed to speak up for fear of offending the congregation or chairman of the trustees; or to protect their reputation they've stood by while their own children had abortions.

There are a lot of guilt feelings here today. And you know what? The reason we feel guilty is usually quite simple—it's because we are guilty. A lot of people think we need to get rid of the guilty feelings. What we need to deal with first is the guilt itself. No matter how often someone may say to you, "You have nothing to feel guilty about," your guilt feelings will remain because deep inside, in your conscience, in your heart, you know better.

By denying reality you can try to avoid guilt feelings, but this denial is unhealthy. It sets you up for emotional trauma whenever something reminds you of the child you once carried or the killing place where your child died. It doesn't help to ignore a cancer. It doesn't help to put a Band-Aid on a cancer. When a person is writhing from the pain of cancer, it isn't truthful and it isn't loving to say to them, "You really have no reason to feel bad."

We all need a permanent cure to the disease of our guilt—a solution based on reality, not denial or pretense. Because as long as we deny we have cancer, we won't get treatment for it. As long as we deny our guilt, we won't experience God's forgiveness and healing.

Look at our sister. God got hold of her life when she faced head-on the reality of her abortions. Probably some people were tempted to say, "It's not so bad." But she knew how bad it was. She had the courage to face it for what it was, and God has gotten hold of this woman and done something amazing, something beautiful with her life. And He wants to do the same with every one of us.

In C. S. Lewis's Chronicles of Narnia, *The Voyage of the Dawn Treader,* there's a part where the boy Eustace becomes a dragon, and he must submit to Aslan, the Lion who is King, to claw away at his dragon skin and make him into a new person. I have felt the claws of the Lion of Judah. I can tell you, it hurts. But I would rather be hurt by my God as He cleanses and heals me than to slowly die without His cleansing and healing because I've tried to protect myself from being hurt.

Transparencies 12–13: God's forgiveness (see Appendix A)

You may feel, "But I don't deserve forgiveness after all I've done." That's exactly right. None of us deserves forgiveness. If we deserved it, we wouldn't need it. Christ got what we deserved on the cross, so we could get what we don't deserve—forgiveness, a clean slate, a fresh start.

No matter what you have done, no sin is beyond the reach of God's grace. The apostle Paul himself was a murderer; he had participated in the killing of Christians. He called himself the "chief of sinners." Do you think God used Paul? Then He can surely use you.

Maybe you imagine that in heaven the skeleton's going to come out of the closet and someone will discover you had an abortion. Well, no skeletons are going to come out of the closet, because there are no skeletons and there are no closets. God knows already. God has seen us at our worst and still loves us.

God loves us as we are, but He loves us too much to let us stay that way. He is determined to bring us to our knees to confess, repent, and be healed.

Once we acknowledge our sin and repent and ask God to forgive us, we must resist the temptation to wallow in guilt feelings, for we are no longer guilty. Christ calls upon us to accept His atonement, not to repeat it. I spoke with a woman recently who said, "I believed God could forgive any sin, except my abortion." She discovered that she had been wrong. She'd been punishing herself for a sin Christ had already taken the punishment for. No sin is too big for the Savior to forgive.

That's the amazing grace of God. Are you thankful for that grace?

There are some unique aspects to abortion that often require a very special healing process. Ninety-five percent of people in the church who've lost children to abortion have never really come to terms with it. There are a number of people hearing this message who've never told a single person they've had an abortion. They've suffered in silence. We need to create a climate that lets them come out of the closet if that's what they want to do.

The church isn't a showcase for saints, it's a hospital for sinners. You're a sinner? Welcome to the club. The truth is, I'm a worse sinner than you know, and you're a worse sinner than I can know. So we're even. You will not be judged and condemned for a sin Christ has forgiven. The rest of us at Good Shepherd are just as human, just as imperfect, just as needy as you are.

In your bulletin and growth group lesson are phone numbers of the HEART programs, fourteen-week Bible study groups designed for women and men touched by abortion. There are also phone numbers of women at our church who have worked with those who've had abortions. At the table in the foyer we have these booklets from Focus on the Family ("Overcoming Post-Abortion Syndrome").

You need the help and support of your church family. This week a woman in our church told me that there are thirteen people in her growth group. She shared her testimony and talked about her abortion, and now five out of the thirteen have acknowledged that they've lost children to abortion. Sometimes it takes one person with the courage to speak up and a group with enough love to put their arms around and weep with those who weep and comfort the hurting.

James 5:16 says, "Confess your sins to each other and pray for each other so that you may be healed." Galatians 6:2 tells us, "Carry each other's burdens, and in this way you will fulfill the law of Christ." We cannot heal on our own or carry all our burdens on our own. God has given us to each other to help carry the load.

Some of you may choose to share in High Ground or Bible study or accountability group or your growth groups this week. There will be no pressure whatsoever. You may not be ready to, or it may not be God's timing for you. That's between you and the Lord. We want what's best for you.

I want to share with you a powerful passage, one which is a prophecy of the ministry of our Lord Jesus, written seven hundred years before He was conceived. It is for anyone who feels as if her life is in ashes, anyone who feels brokenhearted, imprisoned, in darkness, to anyone who mourns and grieves and feels despair:

Transparency 14: Isaiah 61:1–3

The Spirit of the Sovereign LORD is on me, because the LORD has anointed me to preach good news to the poor. He has sent me to bind up the brokenhearted, to proclaim freedom for the captives and release from darkness for the prisoners, to proclaim the year of the LORD's favor and the day of vengeance of our God, to comfort all who mourn, and provide for those who grieve in Zion—to bestow on them a crown of beauty instead of ashes, the oil of gladness instead of mourning, and a garment of praise instead of a spirit of despair. They will be called oaks of righteousness, a planting of the LORD for the display of his splendor.

Transparency 15: Proverbs 31:8–9

Speak up for those who cannot speak for themselves, for the rights of all who are destitute. Speak up and judge fairly; defend the rights of the poor and needy.

What can we do for weak and helpless children? A thousand different things. If you're interested in knowing, call the phone numbers in the bulletin for our local pregnancy resource centers and other prolife groups we have listed.

Last week I heard the director of our PRC's postabortion Bible study program say that one of the biggest things women recovering from abortions have to work through is their anger toward those who knew abortion was child-killing but didn't speak up and try to talk them out of it. I want you to think carefully about that statement. You owe it to others to speak up. To be silent is a sin against God, a sin against the child, and a sin against the person getting the abortion.

It is never the loving thing to do to ignore sin, and it is never in their best interests to encourage or assist people in their sin. If you knew your friend was going to kill her three-year-old, would you consider it an act of friendship to look the other way? If you know someone is going to get an abortion, would you ever say, "I can't risk my friendship by confronting them?" If you understand abortion and you understand friendship and you understand what it means to be a follower of Christ, then you must speak up, or you will have betrayed your friend, an innocent child, and your Lord.

A word to young people: Pregnancy outside marriage can be prevented by not having sex outside of marriage. Even if you don't get pregnant, if you have sex outside marriage you are violating the law of God and setting yourself up for disastrous consequences. I can't overemphasize the importance and the rewards of sexual purity. But if you've gotten pregnant, realize there's a child there. Don't try to cover one sin by committing a greater sin.

Transparency 16: (Picture of preborn child) Remember, this is who we're talking about. This isn't an issue; it's a baby. It's not a choice; it's a child. It's not politics; it's a precious human being created in the image of God.

Edmund Burke said, "All that is necessary for the triumph of evil is that good men do nothing."

Abraham Lincoln said, "To sin by silence when they should protest makes cowards of men."

Silence is never the solution. When churches are silent about abortion, we encourage it. Silence becomes a form of consent, a quiet permission. Let's not be cowards. Let's stand up for truth; let's reach out in compassion.

Whenever I see the face of a child in our church nursery, and I happen to know his mother was going to get an abortion until someone talked her out of it, I praise God that someone spoke up. And I pray that God will make a great champion for Christ out of this precious child whose life was spared.

Transparency 17: Choose life, Deuteronomy 30:19:

"This day I call heaven and earth as witnesses against you that I have set before you life and death, blessings and curses. Now choose life, so that you and your children may live."

Before you leave, remember to pick up the brochures "Identifying and Overcoming Post-Abortion Syndrome" and "The First Nine Months" from the table in the foyer.

In the Next-Step Room to my left are people who would love to talk with you about your relationship with God. Today we have in each service several people who know about abortions and God's grace, including some of the rose carriers. They would consider it an honor to help you in any way they can.

As the worship team comes to lead us, let's pray.

Lord, when we walk out of this service, we're going to go back to a world of lies about this issue. We go back to a godless generation that won't let their children get in the way of their careers and won't let their elderly parents get in the way of their retirements.

We want to be different, God.
We must be different or we have nothing to offer this dying world.

Please, Father, bring healing to those who've had abortions—men and
women. Help them to get the help they need; help our young people to
practice sexual purity; and help all of us not to succumb to the spirit of
our age and sacrifice our children.

Teach us not only to abstain from the wrong, Lord, but to do the
right—to intervene on behalf of unborn children. Our Lord Jesus said,
"Inasmuch as you did it to the least of these my brothers,
so you've done it to me" and
"Inasmuch as you've not done it to these, you've not done it to me."

May we serve You, Lord, by looking out for and standing up for the
weakest and most helpless children You have created.
May we be their defenders and may You be pleased with our efforts
done in Your strength and for Your glory.
Who will stand up for the children? May the answer, Lord, be us.
We ask it in Jesus' name. Amen.

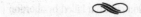

The service concluded with a soloist and our worship team singing "Who Will
Stand Up for the Children?" *An image of an unborn child sucking his thumb was
projected on the screen. As Jim Seymour asked,* "Who will speak up for the children?" *people in the congregation stood to express their commitment.*

*After the five services (all of which were full, a few standing room only,
making about twenty-seven hundred people for the weekend), many wept and
shared their encouragement with the rose carriers, Diane, and the rest of us. We
have heard many wonderful stories. Three years later we still hear people talk
about it. We will not know all the results until eternity, but based on what we've
seen, it's clear that God did an amazing work. May He receive all the glory, and
may His people experience the warmth of His presence and blessing.*

Appendix H

A CHURCH'S POSITION
STATEMENT ON ABORTION

Circulated on Sanctity of Human Life Sunday

I was asked to write this statement to be printed in my church bulletin on Sanctity of Human Life Sunday in 1998. Both believers and visiting unbelievers were in mind as I wrote it. You are welcome to use it in part or in its entirety.

This week is the twenty-fifth anniversary of the Supreme Court decision *Roe* v. *Wade*, which legalized abortion in America in 1973.

Not just our society, but our church has been deeply affected by abortion. In our Sanctity of Life service last year, over fifty of our people, some walking together as families, brought thirty-five roses up the aisle in the services and placed them in a cradle—one rose for each one million children killed by abortion in America since 1973.

Among those rose carriers were these: women who've had abortions; men responsible for abortions; people who helped perform abortions; people who've lost grandchildren and siblings to abortion; a person who survived an abortion and was carried to term; a woman conceived when her thirteen-year-old mother was raped; a woman advised by her doctor to get an abortion but didn't; someone who had an abortion appointment scheduled and canceled it at the last moment; a woman who places flowers outside Portland's Lovejoy abortion clinic on the anniversary of her child's death. These were only a small sampling of lives touched by abortion at our church.

The anniversary of *Roe* v. *Wade*, which some celebrate, is for us a cause for reflection and mourning.

What the Bible Says

At Good Shepherd Community Church we believe the Bible, which says that all people, male and female, are created in the image of God (Genesis 1:27; James 3:9). Each individual has been personally created by God (Malachi 2:10). Personhood is never measured by age, stage of development, or mental, physical, or social skills (Exodus 4:11).

Psalm 139:13–16 paints a graphic picture of the intimate involvement of God with a preborn person. God created David's inmost being, his soul, not at birth, but before birth. David says to his Creator, "You knit me together in my mother's womb." Each person, regardless of his parentage or handicap, has been personally knit together by God in the womb. All the days of his life have been planned out by God before any have taken place (Psalm 139:16).

Scripture says that Mary "was found to be with child through the Holy Spirit." Jesus became a human being at the point of conception. So do all the rest of us.

WHAT SCIENCE SAYS

Dr. Alfred M. Bongioanni, professor of obstetrics at the University of Pennsylvania, states, "I have learned from my earliest medical education that human life begins at the time of conception. I submit that human life is present throughout this entire sequence from conception to adulthood and that any interruption at any point throughout this time constitutes a termination of human life."

Speaking of the early stages of a child's development in the womb, Professor Bongioanni says, "I am no more prepared to say that these early stages represent an incomplete human being than I would be to say that the child prior to the dramatic effects of puberty is not a human being. This is human life at every stage."

Dr. Jerome LeJeune, genetics professor at the University of Descartes in Paris, states, "After fertilization has taken place a new human being has come into being." He says this "is no longer a matter of taste or opinion. Each individual has a very neat beginning, at conception."

Professor Micheline Matthews-Roth of Harvard University Medical School argues, "It is scientifically correct to say that an individual human life begins at conception."

Every indication is that the moment of each person's creation is the moment of his conception. Before that moment the individual (with his unique DNA) did not exist, and from that moment he does.

Even abortionists know this, though they usually don't tell women considering abortion. The owner of the Lovejoy Surgicenter, Oregon's largest abortion clinic, testified under oath that human life "begins at conception."

What Church History Says

Christians throughout church history have affirmed with a united voice the humanity of the preborn child and the duty to protect him. The second-century *Epistle of Barnabas* treats the unborn child as any other human neighbor by saying, "You shall love your neighbor more than your own life. You shall not slay a child by abortion. You shall not kill that which has already been generated" (*Epistle of Barnabas* 19:5).

The Didache, a second-century catechism for young converts, states, "Do not murder a child by abortion or kill a new-born infant" (*Didache* 2:2). Tertullian said, "It does not matter whether you take away a life that is born, or destroy one that is coming to the birth. In both instances, the destruction is murder" (*Apology* 9:4).

Reformer John Calvin said, "The fetus, though enclosed in the womb of its mother, is already a human being and it is a monstrous crime to rob it of the life which it has not yet begun to enjoy. If it seems more horrible to kill a man in his own house than in a field, because a man's house is his place of most secure refuge, it ought surely to be deemed more atrocious to destroy a fetus in the womb before it has come to light."

What Jesus Said

Christ's disciples failed to understand how valuable children were to Him, when they rebuked those who tried to bring them near Him (Luke 18:15–17). Jesus called the children to Him and said, "Let the little children come to me, and do not hinder them, for the kingdom of God belongs to such as these."

We must learn to love children as does God, who "defends the cause of the fatherless" (Deuteronomy 10:18). He calls on us to do the same: "Defend the cause of the weak and fatherless; maintain the rights of the poor and oppressed. Rescue the weak and needy; deliver them from the hand of the wicked" (Psalm 82:3–4).

Jesus said, "Whatever you did for one of the least of these brothers of mine, you did for me" (Matthew 25:40). If the baby Jesus were about to be killed, what would we do on His behalf? We should do it for all little children about to die.

A Civil Rights Issue

Martin Luther King Jr., said, in words prominently displayed on Portland's Justice Center, "Injustice anywhere is a threat to justice everywhere." The daily stories of young people killing already-born children are shocking. But these are simply a logical extension of the abortion mentality. If a parent has the right to take a child's life six months before birth, why not six months after birth? It's the same parent and the same child. Other than size and age, what's the difference?

We believe in civil rights. We believe that just because a boy or girl is young and small doesn't mean we have the right to dispose of him or her. We oppose abortion for the same reason we oppose slavery—it is a fundamental violation of human rights. There is no God-given right to convenience, but there is a God-given right to life. It is not our prerogative to take life, only God's. The concentration camps of Nazi Germany are a testimony to what happens when people start deciding who has the right to live and who doesn't. The sign at Auschwitz says "Never Again." We hope that someday our country will admit that abortion kills children and will say "Never Again."

We affirm the inalienable rights of all people. All people are "created equal," not just "born equal." You don't have to have been born yet to be a person anymore than you have to have walked or talked to be a person.

A Women's Rights Issue

Years of experiences with people in and outside the church who've had abortions have convinced us that an abortion is never in the best interests of the mother.

Early women's rights advocates were prolife, not proabortion. Susan B. Anthony was a radical feminist in her day. She said, "I deplore the horrible crime of child murder.... No matter what the motive, love of ease, or a desire to save from suffering the unborn innocent, the woman is awfully guilty who commits the deed...but oh! thrice guilty is the man who drove her to the desperation which impelled her to the crime."

Anthony's newspaper, *The Revolution,* made this claim: "When a woman destroys the life of her unborn child, it is a sign that, by education or circumstances, she has been greatly wronged."

Another leading feminist, Elizabeth Cady Stanton, commented on abortion this way: "When we consider that women are treated as property, it is degrading to women that we should treat our children as property to be disposed of as we wish."

The early feminists opposed abortion. They were followed by a new breed of feminists, such as Margaret Sanger, founder of Planned Parenthood, who advocated abortion as a means of sexual freedom, birth control, and eugenics.

There are feminists today who still uphold the prolife position. Feminists for Life is a very active group started in the early 1970s. Alice Paul drafted the original version of the Equal Rights Amendment. She called abortion "the ultimate exploitation of women."

If Alcohol Harms Babies, What Does Abortion Do?

Every establishment in Oregon that serves alcohol is required to post a sign which says "Alcohol and Pregnancy Don't Mix." In the picture is a baby clearly visible inside her mother. The message is: "Don't drink alcohol; you've got a baby inside it could harm." Our message is: "Abortion and Pregnancy Don't Mix." Or, "Don't get an abortion; you've got a baby inside it will kill."

We believe the most loving thing we can do for a woman considering an abortion is offer her the scientific facts, a biblical and moral perspective, and help and alternatives, such as those available through Pregnancy Resource Centers.

If we were about to take a medicine that would kill a preborn child, would we want someone to tell us? Yes. We believe it is loving our neighbor to compassionately point out to others the truth that in abortion there are two victims: one dead, one wounded.

The Bible commands us, "Speak up for those who cannot speak for themselves, for the rights of all who are destitute. Speak up and judge fairly; defend the rights of the poor and needy" (Proverbs 31:8–9).

Who is less capable of speaking up for themselves than little boys and girls who haven't yet been born? If we don't speak up for these innocent children, who will?

Our Posture toward Those Who Disagree

We are committed to open and loving dialogue with those who disagree with us in this area. We wish to work through these issues with our people to understand what God says about this critically important subject. If this message is uncomfortable, we ask you to understand that truth is sometimes uncomfortable. We are not pointing the finger at anyone; we are simply trying to be faithful to God's Word. If He points the finger at you or at us, that's up to Him. We are fellow image-bearers; Christ died for the sins of us all; and His forgiveness is freely available to all: "For God so loved the world that he gave his one and only Son, that whoever believes in him shall not perish but have eternal life."

We extend to all our visitors our sincere welcome and the love of Christ. We hope you will accept our invitation to dialogue on this issue and, above all, the issue of the person and work of our Lord Jesus Christ. Our doors and hearts are open to all.

Appendix I

A BIBLE STUDY LESSON
FOR GROUP DISCUSSION

I wrote the following for my church small group Bible studies, for use the week I preached on Sanctity of Life Weekend. Feel free to duplicate and use this study and the accompanying handout as you wish. It can also be accessed at www.epm.org/aboleson.html.

Choosing and Defending Life

1. Read the attached articles, "Abortion in the Bible and Church History" and "A Church's Position Statement on Abortion" (see Appendices B and H). Mark anything that strikes you as significant. Did something in particular stick out to you? (For example: at what point a person is created by God; Scripture's references to people in the womb; where the incarnation of Christ took place; the early church's teaching on abortion; contrasting God's view of children with modern society's.)

2. A real life situation: Your friend is pregnant. She's told by her doctor, "Tests show the fetus has a disease that causes deformity. It will probably live no more than a few weeks after birth, and if it does, it will never be able to walk, talk, see, or have a normal life. I recommend you terminate the pregnancy."

- What would you tell your friend? Why? (Some verses that might help: Deuteronomy 32:39; 1 Samuel 2:6; Exodus 20:13.)
- On the issue of the child's handicaps, how do the following verses help you to respond further? Exodus 4:11 (compare Isaiah 45:9–11); John 9:3; Luke 14:13–14.

3. What do these passages tell you about what God calls us to do when innocent lives are threatened? Proverbs 31:8–9; Psalm 82:3–4; Proverbs 24:11–12. (For further study: Psalm 72:12–14; sin of omission: Jeremiah 21:12; James 4:17.)

4. Another life situation: A young single acquaintance of yours has gotten pregnant. She's called an abortion clinic and made an appointment for tomorrow. You hear about it from a mutual friend. What should you say or do?

- *Consider before answering:* We should not intrude into everyone's life in an attempt to prevent every sin or act of bad judgment. But should the fact that an innocent human being's life is at stake compel us to greater involvement? How much greater? Be specific. What should you do? What should you not do?

5. What does God say to the person who has taken a life or committed any other sin? What does a person need to do to experience what these passages offer? Psalm 103:10–14; Micah 7:18–19; Proverbs 28:13; 1 John 1:9; Romans 8:1.

6. Recent statistics indicate that nearly one in five women who get an abortion identifies herself as an evangelical Christian (up from one in six ten years ago). Does this surprise you? Why do you think abortion happens so often in the church?

7. Among the church family who brought thirty-five roses up the aisle in the services were: women who've had abortions; men responsible for abortions; people who helped perform abortions; people who've lost grandchildren and siblings to abortion; a person who survived an abortion and was carried to term; a woman conceived when her thirteen-year-old mother was raped; a woman advised by her doctor to get an abortion but didn't; someone who had an abortion appointment scheduled and canceled it at the last moment; a woman who places flowers outside an abortion clinic on the anniversary of her child's death. You also heard Diane's testimony. These are only a small sampling of lives touched by abortion at our church. Do any of these stories make you think or touch your heart in a particular way?

8. James 5:16 says, "Confess your sins to one another and pray for each other so that you may be healed." Of course, not all sins need to be confessed in a growth group, but they do need to be confessed to God, and often He leads us to share with others as part of our healing process and to use us to comfort others with similar hurts (2 Corinthians 1:3–7). If you have had a personal or family experience with abortion, and if you think God is leading you to share it with your group, please do so. (There will be no pressure put on anyone to share. This is entirely optional.)

Resources

To get help. If you have been touched by abortion, you are not alone and you *can* experience God's healing. For information on an excellent fourteen week in-depth Bible study for women—and a separate one for men—contact HEART (Healing Encouragement for Abortion Related Trauma) at 503-224-3278. In Sandy, contact BEARS (Bringing Encouragement for Abortion Related Stress) at 503-668-8101.

To touch base personally with a sister from your own church who understands and has volunteered to talk with you, call any of the following: (seven phone numbers listed, followed by pregnancy resource center and church office).

To give help. If you would like to get involved helping the unborn and their mothers, here are three local organizations you can call: (phone numbers for local prolife and abortion alternative organizations).

Book. ProLife Answers to ProChoice Arguments by Randy Alcorn. Includes: "Finding Forgiveness after an Abortion"; "Abortion in the Bible and Church History"; "Fifty Ways to Help Unborn Babies and their Mothers"; "ProLife Resources."

Internet. CareNet (crisis pregnancy centers), www.care-net.org/; National Right to Life, www.nrlc.org; The Ultimate Prolife Resource List, www.prolife.org/ultimate; Eternal Perspective Ministries, www.epm.org.

Questions for Further Reflection and Study

1. If someone in your group chooses now or later to share his or her involvement in an abortion (or any other sin) for which he is repentant, what do the following passages tell you about how you should respond? Galatians 6:2; 1 Peter 4:8; James 2:13; Matthew 5:7.

2. How would you respond to each of the following statements?
- "I believe in a woman's right to choose."
- "The fetus isn't a person; it's just a part of the woman's body."
- "I agree with Planned Parenthood: 'Every child a wanted child.'"
- "I'm against abortion, except in cases of rape, incest, and deformity of the child" (see Deuteronomy 24:16).
- "Abortion is a terribly difficult choice. We shouldn't invade a woman's privacy in making that choice."
- "I'm not proabortion; I'm just prochoice about abortion."

3. What do these passages teach about the importance of churches and Christians coming clean—confessing, repenting, and dealing with sin? Psalm 24:3–4; Psalm 66:18; Proverbs 28:9; Zechariah 7:13; 1 Corinthians 5:6–7.

4. What does Scripture say about a nation that spills innocent blood and does not repent? 2 Kings 24:2–4; Proverbs 6:16–19; Ezekiel 35:6; see 2 Chronicles 7:14. Who does God call upon *first* to repent?

5. Read Psalm 127:3–5. How does the biblical view differ from our culture's view of children? Respond to this statement: "Christians today have bought into society's antichild mentality, which motivates them to see children as an inconvenience, to turn up their noses at large families, and to consider the alternative of abortion when they face an unwanted pregnancy."

Attached to this lesson was a two-page handout by Randy Alcorn,
"Biblical Perspectives on Unborn Children,"
available at www.epm.org/aborbibl.html.
(You may reproduce and use as you wish.)

Appendix J

COMMUNICATING THE PROLIFE MESSAGE

(References to *PlA* are to *ProLife Answers to ProChoice Arguments*. Numbers refer to the respective argument number, and the answers following it, in this book.[789])

1. Tailor your presentation to your audience so that you're speaking to them, not to yourself.
- Realize the vested interests, denial and rationalization surrounding this issue.
- Realize the average person's saturation and indoctrination with media propaganda.

2. Do your homework. The other position can afford to be ignorant of the facts. You can't. (The other position is dependent on diverting attention *from* the central facts; yours is dependent on drawing attention *to* them. To do so, you must know what you're talking about.)

3. Present the facts logically, clearly, and succinctly, citing credible sources (secular whenever possible).

4. Use terms they're familiar with, not prolife buzzwords.

5. Appeal to their curiosity and open-mindedness to hear a suppressed and politically incorrect viewpoint. (Prochoice is the status quo, establishment position. Prolife is the radical, counterculture position.)

6. Surprise your audience. Don't fit the antiabortion stereotype.
- "Actually, I'm prochoice. And you're not." ("I'm prochoice about jobs, clothes, cars, schools, seat belts, smoking, etc. You're antichoice about rape, kidnapping, assault, theft, and child molesting. Aren't you?")

- "I don't believe in unwanted children." ("I just believe the solution is wanting them, not killing them.")
- "I'm committed to women's rights." ("Like Susan B. Anthony and other pioneer feminists, I believe abortion is harmful and demeaning to women. In fact, abortion has become the primary method across the globe of eliminating unwanted females." *PIA* 14) "Abortion is a means for irresponsible men to exploit women, using them sexually, then leaving them alone with the devastating physical and psychological consequences."

7. Be rational and calm. When you're right, there's no need to be defensive. Give the facts and let the listener develop her own emotions based on them. (Don't overwhelm people with *your* emotions. Don't go ballistic in a debate, and nine out of ten times the other side will. People who are listening will see which side is angry and irrational and which is calm and logical.)

8. Be prepared for straw man and ad hominem arguments, but don't use them yourself. When the facts aren't on their side people have nothing left to do but distort issues and call names. The side with the truth need not and should not do this. When the facts are on your side, you draw attention to them. When they're not, you draw attention from them.

9. Be sensitive to the spiritual needs of your audience. (Look and pray for heart change, not just head change.)

10. Ask them questions that will make them think (usually for the first time):
- "You say you want to be called prochoice, not proabortion. Why? What's wrong with abortion?" (The only good reason for feeling bad about abortion—that it kills an innocent child—should compel you to be against *others* doing it also. You should either say it's fine, or oppose it, but you can't logically do both.)
- "See this intrauterine picture of a live unborn at eight weeks (at the time of an early abortion)? What does that look like? (Eye.) That? (Fingers.) That? (Mouth.) That? (Nose.)" Don't tell them. Let *them* answer. Then point out what they said.
- "This baby has a measurable heartbeat at twenty-one days and brainwaves at forty days, before the earliest abortions. What do you call it when there is no longer a heartbeat or brainwaves? (Death.) What do you call it when there *is* a heartbeat and brainwaves? (Life.) What does abortion do? (Kills a living baby.)" *PIA* 3
- "This unborn baby is to a born infant what a born infant is to a toddler (younger and smaller). Do you think it would be more legitimate to kill an unwanted infant than a toddler just because he's younger and smaller?"

- "If abortion isn't fundamentally different than other surgeries, like root canals and tonsillectomies, why are there so many postabortion support groups and hundreds of thousands of women getting psychological counseling and grief therapy related to their abortions? Do you know of any post-root canal counseling and support groups?" *PLA* 27

- "Why do you think it bothers you to see pictures of an abortion more than pictures of root canals or open heart surgery? What's the difference?"

- "Which side in the debate is cruel? The one that shows pictures of dead babies while opposing their killing, or the one that opposes showing the pictures but defends their killing?" *PLA* 32

- "You say the unborn is part of the mother's body? If that's true, then every pregnant woman has two hearts, two brains, two different genetic codes, two sets of fingers with different fingerprints, two heads, two noses, four eyes, two blood types, two circulatory systems, and two skeletal systems. And half the time she also has testicles and a penis." (Location isn't the issue. Are "test tube babies" part of the test tube?) *PLA* 2

- "We all know the 'fetus' is a child." *PLA* 8

- "You say abortion is legal, so we shouldn't oppose it. They said the same about slavery and the Holocaust." *PLA* 16c

- "Abortion in the case of handicap? After they're born, we say they're precious and the family learns so much from them. We cheer them on in the Special Olympics. Then before they're born why do we say, 'We don't want these monsters; let's kill them while we can'?" *PLA* 30

- "Abortion in the case of rape? Rape is never the fault of the child—why punish *him?* Don't you believe a child is a child, regardless of any bad thing his father did to someone? Besides, abortion is not a therapy, it's a *trauma* on a woman who has already undergone the trauma of rape. If you found out your best friend was the 'product of rape' would you think she deserved to live?" *PLA* 31

- "You say it's *men* who are primarily opposed to abortion? Did you know polls consistently show many more women than men oppose abortion? That the single greatest proabortion group in society is young single men? That the great majority of prolife workers are women, not men? That of women who have had abortions, many more become prolife activists than prochoice activists?" *PLA* 34

- "You say prolifers don't really care about the women, or the children once they're born? The fact is that prolife pregnancy centers providing free tests, care, classes, counseling, materials, and housing comprise the single largest grassroots volunteer movement in history. Countless prolifers adopt, open their homes, and volunteer to help children after they're born. The other side gets rich selling abortions. Whose motives should be suspect?" *PLA* 33

- "Will you read this carefully researched presentation? No? I was hoping you were open-minded. Are you choosing to censor this side of the debate from your own consideration? Why? I'll be glad to read anything you have for me from the other side. I'm open-minded. Can you refute anything I've said? Show me. Let's lay out all the evidence, and let the best position win. I'm not afraid of the truth. Are you?"

Appendix K

PROLIFE RESOURCES

Abortion Alternatives and Support for Women

Abort73.com, Email: info@abort73.com, Web site: www.abort73.com

AbortionFacts.com, Web site: www.abortionfacts.com

Bethany Christian Services, (616) 224-7610, Toll Free: (800) 238-4269, 901 Eastern Ave. NE, PO Box 294, Grand Rapids, MI 49501-0294, Web site: www.bethany.org

Heartbeat International, (614) 885-7577, 665 E. Dublin-Granville Road, Suite 440, Columbus, OH 43229-3245, Email: support@heartbeatinternational.org, Web site: www.heartbeatinternational.org

Human Life International, Toll Free: (800) 549-LIFE, Fax: (540) 622-7247, 4 Family Life Lane, Front Royal, VA 22630, Email: hli@hli.org, Web site: www.hli.org

International Life Services, (213) 382-2156, Fax: (213) 382-4203, 2606 1/2 West 8th Street, Los Angeles, CA 90057, Email: lifeservices@juno.com, Web site: www.internationallifeservices.org

Liberty Godparent Foundation, (434) 845-3466, (434) 845-1751, Toll Free: (800) 542-4453, PO Box 4199, Lynchburg, VA 24502, Email: life-keeper@godparent.org, Web site: www.godparent.org

Life Decisions International, (540) 631-0380, P.O. Box 439, Front Royal, VA 22630-0009, Email: ldi@fightpp.org, Web site: www.fightpp.org

Life International, (616) 248-3300, 72 Ransom NE, Grand Rapids, MI 49503, Email: info@lifeinternational.com, Web site: www.lifeinternational.com

Lighthouse, (816) 361-2233, 400 West Meyer Blvd., Kansas City, MO 64113, Web site: www.lighthouse-inc.org. (Mailing Address: Light House Inc., P.O. Box 10145, Kansas City, MO 64171).

Mercy Ministries of America, Nancy Alcorn, Director, (615) 831-6987, P.O. Box 111060, Nashville, TN 37222-1060, Email: info@mercyministries.com, Web site: www.mercyministries.org

National Institute of Family & Life Advocates (NIFLA) (*a ministry providing legal counsel and support to existing pregnancy help centers as well as assisting them in converting to medical clinic status*); Thomas Glessner, President, (540) 372-3930, PO Box 42060, Fredericksburg, VA, 22404, Email: tglessner @nifla.org, Web site: www.nifla.org

National Life Center, (856) 848-1819, Toll Free: (800) 848-LOVE (5683), 686 N. Broad Street, Woodbury, NJ 08096, Email: nlc1stway@snip.net, Web site: www.nationallifecenter.com

Nurturing Network, Development Office, (509) 493-4026, Toll Free: (800) TNN-4MOM, PO Box 1489, White Salmon, WA 98672, Email: TNN@nurturingnetwork.org, Web site: www.nurturingnetwork.org

Pregnancy Centers Online, Toll Free: (800) 395-HELP, Web site: www.pregnancycenters.org

Pregnancy Resource Centers, CareNet, (703) 478-5661, Fax: (703) 478-5668, Toll Free: (800) 395-HELP, 44180 Riverside Parkway, Suite 200, Lansdowne, VA 20176, Email: info@care-net.org, Web site: www.care-net.org.

StandUpGirl.com Foundation, Helpline: (800) 672-2296, Option line: (800) 395-HELP, 4335 River Road N., Salem, OR 97303, Web site: www.standupgirl.com

The following toll-free hotlines for women in crisis pregnancies can be called from anywhere in the United States at no charge:

America's Crisis Pregnancy Helpline: (866) 942-6466, Web site: www.thehelpline.org

Auburne Center (Baltimore, MD): (800) 492-5530 and (800) 521-5530

Bethany Christian Services: (616) 224-7610, Toll Free: (800) 238-4269, 901 Eastern Ave. NE, Grand Rapids, MI 49503-1201, Web site: www.bethany.org

Birthright: (800) 550-4900

CareNet: (703) 478-5661, Fax: (703) 478-5668, Toll Free: (800) 395-HELP, 44180 Riverside Parkway, Suite 200, Lansdowne, VA 20176, Email: info@care-net.org, Web site: www.care-net.org

Catholic Home Bureau: (212) 371-1000, ext. 2117 or 2187 (In New York: [800] 592-HELP), Web site: www.catholiccharitiesny.org

Good Counsel Homes: (800) 723-8331, Web site: www.goodcounselhomes.org

Liberty Godparent Home: (800) 542-4453, Web site: www.godparent.org

National Life Center: (800) 848-LOVE (5683), Web site:
www.nationallifecenter.com

The Nurturing Network: (800) TNN-4MOM, Web site: www.nurturingnetwork.org

Pregnancy Hotline: (800) 848-LOVE (5683)

Several Sources Foundation: (201) 825-7277, Toll Free: 800-NO-ABORT, Web site:
www.severalsourcesfd.org

One or more chapters of these groups, or their equivalents, are located in most
average-sized cities across America, as well as in many smaller ones. Most
states have a number of local pregnancy hotlines that offer counseling and
referrals. Call the national organizations above or see your local Yellow Pages
under "Abortion Alternatives," "Pregnancy Centers," or a similar listing.

A large listing of local prolife groups throughout the United States and Canada can
be purchased from International Life Services, (213) 382-2156, 2606 1/2 West
8th Street, Los Angeles, CA 90057.

Adoption Resources

Adoption Network Law Center, Toll Free: (800) 367-2367, Web site:
www.adoptionnetwork.com/adoption.shtml

Bethany Christian Services, (616) 224-7610, 901 Eastern Ave. NE, PO Box 294,
Grand Rapids, MI 49501-0294, Web site: www.bethany.org

Carolina Hope Christian Adoption Agency (*Domestic and International
Adoptions*), (864) 268-0570, Fax: (864) 370-0036, 1527 Wade Hampton
Blvd., Greenville, SC 29609, Email: office@CarolinaHopeAdoption.org, Web
site: www.carolinahopeadoption.org

Catholic Charities USA, Pregnancy and Adoption Services, 1731 King St., Suite 200,
Alexandria, VA 22314-2756, (800) 227-CARE, Web site:
www.catholiccharitiesusa.org

Christian Family Adoptions, (503) 232-1211, 6040 SE Belmont St., Portland, OR
97215, Web site: www.christianfamilyadoptions.org

Dave Thomas Foundation for Adoption, (800) 275-3832, 525,Metro Place N, Suite
220, Dublin, OH 43017, Email: info@davethomasfoundation.org, Web site:
www.davethomasfoundation.org

Holt International Adoption, (541) 687-2202, PO Box 2880, 1195 City View,
Eugene, OR 97402, Web site: www.holtinternational.org

Human Life International, Toll Free: (800) 549-LIFE, Fax: (540) 622-7247, 4 Family
   Life Lane, Front Royal, VA 22630, Email: hli@hli.org, Web site: www.hli.org

International Life Services, (213) 382-2156, Fax: (213) 382-4203, 2606 1/2 West
   8th Street, Los Angeles, CA 90057, Email: lifeservices@juno.com, Web site:
   www.internationallifeservices.org

Lifesong for Orphans, (309) 747-3556, PO Box 40, · 202 N. Ford St., Gridley, IL
   61744, Web site: www.lifesongfororphans.org

National Committee for Adoption, (202) 328-1200 (*ask for publication list*),
   1930 17th Street NW, Washington, DC 20009, Email: ncfadc.net, Web site:
   www.ncfa-usa.org

Nightlight Christian Adoptions, (714) 278-1020, Fax: (714) 278-1063, 801 East
   Chapman Ave., Suite 106, Fullerton, CA 92831, Email: info@nightlight.org,
   Web site: www.nightlight.org

Orphans Overseas, (503) 297-2006, Fax: (503) 533-5836, Web site:
   www.orphansoverseas.org

PLAN Loving Adoptions Now, Inc., (503) 472-8452, (503) 242-1467 (*Portland
   area*), Birthparent Hotline: (800) 207-4213, 850 SE Booth Bend Rd.,
   McMinnville, OR 97128, Email: info@planlovingadoptions.org, Web site:
   www.planlovingadoptions.org

Precious.org (*international adoptions*), PO Box 1612, Bloomington, IL 61702-
   1612, Web site: www.precious.org

Snowflake Adoption (*frozen embryo adoption*), Web site:
   www.nightlight.org/snowflakeadoption.htm

Financial Help for Adoption:

The ABBA Fund (*uniting families through interest-free, covenant loans for adoption*), Toll Free 1-888-775-3422, PO Box 78800, Charlotte, NC 28271-7042,
   Web site: www.abbafund.org

I CARE (*International Children's Adoption Resource Effort*), PO Box 19020,
   Baltimore, MD 21284, Email: info@intlcare.org, Web site: www.intlcare.org

LifeSong for Orphans, (309) 747-3556, Fax: (309) 747-4647, PO Box 40, 202 N.
   Ford St., Gridley, IL 61744, Email: info@lifesongfororphans.org, Web site:
   www.lifesongfororphans.org

Shaohannah's Hope (*founded by Steven Curtis and Mary Beth Chapman*), (615)
   550-5600, Fax: (615) 595-0850, PO Box 647, Franklin, TN 37065, Web site:
   www.shaohannahshope.org

Post-Abortion Support for Women

Abortion Recovery International, Office-Message: (949) 679-9276, Emergency-Mobile: (949) 378-5149, Toll Free: (866) 4my-recovery, 5319 University Drive #252, Irvine, CA 92612, Email: info@abortionrecovery.org, Web site: www.AbortionRecoveryInternational.org

American Rights Coalition, (800) 634-2224 and (423) 893-7801, 6872 Robin Drive, Chattanooga, TN 37421-1751

American Victims of Abortion, (202) 626-8800, 419 7th Street N.W., Suite 500, Washington, DC 20004

The Elliot Institute, (217) 525-8202, PO Box 7348, Springfield, IL 62791, Email: help@mail.afterabortion.org, Web site: www.afterabortion.org

Healing Hearts, (360) 897-2711, Toll Free: (888) 792-8282, Fax: (360) 897-2400, PO Box 7890, Bonney Lake, WA 98391, Web site: www.healinghearts.org

International Life Services, (213) 382-2156, Fax: (213) 382-4203, 2606 1/2 West 8th Street, Los Angeles, CA 90057, Web site: www.life-services.org

Post Abortion Ministries (PAM), (804) 799-3500, Fax: (804) 799-2082, PO Box 907, Mechanicsville, VA 23111-0907, Email: contact@postabortionministries.com, Web site: www.postabortionministries.com

Post Abortion Reconciliation and Healing (*National Office*), (414) 483-4141, National Referral Line (800) 5WE-CARE, PO Box 070477, Milwaukee, WI 53207, Email: noparh@juno.com, Web site: www.noparh.org

Silent No More, (800) 707-6635, Email: mail@silentnomoreawareness.org, Web site: www.silentnomoreawareness.org

Tell Them I Love Them Ministry, (651) 578-0304, PO Box 25437, Woodbury, MN 55125, Email: business@TellThemILoveThem.org, Web site: www.TellThemILoveThem.org

Educational, Resource, and Legislation-Influencing Groups

Many of the organizations below have regular newsletters available on request at no or nominal charge:

Abort73.com, Email: info@abort73.com, Web site: www.abort73.com

AbortionFacts.com, Web site: www.abortionfacts.com

Students for Life of America, (703) 351-6280, Fax: (866) 582-6420, 4141 N. Henderson Road, Suite 7, Arlington, VA 22203, Email: info@studentsforlife.org, Web site: www.studentsforlife.org

American Life League, Judie Brown, president, (540) 659-4171, Fax: (540) 659-2586, PO Box 1350, Stafford, VA 22555, Email: info@all.org, Web site: www.all.org

Americans United for Life, (312) 492-7234, Fax: (312) 492-7235, 310 S. Peoria, Suite 500, Chicago, IL 60607, Email: info@aul.org, Web site: www.aul.org

Brind, Dr. Joel, PhD. (*Abortion and cancer link*), (646) 660-6240, PO Box 3127, Poughkeepsie, NY 12603, Email: Joel_Brind@baruch.cuny.edu, Web site: www.abortioncancer.com

Catholic Charities, Pregnancy, Parenting, and Adoption Department, (800) CARE002 and (619) 231-2828, Fax: (619) 234-2272, 349 Cedar St., San Diego, CA 92101, Web site: www.ccdsd.org

Christian Coalition of America, (202) 479-6900, 499 S. Capitol Street SW, Suite 615, Washington, DC 20003, Email: coalition@cc.org, Web site: www.cc.org

Concerned Women for America, (202) 488-7000, Fax: (202) 488-0806, 1015 15th St. NW, Suite 1100, Washington, DC 20005, Web site: www.cwfa.org

Eagle Forum (Capitol Hill Office), (202) 544-0353, Fax: (202) 547-6996, 316 Pennsylvania Ave. SE, Suite 203, Washington, DC 20003, Web site: www.eagleforum.org

Ethics and Religious Liberty Commission, Nashville Office: (615) 244-2495, Fax: (615) 242-0065, 901 Commerce St., Suite 550, Nashville, TN 37203-3696; Washington Office: (202) 547-8105, Fax: (202) 547-8165, 505 Second St., NE, Washington, DC 20002, Web site: www.erlc.com

Family Research Council, Toll Free: (800) 225-4008, 801 G Street, NW, Washington, DC 20001, Web site: www.frc.org

Feminists for Life of America, (703) 836-3354, PO Box 320667, Alexandria, VA 22320, Email: info@feministsforlife.org, Web site: www.feministsforlife.org

Focus on the Family, (719) 531-3400, Ordering resources: (800) 232-6459, Colorado Springs, CO 80995, Web site: www.family.org

Life Dynamics, Mark Crutcher, (940) 380-8800, Fax: (940) 380-8700, Toll Free: (800) 401-6494, 204 Cardinal Drive, Denton, TX 76209, Email: ldi1@airmail.net, Web site: www.ldi.org

Life Issues Institute, (513) 729-3600, 1821 Galbraith Road, Cincinnati, OH 45239, Email: info@lifeissues.org, Web site: www.lifeissues.org

LifeNews.com, P.O. Box 1931, Cheyenne, WY 82003, Email: news@lifenews.com, Web site: www.lifenews.com

Life Training Institute (Scott Klusendorf, prolife trainer), (719) 264-7861, P.O. Box 50918, Colorado Springs, CO 80919, Email: comments@prolifetraining.com, Web site: www.prolifetraining.com

National Committee for a Human Life Amendment, (202) 393-0703, Fax: (202) 347-1383, 1500 Massachusetts Ave. NW, Suite 24, Washington, DC 20005, Web site: 222.nchla.org

National Right to Life Committee, Wanda Franz, president, (202) 626-8800, 512 10th Street NW, Washington, DC 20004, Email: NRLC@nrlc.org, Web site: www.nrlc.org

National Right to Life News, (202) 626-8800, ext. 123, 512 10th Street NW, Washington DC 20004, Web site: www.nrlc.org/news

National Teens for Life, 512 10th Street NW, Washington, DC 20004, Web site: www.nrlc.org/outreach/teens.html

Pro-Life America, J. T. Finn, (310)378-0067, Toll Free Pregnancy Hotline: (800) 395-4357, 1840 S. Elena Ave., Suite 103, Redondo Beach, CA 90277, Email: jtfinn@earthlink.net, Web sites: www.lovematters.com and www.prolife.com

Republican National Coalition for Life, (214) 559-4460, Fax: (214) 559-6120, 5009 Harvest Hill Road, Dallas, TX 75244, Email: info@rnclife.org, Web site: www.rnclife.org

Right to Life League of Southern California, (626) 398-6100, Fax: (626) 398-6101, 1028 North Lake Avenue, Suite 207, Pasadena, CA 91104, Web site: www.rtllsc.org

Sidewalk Counseling Web site: http://www.sidewalkcounseling.com/training.asp

StandUpGirl.com Foundation, 4335 River Road N., Salem, OR 97303, Helpline: (800) 672-2296, Option line: (800) 395-HELP, Web site: www.standupgirl.com

Teachers Saving Children, (330) 537-2546, PO Box 125, Damascus, OH 44619-0125, Email: tsc-life@juno.com, Web site: teacherssavingchildren.org

The Ultimate Prolife Resource List *(for prolife books on abortion, euthanasia, and post-abortion information; miscellaneous prolife materials; ultrasound information, abstinence, etc.), includes the option of receiving an outstanding daily e-mail summary of prolife news,* Web site: www.prolifeinfo.org

University Faculty for Life (UFL), 120 New North, Georgetown University, Washington, DC 20057, Email: fehringr@vms.csd.mu.edu, Web site: www.uffl.org

Women 4 Women, (*two-tape set, "Equipping for Life"*), (502) 561-8060,
Waterfront Plaza, 325 West Main Street, Suite 1110, Louisville, KY, Email:
w4w@w4w.org, Web site: www.w4w.org

Human Development Web Sites:

The Endowment for Human Development, "The Biology of Prenatal Development"
DVD, http://www.ehd.org/products_bpd_dvd.php

Human Development Resource Council, Inc., (770) 447-1598, Fax: (770) 447-
0759, Email: info@hdrc.org, Web site: www.hdrc.org

Human Life Foundation, www.humanlifereview.com

The National Institute of Child Health and Human Development, www.nichd.nih.gov

The UNSW Embryology site, Early Human Carnegie Stages pages,
http://embryology.med.unsw.edu.au/medicine/BGDL6s1.pdf

The Virtual Library of Developmental Biology, www.zygote.swarthmore.edu

Natural Family Planning Web Sites and Resources:

BOMA (Billings Ovulation Method), (651) 699-8139, PO Box 2135, St. Cloud,
MN 56302, Email: boma-usa@msn.com, Web site: www.boma-usa.org

Couple to Couple League, (513) 471-2000, Toll Free: (800) 745-8252, PO Box
111184, Cincinnati, OH 45211, Email: ccli@ccli.org, Web site: www.ccli.org

Creighton Model Fertility Care System (*Pope Paul VI Institute for the Study of
Human Reproduction*), (402) 390-6600, ext. 45, Email:
Advancement@popepaulvi.com, Web site: www.creightonmodel.com/

Family of the Americas, Toll Free: (800) 443-3395, Fax: (301) 627-0847, Email:
familyplanning@yahoo.com, Web site: www.familyplanning.net.

Human Life International, Toll Free: (800) 549-LIFE, Fax: (540) 622-7247, 4 Family
Life Lane, Front Royal, VA 22630, Email: hli@hli.org, Web site: www.hli.org

Vida Humana Internacional (Hispanic Division of Human Life International), (305)
260-0525, Fax: (305) 260-0595, 45 SW 71st Ave., Miami, FL 33144, Email:
vhi@vidahumana.org, Web site: www.vidahumana.org

Prolife Minority Groups

AbortionFacts.com, Web site: www.abortionfacts.com

Black Americans for Life, (202) 347-5215, 512 Tenth Street, Washington, DC
20004, Web site: www.nrlc.org/outreach/bal.html

The Heidi Group, (512) 255-2088, Fax: (512) 255-2582, PO Box 5099, Round
   Rock, TX 78683-5099, Email: info@heidigroup.org, Web site:
   www.heidigroup.org
Human Life International, Toll Free: (800) 549-LIFE, Fax: (540) 622-7247, 4 Family
   Life Lane, Front Royal, VA 22630, Email: hli@hli.org, Web site: www.hli.org
Vida Humana Internacional (Hispanic Division of Human Life International), (305)
   260-0525, Fax: (305) 260-0595, 45 SW 71st Ave., Miami, FL 33144, Email:
   vhi@vidahumana.org, Web site: www.vidahumana.org

Prolife Law Firms

American Center for Law and Justice (national office), Legal helpline: (757) 226-
   2489 Toll Free: (800) 296-4529, PO Box 90555, Washington, DC 20090-0555,
   Web site: www.aclj.org
American Rights Coalition, (423) 893-7801, 6872 Robin Drive, Chattanooga, TN
   37421-1751
Americans United for Life, (312) 568-4700, Fax: (312) 568-4747, 310 S. Peoria St.
   #500, Chicago, IL 60607, Email: info@AUL.org, Web site: www.aul.org
CASE, Jay Sekulow, (770) 414-0806, Toll Free: (800) 684-3110, Web site:
   www.aclj.org/OnTheRadio
Center for Law and Justice International (*a project of Catholics United for Life*),
   (502) 549-5454, 6375 New Hope Road, New Hope, KY 40052-6904, Email:
   info@CLJI.org, Web site: www.clji.org
Legal Action for Women (LAW), (888) 9-WOMENS and (800) UCANSUE, Box
   11061, Pensacola, FL 32524,
Liberty Counsel, Toll Free: (800) 671-1776, PO Box 540774, Orlando, FL 32854.
   Email: Liberty@LC.org, Web site: www.lc.org
Rutherford Institute, (434) 978-3888, Fax: (434) 978-1789, PO Box 7482,
   Charlottesville, VA 22906-7482, Email: tristaff@rutherford.org, Web site:
   www.rutherford.org

Prolife Event and Action Organizations

The GAP, Center for Bio-Ethical Reform, (949) 206-0600, PO Box 219, Lake Forest,
   CA 92609, Email: info@cbrinfo.org, Web site: www.abortionNO.org
Justice for All (GAP Project, central region of U.S.), David Lee, director, (316) 683-
   6426, Toll Free: (800) 281-6426, 113 N. Martinson, Wichita, KS 67203, Email:
   jfamail@jfaweb.org, Web site: www.jfaweb.org

Advocates of Life, Helpline: (201) 934-0886, Office: (201) 934-0886, 17 Maple Street, Allendale, NJ 07401

National Life Chain, "Please Let Me Live," Royce Dunn, president, (530) 674-5068, 3209 Colusa Hwy., Yuba City, CA 95993, Email: Director@NationalLifeChain.org, Web site: www.nationallifechain.org

Life Dynamics, Mark Crutcher, (940) 380-8800, Toll free: (800) 401-6494, 204 Cardinal Drive, Denton, TX 76209, Email: ldi1@airmail.net, Web site: www.ldi.org

Life Issues Institute, (513) 729-3600, 1821 Galbraith Road, Cincinnati, OH 45239, Email: info@lifeissues.org, Web site: www.lifeissues.org

March for Life, (202) 543-3377, PO Box 90300, Washington, DC 20090, Email: info@marchforlife.org, Web site: www.marchforlife.org

Operation Rescue, (316) 683-6790, Fax: (916) 244-2636, Toll Free: (800) 705-1175, PO Box 782888, Wichita, KS 67278-2888, Email: info@operationrescue.org, Web site: www.operationrescue.org

Pro-Life Action Ministries (*especially helpful with sidewalk counseling*), (651) 771-1500, PO Box 75368, St. Paul, MN 55175-0368, Email: prolife@plam.org, Web site: www.plam.org

Pro-Life Action League, (773) 777-2900, Fax: (773) 777-3061, 6160 N. Cicero Ave., Suite 600, Chicago, IL 60646, Email: info@prolifeaction.org, Web site: www.prolifeaction.org

Rock for Life, (540) 659-6184, Fax: (540) 659-2586, PO Box 1350, Stafford, VA 22555, Email: rockforlife@all.org, Web site: www.rockforlife.org

Survivors of the Abortion Holocaust, (951) 750-1114, PO Box 52708, Riverside, CA 92517, Email: info@survivors.la, Web site: www.survivors.la

Vital Signs Ministries, Denny & Claire Hartford, (402) 341-8886, PO Box 34278, Omaha, NE 68134, Web site: www.vitalsignsministries.org

Religious/Denominational Prolife Groups

Baptists for Life, (616) 257-6800, Fax: (616) 257-6805, PO Box 3158, Grand Rapids, MI 49501, Email: b4life@bfl.org, Web site: www.bfl.org

Catholics United for Life, (270) 325-3061, Fax: (270) 325-3091, 3050 Gap Knob Road, New Hope, KY 40052, Web site: www.cul.demich.com

Christian Life Commission of the Southern Baptist Convention, (615) 244-2495, 901 Commerce Street, Suite 550, Nashville, TN 37203, Web site: www.christianlifecommission.org

Ethics and Religious Liberty Commission, Nashville Office: (615) 244-2495, Fax: (615) 242-0065, 901 Commerce St., Suite 550, Nashville, TN 37203-3696; Washington Office: (202) 547-8105, Fax: (202) 547-8165, 505 Second St., NE, Washington, DC 20002, Web site: www.erlc.com

Human Life International, Toll Free: (800) 549-LIFE, Fax: (540) 622-7247, 4 Family Life Lane, Front Royal, VA 22630, Email: hli@hli.org, Web site: www.hli.org

Jewish Anti-Abortion League, (718) 336-0053, PO Box 262, Gravesend Station, Brooklyn, NY 11223

Lutherans for Life, (515) 382-2077, Toll Free: (888) 364-LIFE, 1129 South "G" Avenue, Nevada, IA 50201-2774, Email: info@lutheransforlife.org, Web site: www.lutheransforlife.org

National Conference of Catholic Bishops, c/o Fr. John Gouldrick C.M., (202) 541-3000, 3211 4th Street NE, Washington, DC 20017-1194, Web site: nccbuscc.org

National Prolife Religious Council, Inc., (610) 286-6545, Fax: (610) 288-5151, Box 535, Elverson, PA 19520,

NOEL, (412) 749-0422, (800) 707-NOEL, 405 Frederick Avenue, Sewickley, PA 15143

The Prolife Pastor Network, Web site: prolifepastors.tripod.com

Secretariat for Prolife Activities, National Conference of Catholic Bishops, Gail Quinn, *Executive Director,* (202) 541-3000, 3211 4th Street NE, Washington, DC 20017-1194, Web site: www.nccbuscc.org/prolife

Christian Life Resources, Toll Free: (800) 729-9535, Fax: (262) 677-5269, 3070 Helsan Drive, Richfield, WI 53076-9582, Web site: www.christianliferesources.com (*precious feet pins*)

Medical Prolife Groups

American Academy of Medical Ethics (*MDs committed to preserving life as set forth in the Hippocratic Oath*), (423) 844-1095, PO Box 451, Bristol, TN 37621, Email: main@ethicalhealthcare.org, Web site: www.ethicalhealthcare.org

American Association of Pro Life Obstetricians and Gynecologists (AAPLOG), (616) 546-2639, 339 River Ave., Holland, MI 49423, Email: info@aaplog.org, Web site: www.aaplog.org

Association of American Physicians and Surgeons, Inc., (AAPS), Toll Free: (800)

635-1196, 1601 N. Tucson Blvd., Suite 9, Tucson, AZ 85716-3450, Email: aaps@aapsonline.org, Web site: www.aapsonline.org

Canadian Physicians for Life, (613) 728-5433, PO Box 1289, Ottawa, ON K0A2Z0, CANADA Email: info@physiciansforlife.ca, Web site: www.physiciansforlife.ca

Catholic Association of Scientists and Engineers (CASE), Dr. Francis Kelly, president, (301) 422-9035, 8308 Rambler Drive, Adelphi, MD 20783, Email: kellyfj@aol.com

Christian Medical and Dental Society (CMDS), David Stevens, M.D., executive director, (423) 844-1000, Fax: (423) 844-1005, PO Box 7500, Bristol, TN 37621, Web site: www.cmda.org

Dentists for Life, (540) 659-4171, Fax: (540) 659-2586, PO Box 1350, Stafford, VA 22555, Email: info@dentistsforlife.org, Web site: www.all.org/dentists

Do No Harm: The Coalition of Americans for Research Ethics, (202) 347-6840, Fax: (202) 347-6849, 1100 H St. NW, Suite 700, Washington, DC 20005, Email: media@stemcellresearch.org, Web site: www.stemcellresearch.org

Healthy Beginnings (*medical care for pregnant, uninsured women*), www.healthybeginnings.org

National Association of Pro-Life Nurses, (501) 992-5905, PO Box 8236, Hot Springs Village, AR 71910-8236, Email: director@nursesforlife.org, Web site: www.nursesforlife.org

Pharmacists for Life International, Bogomir Kuhar, director, (740) 881-5520, Fax: (570) 521-0892, Toll Free: (800) 227-8359, PO Box 1281, Powell, OH 43065-1281, Email: pfli@pfli.org, Web site: www.pfli.org

Society of Catholic Social Scientists (SCSS), Dr. Stephen Krason, president, Political Science Program, (740) 284-5377, Fax: (740) 283-6401, Franciscan University of Steubenville, 1235 University Boulevard, Steubenville, OH 43952, Email: catholicsocialscientists@gmail.com, Web site: www.catholicsocialscientists.org

Quality Brochures for Personal or Mass Distribution

American Life League, (540) 659-4171, Questions about orders: (866) LET-LIVE, 1179 Courthouse Road, PO Box 1350, Stafford, VA 22555, Web site: www.americanlifeleague.stores.yahoo.net: "The Paramount Human Life Amendment," "Human Cloning," "My Secret Life," "A person's a person, no matter how small," "Moral and logical arguments against abortion," "Human personhood begins at conception"

CareNet, (703) 478-5661, Fax: (703) 478-5668, 44180 Riverside Parkway, Suite 200, Lansdowne, VA 20176, Email: info@care-net.org, Web site: www.care-net.org: Bulletin inserts for "Sanctity of Human Life Sunday," "100 Things to Know When Dating," "Abortion and Psalm 139," "Before You Decide" (*both English and Spanish*), "The Morning After Pill," "Post-Abortion Stress in Men," "Why Wait?" (*biblical and medical reasons for abstinence before marriage*), "You are Not Alone"

Christian Life Resources, Toll Free: (800) 729-9535, Fax: (262) 677-5269, 3070 Helsan Drive, Richfield, WI 53076-9582, Web site: www.christianliferesources.com: "Birth Control Facts You Should Know About," "I Just Can't Forgive Myself" (*man and woman's versions*), "Natural Family Planning," "The Truth About Sex Before Marriage," "The First Nine Months," "PAS: There's a Way Back" (*post-abortion syndrome*), "Wonderfully Made"

Focus on the Family, (800) 232-6459, Colorado Springs, CO 80995: "How to Really Love Your Pregnant Teen," "What Does God Say About Abortion?," "RU-486: Know the Facts About the 'Abortion Pill' Before You Decide," "Plan B the Morning After Pill," "Before You Decide: An Abortion Education Resource"

Last Days Ministries, (214) 963-8671, Box 40, Lindale, TX 75771

Post-Abortion Ministries, (901) 837-3343, PO Box 649, Atoka, TN 38004, Email: PAMKOERBEL@aol.com, Web site: www.lastdaysministries.org: "Children...Things We Throw Away?" "Abortion: Attitudes for Action," "The Questions Most People Ask About Abortion," "Message of Hope for Post Abortive Women"

The National Life Chain, Royce Dunn, president, (530) 674-5068, 3209 Colusa Hwy., Yuba City, CA 95993, Email: Director@NationalLifeChain.org, Web site: www.nationallifechain.org: "America Must Decide," "Contraception: The Tragic Deception," "What the Facts Reveal about Planned Parenthood."

Heritage House, (800) 858-3040, 919 S. Main St., Snowflake, AZ 85937, Web site: www.heritagehouse76.com: "Do You Really Want an Abortion?" "Abortion and the Christian," "Abortion: The Black Woman's Voice," "A Sensible Choice, Presenting Adoption to the Abortion-Minded Client," "Choose Life," "Facts of Life," "For Men Only," "Inches from Infanticide," "Inches from Life, Partial-Birth Abortion," "Is Virginity Missing in Your Life?" "Know the Facts Before You Choose," "Let's Talk," "Mifepristone: Are Women at Risk?" (RU-486), "Mixed Messages," "Partial-Birth Abortion, An Eyewitness Account," "Pregnant? Now

What?" "Selling Teen Abortions," "What I Saw in the Abortion Industry," "Why Didn't They Tell Me?" (*emphasizes parental consent laws*), "You Have a Right to Know,"

Life Issues Institute, (513) 729-3600, 1821 Galbraith Road, Cincinnati, OH 45239, Email: info@lifeissues.org, Web site: www.lifeissues.org: "2 Basic Questions (When Does Life Begin?), " "Choice," "Life or Death," "Women Hurt," "Men Hurt Too," "Never Again? Never Was!" "Planned Parenthood," "RU-486, A Human Pesticide"

Right to Life of Michigan Educational Fund, (616) 532-2300, 2340 Porter Street SW, PO Box 901, Grand Rapids, MI 49509, Email: info@rtl.org, Web site: www.rtl.org: "If they say…" "Life Is Precious" fliers and bulletin inserts

Life Cycle Books, (416) 690-5860, PO Box 420, Lewiston, NY 14092, Web site: www.lifecyclebooks.com: "Breast Cancer And Abortion—What's the Connection," "Life or Death," "Adoption—A Loving Choice," "How At Risk Are You", "If Someone You Know Considers an Abortion," "Secret Sorrow" (*post-abortion*), "Forgotten Fathers," "A Christian Response To Abortion," "How You Began" and "The First Nine Months" (*prenatal development*).

Human Development Resource Council, Inc., (770) 447-1598, Fax: (770) 447-0759, 3941 Holcomb Bridge Rd., Suite 300, Norcross, GA 30092-2292, Email: info@hdrc.org, Web site: www.hdrc.org: "I think I'm Really in Love", "Why Do Teens Say 'Yes' To Sex?"

Human Life International, Toll Free: (800) 549-LIFE, Fax: (540) 622-7247, 4 Family Life Lane, Front Royal, VA 22630, Email: hli@hli.org, Web site: www.hli.org: "Abortion Raises Breast Cancer Risk," "Caring For Yourself After An Abortion," "Planned Parenthood: It's Not What You Think," "You Have A Right To Know"

StandUpGirl.com Foundation, Helpline: (800) 672-2296, Option line: (800) 395-HELP, 4335 River Road N., Salem, OR 97303, Web site: www.standupgirl.com: "You Have the Right to Choose: Make Your Choice Wisely"

Vida Humana Internacional (*a division of Human Life International*), (305) 260-0525, Fax: (305) 260-0595, 45 SW 71 Ave., Miami, FL 33144, Email: vhi@vidahumana.org, Web site: www.vidahumana.org: Miscellaneous brochures written in Spanish, including: "Love and Let Live," and Natural Family Planning brochures

Pope Paul VI Institute for the Study of Human Reproduction, (402) 390-6600, 6901 Mercy Road, Omaha, NE 68106, Web site: www.popepaulvi.com: brochures on infertility, natural family planning

Post Abortion Ministries, (804) 799-3500, Fax: (804) 799-2082, PO Box 907, Mechanicsville, VA 23111-0907, Email: contact@postabortionministries.com, Web site: www.postabortionministries.com: "Abortion. No One Told Me I Would Feel Like This" (*also in Spanish*), "After Your Abortion, Did You Ever Wonder...," "Denial & Abortion," "If I Had only Known," "Up in the Air About Having an Abortion?" (*also in Spanish*) "She Had the Abortion...But It Was My Baby Too," "How to Help Your Wife Deal with Her Abortion," "Silent Sorrow," "Abortion: One Woman's Journey"

Brochures to Use with Women Outside Abortion Clinics or Considering Abortion (in addition to some of the above)

CareNet, (703) 478-5661, Fax: (703) 478-5668, 44180 Riverside Parkway, Suite 200, Lansdowne, VA 20176, Email: info@care-net.org, Web site: www.care-net.org: "An Unplanned Pregnancy is a Hard Thing to Face," "Open Your Eyes"

Post-Abortion Ministries, (901) 837-3343, PO Box 649, Atoka, TN 38004, Email: contact@postabortionministries.com, Web site: www.postabortionministries.com: "Abortion. No One Told Me I Would Feel Like This" (*also in Spanish*), "After Your Abortion, Did You Ever Wonder...," "Denial & Abortion," "If I Had Only Known," "Up in the Air About Having an Abortion?" (*also in Spanish*) "She Had the Abortion...But It Was My Baby Too," "How to Help Your Wife Deal with Her Abortion," "Silent Sorrow," "Abortion: One Woman's Journey"

Prolife Videos and Films

"The Biology of Prenatal Development" DVD, The Endowment for Human Development, Web site: www.ehd.org/products_bpd_dvd.php

"A Doctor Explains the Abortion Procedure," "Abortion Questions and Answers," "The Least of These: What Everyone Should Know About Abortion," "Reversing Roe—The Norma McCorvey Story," "The Silent Scream," "Letting Go" (*when placing a baby for adoption*), "Living With Grief," Christian Life Resources, Toll Free: (800) 729-9535, 3070 Helsan Drive, Richfield, WI 53076, Email: AV@ChristianLifeResources.com, Web site: christianliferesources.com

"The Silent Scream," "The Heart of the Matter," "Matter of Life and Death" (*two versions, graphic and non-graphic, fetal development*), "Matter of Choice," "Dear Children" (*post abortion grief*),"The Hard Truth," "Abortion

Techniques," "A Better Way," "Hidden Holocaust," "Assignment: Life," "Your
Crisis Pregnancy," American Portrait Films, (216) 531-8600, (800) 736-4567,
P. O. Box 809, Brunswick, OH 44212, Web site: www.amport.com

"Abortion in the Church," "Choice Blues," Center for Bio-Ethical Reform, (949)
206-0600, PO Box 219, Lake Forest, CA 92609, Email: info@cbrinfo.org, Web
site: www.cbrinfo.org/videos_in.html

"Conceived in Rape: From Worthless to Priceless," story of Rebecca Wasser-
Kiessling, Email: Rebecca@rebeccakiessling.com, Web site:
www.rebeccakiessling.com

"Living Proof," Pope Paul VI Institute for the Study of Human Reproduction, (402)
390-6600, 6901 Mercy Road, Omaha, NE 68106, Web site:
www.popepaulvi.com

"Baby Parts For Sale," Jeremiah Films, Toll Free: (800) 828-2290, PMB 246, Ste
B18, 3-2600 Kaumualii Hwy., Lihue, HI 96766, Email:
admin@jeremiahfilms.com, Web site: www.jeremiahfilms.com

"Whatever Happened to the Human Race?" with Francis Schaeffer and Dr. C. Everett
Koop; three-tape series, Gospel Films, (231) 773-3361, Box 455, Muskegon,
MI 49443, Web site: www.gospelcom.net

"Abortion Breast Cancer Link", "Facing Life Head-on", "Truth Unmasked" (for
youth), "Abortion 101", "Can You Hear Their Pain" (men and abortion), 4D
Ultrasounds, Life Issues Institute, (513) 729-3600, 1821 Galbraith Road,
Cincinnati, OH 45239, Email: info@lifeissues.org, Web site: www.lifeissues.org

"No Greater Joy: Sidewalk Counseling" available from the Pro-Life Action League
(*documentary about the life-saving sidewalk counseling*), (773) 773-777-
2900, Fax: (773) 777-3061, 6160 N. Cicero Ave., Suite 600, Chicago, IL
60646, Email: info@prolifeaction.org, Web site: www.prolifeaction.org

"Making Abortion Unthinkable" (VHS & CD-ROM Training), Klusendorf, Scott &
Koukl, Gregory, Stand to Reason Interactive, 2001. Web site: www.str.org

"Training Program for Crisis Pregnancy Centers," "The Silent Scream," "Hard
Truth," "Window to the Womb," "The Eclipse of Reason," "Dear Children"
(*post abortive*), "The Truth About Abortion," "Hope After Abortion," "A
Mother's Regret," Vida Humana Internacional (*a division of Human Life
International*), (305) 260-0525, Fax: (305) 260-0595, 45 SW 71 Ave.,
Miami, FL 33144, Email: vhi@vidahumana.org, Web site: www.vidahumana.org

Miscellaneous Literature, DVD/CD-ROM, and Information

"Abortion-Breast Cancer," a thorough examination of the induced abortion/breast cancer link, Web site: www.abortioncancer.com

American Life League, (540) 659-4171, Fax: (540) 659-2586, PO Box 1350, Stafford, VA 22555, Email: info@all.org, Web site: www.all.org

"Born Silent," a sixty-second promotion, Web site: www.bornsilent.com

Center for Bio-Ethical Reform, (949) 206-0600, PO Box 219, Lake Forest, CA 92609, Email: info@cbrinfo.org, , Web site: www.abortionNO.org

Couple to Couple League International, (513) 471-2000, Toll Free: (800) 745-8252, PO Box 111184, Cincinnati, OH 45211-1184, Email: ccli@ccli.org, Web site: www.ccli.org

"First 9 Months," an animated journey highlighting human development from conception through birth, Web site: http://parenting.ivillage.com/pregnancy/calendar

Focus on the Family, (719) 531-3400, Ordering resources: (800) 232-6459, Colorado Springs, CO 80995, Web site: www.family.org

Frontlines Publishing, (616) 248-4300, 72 Ransom Ave NE, Grand Rapids, MI 49503, Email: (*to order products*) order@frontlines.org, Web site: www.frontlines.org

Hayes Publishing Co. (*slide presentations, etc.*), (513) 681-7559, Fax: (513) 681-9298, 6304 Hamilton Ave., Cincinnati, OH 45224, Email: hayespub@aol.com, Web site: www.hayespub.tripod.com

Human Life International, Toll Free: (800) 549-LIFE, Fax: (540) 622-7247, 4 Family Life Lane, Front Royal, VA 22630, Email: hli@hli.org, Web site: www.hli.org

Right to Life of Michigan, (616) 532-2300, 2340 Porter Street SW, PO Box 901, Grand Rapids, MI 49509, Web site: www.rtl.org

Special Prolife Products

Abort73.com, (*prolife apparel*), Email: info@abort73.com, Web site: www.abort73.com

American Life League's Pro-Life Store, questions about orders: (866) LET-LIVE, 1179 Courthouse Road, PO Box 1350, Stafford, VA 22555, (540) 659-4171, Web site: www.americanlifeleague.stores.yahoo.net

Right to Life of Michigan, (616) 532-2300, 2340 Porter Street SW, PO Box 901, Grand Rapids, MI 49509, Web site: www.rtl.org: *Large attractive photographs, posters, and billboards of intrauterine preborn babies.*

National Right to Life, (202) 626-8800; 512 10th St. NW, Washington, D.C. 20004,
    posters: Victory Won, (800) 767-7258, Email: NRLC@nrlc.org, Web site:
    www.nrlc.org

Lifehouse Books & Coffee, (405) 236-5433, 1 NW 12th St., Oklahoma City, OK
    73103-4801, *Newspaper supplement samples,* Web site: www.lifehouse.org.

Heritage House, (800) 858-3040, 919 S. Main St., Snowflake, AZ 85937, Web site:
    www.heritagehouse76.com: *"Precious Feet" pins, buttons, mailing stickers,*
    bumper stickers, checks, books, and literature.

Books on Abortion

Alcorn, Randy. *Does the Birth Control Pill Cause Abortions?* 8th ed., Sandy, OR:
    Eternal Perspective Ministries, 2007.

Alcorn, Randy. *ProLife Answers to ProChoice Arguments,* Colorado Springs, CO:
    Multnomah Books, 2000, 2008.

Alcorn, Randy. *Why ProLife?: Caring for the Unborn and Their Mothers,* Colorado
    Springs, OR: Multnomah Books, 2004.

Ankerberg, John and John Weldon. *When Does Life Begin?* Brentwood, TN:
    Wolgemuth and Hyatt, 1990.

Beckwith, Francis. *Politically Correct Death.* Grand Rapids, MI: Baker Book House,
    1994.

Brennan, William. *Dehumanizing the Vulnerable: When Word Games Take Lives.*
    Niagara Falls, NY: Life Cycle Books, Ltd., 2000.

Brennan, William. *The Abortion Holocaust: Today's Final Solution.* St. Louis, MO:
    Landmark Press, 1983.

Brown, Judie, Jerome LeJeune and Robert G. Marshall. *RU-486: The Human*
    Pesticide. Stafford, VA: American Life League, n.d.

Camasso, Michael, Family Caps, *Abortion and Women of Color: Research*
    Connection and Political Rejection. Oxford University Press, 2007.

Campbell, James J. *Abortion, Applying Objective Reason to the Debate.* Salinas, CA:
    Eudaimonia Publications, 1999.

Davis, John J. *Abortion and the Christian.* Phillipsburg, NJ: Presbyterian and
    Reformed, 1984.

Fowler, Paul. *Abortion: Toward an Evangelical Consensus.* Portland, OR:
    Multnomah Press, 1987.

Garth, Lakita, *The Naked Truth About Sex, Love and Relationships.* Ventura, CA:
    Regal Books, 2007.

Garton, Jean. *Who Broke the Baby?* Minneapolis: Bethany House Publishers, 1998.

Hoffmeier, James, ed. *Abortion: A Christian Understanding and Response.* Grand Rapids, MI.: Baker Book House, 1987.

Johnson, Lois Walfrid. *You Are Wonderfully Made!* Minneapolis, MN: Bethany House Publishers, 1999.

Kennedy, D. James. *Abortion: Cry of Reality.* Ft. Lauderdale, FL: Coral Ridge Ministries, 1989.

Koerbel, Pam. *Telling Your Child about Your Abortion.* Post-Abortion Ministries, PO Box 907, Mechanicsville, VA 23111-0907, (804) 799-3500, Fax: (804) 799-2082, Email: contact@postabortionministries.com, Web site: www.postabortionministries.com.

Koerbel, Pam. *Abortion's Second Victim.* Colorado Springs, CO: Scripture Press Publications, 1986.

Koerbel, Pam. *Does Anyone Else Feel Like I Do? And Other Questions Women Ask Following an Abortion.* Bel Air, CA: Galilee Trade, 1990.

Mathewes-Green, Frederica. *Real Choices.* Ben Lomond, CA: Conciliar Press, 1997.

McCorvey, Norma. *Won By Love: Norma McCorvey, Jane Roe of Roe V. Wade, Speaks Out for the Unborn As She Shares Her New Conviction for Life.* Nashville, TN: Thomas Nelson Publishers, 1998.

Mosher, Steven W. *A Mother's Ordeal.* New York: Harcourt, Brace and Co., 1993.

Nathanson, Bernard. *The Hand of God: A Journey from Death to Life by the Abortion Doctor Who Changed His Mind.* Washington, DC: Regnery Publishing, Inc., 2001.

Olasky, Marvin. *Abortion Rites: A Social History of Abortion in America.* Wheaton, IL: Crossway Books, 1992.

Powell, John. *Abortion: The Silent Holocaust.* Allen, TX: Tabor Publishing, 1981.

Reagan, Ronald and C. Everett Koop. *Abortion and the Conscience of a Nation.* Sacramento, CA: New Regency Publishing, 2001.

Reardon, David. *Making Abortion Rare: A Healing Strategy for a Divided Nation.* Kansas City, MO: Acorn Books, 1996.

Reardon, David. *Aborted Women: Silent No More.* Kansas City, MO: Acorn Books, 2002.

Schaeffer, Francis and C. Everett Koop. *Whatever Happened to the Human Race?* Westchester, IL: Crossway Books, 1983.

Shaver, Jessica. *Gianna: Aborted. . .And Lived to Tell About It.* Colorado Springs, CO: Focus on the Family, 2000.

Shettles, Landrum and David Rorvik. *Rites of Life: The Scientific Evidence for Life Before Birth*. Grand Rapids, MI: Zondervan Publishing House, 1983.

Smith, F. LaGard. *When Choice Becomes God*. Eugene, OR: Harvest House Publishers, 1990.

Sproul, R. C. *Abortion: A Rational Look at an Emotional Issue*. Colorado Springs, CO: NavPress, 1990.

Stanford-Rue, Susan M., PhD. *Will I Cry Tomorrow? Healing Post Abortion Trauma*. Ada, MI: Fleming H. Revell Co., 1990.

Swindoll, Charles. *Sanctity of Life*. Waco, TX: Word Publishing, 1990.

Tsiaras, Alexander, *From Conception to Birth: A Life Unfolds*. Doubleday, 2002.

Willke, Dr. & Mrs. John. *Abortion Questions and Answers*. Cincinnati, OH: Hayes Publishing Co., 2003.

Young, Curt. *The Least of These: What Everyone Should Know About Abortion*. Chicago, IL: Moody Press, 1984.

Books on the Abortion Industry

Crutcher, Mark. *Lime 5, Exploited by Choice*. Denton, TX: Life Dynamics, Inc., 1996.

Everett, Carol. *Blood Money: Getting Rich Off a Woman's Right to Choose*. Sisters, OR: Multnomah Publishers, 1992.

Grant, George. *Grand Illusions: The Legacy of Planned Parenthood*. Revised version, Cumberland House, 1999.

Grant, George. *Killer Angel: A Biography of Planned Parenthood's Founder, Margaret Sanger*. England: Highland Books, Revised Version, 2001.

Nathanson, Bernard. *The Hand of God: A Journey from Death to Life by the Abortion Doctor Who Changed His Mind*. Washington, DC: Regnery Publishing, Inc., 2001.

Nathanson, Bernard. *The Abortion Papers: Inside the Abortion Mentality*. New York: Frederick Fell, 1983.

Nathanson, Bernard. *Aborting America*. New Zealand: Pinnacle Books, 1981.

Rini, Suzanne. *Beyond Abortion: A Chronicle of Fetal Experimentation*. Rockford, IL: Tan Books and Publishers, 1993.

Books on Prolife Action and Strategies

Alcorn, Randy. *Is Rescuing Right?* Downers Grove, IL: InterVarsity Press. 1990. To order, contact EPM, (503) 668-5200.

Belz, Mark. *Suffer the Little Children*. Westchester, IL: Crossway Books, 1989.

Campbell, James J. *ABORTION, Applying Objective Reason to the Debate.* Salinas, CA: Eudaimonia Publications, 1999.

Crutcher, Mark. *On Message, The Pro-Life Handbook.* Lewisville, TX: Life Dynamics, 2005.

Pavone, Fr. Frank A., *Ending Abortion, Not Just Fighting It.* Catholic Book Publishing Company, 2006.

Pierson, Anne. *52 Simple Things You Can Do to Be Prolife.* Minneapolis, MN: Bethany House Publishers, 1991.

Scheidler, Joseph. *Closed: 99 Ways to Stop Abortion.* Rockford, IL: Tan Books & Publishers, 1994.

Books for Women's Counselors and Helpers

Black, Karen, *Sidewalk Counseling Handbook (Can be downloaded from: http://members.tripod.com/~joseromia/black.htm),* Inglewood, CA: Inglewood Women's Outreach, n.d.

Curro, Ellen. *Caring Enough to Help: Counseling at a Crisis Pregnancy Center.* Grand Rapids, MI: Baker Book House, 1990.

Dillon, Rev. John J. *A Path to Hope: For Parents of Aborted Children and Those Who Minister to Them.* Catholic Book Publishing Company, 1990.

Hayford, Jack W. *I'll Hold You in Heaven: Healing and Hope for Parents of a Miscarried, Aborted or Stillborn Child.* Ventura, CA: Regal Books, 2003.

Hill, Jeannie. *Sidewalk Counseling Workbook.* Jefferson City, MO: Easton Publishing Co., 1986.

Klusendorf, Scott, *The Case for Life: Equipping Christians to Engage the Culture.* Wheaton, IL: Crossway Books, 2009.

Klusendorf, Scott, *Pro-Life 101: A Step-by-Step Guide to Making Your Case Persuasively.* Signal Hill, CA: Stand to Reason Press, 2002.

Masse, Sydna and Joan Phillips. *Her Choice to Heal: Finding Spiritual and Emotional Peace After Abortion.* Colorado Springs, CO: David C. Cook, 2009.

Michels, Nancy. *Helping Women Recover from Abortion.* Minneapolis, MN: Bethany House Publishers, 1988.

Perry, Linda. *How to Survive Your Teen's Pregnancy.* Dumfries, VA: Chalfont House, 2003.

Pierson, Anne. *Mending Hearts, Mending Lives: A Guide to Extended Family Living.* Shippensburg, PA: Destiny Image Publishers, 1987.

"Pregnancy Counseling for Success: A Guide to Effective Counseling." New York: Bethany Christian Service, 1990.

Schmidt, Sheila, *Pregnant and Blown Off: When Abortion Is Not An Option.*
    America House, 2001.
Schooler, Jayne E., *Mom, Dad...I'm Pregnant: When Your Daughter or Son Faces
    an Unplanned Pregnancy.* Colorado Springs, CO: NavPress, 2004.
Tsiaras, Alexander, *From Conception to Birth: A Life Unfolds.* Doubleday, 2002.
Walton, Charlie. *Twelve Faces of Grief: A Grief-Recovery Handbook for group or
    Personal Use.* St. Meinrad, IN: Abbey Press, 1998.
Wilson, Barbara, *The Invisible Bond: How to Break Free from Your Sexual Past.*
    Colorado Springs, CO: Multnomah Books, 2006.
Zimmerman, Martha. *Should I Keep My Baby?* Minneapolis, MN: Bethany House
    Publishers, 1997.

Books on Post-Abortion Healing for Women and Their Helpers

Cochrane, Linda. *Forgiven and Set Free: A Post-Abortion Bible Study for Women.*
    Grand Rapids, MI: Baker Books, 1996.
Dillon, Rev. John J. *A Path to Hope: For Parents of Aborted Children and Those
    Who Minister to Them.* Catholic Book Publishing Company, 1990.
Hayford, Jack W. *I'll Hold You in Heaven: Healing and Hope for Parents of a
    Miscarried, Aborted, or Stillborn Child.* Ventura, CA: Regal Books, 2003.
Masse, Sydna and Joan Phillips. *Her Choice to Heal: Finding Spiritual and
    Emotional Peace After Abortion.* Colorado Springs, CO: David C. Cook, 2009.
Mannion, Michael. *Abortion and Healing: A Cry to Be Whole.* Kansas City, MO:
    Sheed and Ward, 1986.
O'Neill, Jennifer, *You're Not Alone: Healing Through God's Grace After Abortion.*
    Deerfield Beach, FL: Faith Communications, 2005.
Peretti, Frank. Tilly. Westchester, IL: Crossway Books, 2003.
Reardon, David, PhD. *The Jericho Plan: Breaking Down the Walls Which Prevent
    Post-Abortion Healing.* Kansas City, MO: Acorn Books, 1996.
Reisser, Teri and Paul. *Help for the Post-Abortion Woman.* Grand Rapids, MI:
    Zondervan Publishing House, 1989.
Reisser, Teri and Paul, *A Solitary Sorry: Finding Healing and Wholeness After
    Abortion.* Colorado Springs, CO: Shaw Books, 2000.
Riols, Noreen. *My Unknown Child.* Sisters, OR: Multnomah Publishers, 1999.
Selby, Terry. *The Mourning After.* Grand Rapids, MI: Baker Book House, 1990.

Books on Adoption

Christianson, Laura. *The Adoption Decision: 15 Things You Want to Know Before Adoptin.* Eugene, OR: Harvest House Publishers, 2007

Donnelly, Douglas. *A Guide to Adoption.* Colorado Springs, CO: Focus on the Family, 1988.

Ezell, Lee. *The Missing Piece: The True Story of a Mother's Painful Loss of Her Daughter—And Their Triumphant Reunion.* Ventura, CA: Regal Books, 2004.

Gillespie, Natalie Nichols. *Successful Adoption: A Guide for Christian Families.* Nashville, TN: Thomas Nelson, 2006.

National Committee on Adoption. *The Adoption Fact Book.* Washington, DC: NCA, 1989.

Roggow, Linda. *Pregnant and Single: Help for Tough Choices.* Scottdale, PA: Herald Press, 1998.

Sanford, David & Renee. *Handbook on Thriving as an Adoptive Family: Real-Life Solutions to Common Challenges.* Colorado Springs, CO: Focus on the Family, 2008.

Zimmerman, Martha. *Should I Keep My Baby?* Minneapolis, MN: Bethany House Publishers, 1997.

Prochastity Curricula and Abstinence Education

Alliance for Chastity Education, (703) 659-4171, PO Box 1350, Stafford, VA 22554, Email: info@reallove.net, Web site: www.reallove.net

CareNet, (703) 478-5661, Fax: (703) 478-5668, 44180 Riverside Parkway, Suite 200, Lansdowne, VA 20176, Email: info@care-net.org, Web site: www.care-net.org

Character Curriculums, Inc., (361) 275-5024, 112 E. Church St., Cuero, TX 77954

Human Life International, Toll Free: (800) 549-LIFE, Fax: (540) 622-7247, 4 Family Life Lane, Front Royal, VA 22630, Email: hli@hli.org, Web site: www.hli.org

National Association for Abstinence Education, (202) 248-5420, Fax: (202) 580-6559, 1701 Pennsylvania Avenue, NW, Suite 300, Washington, DC 20006, Email: info@abstinenceassociation.org, Web site: www.abstinenceassociation.org

Teen-Aid, (509) 482-2868, Fax: (509) 482-7994, Toll Free: (800) 357-2868, 723 E. Jackson, Spokane, WA 99207, Web site: www.teen-aid.org

Prolife Speakers and Trainers (Contact other listed organizations as well)

Ambassador's Speakers Bureau, (615) 370-4700, Fax: (615) 661-4344, PO Box 50358, Nashville, TN 37205, Email: info@ambassadoragency.com, Web site: www.AmbassadorSpeakers.com

Judie Brown (*and others*), American Life League, (540) 659-4171, PO Box 1350, Stafford, VA 22555, Email: info@all.org, Web site: www.all.org

CareNet, (703) 478-5661, Fax: (703) 478-5668, 44180 Riverside Parkway, Suite 200, Lansdowne, VA 20176, Email: info@care-net.org, Web site: www.care-net.org

ChristianSpeakers.com, (615) 771-9400, Fax: (615) 771-2177, 277 Mallory Station Road, Suite 128, Franklin, TN 37067, Email: info@christianspeakers.com, Web site: www.christianspeakers.com

Jamie L. Clague, (724) 424-1172, 1924 Snyder Ave., Greensburg, PA 15601, Email: jamielynnhis@yahoo.com

Mark Crutcher, Life Dynamics, (940) 380-8800, Fax: (940) 380-8700, Toll Free: (800) 401-6494, 204 Cardinal Drive, Denton, TX 76209, Email: ldi1@airmail.net, Web site: www.ldi.org

Gregg Cunningham, Center for BioEthical Reform, (949) 206-0600, PO Box 219, Lake Forest, CA 92609, Email: info@cbrinfo.org, Web site: www.cbrinfo.org

Carol Everett, The Heidi Group, (512) 255-2088, Fax: (512) 255-2582, PO Box 5099, Round Rock, TX 78683-5099, Email: info@heidigroup.org, Web site: www.heidigroup.org

Michaelene Fredenburg, Abortion Changes You, PO Box 600533, San Diego, CA 92160-0533, Email: contact@abortionchangesyou.com, Web site: www.abortionchangesyou.com

Feminists for Life of America, *Speakers: Serrin Foster, president, Molly Pannell, advocacy and outreach coordinator,* (703) 836-3354, PO Box 320667, Alexandria, VA 22320, Email: info@feministsforlife.org, Web site: www.feministsforlife.org

Wanda Franz (*and others*), National Right to Life Committee, (202) 626-8800, 512 10th Street NW, Washington, DC 20004, Email: NRLC@nrlc.org, Web site: www.nrlc.org

Olivia Gans, *director of American Victims of Abortion,* National Right to Life Committee, (202) 626-8800, 512 10th Street NW, Washington, DC 20004, Email: NRLC@nrlc.org, Web site: www.nrlc.org

Lakita Garth (singer, Abstinence Speaker, Dominion Enterprises), (562) 429-0357, Fax: (310) 891-6932, 800 S. Pacific Coast Hwy., #8501, Redondo Beach, CA 90277, Email: info@lakitagarth.com, Web site: www.lakitagarth.com

Doug Gresham (*stepson of C. S. Lewis, ran a post-abortion ministry in Ireland with his wife Merrie for thirteen years, now resides in Malta*), Email: dgresham@maltamail.com

Gianna Jessen (*abortion survivor*), Email: bookings@giannajessen.com, Web site: www.giannajessen.com

Scott Klusendorf, Life Training Institute, (719) 264-7861, PO Box 50918, Colorado Springs, CO 80919, Email: info@prolifetraining.com, Web site: www.prolifetraining.com

Paul McKenzie (*prolife musician*), Paul McKenzie Ministries, (734) 692-0036, PO Box 136, Rockwood, MI 48173, Email: pmmin1@yahoo.com, Web site: www.paulmckenzieministries.com

Dr. Beverly McMillan, (601) 981-8377, 1004 Buckley, Jackson, MS 39206-8377

Marc Newman, PhD. (*speaking and training*), (865) 429-5523, 2005 Green Pine Lane, Sevierville, TN 37862, Email: marc@movieministry.com

Jennifer O'Neill, Jennifer O'Neill Ministries, (615) 463-3126,1811 Beech Avenue, Nashville, TN 37203, Email: jenniferoneill@bellsouth.net, Web site: www.jenniferoneill.com/pages/ministryPress.php

David Reardon (*director of the Elliot Institute, women's issues*), (217) 525-8202, PO Box 9079, Springfield, IL 62791, Web site: www.afterabortion.org

Joseph M. Scheidler, ProLife Action League, (773) 777-2900, Fax: (773) 777-3061, 6160 N. Cicero Avenue, Chicago, IL 60646, Email: info@prolifeaction.org, Web site: www.prolifeaction.org

Michael Spielman, Abort73.com (*A division of Loxafamosity Ministries*), PO Box 2256 Loves Park, IL 61111, Email: info@abort73.com, Web site: www.abort73.com

Stand to Reason, Toll Free: (800) 2-REASON, (562) 595-7333, 1438 East 33rd Street, Signal Hill, CA 90755, Email: questions@str.org, Web site: www.str.org

Pam Tebow (refused doctors-recommended abortion of last pregnancy), (904) 266-2408, Email: pamtebow@yahoo.com

Rebecca Wasser-Kiessling (*attorney, conceived in rape*), Email: Rebecca@rebeccakiessling.com, Web site: www.rebeccakiessling.com

Barbara Wilson, (916) 224-4039, Email: comments@barbarawilson.org, Web site: www.barbarawilson.org

ABOUT THE AUTHOR

Randy Alcorn is the founder and director of Eternal Perspective Ministries (EPM). Prior to 1990, when he started EPM, he served as a pastor for fourteen years. He has spoken around the world and has taught on the adjunct faculties of Multnomah University and Western Seminary in Portland, Oregon.

Randy is the best-selling author of more than thirty books (3.5 million in print), including the novels *Deadline, Dominion,* and *Deception* as well as *Lord Foulgrin's Letters,* the Gold Medallion winner *Safely Home, Wait Until Then* (children's picture book about Heaven) and *Tell Me About Heaven* (picture book illustrated by Ron DiCianni). His nonfiction works include *Money, Possessions, and Eternity; ProLife Answers to ProChoice Arguments; In Light of Eternity; The Treasure Principle; The Grace and Truth Paradox; The Purity Principle; The Law of Rewards; Why ProLife; Heaven; Heaven for Kids (8–12 year olds); Fifty Days of Heaven* (meditations on Heaven); and *TouchPoints: Heaven.*

Randy has written for many magazines and produces the popular periodical *Eternal Perspectives.* He's been a guest on more than 600 radio and television programs including *Focus on the Family, The Bible Answer Man, Family Life Today, Revive Our Hearts, Truths That Transform,* and *Faith Under Fire.*

The father of two married daughters, Randy lives in Gresham, Oregon, with his wife and best friend, Nanci. Randy enjoys hanging out with his family, biking, tennis, research, and reading.

Feedback on books and inquiries regarding publications and other matters can be directed to Eternal Perspective Ministries (EPM), 39085 Pioneer Boulevard, Suite 200, Sandy, Oregon 97055; 503-668-5200. For information on EPM or Randy Alcorn, and for resources on missions, persecuted church, prolife issues, and matters of eternal perspective, see www.epm.org. And visit Randy Alcorn's blog: www.randyalcorn.blogspot.com.

NOTES

INTRODUCTION TO THE REVISED EDITION

1. Randy Alcorn, *"Should We Have a Pro-Life Platform?"* 1996 Oregon High School Model Republican Convention, www.epm.org/hsprolif.html.

2. 1 Premio Internazionale Letterario, "Tito Casini," Borgo S.Lorenzo (FI), Premio Cultura, 5 Giugno 1996.

3. Mother Teresa, National Prayer Breakfast, 3 February 1994, www.epm.org/motherteresa.html.

4. Francis J. Beckwith, *Politically Correct Death: Answering Arguments for Abortion Rights* (Grand Rapids, Mich.: Baker Book House, 1993).

5. Mark Crutcher, *Lime 5* (Denton, Tex.: Life Dynamics, Inc., 1996).

6. Naomi Wolf, "Our Bodies, Our Souls," *New Republic,* 16 October 1995, www.epm.org/naomiwolf.html.

7. "Left for Dead," *World,* 22 January 2000, 25–6.

8. David Gibson, "Teens Accused in Death of Baby; Infant Beaten after Delivery," *Bergen Record,* 17 November 1996, A1, excerpted from Dr. James Dobson, *Family News from Focus on the Family,* May 1998.

9. Laurie Goodstein, "Of Birth and Death and the Prom," *Washington Post,* 10 June 1997, A3, excerpted from Dr. James Dobson, *Family News from Focus on the Family,* May 1998.

10. "Police: Teen Threw Baby into River," Associated Press, 8 June 2000.

11. See Randy Alcorn, "Who Do We Think We Are?" (Physician-Assisted Suicide), www.epm.org/physuici.html.

12. Erin Hoover Barnett, "Is Mom Capable of Choosing to Die?" *Oregonian,* 17 October 1999, G1–2.

13. Dr. William Toffler, M.D., Director of Physicians for Compassionate Care, "Oregon Patient with Dementia Given Suicide: Decision Falls upon HMO Administrator," 18 October 1999.

14. Gregg Cunningham, director of Center for Bio-Ethical Reform, phone conversation, 8 May 2000.

15. Feminists for Life press release, "Proabortion Republican Senator Invites Prolife Feminist for Debate," *Prolife Infonet,* 12 March 2000. See related

article by Melissa Healy, "Feminists for Life Keys on Prevention, Not Abortion," *Los Angeles Times,* 21 January 1997, www.prolifeinfo.org/fact4.html.

16. Nancy R. Pearcy, "The Evolution Backlash: Debunking Darwin," *World,* 1 March 1977, 13–5.

17. Michael J. Behe, *Darwin's Black Box: The Biochemical Challenge to Evolution* (New York: Free Press, 1996); William A. Dembski, ed., Hugh Ross and Michael J. Behe, contr., *Mere Creation: Science, Faith and Intelligent Design* (Downers Grove, Ill.: InterVarsity Press, 1998); William A. Dembski and Michael J. Behe, *Intelligent Design: The Bridge Between Science and Theology* (Downers Grove, Ill.: InterVarsity Press, 1999); Lee M. Spetner, *Not By Chance* (New York: Judaica Press, 1998).

18. The Gallup Organization, April 2000, www.gallup.com/poll/indicators/indabortion.asp.

19. Lydia Saad, "Americans Divided Over Abortion Debate," 18 May 1999, Gallup News Service Poll Releases, www.gallup.com/poll/releases/pr990518.asp.

20. Associated Press, 10 March 2000.

21. "Unborn Victims of Violence Act Will See Senate Action This Term," Gannett News Service, 6 March 2000.

22. Susan Olasky, "Abstinence Video: You Ought to Know," *World,* 22 January 2000, 18–20.

23. Candi Cushman, "Freedom from Fear," *World,* 22 January 2000, 16–8.

24. "Senate Committee Considers Stem Cell Research Source," Associated Press, 26 April 2000.

25. National Institute of Health, "Stem Cell Research," www.nih.gov/news/stemcell/draftguidelines.htm.

26. "Deadline Extended for Comment to NIH on Stem Cells Harvesting," *Prolife Infonet,* 31 January 2000.

27. "Dr. Bernard Nathanson Testifies before Congress on Reproductive Technologies," *Washington Times,* 10 February 2000.

28. Opening Lines, A Division of Consultants and Diagnostic Pathology, Inc. PO Box 508, West Frankfort, IL 62896; 1-800-490-9980; www.trosch.org/for/body-parts.html.

29. Les Sillars, "Cracking the Code," *World,* 29 April 2000, 18.

30. *London Telegraph,* 11 March 2000.

31. Sillars, "Cracking the Code," 19.

32. "Designer Babies," ZENIT News Agency, 28 January 2000.

33. Chuck Colson, "Life and Death Decisions: Praying for the Supremes," *BreakPoint Commentary* #000425, 25 April 2000.

34. "Baby Samuel and Mother Doing Well after Fetal Surgery," *WorldNet Daily,* 16 February 2000.

35. ABC News press release, 6 March 2000.

36. "ABC Airs Bogus Report on Fetal Tissue Marketing," Washington: American Life League press release, 9 March 2000.

37. Press release on *"20/20* Fetal Body Parts Scandal," Life Dynamics, March 2000.

38. Ibid.

39. Charles Colson, *How Now Shall We Live?* (Wheaton, Ill. Tyndale House Publishers, 1999), x–xi.

WHY THIS BOOK IS NECESSARY

40. National Center for Health Statistics, Atlanta, GA.

41. "Abortion: Facts at a Glance" (New York: Planned Parenthood of America), 1.

42. Edward Lenoski, *Heartbeat* 3 (December 1980), cited by John Willke, *Abortion Questions and Answers* (Cincinnati: Hayes Publishing Co., 1988), 140–1.

43. U.S. Department of Health and Human Services, Center for Disease Control, Abortion Surveillance Report, May 1983.

44. "Facts in Brief," rev. February 2000, the Alan Guttmacher Institute, www.agi-usa.org/pubs/fb_induced_abortion.html.

45. Centers for Disease Control and Prevention, "Abortion Surveillance: Preliminary Analysis—United States," 1996; *MMWR Mortal Wkly. Rep.* 47 (1998): 1025–8, 1035.

46. S. K. Henshaw, "Abortion Incidence and Services in the United States," 1995–1996, *Family Planning Perspective* 30 (1998): 263–70, 287.

47. S. K. Henshaw, "Unintended Pregnancy in the United States," *Family Planning Perspective* 30 (1998): 24–9, 46.

48. James Patterson and Peter Kim, *The Day America Told the Truth* (New York: Prentice Hall Press, 1991), 32.

49. *Newsweek,* 14 January 1985, 22.

50. Lydia Saad, "Americans Divided Over Abortion Debate," Gallup News Service Poll Releases, 18 May 1999, www.gallup.com/poll/releases/pr990518.asp.

51. Gene Edward Veith, "Salvation by Transgression," *World,* 15 April 2000, 17.

52. Marvin Olasky, *The Prodigal Press* (Westchester, Ill.: Crossway Books, 1988), 116.

53. *Between the Lines,* May 1989.

54. *Washington Post,* 9 April 1989.

55. David Shaw, "Abortion Foes Say Media Bias Most Evident in Terminology," *Oregonian,* 6 August 1990, A2.

56. John Leo, "Is the Press Straight on Abortion?" *U.S. News and World Report,* 16 July 1990, 17.

57. David Kupelian and Mark Masters, "Prochoice 1990: Skeletons in the Closet," *New Dimensions,* October 1990, 22.

58. Shaw, "Abortion Foes."

59. Ibid.

60. Jerry Adler, "Taking Offense," *Newsweek,* 24 December 1990, 54.

61. Francis J. Beckwith, *Politically Correct Death: Answering the Arguments for Abortion Rights* (Grand Rapids, Mich.: Baker Book House, 1993), 27–8.

PART ONE: ARGUMENTS CONCERNING LIFE, HUMANITY, AND PERSONHOOD

Argument 1

62. American Life League, *Communique,* 25 May 2000.

63. Polly Rothstein and Marian Williams, "Choice" (New York: Westchester Coalition for Legal Abortion, 1983), printed and distributed by the NARAL Foundation, Washington, DC.

64. Bradley M. Patten, *Human Embryology,* 3d ed. (New York: McGraw Hill, 1968), 43.

65. Keith L. Moore, *The Developing Human: Clinically Oriented Embryology,* 2d ed. (Philadelphia, Penn: W.B. Saunders, 1977), 1.

66. Ibid., 12.

67. J. P. Greenhill and E. A. Friedman, *Biological Principles and Modern Practice of Obstetrics* (Philadelphia, Penn.: W. B. Saunders, 1974), 17 (cf. 23).

68. Louis Fridhandler, "Gametogenesis to Implantation," *Biology of Gestation,* vol. 1, ed. N. S. Assau (New York: Academic Press, 1968), 76.

69. E. L. Potter and J. M. Craig, *Pathology of the Fetus and the Infant,* 3d ed. (Chicago: Year Book Medical Publishers, 1975), vii.

70. *Time* and Rand McNally, *Atlas of the Body* (New York: Rand McNally, 1980), 139, 144.

71. "Pregnancy," *New Encyclopedia Britannica,* 15th ed., Macropedia, vol. 14 (Chicago, Ill.: Encyclopedia Britannica, 1974), 968.

72. Subcommittee on Separation of Powers to Senate Judiciary Committee S-158, *Report,* 97th Cong., 1st Sess., 1981.

73. Landrum Shettles and David Rorvik, *Rites of Life: The Scientific Evidence for Life Before Birth* (Grand Rapids, Mich.: Zondervan Publishing House, 1983), 113.

74. Ashley Montague, *Life Before Birth* (New York: Signet Books, 1977), vi.

75. Bernard N. Nathanson, "Deeper into Abortion," *New England Journal of Medicine* 291 (1974): 1189–90.

76. Bernard Nathanson, *Aborting America* (Garden City, N.Y.: Doubleday, 1979).

77. Shettles and Rorvik, *Rites of Life,* 103.

78. John C. Willke, *Abortion Questions and Answers* (Cincinnati, Ohio: Hayes Publishing, 1988), 42.

79. Report, Subcommittee on Separation of Powers to Senate Judiciary Committee S-158, 97th Congress, 1st Session 1981, 7.

80. Norquist, www.epm.org/opposed.html.

81. Matt Ridley, "Will We Still Need to Have Sex?" *Time,* 8 November 1999, 66, quoted by Dr. James Dobson in *Family News from Focus on the Family,* January 2000.

Argument 2

82. Mortimer J. Adler, *Haves Without Have-Nots: Essays for the 21st Century on Democracy and Socialism* (New York: Macmillan, 1991), 210.

83. John J. Davis, *Abortion and the Christian* (Phillipsburg, N.J.: Presbyterian & Reformed Publishing Co., 1984), 23.

84. "Brain Dead Woman Gives Birth," *Oregonian,* 31 July 1987.

85. From a November 1970 speech titled "The Termination of Pregnancy or the Extermination of the Fetus," cited by Jean Garton, *Who Broke the Baby?* (Minneapolis, Minn.: Bethany House Publishers, 1979), 41–2.

86. Dr. Peter Nathanielsz, cited by Sharon Begley, "Do You Hear What I Hear?" *Newsweek,* special summer edition 1991, 14.

87. Mark Crutcher, "Abortion Questions They'd Rather Duck," *Focus on the Family Citizen,* 20 May 1991, 4.

88. George P. Smith II, "Australia's Frozen Orphan Embryos: A Medical, Legal, and Ethical Dilemma," *Journal of Family Law* 24 (1985–86): 27–41.

89. Samuel B. Casey, "The Chosen and Frozen," in *The Reproduction Revolution: A Christian Appraisal of Sexuality,* ed. John F. Kilner, Paige C. Cunningham,

and W. David Hager (Grand Rapids, Mich.: Wm. B. Eerdmans Publishing Co., 2000), 172.

90. Robert W. Evans, "The Moral Status of Embryos," in *The Reproduction Revolution,* 60.

91. Casey, "The Chosen and Frozen," 164.

92. Lori B. Andrews, "Embryonic Confusion," *Washington Post,* 2 May 1999, B1, B4.

93. IVF Phoenix Infertility Information Booklet, www.ihr.com/fertbook/treatment.htm, cited by Casey, "The Chosen and Frozen," 164.

94. Leon Speroff, *Clinical Gynecologic Endocrinology and Infertility* (Baltimore, Md.: Williams and Wilkins, 5th ed., 1994), 937–9.

95. Dr. Jerome LeJeune, *The Concentration Can: When Does Human Life Begin? An Eminent Geneticist Testifies* (San Francisco, Calif.: Ignatius Press, 1992).

96. "The Custody Dispute over Seven Human Embryos: The Testimony of Professor Jerome LeJeune, M.D., Ph.D.," Christian Legal Society, 4208 Evergreen Lane, Annandale, VA 22003-3264.

97. James Walsh, "A Bitter Embryo Imbroglio," *Time,* August 1996, 10.

98. Reuters News Service, "Thousands of Unwanted Embryos Perish in England," *Prolife Infonet,* 14 April 2000.

99. Focus on the Family, *Physician,* January–February 2000.

Argument 3

100. Dr. Eugene F. Diamond, "Word Wars: Games People Play about the Beginning of Life," Focus on the Family, *Physician,* November–December 1992, 14–5.

101. "Deadline Extended for Comment to NIH on Stem Cells Harvesting," *Prolife Infonet,* 31 January 2000.

102. Dorothea Kerslake and Donn Casey, "Abortion Induced by Means of the Uterine Aspirator," *Obstetrics and Gynecology* 30 (July 1967): 37, 43.

103. Naomi Wade, "Aborted Babies Kept Alive for Bizarre Experiments," *National Examiner,* 19 August 1980, 20–1.

104. Raul Hilberg, *The Destruction of European Jews* (Chicago: Quadrangle Books, 1967), 567–8.

105. Davis, *Abortion and the Christian,* 23. Davis cites as a source R. Houwink, *Data: Mirrors of Science* (1970), 104–90.

106. Lennart Nilsson, "Drama of Life Before Birth," *Life,* 30 April 1965.

107. Begley, "Do You Hear What I Hear?" 14.

108. "The Facts of Life" (Norcross, Ga.: Human Development Resource Council), 2.

109. These are well-established scientific facts. See, for instance, Shettles and Rorvik, *Rites of Life*, 41–66.

110. "Facts in Brief," rev. February 2000, the Alan Guttmacher Institute, www.agi-usa.org/pubs/fb_induced_abortion.html.

111. "The Doctor's Dilemma," *Newsweek*, 17 July 1989, 25.

112. Dr. Hicks's audiotape of an unborn child's beating heart at six weeks and five days of development is available for $3.00 from Cincinnati Right to Life, 1802 W. Galbraith Road, Cincinnati, OH 45239.

113. Nathanson, *Aborting America*.

114. *Life*, August 1990.

115. Lennart Nilsson, *A Child Is Born* (New York: Delacorte Press, 1977).

116. Ellen Kreuger, quoted by *Winnipeg Sun*, cited in *Kansans for Life*, May 1991, 9.

117. Ibid.

118. "Abortion: For Survival," a video produced by the Fund for the Feminist Majority.

119. Leonide M. Tanner, ed., "Developing Professional Parameters: Nursing and Social Work Roles in the Care of the Induced Abortion Patient," *Clinical Obstetrics and Gynecology* 14 (December 1971): 1271.

120. Paul Marx, *The Death Peddlers: War on the Unborn* (Collegeville, Minn: St. John's University Press, 1971), 21.

121. *Feminists for Life Debate Handbook* (Kansas City, Mo.: Feminists for Life of America, n.d.), 3.

Argument 4

122. Faye Wattleton, in a debate following TNT's airing of "Abortion: For Survival," produced by the Fund for the Feminist Majority.

123. Carl Sagan and Ann Druyan, "Is It Possible to Be Prolife and Prochoice?" *Parade*, 22 April 1990, 4.

124. *The First Nine Months* (Colorado Springs, Colo.: Focus on the Family), 3.

125. *Preview of a Birth* (Norcross, Ga: Human Development Resource Center, 1991), 4.

126. Dr. Warren Hern, "Operative Procedures and Technique," *Abortion Practice* (Boulder, Colo.: Alpenglo Graphics, Inc., 1990), 154.

127. Dr. Thomas W. Hilgers, Dennis J. Horan and David Mall, eds., *New Perspectives on Human Abortion* (Frederick, Md.: University Publications of America Inc./Aletheia Books, 1981), 351.

128. Paul Ramsey, "Points in Deciding About Abortion," *The Morality of Abortion: Legal and Historical Perspectives,* ed. John T. Noonan (Cambridge, Mass.: Harvard University Press, 1970), 66–7.

Argument 5

129. Roland M. Nardone, "The Nexus of Biology and the Abortion Issue," *Jurist,* Spring 1973, 154.

130. A good treatment of this critical issue of what constitutes personhood is Ron Norquist's "PERSONally Opposed," http://www.epm.org/opposed.html.

131. Sagan and Druyan, "Is It Possible to Be Prolife and Prochoice?" 5.

132. Dr. Seuss, *Horton Hears a Who* (New York: Random House, 1954).

133. Joseph Fletcher, *Situation Ethics: The New Morality,* cited by Mark O'Keefe, "Personhood: When Does It Begin...or End?" *Oregonian,* 12 February 1995, B1.

134. Ashley Montague, *Sex, Man and Society* (New York: G. P. Putnam and Sons, 1967), cited by Paul Fowler, *Abortion: Toward an Evangelical Consensus* (Portland, Ore.: Multnomah Press, 1987), 34–5.

135 *Roe* v. *Wade,* 410 U.S., 1973.

136. Associated Press, cited in Christian Action Council's *Action Line,* March–April 1991.

137. Begley, "Do You Hear What I Hear?" 12.

138. Ibid.

139. T. Verney and J. Kelley, *The Secret Life of the Unborn Child* (New York: Delta Books, 1981).

140. H. B. Valman and J. F. Pearson, "What the Fetus Feels." (This is a printed article with no reference to the publication in which it appeared. Dr. Valman is consultant pediatrician at Northwick Park Hospital and Clinical Research Center in Harrow; Pearson is senior lecturer and consultant obstetrician and gynecologist at Welsh National School of Medicine in Cardiff.)

141. John Willke, *Abortion Questions and Answers* (Cincinnati, Ohio: Hayes Publishing Co., 1988), 53.

142. Begley, "Do You Hear What I Hear?" 14.

143. Peter Singer, *Animal Liberation* (New York: Avon Books, 1975), 215.

144. Peter Singer, *Animal Liberation,* rev. ed. (New York: Avon Books, 1990), 6.

145. Peter Singer, *Practical Ethics* (1979), cited in "Peter Singer in His Own Words," Accuracy in Academia, www.academia.org/singerquotes.html.

146. Singer, *Practical Ethics* (1979), 97, cited by Charles E. Rice, *Fifty Questions* (New Hope, Ky.: Cashel Institute, 1986), 64–5.

147. Peter Singer, "Sanctity of Life or Quality of Life," *Pediatrics*, July 1983, 129.

148. Winston L. Duke, "The New Biology," *Reason*, August 1972.

149. Ingrid Newkirk, cited in Richard Milne, "Animal Liberation: Do the Beasts Really Benefit?" www.probe.org/docs/anim-rts.html.

150. Singer, "In His Own Words."

151. Ibid.

152. George Will, "Life and Death at Princeton," *Newsweek*, 7 September 1999, www.npnd.org/will.htm.

153. Jim Newhall, cited by Maureen O'Hagan, "Cross Hairs to Bear," *Willamette Week*, 3 May 1995.

154. "Prelude to the New Holocaust, Part II, (The MOD Brings the Eugenic Spirit Home)," The Michael Fund (a prolife alternative to the March of Dimes), 500 A Garden City Drive, Pittsburgh, PA 15146, (724) 823-6380, www.michaelfund.org.

155. Charles Hartshorne, "Concerning Abortion: An Attempt at a Rational View," *Christian Century*, 21 January 1981, 42–5.

Argument 6

156. Nathanson, *Aborting America*, 216.

157. Robert Wennberg, *Life in the Balance: Exploring the Abortion Controversy* (Grand Rapids, Mich.: Wm. B. Eerdmans Publishing Co., 1985), 71, cited in Francis J. Beckwith, *Politically Correct Death: Answering the Arguments for Abortion Rights* (Grand Rapids, Mich.: Baker Book House, 1993), 97.

158. *Roe* v. *Wade*, 410 U.S. 113 (1973), 38.

159. Molly Yard, quoted in "Voices of the Abortion Debate," *New Dimensions*, October 1990, 109.

160. Kate Taylor, "Hanging in There at 1½ Pounds," *Oregonian*, 7 April 2000.

161. Micahel Ottey, "Oregon's Tiniest Goes Home, Sweet Home," *Oregonian*, 3 June 2000, B1.

162. Kenneth L. Woodward, "The Hardest Question," *Newsweek*, 14 January 1985, 29.

163. Davis, *Abortion and the Christian*, 101.

164. Harold O. J. Brown, *Death Before Birth* (Nashville, Tenn.: Thomas Nelson Publishers, 1977), 124, cited in Beckwith, *Politically Correct Death*, 97.

165. F. LaGard Smith, *When Choice Becomes God* (Eugene, Ore.: Harvest House Publishers, 1990), 146.

Argument 8

166. Jean Staker Garton, *Who Broke the Baby?* (Minneapolis, Minn.: Bethany House Publishers, 1979), 7–8.

167. Gina Kolata, "Infant Healthy after Surgery in the Womb," *Oregonian*, 31 May 1990, A16.

168. Pat Ohlendorf-Moffat, "Surgery Before Birth," *Discover*, February 1991, 59.

169. "A New Ethic for Medicine and Society," editorial, *California Medicine* (September 1970), 68.

170. Dr. Warren Hern, "Operative Procedures and Technique," 154.

171. "Baby Samuel Photo Changes Family for Life," *Atlanta Journal Constitution*, 8 April 2000, *Prolife Infonet*, 10 April 2000.

172. "Baby Samuel and Mother Doing Well after Fetal Surgery," *WorldNet Daily*, 16 February 2000.

173. Naomi Wolf, "Our Bodies, Our Souls," *New Republic*, 16 October 1995, www.epm.org/naomiwolf.html.

174. Fred Leeson, "Judge Sends Mother to Jail to Protect Unborn Child," *Oregonian*, 9 December 1989, A1.

175. Associated Press, 28 February 2000.

176. Ann McDaniel, "Home Remedy Abortions," *Newsweek*, 17 July 1989, 25.

177. Marvin Olasky, *Prodigal Press* (Westchester, Ill.: Crossway Books, 1988), 116.

178. Barbara Cornell, "Do the Unborn Have Rights?" *Time*, special fall edition 1990, 23.

179. Volvo advertisement, *Time*, 29 October 1990, inside back cover.

180. Chrysler advertisement, *Time*, 15 October 1990, 28–9.

181. "The Unborn and the Born Again," editorial, *New Republic*, 2 July 1977, 6.

182. Magda Denes, "The Question of Abortion," *Commentary* 62 (December 1976): 6.

183. Singer, "In His Own Words."

184. Beckwith, *Politically Correct Death*, 92.

PART TWO: ARGUMENTS CONCERNING RIGHTS AND FAIRNESS

Argument 9

185. *Roe* v. *Wade*, 410 U.S., 1973.

186. Cited by John Leo in "The Moral Complexity of Choice," *U.S. News & World Report*, 11 December 1989, 64.

187. Ibid.

188. Naomi Wolf, "Our Bodies, Our Souls," *New Republic*, 16 October 1995, www.epm.org/naomiwolf.html.

189. Francis J. Beckwith, *Politically Correct Death: Answering the Arguments for Abortion Rights* (Grand Rapids, Mich.: Baker Book House, 1993), 91.

190. William Tillman, *Christian Ethics: A Primer* (Nashville, Tenn.: Broadman Press, 1986), 114.

191. Peter Singer and Helen Kuhse, "On Letting Handicapped Infants Die," in *The Right Thing to Do: Basic Readings in Moral Philosophy*, ed. James Rachels (New York: Random House, 1989), 146.

192. Planned Parenthood Federation of America, "Abortion: Facts at a Glance," 1.

193. Judith Jarvis Thomson, *Philosophy and Public Affairs* 1 (1971): 47–66.

Argument 10

194. Beckwith, *Politically Correct Death*, 12.

195. Mary O'Brien Drum, "Meeting in the Radical Middle," *Sojourners*, November 1980, 23.

Argument 11

196. Mary Anne Warren, "On the Moral and Legal Status of Abortion," in *The Problem of Abortion*, 2d ed., ed. Joel Feinberg (Belmont, Calif.: Wadsworth, 1984), 103.

197. *Feminists for Life Debate Handbook* (Kansas City, Mo.: Feminists for Life of America, n.d.), 16.

Argument 12

198. Randy Alcorn, *Christians in the Wake of the Sexual Revolution* (Portland, Ore.: Multnomah Press, 1985), 175–87.

199. Robert Jay Lifton, *The Nazi Doctors: Medical Killing and the Psychology of Genocide* (New York: Basic Books, 1986).

200. Mark Baker, "Men on Abortion," *Esquire*, March 1990, 114–25.

Argument 13

201. Frederica Mathews-Green, *Real Choices* (Sisters, Ore.: Multnomah Publishers, 1995), 14–15.

202. Cited by Charmaine Yoest, "Why Is Adoption So Difficult?" *Focus on the Family Citizen*, 17 December 1990, 10.

203. The National Council for Adoption, *1989 Adoption Factbook* (Washington, D.C., June 1989), 158. Per a phone conversation on 5/8/00 with a representative of NCFA, these figures are relatively the same in 2000, confirming that at least one million couples of childbearing age constitute the minimum adoption demand for newborns in the U.S.
204. Yoest, "Why Is Adoption So Difficult?" 10.
205. Ibid.

Argument 14

206. Susan B.Anthony, *Revolution*, 8 July 1869, 4.
207. Mattie Brinkerhoff, *Revolution*, 9 April 1868, 215–6.
208. Elizabeth Cady Stanton, from a letter in Julia Ward Howe's journal, 16 October 1873, available at Houghton Library, Harvard University.
209. R. C. Sproul, *Abortion: A Rational Look at an Emotional Issue* (Colorado Springs, Colo.: NavPress, 1990), 117–8.
210. Guy M. Condon, "You Say Choice, I Say Murder," *Christianity Today*, 24 June 1991, 22.
211. Feminists for Life of America, 811 East 47th Street, Kansas City, Mo. 64110.
212. Mary Ann Schaefer, quoted by Catherine and William Odell, *The First Human Right* (Toronto: Life Cycle Books, 1983), 39–40.
213. Kate Michelman, quoted in *New York Times*, 10 May 1988.
214. *Feminists for Life Debate Handbook*, 17.
215. Rosemary Bottcher, "Feminism: Bewitched by Abortion," in *To Rescue the Future*, ed. Dave Andrusko (New York: Life Cycle Books, 1983).
216. D. James Kennedy, *Abortion: Cry of Reality* (Ft. Lauderdale, Fla.: Coral Ridge Ministries, 1989), 13.
217. Wolf, "Our Bodies, Our Souls."
218. Dr. Jose A. Bufill, "What Ills the Pill Has Wrought," *Chicago Tribune*, 8 March 2000, www.chicagotribune.com/reg/tools/search/archives/form.
219. "Lawmakers Seek Investigation of US Money for Forced Abortions in Peru," Conservative News Service, 14 March 2000.
220. Supreme Court 476 U.S. at 762, *Thornburgh*.
221. *Feminists for Life Debate Handbook*, 7.
222. Ibid., 16.
223. Robert Stone, "Women Endangered Species in India," *Oregonian*, 14 March 1989, B7.

224. Jo McGowan, "In India They Abort Females," *Newsweek*, 13 February 1989.

225. "Asia: Discarding Daughters," *Time*, special fall edition 1990, 40.

226. *Straits Times* report, Beijing, 7 February 2000; related stories at www.lifesite.net.

227. *Medical World News*, 1 December 1975, 45.

228. John Leo, "Baby Boys, to Order," *U.S. News and World Report*, 9 January 1989, 59.

Argument 15

229. F. LaGard Smith, *When Choice Becomes God* (Eugene, Ore.: Harvest House Publishers, 1990), 192–3.

230. David Reardon, *Aborted Women: Silent No More* (Westchester, Ill.: Crossway Books, 1987), 10.

231. Testimonies of clinic workers in "The Abortion Providers," a video produced by Prolife Action League, Chicago. Confirmed by former abortion clinic owner Carol Everett, in private telephone conversation between her, Frank Peretti, and the author on 24 May 1991.

232. *Feminists for Life Debate Handbook*, 12.

233. Ibid., 15.

234. "Abortion: Facts at a Glance," 1.

Argument 16

235. Roger B. Taney, cited by James C. Dobson and Gary L. Bauer, *Children at Risk* (Waco, Tex.: Word Publishing, 1990), 141.

236. Ibid.

237. Beckwith, *Politically Correct Death*, 87.

PART THREE: ARGUMENTS CONCERNING SOCIAL ISSUES

Argument 17

238. D. James Kennedy, *Abortion: Cry of Reality* (Ft. Lauderdale, Fla.: Coral Ridge Ministries, 1989), 21.

239. The Michael Fund, 400 Penn Center, Pittsburgh, PA 15146.

240. "Adoption: The Forgotten Alternative," *New Dimensions*, October 1990, 32.

241. Planned Parenthood Federation of America, "Born Unwanted: Developmental Consequences for Children of Unwanted Pregnancies," n.d.

242. *Nine Reasons Why Abortion Is Legal* (New York: Planned Parenthood
     Federation of America, 1989), 6.

243. Planned Parenthood Federation of America 1999 Services Report.

Argument 18

244. Edward Lenoski, *Heartbeat* 3 (December 1980), cited by John Willke, *Abortion
     Questions and Answers* (Cincinnati, Ohio: Hayes Publishing Co., 1988), 140–1.

245. Report of the National Center of Child Abuse and Neglect, U.S. Department of
     Health and Human Services, 1973–1982.

246. Ibid.

247. U.S. Department of Health and Human Services Report; National Study on Child
     Abuse and Neglect Reporting, The American Humane Association, 1981 and
     1991; 1977 Analysis of Child Abuse and Neglect Research, U.S. Dept. of H.E.W.,
     1978.

248. Child Abuse and Neglect Statistics from the National Committee to Prevent
     Child Abuse, 1995, www.vix.com/pub/men/abuse/studies/child-ma.html.

249. Child Abuse and Neglect Reports 1997,
     www.geocities.com/CapitolHill/Lobby/8460/1997abstattables.html.

250. Child Abuse and Neglect Statistics from the National Committee to Prevent
     Child Abuse, 1995, www.vix.com/pub/men/abuse/studies/child-ma.html.

251. Peter Singer, *Rethinking Life and Death,* cited in "Peter Singer in His Own
     Words," Accuracy in Academia, www.academia.org/singerquotes.html.

252. Nancy Michels, *Helping Women Recover from Abortion* (Minneapolis, Minn:
     Bethany House Publishers, 1988), 168.

253. Philip G. Ney, "A Consideration of Abortion Survivors," *Child Psychiatry and
     Human Development* (Spring 1983): 172–3.

254. Philip G. Ney, "Relationship between Abortion and Child Abuse," *Canadian
     Journal of Psychiatry* (November 1979): 611–2.

255. Michels, *Helping Women,* 169–70.

256. Cited by James Dobson, *Focus on the Family* radio broadcast, 21 June 1991.

257. Peter Singer, *Rethinking Life and Death* (New York: St. Martin's Griffin,
     1996), 217.

Argument 19

258. *Nine Reasons Why Abortion Is Legal* (New York: Planned Parenthood
     Federation of America, 1989), 5.

259. "Facts in Brief: Induced Abortion," 1998, the Alan Guttmacher Institute; www.agi-usa.org/pubs/fb_induced_abort.html.

260. Frederica Mathewes-Green, *Real Choices* (Sisters, Ore.: Multnomah Publishers, 1995), 19.

261. John J. Davis, *Abortion and the Christian* (Phillipsburg, N.J.: Presbyterian & Reformed Publishing Co., 1984), 68–9.

262. Stanley K. Henshaw and Kathryn Kost, "Abortion Patients in 1994–95: Characteristics and Contraceptive Use," *Family Planning Perspectives* 28 (July–August 1996), www.agi-usa.org/pubs/journals/2814096.html.

263. A. E. Laing, et al., "Breast Cancer Risk Factors in African-American Women: The Howard University Registry Experience," *Journal of the National Medical Association* 85 (December 1993): 931–9.

264. Some quotations attributed to Margaret Sanger in prolife sources are inaccurate, or at least the citations are inaccurate. Since I have not located these statements in any original documents, I can only assume that they are not authentic. Citations from Sanger and the *Birth Control Review* in this edition are limited to quotations from copies of original documents in my possession.

265. Margaret Sanger, *Pivot of Civilization* (New York: Brentano's Publishers, 1922), 176.

266. Ibid., 177.

267. Ibid., 112, 116.

268. Ibid., 113.

269. Ibid., 115.

270. Dr. Havelock Ellis, "The World's Racial Problem," *Birth Control Review*, October 1920, 14–6; Theodore Russell Robie, "Toward Race Betterment," *BCR*, April 1933, 93–5; Ernst Rudin, "Eugenic Sterilization: An Urgent Need," *BCR*, April 1933, 102–4.

271. C. O. McCormick, "Defective Families," *Birth Control Review*, April 1933, 98.

272. Dr. Havelock Ellis, "Birth Control and Sterilization," *Birth Control Review*, April 1933, 104.

273. Marvin Olasky, *Abortion Rites: A Social History of Abortion in America* (Wheaton, Ill.: Crossway Books, 1992), 256–7.

274. Ibid., 258.

275. Ibid., 259.

276. Ibid., 259–63.

277. Sanger, *Pivot of Civilization*, 116–7.

Argument 20

278. Willke, *Abortion Questions*, 158.

279. ABC News, "Running Out of Russians," 18 May 2000, *Prolife Infonet*.

280. Landrum Shettles and David Rorvik, *Rites of Life: The Scientific Evidence for Life before Birth* (Grand Rapids, Mich.: Zondervan Publishing House, 1983), 152–3; Willke, *Abortion Questions*, 232–3.

281. "Investigational Contraceptives," *Drug Newsletter,* May 1987, 34; *Contraceptive Technology Update,* January 1990, 5.

282. Randy Alcorn, *Does the Birth Control Pill Cause Abortions?* (Gresham, Ore.: Eternal Perspective Ministries, 5th ed., 2000), www.epm.org/prolife.html.

283. See Randy Alcorn, "A Dialogue about Birth Control," www.epm.org/dialogue.html.

284. *Newsweek,* 30 March 1981, cited by Willke, *Abortion Questions,* 159.

285. Roy Clinebelle, *Abortions: Alarming Socioeconomic Losses* (Stafford, Va.: American Life Lobby, n.d.), 3.

286. Willke, *Abortion Questions*, 162.

287. Clinebelle, *Abortions,* 11.

288. Willke, *Abortion Questions,* 163.

289. For a treatment of the biblical and ethical issues involved in euthanasia, see Randy Alcorn's "Euthanasia: Mercy or Murder?" www.epm.org/euthanas.html.

290. Marilyn vos Savant, "The World," *Reader's Digest,* February 1992, 91.

291. Robert Evangelisto, *The Moral and Logical Arguments against Abortion* (Stafford, Va.: American Life League, n.d.), 1.

292. "Abortion, Depopulation Plague Russia," Agence France Presse English, 22 February 2000.

293. John Whitehead, *The End of Man* (Westchester, Ill.: Crossway Books, 1986), 195.

294. Bently Class, quoted by George F. Will in *The Pursuit of Happiness and Other Sobering Thoughts* (New York: Harper Colophon, 1978), 61.

295. "Prochoice or No Choice?" *Christianity Today,* 4 November 1988.

296. George Grant, *Grand Illusions: The Legacy of Planned Parenthood* (Brentwood, Tenn.: Wolgemuth and Hyatt, 1988), 25.

297. Leo Alexander, "Medical Science under Dictatorship," *New England Journal of Medicine* (July 1989): 39–47.

298. Mother Teresa, National Prayer Breakfast, 3 February 1994, www.epm.org/motherteresa.html.

Argument 21

299. Rita J. Simon, *Abortion: Statutes, Policies, and Public Attitudes the World Over* (London: Praeger Publishers, 1998), 143–4.

300. Martin Luther King Jr., *Strength to Love* (New York: William Collins and World Publishing, 1963), 33.

301. Marvin Olasky, *Abortion Rites: A Social History of Abortion in America* (Wheaton, Ill.: Crossway Books, 1992).

302. Bernard Nathanson, *Aborting America* (New York: Doubleday, 1979), 40–1.

303. Daniel Callahan, "Abortion: Thinking and Experiencing," *Christianity and Crisis,* 8 January 1973, 296.

304. David C. Reardon, *Aborted Women: Silent No More* (Westchester, Ill.: Crossway Books, 1987), 333.

Argument 22

305. *The Boston Globe,* 31 March 1989.

306. Ibid.

307. *Los Angeles Times* poll, cited by Charles Colson, "A Time to Disobey?" *Focus on the Family Citizen,* June 1989, 15.

308. *New York Times* poll cited in *Washington Times,* 28 February 1991, 1.

309. "Poll: Abortion Key for Voters," *USA Today,* 2 January 1990, 1A, 2A.

310. "Abortion Legislation Poll," *Newsweek,* 17 July 1989, 20.

311. "Abortion and Moral Beliefs: A Survey of American Opinion," conducted by the Gallup Organization, commissioned by Americans United for Life, Washington, DC, 1991, 10.

312. Ibid., 4.

313. Ibid., 5.

314. Ibid., 9.

315. Ibid., 11.

316. Ibid.

317. Ibid., 5.

318. Lydia Saad, "Americans Divided Over Abortion Debate," 18 May 1999, Gallup News Service Poll Releases, www.gallup.com/poll/releases/pr990518.asp.

319. "Gallup Poll: America is Prolife," *Washington Times,* 28 February 1991, 1.

320. "Abortion and Moral Beliefs," 1991 Gallup Poll, 13.

321. Ibid., 15.

322. Ibid., 14.

323. News Release on Gallup Poll on Abortion, Americans United for Life, 28 February 1991, 2.

324. "Abortion and Moral Beliefs," 49.

325. Ibid.

326. Ibid., 17.

327. Willke, *Abortion Questions,* 19–20.

328. Ibid.

329. Bob Woodward and Scott Armstrong, *The Brethren: Inside the Supreme Court* (New York: Avon Books, 1979), 215.

330. Ibid., 276.

331. David Kaplan, "Is *Roe* Good Law?" *Newsweek,* 27 April 1992, 50.

332. *Doe* v. *Bolton,* U.S. Supreme Court, January 1973, No. 70-40, IV, 11.

333. Essentially, the Supreme Court's 1989 *Webster Decision* empowered states to regulate abortion after the point of viability. In addition, the Court allowed the state of Missouri to restrict the use of public funds, facilities, and personnel for abortion.

334. Ronald Reagan, *Abortion and the Conscience of the Nation* (Nashville, Tenn.: Thomas Nelson Publishers, 1984), 15.

335. Ibid., 16.

Argument 23

336. "Gallup Poll: America Is Prolife," *Washington Times,* 28 February 1991, 1.

337. Anne Catherine Speckhard, "The Psycho-Social Aspects of Stress Following Abortion" (Arlington, Va.: Family Systems Center, 1985), 1.

338. Marvin Olasky, "The Village's Prolife Voice," *Christianity Today,* 24 June 1991, 24.

339. Ibid., 24–6.

340. Nathanson, *Aborting America,* 227.

341. Ibid.

342. Ibid.

343. Laurence Tribe, *Abortion: The Clash of Absolutes* (New York: Norton, 1990), 116, cited in Francis Beckwith, *Politically Correct Death: Answering the Arguments for Abortion Rights* (Grand Rapids, Mich.: Baker Book House, 1993), 81.

344. George Grant, *Trial and Error* (Brentwood, Tenn.: Wolgemuth and Hyatt, 1989), 94.

345. Walker P. Whitman, *A Christian History of the American Republic: A Textbook for Secondary Schools* (Boston, Mass.: Green Leaf Press, 1939, 1948), 42, cited by Grant, *Trial and Error,* 75.

346. Harold K. Lane, *Liberty! Cry Liberty!* (Boston: Lamb and Lamb Tractarian Society, 1939), 31.

347. David Barton, *The Myth of Separation* (Aledo, Tex.: Wall Builder Press, 1991).

348. James Patterson and Peter Kim, *The Day America Told the Truth* (New York: Prentice Hall Press, 1991).

349. Ibid., 27, 34.

350. Ibid., 61, 201.

PART FOUR: ARGUMENTS CONCERNING HEALTH AND SAFETY

Argument 24

351. Alfred Kinsey, cited by John Willke, *Abortion Questions and Answers* (Cincinnati, Ohio: Hayes Publishing Co., 1988), 169.

352. Mary Calderone, "Illegal Abortion as a Public Health Problem," *American Journal of Health* 50 (July 1960): 949.

353. Bernard Nathanson, *Aborting America* (New York: Doubleday, 1979), 193.

354. Ibid, 42.

355. U.S. Bureau of Vital Statistics.

356. Ibid.

357. Germain Grisez, *Abortion: The Myths, the Realities, and the Arguments* (New York: Corpus Books, 1972), 70.

358. J. C. Willke, "Clear Evidence: If Forbidden, Abortion Will Not Return to the Back Alley," *Life Issues Connector,* Life Issues Institute, April, 2000, 1, 3.

359. "Abortion: For Survival," a video produced by the Fund for the Feminist Majority.

360. Hani K. Atrash, M.D., Theodore Cheek, M.D., and Carol Hogue, Ph.D., "Legal Abortion Mortality and General Anesthesia," *American Journal of Obstetrics and Gynecology* (February 1988): 420.

361. Michael Kaffrissen, et al., "Cluster of Abortion Deaths at a Single Facility," *Obstetrics and Gynecology* (September 1986): 387.

362. "Jury Orders Abortionist to Pay $25 Million Judgment," *Life Advocate,* June 1991, 25.

363. Dawn Stover, "Cause of Death: Legal Abortion," *Life Advocate,* August 1991, 3.

364. Carol Everett, personal conversation with the author and Frank Peretti on 24 May 1991.

365. U.S. Center of Vital Statistics.

366. James A. Miller, "A Tale of Two Abortions," *Human Life International Reports*, March 1991, 1.

367. Willke, *Abortion Questions*, 99.

368. Frank E. Peretti, *Prophet* (Wheaton, Ill.: Crossway Books, 1992).

369. Dr. Dennis Cavanaugh, "Effect of Liberalized Abortion on Maternal Mortality Rates," *American Journal of Obstetrics and Gynecology* (February 1978): 375.

370. Gina Kolata, "Self-Help Abortion Movement Gains Momentum," *New York Times*, 23 October 1989, B12; Janice Perrone, "Controversial Abortion Approach," *American Medical News*, 12 January 1990, 9.

371. David C. Reardon, *Aborted Women: Silent No More* (Westchester, Ill.: Crossway Books, 1987), 301.

Argument 25

372. *American Medical Association Encyclopedia of Medicine*, ed. Charles B. Clayton (New York: Random House, 1989), 58.

373. Reardon, *Aborted Women*, 113.

374. Ibid.

375. "Abortion Nearly Four Times Deadlier Than Childbirth," 16 June 2000, www.afterabortion.org/PAR/V8/n2/finland.html.

376. Reardon, *Aborted Women*, 113–4.

377. *Family Planning Perspectives*, March–April 1983, 85–6.

378. Ann Aschengrau Levin, "Ectopic Pregnancy and Prior Induced Abortion," *American Journal of Public Health* (March 1982): 253.

379. U.S. Department of Health and Human Services, *Morbidity and Mortality Weekly Report* 33 (April 1984).

380. Allan Osser, M.D. and Kenneth Persson, M.D., "Postabortal Pelvic Infection Associated with Chlamydia Tracomatis and the Influence of Humoral Immunity," *American Journal of Obstetrics and Gynecology* (November 1984): 669–703.

381. Lars Heisterberg, M.D., et al., "Sequelae of Induced First-Trimester Abortion," *American Journal of Obstetrics and Gynecology* (July 1986): 79.

382. Ronald T. Burkman, M.D., "Culture and Treatment Results in Endometritis Following Elective Abortion," *American Journal of Obstetrics and Gynecology* (July 1977): 556–9.

383. David A. Grimes, "Fatal Hemorrhage from Legal Abortion in the United States," *Surgery, Gynecology and Obstetrics* (November 1983): 461–6.

384. Ann Anschengrau Levin, "Association of Induced Abortion with Subsequent Pregnancy Loss," *Journal of the American Medical Association* (June 1980): 2495–9; Carol Madore, "A Study on the Effects of Induced Abortion on Subsequent Pregnancy Outcome," *American Journal of Obstetrics and Gynecology* (March 1981): 516–21; Shari Linn, M.D., "The Relationship Between Induced Abortion and Outcome of Subsequent Pregnancies," *American Journal of Obstetrics and Gynecology* (May 1983): 136–40.

385. Janet R. Daling, Ph.D., "Tubal Infertility in Relation to Prior Induced Abortion," *Fertility and Sterility* (March 1985): 389–94.

386. Madore, "Effects of Induced Abortion," 516–21; Linn, "Outcome of Subsequent Pregnancies," 136–40.

387. Linn, "Outcome of Subsequent Pregnancies," 136–40.

388. John A. Richardson and Geoffrey Dixon, "Effects of Legal Termination on Subsequent Pregnancy," *British Medical Journal* (1976): 1303–4.

389. The Elliot Institute, www.afterabortion.org.

390. Jeffrey M. Barrett, M.D., "Induced Abortion: A Risk Factor for Placental Previa," *American Journal of Obstetrics and Gynecology* (December 1981): 769.

391. Reardon, *Aborted Women,* 106.

392. Thomas W. Hilgers and Dennis J. Horan, *Abortion and Social Justice* (Thaxton, Va.: Sun Life, 1980), 58, 77.

393. M. C. Pike, "Oral Contraceptive Use and Early Abortion as Risk Factors for Breast Cancer in Young Women," *British Journal: Cancer 1981,* 72–6.

394. Dr. Joel Brind, "Comprehensive Review and Meta-Analysis of the Abortion/Breast Cancer Link," members.aol.com/DFjoseph/brind.html.

395. Dr. Joel Brind, text of oral testimony given before the Reproductive Health Drugs Advisory Committee of the Food and Drug Administration at its public meeting of 19 July 1996, www.epm.org/brindtest.html.

396. Dr. Mads Melbye, et. al., *New England Journal of Medicine* (336): 81–5.

397. *The Wall Street Journal,* 9 January 1997, B1.

398. *New York Times,* 10 January 1997, A32.

399. Dr. Joel Brind, "Rotten in Denmark," www.abortioncancer.com/denmark.htm.

400. Ibid.

401. For a partial list of studies linking abortion and breast cancer, see www.epm.org/breastcancer.html.

402. Dr. Joel Brind, "May Cause Cancer," *National Review,* 25 December 1995, 38.

403. Stephen L. Corson, M.D., "Clinical Perspectives: Morbidity and Morality from Second-Trimester Abortions," *Journal of Reproductive Medicine* (July 1985): 505–14.

404. Everett, personal conversation.

405. Miller, "Tale of Two Abortions," 2.

406. Everett, personal conversation.

407. Reardon, *Aborted Women,* 234.

408. Ibid., 106–7.

Argument 26

409. Six actual fifteen- to twenty-two-week babies, victims of saline abortions, are shown in "Baby Choice," a 1986 video available from Americans Against Abortion, PO Box 2680, Hayden Lake, ID 83835.

410. Dorothy F. Chappel, "A Biologist's Concern for Mother and Child," *Abortion: A Christian Understanding and Response,* ed. James K. Hoffmeier (Grand Rapids, Mich.: Baker Book House, 1987), 163.

411. Curt Young, *The Least of These* (Chicago: Moody Press, 1984), 96.

412. Drawing by Jenny Westberg, originally appeared in *Life Advocate* magazine, February 1993.

413. Chappel, "A Biologist's Concern," 161.

414. Everett, personal conversation.

415. David Grimes, "A Twenty-Six-Year-Old Seeking an Abortion," *Journal of the American Medical Association* 282 (22–29 September 1999), http://jama.ama-assn.org/issues/v282n12/full/jxr90004.html.

416. Mark Baker, "Men on Abortion," *Esquire,* March 1990, 120.

417. James Patterson and Peter Kim, *The Day America Told the Truth* (New York: Prentice Hall Press, 1991), 33.

418. Reardon, *Silent No More,* 229.

419. Warren Hern and Billie Corrigan, "What About Us? Staff Reactions to the D & E Procedure," paper presented to the Association of Planned Parenthood Physicians, 26 October 1978, 7.

420. Ibid., 1, 4, 5, 6.

421. Magda Denes, *In Necessity and Sorrow: Life and Death in an Abortion Hospital* (New York: Basic Books, 1976), 50, 58–61.

422. Ibid., 222–3.

423. *Washington Post,* 3 March 1980.
424. Sallie Tisdale, "We Do Abortions Here," *Harper's Magazine,* October 1987.
425. *New York Times,* 19 October 1994.
426. Denes, *In Necessity and Sorrow.*
427. "Meet the Abortion Providers III: The Promoters," audiotape, Prolife Action League Conference, Chicago, 3 April 1993.
428. Nathanson, *Aborting America.*
429. Everett, personal conversation.
430. *National Review,* 18 November 1991, 14.
431. "The Abortion Providers," a 1989 video available from Prolife Action League, 6160 N. Cicero, Chicago, IL 60646, (312) 777-2900.
432. Ibid.
433. Ibid.
434. Letter to President Reagan, cited by John Willke, *Abortion Questions,* 64–5.
435. Willke, *Abortion Questions,* 68.
436. "The Silent Scream," available from American Portrait Films, PO Box 809, Brunswick, OH 44212, (800) 736-4567.
437. Ibid.
438. Vincent J. Collins, M.D., Steven R. Zielinski, M.D., and Thomas J. Marzen, Esq., *Fetal Pain and Abortion: The Medical Evidence, Studies in Law & Medicine* (Chicago: Americans United for Life Legal Defense Fund, 1984), 8.
439. "Fetuses Can Feel Pain," http://maxx.mc.net/~dougp/ftrnew26.htm.
440. Julie Foster, "Baby Samuel, Mom Doing Well," *WorldNet Daily,* 16 February 2000.
441. Excerpted from statement of Brenda Pratt Shaver, R. N., before the Subcommittee on the Constitution Committee on the Judiciary, U.S. House of Representatives, Hearing on the Partial Birth Abortion Ban Act (HR 1833), 21 March 1996, (partially repeated 1 April 1996).

Argument 27
442. Mark Baker, "Men on Abortion," *Esquire,* March 1990, 125.
443. "Abortion's Adverse Physical and Psychological Effects on Women" (list of studies), www.abortionresearch.com/articles.htm#adverse.
444. For this and other studies, see Elliot Institute, www.afterabortion.org.
445. Elliot Institute press release, 20 March 2000.
446. "Tearing Down the Wall," *LifeSupport,* Spring–Summer 1991, 1–3.

447. Reardon, *Aborted Women*, 129.

448. Martina Mahler, "Abortion: The Pain No One Talks About," *Women's World*, 24 September 1991, 6.

449. "Tearing Down the Wall," 3.

450. American Psychiatric Association, *Diagnostic and Statistical Manual of Mental Disorders*, rev. ed. (1987), 250.

451. Nancy Michels, *Helping Women Recover from Abortion* (Minneapolis, Minn: Bethany House Publishers, 1988), 35–6.

452. Vincent M. Rue, et al., *A Report on the Psychological Aftermath of Abortion*, 15 September 1987, 7. Submitted to the Surgeon General by the National Right to Life Committee.

453. "Exclusive Interview: U.S. Surgeon General C. Everett Koop," *Rutherford Journal* (Spring 1989): 31.

454. Ibid.

455. Catherine A. Barnard, Ph.D., "Stress Reactions in Women Related to Induced Abortion," Association for Interdisciplinary Research in Values and Social Change (AIRVSC) *Newsletter*, Winter 1991, 1–3.

456. James L. Rogers, "Psychological Consequences of Abortion," an adaptation of a technical study presented to the American Psychological Association and the American Public Health Association, in *Abortion: A Christian Understanding and Response*, 186.

457. Ibid., 187.

458. Reardon, *Aborted Women*, 119.

459. John Leo, "Moral Complexity of Choice," *U.S. News and World Report*, 11 December 1989, 64.

460. "Psychological Sequelae of Therapeutic Abortion," editorial, *British Medical Journal* (May 1976): 1239.

461. J. R. Ashton, "The Psychological Outcome of Induced Abortion," *British Journal of Obstetrics and Gynecology* (December 1980): 1115–22.

462. Ibid.

463. "Report on the Committee on the Operation of the Abortion Law," Ottawa, Canada, 1977, 20–1.

464. Ibid.

465. Reardon, *Aborted Women*, 116.

466. "Exclusive Interview: C. Everett Koop," 31.

467. *Los Angeles Times*, 19 March 1989.

468. Judith S. Wallerstein, "Psychosocial Sequelae of Therapeutic Abortion in Young Unmarried Women," *Archives of General Psychiatry* 27 (December 1972); Carl Tishler, Ph.D., "Adolescent Suicide Attempts Following Elective Abortion: A Special Case of Anniversary Reaction," *Pediatrics* 68 (November 1981): 670–1.

469. Tishler, "Adolescent Suicide."

470. Reardon, *Aborted Women,* 250.

471. Ibid.

472. David Kupelian and Jo Ann Gasper, "Abortion, Inc.," *New Dimensions,* October 1991, 16.

473. Audrey Stout, Marietta, GA, e-mail to Randy Alcorn, 12 February 2000.

474. Kupelian and Gasper, "Abortion, Inc.," 14.

475. Ibid., 23.

476. Anne Catherine Speckhard, Ph.D., "The Psycho-Social Aspects of Stress Following Abortion" (Arlington, Va.: Family Systems Center, 1985), 1.

477. Reardon, *Aborted Women,* 134.

Argument 28

478. Planned Parenthood Federation of America, "Abortion: Facts at a Glance," n.d., 2.

479. *Miami Herald,* 17 September 1989.

480. American Rights Coalition, "Governor Closes 10% of Florida's Clinics," *The Abortion Injury Report,* May 1990, 1.

481. *Chicago Sun-Times,* 12 November 1978, cited by Marvin Olasky, *The Prodigal Press* (Westchester, Ill.: Crossway Books, 1988), 134.

482. Pamela Zekman and Pamela Warrick, "The Abortion Profiteers," *Chicago Sun-Times,* special reprint, 3 December 1978 (original publication 12 November 1978), 15.

483. Ibid., 11–5.

484. Reardon, *Aborted Women,* 245.

485. *New York Times,* 16 February 2000.

486. "Incompetent Abortion Practitioner Could Get Back License," Associated Press, 24 March 2000.

487. "Ohio Legislators Want to Close Abortion Facilities," *Prolife Infonet,* 19 February 2000, www.prolifeinfo.org.

488. Mark Crutcher, *Lime 5: Exploited by Choice* (Denton, Tex.: Life Dynamics, 1996), 19–82.

489. Ibid., 83–170.

490. Willke, *Abortion Questions,* 79.

491. Everett, personal conversation.

492. Willke, *Abortion Questions,* 79.

493. Cited by www.ohiolife.org/aborters/busi.htm.

494. Willke, *Abortion Questions,* 186.

495. Ibid.

496. "Prochoice 1990: Skeletons in the Closet," *New Dimensions,* October 1990, 31.

497. Ibid.

498. Carol Everett, *Blood Money* (Sisters, Ore.: Multnomah Publishers, 1992).

499. "Prochoice 1990," 27.

500. "Meet the Abortion Providers."

501. "Prochoice 1990," 27.

502. Everett, personal conversation.

503. "Meet the Abortion Providers."

504. Ibid.

505. Hern and Corrigan, "What about Us?" 7–8.

506. Warren M. Hern, M.D., M.P.H., *Abortion Practice* (Boulder, Colo.: Alpenglo Graphics, Inc.,1990), 132.

507. Ibid., 134

508. Hern and Corrigan, "What about Us?" 7–8.

509. Hern, *Abortion Practice,* 142.

510. Ibid., 151, 154.

511. "Court Limits Anti-Abortion Protests," staff and wire reports, *Oregonian,* 29 June 2000.

512. Dr. Carhart's clinic's web site is www.abortionclinics.org/. Information about Dr. Carhart is furnished by the clinic under "Our Doctor" at www.abortionclinics.org/our.htm. The clinic also provides large pictures and other information about "antichoice" individuals under "Our Protestors" at www.abortionclinics.org/our1.htm, instructing people to "avoid contact" with them.

513. Testimony of Leroy Carhart, M.D., www.texasrighttolife.com/whatsnew/abortionists_testimony.html; also, scanned documents of Carhart's testimony are at www.operationsaveamerica.org/streets/ne/carhart.html.

514. Randy Alcorn, "Partial Birth Abortions: What's the Big Deal?"
www.epm.org/partbirt.html.

515. Richard Carelli, (AP), "Court Blocks Nebraska Abortion Ban," *Oregonian*,
29 June 2000.

516. George F. Will, "Court Locked Itself into Terrible Choice on Abortion,"
Oregonian, 29 June 2000, D9.

517. Drawing by Jenny Westberg, originally printed in the *Life Advocate*, "D & X—
Grim Technology for Abortion's Older Victims," February 1993.

518. Linda Bowles, Creator's Syndicate, September 23, 1996,
www.epm.org/partbirt.html.

519. Ellen Goodman, "Abortion Case Draws Justices into Maelstrom," *Oregonian*,
25 April 2000, E13.

520. Stephen D. Schwarz, *The Moral Question of Abortion* (Chicago, Ill.: Loyola
University Press, 1990), 143.

521. Ann Tilson, "Exposé on Abortion in Wichita," *Kansans for Life*, May 1991, 10.

522. Robert D. Orr, M.D. and Norman Pang, M.D, *A Review of 20th Century
Practice and a Content Analysis of Oaths Administered in Medical Schools
in the U.S. and Canada in 1993*.

523. Ibid.

524. Robert Jay Lifton, *The Nazi Doctors* (New York: Basic Books, 1986), 337–83.

525. *National Review*, 2 March 1992, 12.

526. *World Medical Association Bulletin* 1 (April 1949): 22.

527. *World Medical Association Bulletin* 2 (January 1950): 6–34.

528. American Medical Association statement on abortion, *Medical Holocausts* 1
(Houston, Tex.: Nordland Publishing International, n.d.): 28–30.

PART FIVE: ARGUMENTS CONCERNING THE HARD CASES

Argument 29

529. Alan F. Guttmacher, "Abortion—Yesterday, Today and Tomorrow," in *The Case
for Legalized Abortion Now* (Berkeley, Calif.: Diablo Press, 1967).

530. Landrum Shettles and David Rorvik, *Rites of Life* (Grand Rapids, Mich.:
Zondervan Publishing House, 1983), 129.

531. Mimi Hall, "Even When a Life Saved, Abortion a Divisive Issue," *USA Today*,
26 July 1991, 2A.

Argument 30

532. Asbel S. Green, "Appeals Court Rules against Suit about Fetus," *Oregonian,* 2 March 2000.

533. David C. Reardon, *Aborted Women: Silent No More* (Westchester, Ill.: Crossway Books, 1987), 172.

534. "Abortion in the United States," *Facts in Brief,* Alan Guttmacher Institute, n.d.

535. Susan Kitching, *London Sunday Times,* 11 February 1990.

536. Thomas Hilgers, Dennis Horan, and David Mall, *New Perspectives on Human Abortion* (Frederick, Md.: University Publications of America, 1981), 54.

537. Reardon, *Aborted Women,* 173.

538. Hymie Gordon, "Amniocentesis," *Primum Non Nocere,* September 1980, 4–6.

539. Ibid.

540. C. Everett Koop and Francis Schaeffer, *Whatever Happened to the Human Race?* (Westchester, Ill.: Crossway Books, 1979), 36.

541. John Willke, *Abortion Questions and Answers* (Cincinnati, Ohio: Hayes Publishing Co., 1988), 211.

542. C. Everett Koop, "The Slide to Auschwitz," in Ronald Reagan, *Abortion and the Conscience of the Nation* (Nashville, Tenn.: Thomas Nelson, 1984), 45–6.

543. Gregg Cunningham, "Abortion and the New Disability Cleansing," *National Review,* 10 November 1997, www.cbrinfo.org/articles.html.

544. Curtis Young, *The Least of These* (Chicago: Moody Press, 1983), 118.

545. W. Peacock, "Active Voluntary Euthanasia," *Issues in Law and Medicine,* 1987, cited by Willke, *Abortion Questions,* 212.

546. Story told by Jerome LeJeune, cited by Willke, *Abortion Questions,* 211.

547. J. Lloyd and K. Laurence, "Response to Termination of Pregnancy for Genetic Reasons," *Zeitschrift fur Kinderchirurgie* 38, suppl. 2 (1983): 98–9.

548. B. Blumberg, et al., "The Psychological Sequelae of Abortion Performed for Genetic Indication," *American Journal of Obstetrics and Gynecology* 2 (1975): 215–24.

549. R. Furlong and R. Black, "Pregnancy Termination for Genetic Indications: The Impact on Families," *Social Work Health Care* 10 (1984): 17–34.

550. Philip Ney, "A Consideration of Abortion Survivors," *Child Psychiatry in Human Development* 13 (1983): 168–79.

551. *Feminists for Life Debate Handbook* (Kansas City, Mo.: Feminists for Life of America, n.d.), 18.

552. "Dr. Bernard Nathanson Testifies Before Congress on Reproductive Technologies," *Washington Times,* 10 February 2000.

553. Carey Goldberg, "On Web, Models Auction Their Eggs to Bidders for Beautiful Children," *New York Times,* 23 October 1999, A11, excerpted from Dr. James Dobson, *Family News from Focus on the Family,* January 2000.

Argument 31

554. Jean Staker Garton, *Who Broke the Baby?* (Minneapolis, Minn: Bethany House Publishers, 1979), 76.

555. "Who Has Abortions?" The Alan Guttmacher Institute, www.agi-usa.org/pubs/fb_induced_abortion.html.

556. "Abortion: Facts at a Glance," Planned Parenthood Federation of America, n.d., 1.

557. Willke, *Abortion Questions,* 146–50.

558. Kathleen C. Basile and Linda E. Saltzman, "Sexual Violence Surveillance: Uniform Definitions and Recommended Data Elements," 4.18, p.67, Centers for Disease Control, November 2002.

559. Sue Reily, "Life Uneasy for Woman at Center of Abortion Ruling," *Oregonian,* 9 May 1989, A2.

560. Garton, *Who Broke the Baby?* 77.

561. "Alan Keyes Continues His Campaign, Hammers on Abortion," *Prolife Infonet,* www.prolifeinfo.org, 27 February 2000.

562. *Feminists for Life Debate Handbook,* 14.

Final Thoughts on the Hard Cases

563. U.S. Department of Health and Human Services, Centers for Disease Control, *Abortion Surveillance Report,* May 1983.

PART SIX: ARGUMENTS AGAINST THE CHARACTER OF PROLIFERS

Argument 32

564. Naomi Wolf, "Our Bodies, Our Souls," *New Republic,* 16 October 1995, www.epm.org/naomiwolf.html.

565. Gregg Cunningham, *Hard Truth User's Guide* (Cleveland, Ohio: American Portrait Films, 1991), 5–6, 19.

566. The Genocide Awareness Project, www.cbrinfo.org/gap.html.

567. Gregg Cunningham, director of Center for Bio-Ethical Reform, phone conversation, 10 May 2000.

568. "Negative Psychological Impact of Sonography in Abortion," *Ob. Gyn. News,* 15–28 February 1986.

569. Thomas Hilgers and Dennis Horan, eds., *Abortion and Social Justice* (New York: Sheed & Ward, 1972), 292.

570. John Willke, *Abortion Questions and Answers* (Cincinnati, Ohio: Hayes Publishing Co., 1988), 200–2.

571. Ibid, 203; R. Collins, *Arizona Republic,* 26 March 1981.

572. Thomas Glessner, *Achieving an Abortion-Free America by 2001* (Portland, Ore.: Multnomah Press, 1990), 39.

573. *Abortion "As Birth Control" and Abortion for Gender Selection,* Fact Sheet (New York: Planned Parenthood Federation of America, n.d.), 3.

574. Tom Ehart, "She Was an Aborted Baby...and Lived," *Brio,* April 1992, 14–7.

575. Jon E. Dougherty, "New Definition for Therapeutic Abortions? Hospital Delivers Problem Babies, Then Lets Them Die," WorldNetDaily.com, 1 October 1999; www.tpcc.net/criticalconcerns/arch018.htm.

Argument 33

576. Polly Rothstein and Marian Williams, "Choice" (New York: Westchester Coalition for Legal Abortion, 1983), printed and distributed by the NARAL Foundation, Washington, D.C.

577. Abigail Van Buren, "Questions for the Foes of Abortion," *Universal Press Syndicate,* n.d.

578. Francis J. Beckwith, *Politically Correct Death: Answering the Arguments for Abortion Rights* (Grand Rapids, Mich.: Baker Book House, 1993), 16.

579. John Willke, "The Real Woman's Movement," *National Right to Life News,* 14 December 1989, 3.

580. Guy Condon, "You Say Choice; I Say Murder," *Christianity Today,* 24 June 1991, 23.

581. Several news programs have attempted to discredit abortion alternative centers as "phony abortion clinics" that deceive women and give them inaccurate medical information. Out of thousands of such clinics, they were able to find a few that could be presented unfavorably. However, even if their portrayal were accurate, this would not discredit the 99 percent of clinics that provide accurate information and loving assistance to women. Many more women have come forward to say that it is abortion clinics, not abortion alternative centers, that have misled them and disseminated inaccurate medical information (see Part 4: Arguments Concerning Health and Safety).

Unfortunately, it does not serve the "politically correct" posture of the television networks to do exposés of abortion clinics.

582. "Prolifers Shut Out of Hearing," *Life Advocate*, November 1991, 8.

583. Lynn Vincent, "Can't Beat 'em? Smear 'em," *World*, 22 January 2000, 22.

584. "The Deceptive Practices of Crisis Pregnancy Centers," www.wcla.org/98-autumn/au98-23.htm.

585. CareNet, www.care-net.org.

586. "Anti-Abortion Counseling Centers: A Consumer's Alert to Deception, Harassment, and Medical Malpractice," www.plannedparenthood.com/library/opposition/antiabcenters.htm.

587. Brooklyn Prochoice Network, www.echonyc.com/~bpcn/fakeclinic.html.

588. Mark Crutcher, "Abortion Questions They'd Rather Duck," *Focus on the Family Citizen*, 20 May 1991, 2.

589. "Abortion Providers Tell Their Stories," www.catholic-church.org/prolifeaction/stories.

Argument 34

590. Lydia Saad, "Americans Divided Over Abortion Debate," Gallup News Service Poll Releases, 18 May 1999, www.gallup.com/poll/releases/pr990518.asp.

591. Willke, "Woman's Movement," 3.

592. *Feminists for Life Debate Handbook* (Kansas City, Mo.: Feminists for Life of America, n.d.), 21.

593. "Abortion and Moral Beliefs: A Survey of American Opinion," conducted by the Gallup Organization, 1991, 4–7.

594. Willke, "Woman's Movement," 3.

595. Condon, "You Say Choice," 23.

596. David C. Reardon, *Aborted Women: Silent No More* (Westchester, Ill.: Crossway Books, 1987), 71.

597. Willke, "Woman's Movement," 3.

598. Ibid.

599. Clifton Fadimar, ed., *The Little, Brown Book of Anecdotes* (Boston, Mass.: Little, Brown and Co., 1985), 18.

600. Frederica Mathewes-Green, *Real Choices* (Sisters, Ore.: Multnomah Publishers, 1994), 11.

601. Donald Granberg, "The Abortion Activists," *Family Planning Perspectives*, July–August 1981, 157–63.

602. Reardon, *Aborted Women*, 70–1.

Argument 35
603. Rothstein and Williams, "Choice."
604. Willke, *Abortion Questions*, 180.

Argument 36
605. Bob Jones, "God Save the United States, *World*, 6 May 2000,
     www.worldmag.com/world/issue/05-06-00/cover_1.asp.
606. Ann Scheidler, "Should Abortion Providers Face FACE?" www.hli.org.
607. "1999 Year-End Analysis of Trends of Violence and Disruption Against
     Reproductive Health Care Clinics," 19 January 2000,
     www.prochoice.org/violence/vdanaly99.htm.
608. James T. Burtchaell, "Media's Blind (and Biased) Eye," *Oregonian*,
     15 September 1991, BI–B3.
609. *USA Today*, 22 August 1991.
610. Michael Ebert, "Violence! Mayhem! or How the Media Blew It," *Focus on the
     Family Citizen*, 18 November 1991, 7.
611. Ibid., 6.
612. Ibid.
613. Burtchaell, "Media's Blind (and Biased) Eye," B1.
614. William Cotter, *The Boston Globe*, 4 May 2000, A23.
615. Ibid.
616. Randy Alcorn, *Is Rescuing Right?* (Downers Grove, Ill.: InterVarsity Press,
     1990), 169. A brief summary of the major tenets of this book can be found at
     www.epm.org/rescue6.html .
617. Ibid., 150–1.
618. Ibid., 84–99.
619. Ibid., 40–56, 100–22.
620. B. D. Colen, "The Anti-Abortion High Ground," *New York Newsday*, 8 November
     1988.
621. St. Louis Circuit Court, St. Louis County, MO, 16 August 1989.
622. Alcorn, *Is Rescuing Right?* 163–4.
623. K. L. Billingsley, "The J Street Five," *National Review*, 16 December 1991, 25.
624. Alcorn, *Is Rescuing Right?* 9.

625. "Victims of 'ProLife' Violence," *Abortion Rights Activist,*
     www.cais.com/agm/main/index.html.

626. National Abortion Federation, "Incidents of Violence and Disruption against
     Abortion Providers" (Washington, DC: NAF, 1992).

627. National Abortion Federation, "Extreme Violence Against Providers,"
     1 February 2000, www.prochoice.org.

628. David Moore, "Vandals Hit Jakobowski's Clinic," *Life Advocate,* November
     1991, 16–7.

Argument 37

629. Francis Beckwith, "Answering the Arguments for Abortion Rights," *Christian
     Research Journal,* four-part analysis (Fall 1990, Winter 1991, Spring 1991,
     Summer 1991).

630. Planned Parenthood of New York City fundraising letter, "A Century of
     Progress in Peril," cited by Robert Marshall and Charles Donovan, *Blessed Are
     the Barren: The Social Policy of Planned Parenthood* (San Francisco:
     Ignatius, 1991), 203.

631. *Washington Post,* 14 February 1990.

632. Marshall and Donovan, 203.

633. Beckwith, *Politically Correct Death,* 57.

634. Landrum Shettles and David Rorvik, *Rites of Life* (Grand Rapids, Mich.:
     Zondervan Publishing House, 1983), 112–3.

635. "Plan Your Children for Health and Happiness" (New York: Planned
     Parenthood—World Population, 1963), 1.

636. Planned Parenthood of Chicago fact sheet "Abortion," 2.

637. "Abortion and Moral Beliefs: A Survey of American Opinion," conducted by the
     Gallup Organization, 1991, 4–5.

638. Ibid.

639. George Will, "The Case of the Unborn Patient" in *The Pursuit of Virtue and
     Other Tory Notions* (New York: Touchstone, 1982), 109.

640. "Abortion: For Survival," a video produced by the Fund for the Feminist Majority.

641. Ibid.

642. "Nine Reasons Why Abortions Are Legal" (New York: Planned Parenthood
     Federation of America, 1989), 8–9.

643. Rothstein and Williams, "Choice."

644. Shirley McSilvers, "'Jane Roe Reaffirms Her Faith, Prolife Stance," *Christian
     News Northwest,* April 2000, 11.

645. "Norma McCorvey Wows Conference," *Life in Oregon*, April–May 2000.

646. Ann Scheidler, an interview with Norma McCorvey, the "Roe" of "Roe vs. Wade" and Sandra Cano, the "Doe" of "Doe vs. Bolton," Chicago Prolife Action League, 20 April 1996.

647. *Doe* v. *Bolton*, U.S. Supreme Court, January 1973, No. 70-40, IV, 11.

648. Scheidler, *An Interview*.

Argument 38

649. *Los Angeles Times*, 17 October 1986.

650. Centers for Disease Control, www.cdc.gov/nchs/releases/00facts/trends.htm.

651. Frederica Mathewes-Green, "Embryonic Trend: How Do We Explain the Drop in Abortions?" *Policy Review*, Summer 1995, no.73.

652. David Kupelian and Jo Ann Gasper, "Abortion, Inc.," *New Dimensions*, October 1991, 18.

653. "Three Face Charges in Teen's Abortion," *Oregonian*, 28 April 1994, A1, A16.

654. Ibid.

655. PPAC Issue Library, www.ppacca.org/issues/index.asp.

656. Ibid.

657. Ibid., 19.

658. Ibid.

659. Alan Guttmacher Institute, *Issues in Brief* 4 (March 1984): 3.

660. Robert Ruff, "An Ingenious System for Milking Tax Payers," *New Dimensions*, October 1991, 17.

661. Transcript of Planned Parenthood presentation, 21 April 1986, Ramona High School, Riverside, CA.

662. Lynn Vincent, "Profiting from Losses," *World*, 22 April 2000, 36.

663. Ibid.

664. Press release on *20/20* Fetal Body Parts Scandal, *Life Dynamics*, March 2000.

665. Rochelle Sharpe, "She Died Because of a Law," *Ms.*, July–August 1990, 80–1.

666. Frederica Mathewes-Green, "The Becky Bell Tragedy," *Sisterlife*, Fall 1990, 1.

667. Bernard Nathanson, "In Memoriam," *Bernadell Technical Bulletin*, November 1990, 4.

668. James A. Miller, "A Tale of Two Abortions," *Human Life International Reports*, March 1991, 1.

669. Cal Thomas, "New Combatants Join Parental Consent Fight," *The Milwaukee Journal*, 9 August 1990.

670. Nathanson, "In Memoriam," 4.
671. "Exploiting the Bells' Tragic Situation," *National Right to Life News,* 16 August 1990, 14.
672. Thomas, "New Combatants."
673. Ibid.
674. "Exploiting the Bells' Tragic Situation," 14.
675. Miller, "Two Abortions," 11.

SUMMARY ARGUMENT

Argument 39

676. Antoinette Bosco, "Touch of Life," *Reader's Digest,* July 1991, 125–6.
677. James Dobson and Gary Bauer, *Children at Risk* (Waco, Tex: Word Books, 1990), 151.
678. Figure based on number of abortions in 1997.
679. *Mother Jones,* May–June 1991, 31ff.
680. Donald Robinson, "Save Our Babies," *Parade Magazine,* 30 June 1991, 8.
681. "Slaughtering Other Babies," *Sunday Oregonian,* 18 August 1991, B8.
682. Bernard Nathanson, "Prochoice 1990," *New Dimensions,* October 1990, 38.
683. Rothstein and Williams, "Choice," 5.
684. 49 N. J. 22, 227A.2d 689 (1967), cited by Cal Thomas, *Uncommon Sense* (Brentwood, Tenn.: Wolgemuth and Hyatt, 1990), 6.
685. George Will, *The Pursuit of Happiness and Other Sobering Thoughts* (New York: Harper Colophon, 1978), 61.
686. Herbert London, "Legalized Abortions and Infanticide," *New Dimensions,* June 1991, 71.
687. Ibid.
688. Peter Singer, *Rethinking Life and Death* (New York: St. Martin's Griffin, 1996), 217.
689. Will, *Pursuit of Happiness,* 62–3.
690. "Bad Looks Lead to Abortion in England," *Prolife Infonet,* 2 June 1998.
691. *Feminists for Life Debate Handbook* (Kansas City, Mo.: Feminists for Life of America, n.d.), 9.
692. Judie Brown, Jerome LeJeune, and Robert G. Marshall, *RU-486: The Human Pesticide* (Stafford, Va.: American Life League, n.d.).
693. George Grant, *The Quick and the Dead: RU-486 and the New Chemical*

Warfare Against Your Family (Westchester, Ill.: Crossway Books, 1991).

694. Silvestre, et. al., "Interruption of Pregnancy with RU-486 and Prostaglandin," *New England Journal of Medicine* 322 (8 March 1990).

695. A. Riding, "Frenchwomen's Death...," *New York Times,* 10 April 1991, A-10.

696. Ulmann, et. al., "Termination...With RU-486 and a Prostaglandin Analogy," *Acta OBGYN Scand.* 71 (1992): 166.

697. Testimony, M. Louviere, M.D., at USFDA hearing, 19 July 1996.

698. R. Henrion, "RU-486 Abortions," *Nature* 338 (9 March 1989): 110; Pons, "RU-486 Teratogenocity," *Lancet* 338 (23 November 1991): 1333.

699. "RU-486 A Human Pesticide," Hayes Publishing Co., 1997.

700. "Efficacy of Mifepristone and Prostaglandin in First Trimester Abortion," UK Multicentre Trial, *Br. J. OB-Gyn* 97 (June 1990): 480–6.

701. "Drug Firm Defends Marketing Strategy," *Le Monde* (French), *Guardian Weekly* (English), 19 August 1990, 16.

702. Richard D. Glasow, "RU-486's Dangers Begin to Surface in Media," *National Right to Life News,* 13 August 1991, 6.

703. Charlotte Allen, "Safe and Easy? Not RU-486," *Focus on the Family Citizen,* 16 September 1991, 14–5.

704. Janice Raymond, Renate Klein, and Lynette J. Dumble, *RU-486: Misconceptions, Myths and Morals* (Cambridge: Massachusetts Institute of Technology, 1991).

705. Mary Voboril, "The Abortion Pill," *Miami Herald,* 13 October 1991, 1J, 4J.

706. "RU-486 Myths," *Life in Oregon,* February–March 2000.

707. "Singer's Sanctimonious Song," *Federalist Digest,* 18 January 2000.

Final Appeals

708. George Gilder, *Men and Marriage* (Gretna, La.: Pelican, 1992).

709. *Family Planning Perspectives,* July–August 1996, 12.

710. Wolf, www.epm.org/naomiwolf.html.

711. Reardon, *Aborted Women,* 31.

712. Bernard Nathanson, keynote address, National Right to Life Convention, Anaheim, CA, 26 June 1980.

713. Cal Thomas, *Uncommon Sense* (Brentwood, Tenn.: Wolgemuth and Hyatt, 1990), 7.

714. "News Briefs," *Action,* newsletter of the Rutherford Institute, October 1991, 7.

715. Dr. Bernard Nathanson, *The Abortion Papers* (New York: Frederick Fell, 1983), 170.

716. Ibid.

717. Randy Alcorn, *Does the Birth Control Pill Cause Abortions?* (Gresham, Ore.: Eternal Perspective Ministries, 5th ed., 2000), www.epm.org/prolife.html.

718. "Abortion and Moral Beliefs: A Survey of American Opinion," conducted by the Gallup Organization, 1991, 17.

719. Ibid.

720. Lydia Saad, "Americans Divided Over Abortion Debate," 18 May 1999, Gallup News Service Poll Releases; www.gallup.com/poll/releases/pr990518.asp.

721. *Eugene* (Ore.) *Register Guard*, 7 November 1990.

722. Ibid.

723. *Family Planning Perspectives*, July–August 1996, 12.

724. The "Hard Truth" video is available from American Portrait Films, PO Box 809, Brunswick, OH 44212, (800) 736-4567. The "Harder Truth" video is available from the Center for Bio-Ethical Reform, PO Box 8056, Mission Hills, CA 91346, 1-818-360-2477.

725. Randy Alcorn, *Lord Foulgrin's Letters* (Sisters, Ore.: Multnomah Publishers, 2000).

726. Randy Alcorn, "Life Issues: Distraction from the Great Commission or Part of It?" www.epm.org/greatcom.html.

727. Gregg Cunningham of the Center for Bio-Ethical Reform offers an excellent one-day seminar and printed materials concerning the development of such a strategy for churches and prolife groups. He can be contacted at PO Box 8056, Mission Hills, CA 91346, (818) 360-2477.

728. Charles Colson, *Kingdoms in Conflict* (Grand Rapids, Mich.: Zondervan Publishing House, 1988), 102.

APPENDIX A: FINDING FORGIVENESS AFTER AN ABORTION

729. Naomi Wolf, "Our Bodies, Our Souls," *New Republic*, 16 October 1995, www.epm.org/naomiwolf.html.

APPENDIX B: ABORTION IN THE BIBLE AND CHURCH HISTORY

730. Virginia Ramey Mollenkott, "Reproductive Choice: Basic to Justice for Women," *Christian Scholar's Review*, March 1988, 291.

731. James Hoffmeier, *Abortion: A Christian Understanding* (Grand Rapids, Mich.: Baker Book House, 1987), 46, 50; Eugene Quay, "Abortion: Medical

and Legal Foundations," *Georgetown Law Review* (1967): 395, 420; Meredith G. Kline, *"Lex Talionis* and the Human Fetus," *Journal of the Evangelical Theological Society* (September 1977): 200–1.

732. Lawrence O. Richards, *Expository Dictionary of Bible Words* (Grand Rapids, Mich.: Zondervan Publishing House, 1985), 156–7.

733. James Hoffmeier, ed., *Abortion: A Christian Understanding and Response* (Grand Rapids, Mich.: Baker Book House, 1987), 62.

734. John Jefferson Davis, *Abortion and the Christian* (Phillipsburg, N.J.: Presbyterian and Reformed, 1984), 52.

735. Kline, *"Lex Talionis,"* 193.

736. *A Prochoice Bible Study* (Seattle, Wash.: Episcopalians for Religious Freedom, 1989).

737. Hoffmeier, *Abortion,* 53.

738. See George Grant, *Grand Illusions: The Legacy of Planned Parenthood* (Brentwood, Tenn: Wolgemuth and Hyatt, 1988), 190–1.

739. Michael Gorman, *Abortion and the Early Church* (Downers Grove, Ill.: InterVarsity Press, 1982), 9.

740. John Calvin, *Commentary on Pentateuch,* cited in *Crisis Pregnancy Center Volunteer Training Manual* (Washington, D.C.: Christian Action Council, 1984), 7.

741. Dietrich Bonhoeffer, *Ethics* (New York: Macmillan, 1955), 131.

742. Karl Barth, *Church Dogmatics,* vol. 3, ed. Geoffrey Bromiley (Edinburgh: T & T Clark, 1961), 415, 418.

743. An excellent refutation of the various "Christian" prochoice arguments is made by philosophy professor Francis Beckwith in "A Critical Appraisal of Theological Arguments for Abortion Rights," *Bibliotheca Sacra* (July/September 1991): 337–55.

APPENDIX D: CHEMICAL ABORTIONS IN LIGHT OF HISTORY AND SCRIPTURE

744. *Family Planning Perspectives,* July–August 1996, 12.

745. Peter Brimelow, "Who Has Abortions?" *Forbes,* 18 October 1999, www.forbes.com/forbes/99/1018/6410110a.htm.

746. Irving Sivin, "IUDs are Contraceptives, Not Abortifacients: A Comment on Research and Belief," *Studies in Family Planning,* vol. 20, no. 6 (November–December 1989), 355–9.

747. Drug Facts and Comparisons, 1996, 419.

748. Robert W. Kistner, ed. *Gynecology: Principles and Practices,* 3rd ed.(St. Louis, Mo.: YearBook Medical Publishers, 1979), 735.

749. Dr. Joseph W. Goldzieher states, "Endometrial resistance to implantation is an important mechanism of the minipill," in *Hormonal Contraception: Pills, Injections and Implants,* 35 (Essential Medical Information Systems, PO Box 811247, Dallas, TX).

750. *Physician's Desk Reference,* 1996 edition (page 1872).

751. "FDA Panel: Birth Control Pills Safe As Morning-After Drug," *Virginian-Pilot,* 29 June 1996, A1, A6.

752. Peter Modica, "FDA Nod to 'Morning-After' Pill Is Lauded," *Medical Tribune News Service,* 26 February 1997.

753. *World,* 8 March, 1997, 9.

754. Marilyn Elias, "Docs Spread Word: Pill Works on Morning After," *USA Today,* 29 April 1997, 1A.

755. Fr. Frank Pavone, "Wishful Thinking," *Prolife Infonet,* 1 February 2000.

APPENDIX E: DOES THE BIRTH CONTROL PILL CAUSE ABORTIONS?

756. Randy Alcorn, *ProLife Answers to ProChoice Arguments* (Sisters, Ore.: Multnomah Publishers, 1992, 1994), 118.

757. *Danforth's Obstetrics and Gynecology,* 7th ed. (Philadelphia, Pa.: J. B. Lippincott Co., 1994), 626.

758. Nine Van der Vange, "Ovarian Activity During Low Dose Oral Contraceptives," in *Contemporary Obstetrics and Gynecology,* G. Chamberlain, ed. (London: Butterworths, 1988), 315–6.

759. *Hippocrates,* May–June 1988, 35.

760. Pharmacists for Life, *Oral Contraceptives and IUDs: Birth Control or Abortifacients?* November 1989, 1.

761. *Physician's Desk Reference* (Montvale, N.J.: Medical Economics, 1998).

762. *PDR,* 1995, 1782.

763. Stephen G. Somkuti, et al., "The Effect of Oral Contraceptive Pills on Markers of Endometrial Receptivity," *Fertility and Sterility,* vol. 65, no. 3 (March 1996), 488.

764. "Escape Ovulation in Women Due to the Missing of Low Dose Combination Oral Contraceptive Pills," *Contraception,* September 1980, 241.

765. G. Virginia Upton, "The Phasic Approach to Oral Contraception,"

International Journal of Fertility, vol. 28 (1988), 129.

766. E. K. Kastrup, ed., *Drug Facts and Comparisons,* annual edition (St. Louis, Mo.: Facts and Comparisons, 1997).

767. H. I. Abdalla, A. A. Brooks, M. R. Johnson, A. Kirkland, A. Thomas, and J. W. Studd "Endometrial Thickness: A Predictor of Implantation in Ovum Recipients?" *Human Reprod* 9 (1994): 363–5.

768. J. M. Bartoli, G. Moulin, L. Delannoy, C. Chagnaud, and M. Kasbarian, "The Normal Uterus on Magnetic Resonance Imaging and Variations Associated with the Hormonal State," *Surg Radiol Anat* 13 (1991): 213-20; B. E. Demas, H. Hricak, and R. B. Jaffe, "Uterine MR Imaging: Effects of Hormonal Stimulation," *Radiology* 159 (1986): 123-6; S. McCarthy, C. Tauber, and J. Gore, "Female Pelvic Anatomy: MR Assessment of Variations during the Menstrual Cycle and with Use of Oral Contraceptives," *Radiology* 160 (1986): 119–23.

769. H. K. Brown, B. S. Stoll, S. V. Nicosia, J. V. Fiorica, P. S. Hambley, L. P. Clarke, and M. L. Silbiger, "Uterine Junctional Zone: Correlation between Histologic Findings and MR Imaging," *Radiology* 179 (1991): 409–13.

770. Abdalla, et al., "Endometrial thickness"; R. P. Dickey, T. T. Olar, S. N. Taylor, D. N. Curole, and E. M. Matulich, "Relationship of Endometrial Thickness and Pattern to Fecundity in Ovulation Induction Cycles: Effect of Clomiphene Citrate Alone and with Human Menopausal Gonadotropin," *Fertil Steril* 59 (1993): 756–60; Y. Gonen, R. F. Casper, W. Jacobson, and J. Blankier, "Endometrial Thickness and Growth During Ovarian Stimulation: A Possible Predictor of Implantation in In-Vitro Fertilization," *Fertil Steril* 52 (1989): 446–50; L. B. Schwartz, A. S. Chiu, M. Courtney, L. Krey, and C. Schmidt-Sarosi, "The Embryo Versus Endometrium Controversy Revisited As It Relates to Predicting Pregnancy Outcome in In-Vitro Fertilization-Embryo Transfer Cycles," *Hum Reprod* 12 (1997): 45–50; Z. Shoham Z, et al., "Is It Possible to Run a Successful Ovulation Induction Program Based Solely on Ultrasound Monitoring: The Importance Of Endometrial Measurements," *Fertil Steril* 56 (1991): 836–841; N. Noyes, H. C. Liu, K. Sultan, G. Schattman, and Z. Rosenwaks, "Endometrial Thickness Appears to Be a Significant Factor in Embryo Implantation in In-Vitro Fertilization," *Hum Reprod* 10 (1995): 919–22; J. A. Vera, B. Arguello, and C. A. Crisosto, "Predictive Value of Endometrial Pattern and Thickness in the Result of In Vitro Fertilization and Embryo Transfer," *Rev Chil Obstet Gynecol* 60 (1995): 195–8; J. H. Check, K. Nowroozi, J. Choe, D. Lurie, and C. Dietterich, "The Effect of Endometrial

Thickness and Echo Pattern on In Vitro Fertilization Outcome in Donor Oocyte-Embryo Transfer Cycle," *Fertil Steril* 59 (1993): 72–5; J. B. Oliveira, R. L. Baruffi, A. L. Mauri, C. G. Petersen, M. C. Borges, and J. G. Franco Jr, "Endometrial Ultrasonography As a Predictor of Pregnancy in an In-Vitro Fertilization Programme after Ovarian Stimulation and Gonadotrophin-Releasing Hormone and Gonadotrophins," *Hum Reprod* 12 (1997): 2515–8; C. Bergh, T. Hillensjo, and L. Nilsson, "Sonographic Evaluation of the Endometrium in In-Vitro Fertilization IVF Cycles. A Way To Predict Pregnancy?" *Acta Obstet Gynecol Scand* 71 (1992): 624–8.

771. H. I. Abdalla, et al., "Endometrial Thickness"; Dickey, et al., "Relationship of Endometrial Thickness"; Gonen, et al., "Endometrial Thickness and Growth"; Oliveira, et al., "Endometrial Ultrasonography As a Predictor"; Bergh, et al., "Sonographic Evaluation of the Endometrium."

772. The 5mm figure is from A. Glissant, J. de Mouzon, and R. Frydman, "Ultrasound Study of the Endometrium during In Vitro Fertilization Cycles," *Fertil Steril* 44 (1985): 786–90. The 13mm figure is from R. Rabinowitz, N. Laufer, A. Lewin, D. Navot, I. Bar, E. J. Margalioth, and J. J. Schenker, "The Value of Ultrasonographic Endometrial Measurement in the Prediction of Pregnancy Following In Vitro Fertilization," *Fertil Steril* 45 (1986): 824–8.

773. McCarthy, et al., "Female Pelvic Anatomy."

774. *Physician's Desk Reference*; Kastrup, "Drug Facts."

775. Kristine Severyn, "Abortifacient Drugs and Devices: Medical and Moral Dilemmas," *Linacre Quarterly,* August 1990, 55.

776. Walter L. Larimore and Joseph Stanford, "Postfertilization Effects of Oral Contraceptives and Their Relation to Informed Consent," *Archives of Family Medicine* 9 (February, 2000); Walter L. Larimore, "The Abortifacient Effect of the Birth Control Pill and the Principle of Double Effect," *Ethics and Medicine,* January 2000.

777. Walter L. Larimore and Randy Alcorn, "Using the Birth Control Pill is Ethically Unacceptable," in John F. Kilner, Paige C. Cunningham,and W. David Hager, eds., *The Reproduction Revolution* (Grand Rapids, Mich.: Wm. B. Eerdmans Publishing Co., 2000), 179–91.

778. Susan Crockett, Joseph L. DeCook, Donna Harrison, and Camilla Hersh, "Using Hormone Contraceptives Is a Decision Involving Science, Scripture, and Conscience," in John F. Kilner, Paige C. Cunningham, and W. David Hager, eds., *The Reproduction Revolution* (Grand Rapids, Mich.: Wm. B. Eerdmans

Publishing Co., 2000), 192–201.

779. J. B. Stanford and K. D. Daly, "Menstrual and Mucus Cycle Characteristics in Women Discontinuing Oral Contraceptives (Abstract)," *Paediatr Perinat Epidemiol* 9 (1995): A9.

780. V. Chowdhury, U. M. Joshi, K. Gopalkrishna, S. Betrabet, S. Mehta, and B. N. Saxena, "'Escape' Ovulation in Women Due to the Missing of Low Dose Combination Oral Contraceptive Pills," *Contraception* 22 (1980): 241–7.

781. J. Thorburn, C. Berntsson, M. Philipso, and B. Lindbolm, "Background Factors of Ectopic Pregnancy—I. Frequency Distribution in a Case-Control Study," *Eur J Obstet Gynecol Reprod Biol* 23 (1986): 321–31 (the original data was reevaluated by B. W. J. Mol, W. M. Ankum, P. M. M. Bossuyt, and F. Van deeeer Veen, "Contraception and the Risk of Ectopic Pregnancy: A Meta Analysis," *Contraception* 52 (1995): 337–41); J. Coste, N. Job-Spira, H. Fernandez, E. Papiernik, and A. Spira, "Risk Factors for Ectopic Pregnancy: A Case-Control Study in France, with Special Focus on Infectious Factors," *Am J Epidemiol* 133 (1991): 839–49.

782. Coste, et al., "Risk Factors For Ectopic Pregnancy."

783. Thorburn, et al., "Background Factors of Ectopic Pregnancy."

784. Larimore and J. B. Stanford, "Postfertilization Effects"; Thorburn, et al., "Background Factors" (the original data was reevaluated by Mol, et al., "Contraception and the Risk").

785. Alcorn, *Does the Birth Control Pill Cause Abortions?*; W. L. Larimore and J. B. Stanford, "Postfertilization Effects of Oral Contraceptives and Their Relation to Informed Consent"; W. L. Larimore, "The Growing Debate about the Abortifacient Effect of the Birth Control Pill and the Principle of the Double Effect," *Ethics and Medicine: In Review.*

786. J. L. DeCook, J. McIlhaney, et al. *Hormonal Contraceptives: Are they Abortifacients?* (Sparta, Mich.: Frontlines Publishing, 1998).

787. Randy Alcorn, *Does the Birth Control Pill Cause Abortions?* 5th ed. (Gresham, Ore.: Eternal Perspective Ministries), 50–73.

APPENDIX F: FIFTY WAYS TO HELP UNBORN BABIES AND THEIR MOTHERS

788. Royce Dunn, Director, "Please Let Me Live," *Life Chain Coordinators Manual,* 6–7.

APPENDIX J: COMMUNICATING THE PROLIFE MESSAGE

789. This appendix also appears at www.epm.org/abocomun.html.

INDEX

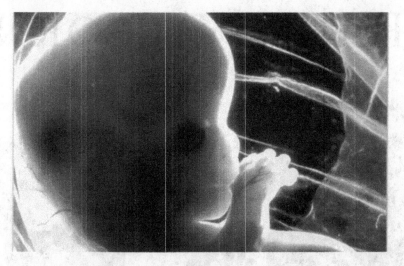

Live unborn child fifty-six days after conception.

"While giving an anesthetic for a ruptured ectopic pregnancy...I was handed what I believe was the smallest living human ever seen.... This tiny human was perfectly developed, with long, tapering fingers, feet and toes.... The baby was extremely alive and swam about the sac approximately one time per second, with a natural swimmer's stroke."

Paul Rockwell, M.D.

BEST-SELLING FICTION FROM
RANDY ALCORN

DEADLINE

After tragedy strikes those closest to him, journalist Jake Woods is drawn into a complex murder investigation that ultimately forces him to seek answers to the meaning of his existence.

DOMINION

When two murders drag a columnist into the world of gangs and racial conflict, Clarence Abernathy seeks revenge for the killings and answers to hard issues regarding race and faith.

DECEPTION

A jumbled mess of lies and secrets find Ollie Chandler investigating a perplexing, dangerous murder mystery. Bristling with tension and suspicion, *Deception* will take you to heaven and hell...and back again.

RANDY ALCORN
MORE GREAT FICTION

LORD FOULGRIN'S LETTERS

Foulgrin, a high-ranking demon, instructs his subordinate on how to deceive and destroy Jordan Fletcher and his family. It's like placing a bugging device in hell's war room, where we overhear our enemies assessing our weaknesses and strategizing attacks. *Lord Foulgrin's Letters* is a *Screwtape Letters* for our day, equally fascinating yet distinctly different—a dramatic story with earthly characters, setting, and plot. A creative, insightful, and biblical depiction of spiritual warfare, this book will guide readers to Christ-honoring counterstrategies for putting on the full armor of God and resisting the devil.

THE ISHBANE CONSPIRACY

Jillian is picture perfect on the outside, but terrified of getting hurt on the inside. Brittany is a tough girl who trusts almost no one. Ian is a successful athlete who dabbles in the occult. And Rob is a former gangbanger who struggles with guilt, pain, and a newfound faith in God. These four college students will face the ultimate battle between good and evil in a single year. As spiritual warfare rages around them, a dramatic demonic correspondence takes place. Readers can eavesdrop on the enemy, and learn to stave off their own defeat, by reading *The Ishbane Conspiracy*.

Nonfiction titles from
RANDY ALCORN

THE PURITY PRINCIPLE:
God's Safeguards for Life's Dangerous Trails
God has placed warning signs and guardrails to keep us from plunging off the cliff. Find straight talk about sexual purity in Randy Alcorn's one-stop handbook for you, your family, and your church.

THE GRACE AND TRUTH PARADOX:
Responding with Christlike Balance
Living like Christ is a lot to ask! Discover Randy Alcorn's two-point checklist of Christlikeness—and begin to measure everything by the simple test of grace and truth.

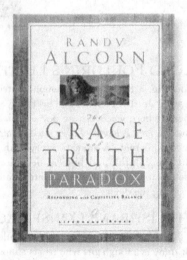

THE TREASURE PRINCIPLE:
UNLOCKING THE SECRET OF JOYFUL GIVING

"WHERE YOUR TREASURE IS, THERE WILL YOUR HEART BE ALSO."

—MATTHEW 6:21

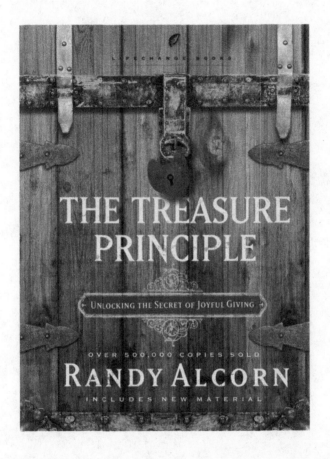

In *The Treasure Principle*, Alcorn introduces readers to a revolution in material freedom and radical generosity that is changing people's lives around the world. Alcorn's inspiring, down-to-earth advice helps readers understand the real meaning of stewardship, how we can get our heart and our checkbook going in the same direction, and—most of all—how we can celebrate the joys of the generous life.